MACHINE MADE

MACHINE MADE

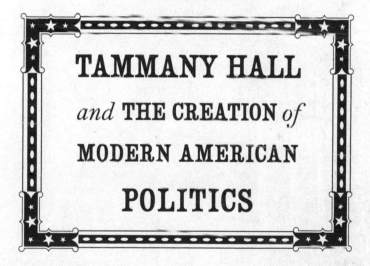

TAMMANY HALL
and THE CREATION *of*
MODERN AMERICAN
POLITICS

TERRY GOLWAY

LIVERIGHT PUBLISHING CORPORATION

A Division of W. W. Norton & Company   *New York* • *London*

For information about permission to reproduce selections from this book, write to
Permissions, Liveright Publishing Corporation, a division of W. W. Norton & Company,
Inc., 500 Fifth Avenue, New York, NY 10110

For information about special discounts for bulk purchases, please contact
W. W. Norton Special Sales at specialsales@wwnorton.com or 800-233-4830

Manufacturing by RR Donnelley, Harrisonburg
Book design by Dana Sloan
Production manager: Devon Zahn

Library of Congress Cataloging-in-Publication Data

Golway, Terry, 1955–
Machine made : Tammany Hall and the creation of modern
American politics / Terry Golway. — First edition.
pages cm
Includes bibliographical references and index.
ISBN 978-0-87140-375-9 (hardcover)
1. Tammany Hall—History. 2. New York (N.Y.)—Politics and
government—To 1898. 3. New York (N.Y.)—Politics and government—1898–1951.
4. Irish Americans—New York (State)—New York—Politics and government. 5.
Immigrants—Political activity—New York (State)—New York—History.
6. Progressivism (United States politics)—History. 7. Municipal government—
New York (State)—New York—History. 8. Politics, Practical—New York (State)—
New York—History. 9. Political corruption—New York (State)—New York—History.
I. Title.
F128.44.G65 2014
974.7'04—dc23

2013045565

Liveright Publishing Corporation, 500 Fifth Avenue, New York, NY 10110
www.wwnorton.com

W. W. Norton & Company Ltd.
Castle House, 75/76 Wells Street, London W1T3QT

1 2 3 4 5 6 7 8 9 0

For Peter Quinn

CONTENTS

MACHINE MADE

INTRODUCTION

The Fourth of July always was a star-spangled day at Tammany Hall. Each year hundreds of New Yorkers made a patriotic pilgrimage to the headquarters of Manhattan's all-powerful Democratic Party, where they heard politicians from the neighborhood and from all over the United States remind them why their ancestors left behind their homes and families and old identities to come to this new land, to this city where people spoke and ate and worshipped—and voted—in ways that other Americans could barely comprehend.

Tammany Hall, the building, was home to Tammany Hall, the controlling body of the Democratic Party of New York County, better known as Manhattan. And Tammany Hall, the organization, knew how to throw a party. There were bands and singers and plenty of red-white-and-blue bunting. Somebody always read aloud the Declaration of Independence—the good parts, anyway—and a couple of honored guests delivered what were called, somewhat forbiddingly, the "long talks." Invariably these were windy and earnest, civics lessons for those only a generation or two removed from a voyage westward across the Atlantic.

All of this was on the agenda for the Fourth of July in 1929. But that year's ceremony was unlike any other in the long history of the Society of St. Tammany or Columbian Order, the full formal name of the organization. On that cloudy summer morning, the city's powerful and mighty assembled near Manhattan's Union Square to commemorate not just the anniversary of the nation's independence but also the opening of a brand-new Tammany Hall on Seventeenth Street, just off the bustling square. Generations of New York politicians had come of age in the Hall's old building on Fourteenth Street, site of the Democratic National Convention in 1868, but the place was too small for an ambitious organization at the height of its power. The new Tammany Hall was built for the ages, with its classical columns, solid brick-and-granite exterior, and the words *Society of Tammany or Columbian Order* etched in stone on the façade. This was the biggest and best Tammany Hall yet, the architectural representation of the organization's hopes for a long and successful future.

The occasion demanded an exhibition of Tammany at its grandest. The crowds were not disappointed. There, on the stage, was Al Smith, the four-term governor of New York, a Tammany member ever since a saloonkeeper named Tom Foley put him to work for the organization in the early twentieth century. Less than a year earlier, Al Smith, a child of the Lower East Side who dropped out of grade school to support his widowed mother, was the Democratic Party's nominee for the office of president of the United States. But he was annihilated in the general election because, Tammany loyalists said, he was a Catholic, because he was a New Yorker, because he was a Tammany man, and because he thought it was silly for the government to prevent working people from taking a drink if they wanted one. Al Smith liked a drink himself, and the hell with Prohibition. Most of the people waiting to hear him speak felt the same way.

And there was the mayor of New York, James J. Walker, a Celtic peacock with his movie-star looks and well-tailored suits, an immensely likable man always ready with a quip, a smile, and a handshake. Jimmy Walker was a Tammany man, too, with a fine record of support for social legislation during his years as a state lawmaker in Albany. He was up for reelection in 1929, but he had no reason to worry. Word on the street had it that a Republican congressman and rabble-rouser named Fiorello La Guardia would challenge him in the fall. Few gave the pudgy little man a chance—times were good in July 1929, and the people loved sharp-looking Jimmy Walker even if he spent the night hours in places few would consider respectable. In fact, they loved him because of his defiance of respectability, because he paid no attention to the bluenose moralists who were so quick to divide the world between good and evil, between Plymouth Rock and Ellis Island, between reformer and hack.

From City Hall to national politics, Tammany Hall's outsize influence on this Fourth of July merited the grander-than-usual ceremonies. Just last November, a member of Tammany's finance committee, Herbert H. Lehman, was elected lieutenant governor, the first Jewish New Yorker to win statewide office. In the United States Senate, a German immigrant and longtime Tammany member, Robert F. Wagner, was developing a reputation as one of Capitol Hill's most effective legislators.

Smith, Walker, Lehman, and Wagner were no strangers to the fifteen hundred flag-waving Tammany stalwarts gathered in the new building's main meeting hall. But the day's main speaker, well, he was not exactly a frequent visitor. He lived on an estate in the Hudson River Valley, far from the problems and realities of life in the city. He was an aristocrat, a patrician. When he served in the State Senate nearly two decades earlier, he'd made a grand show of his contempt for Tammany. Smith and Walker, who served with him back in those days, called him "Frank." Now Franklin D. Roosevelt was governor of New York, successor to Al Smith, and he was seated on the flag-bedecked stage, waiting for his chance to speak.

Franklin Delano Roosevelt in Tammany Hall! No wonder two of the city's radio stations, WOR and WNYC, chose to cover the speeches via a live hookup.

The governor, wearing a bow tie and sporting a ribbon on his left lapel, seemed pleased to be there. He opened his remarks with a salute to Tammany's ceremonial leader, John R. Voorhis, who was about to turn a hundred years old. Voorhis was a small man, bent with age, but not hard to spot: he was the only man in the room wearing a silk top hat. Governor Roosevelt lifted his chin and smiled that wonderful smile as he told of shaking hands with Voorhis when he was a youngster, four decades earlier. Voorhis, Roosevelt slyly noted, "was already approaching old age" when they met all those years ago. The Tammany crowd loved it.

Roosevelt moved on to his main theme, the growing gap between rich and poor in the 1920s. With the assistance of friendly political figures, monopolies and huge corporations were placing wealth and property "in the hands of a few" while ordinary citizens were becoming "serfs," Roosevelt said. This was not the sort of rhetoric that young State Senator Roosevelt had used during his short stint as an anti-Tammany reformer in Albany two decades earlier. Much had changed since those early days, not least Roosevelt's opinion of the men with whom he shared a stage on this Fourth of July. Turning to Al Smith, the pride of Tammany, Roosevelt said, "The fight against business-controlled government at Albany has been made by Al and me for the last ten years, and with all my efforts I am going to keep that fight going on."

It was quite a show all right. Smith was next to speak, and as Roosevelt carefully moved away from the podium to make way for his predecessor, his legs locked in steel braces, the 69th Regimental Band broke into a rendition of Smith's campaign song, "The Sidewalks of New York."

Smith, his thin gray hair parted in the middle, a ceremonial Tammany apron around his neck and falling down to his thickening waistline, gave a fiery speech against Prohibition, warning of further assaults on the pleasures of ordinary people. Imagine, he said, a day when "you may find yourself unable to stand at Forty-Second Street and Broadway and smoke a cigar." Most in the crowd no doubt found this unthinkable, but Smith insisted it was possible.[1]

It might have seemed on that July morning in 1929 that Tammany had friends in all the right places, that its future never looked brighter. Men such as Al Smith and Robert Wagner—the "Tammany Twins," as a skeptical press corps once dubbed them—already had written and passed sweeping social reforms that made life for families like their own just a little easier, less exposed to the cruelties of the marketplace. And they were still in the prime of life. Now, a onetime foe, Franklin Roosevelt, was pressing the flesh with them, joking with them, speaking their language. And people thought he might be president one day.

Yes, it was a Fourth of July like no other.

But Tammany's bright future barely lasted a decade. By 1943, the Tammany Hall edifice was little more than a museum to past glory. The power that once resided there was gone. The building was sold; the organization moved to rented office space uptown.

. . .

Tammany Hall has an unenviable place in American memory. It remains, long after it ceased to be a power in New York politics, a symbol of all that was wrong with urban government in the nineteenth and twentieth centuries. Its leaders are remembered as sleazy, unprincipled crooks who shook down the decent and indecent alike in pursuit of an illicit buck. The ordinary people who gave Tammany its power generally have been treated no more sympathetically, depicted as ignorant tools of a conspiracy organized not to bring about political change but to plunder the public treasury for the benefit of well-connected politicians and their friends.

The story of Tammany is linked indelibly to the story of New York's Irish-American community, although native-born Americans founded the society long before the Irish arrived in great numbers. Tammany already was the dominant faction in the city's Democratic Party when tens of thousands of starving Irish arrived during the Great Famine years of the 1840s and '50s. As these impoverished rural people reorganized their lives in a great and alien city, they saw Tammany as an ally—an ally who did not judge their poverty, their religion, their culture. And so the narratives of Tammany and Irish America became one.

That narrative is generally told as a true-crime story, a tale of larceny on a grand scale. Tammany, at its worst, certainly was guilty of many of the charges arrayed against it. But the accusations of political and moral corruption were often linked to a profound bigotry rooted in a transatlantic, Anglo-Protestant analysis of Irish character defects, not least of them being their stubborn adhesion to the venal institution known as the Roman Catholic Church. Tammany's critics in New York might not have been aware of it, but the Irish had heard it all before: They were poor because they were lazy, they were lazy because they were Catholic, they were Catholic because they were Irish, and no more needed to be said. This was the transatlantic consensus about Irish Catholics, and it was preached from the finest pulpits and most polite salons in London and uptown Manhattan.

There is little question that Tammany displayed a contempt for law and process that enraged reformers and that continues to define its image in memory and history. Men like Richard Croker, an Irish immigrant and onetime gang leader, grew wealthy from graft extorted from contractors, office-seekers, and the merchants of vice as Tammany's boss in the late nineteenth century. Croker and his better-known predecessor, William M. Tweed, remain the florid faces of Tammany Hall in popular imagery and academic history.

They were hardly the only faces of Tammany Hall—just the most familiar. For the family of young Al Smith, the face of Tammany Hall belonged to saloonkeeper Tom Foley, a local power broker who lived near the Smiths' apartment on Manhattan's Lower East Side. A large man with an even larger presence in his neighborhood, Foley held annual picnics for families who shared the uncertainties and deprivations of a society that believed government had no role to play in mediating the excesses of property and capital. Foley knew that for families like the Smiths, packed into crowded tenements and living on the smallest of margins, there was no safety net, no rainy-day fund, no government agency to hear their appeals for assistance. There was only the local Tammany ward heeler, invariably described in the press as a henchman, a tool of evil political bosses and their corrupt machine.

They were men like Tom Foley, left fatherless at the age of thirteen and forced to quit school and find work as a blacksmith, eventually working his way into the liquor trade, which led inevitably to smoke-wreathed conversations with Tammany operatives for whom the saloon was a listening post, a village green, a meeting hall, and a private confessional. It was Tom Foley who helped take care of the Smith family after Al, too, lost his father as a young boy. Foley gave Al a patronage job in the city's court system after Smith showed his mettle as a hard worker for Foley's Tammany allies. Reformers loathed this blatant abuse of the public payroll; they demanded higher standards and civil-service tests for potential government employees in order to prevent Tammany saloonkeepers like Tom Foley from handing out jobs to grade-school dropouts like Al Smith.

From the moment they landed in Lower Manhattan, the Irish embraced what Daniel Patrick Moynihan called the "possibilities of politics." Their enthusiasm for the hard work of organization as well as the grand spectacle of political performance has been attributed to their command of the English language—although many immigrants arrived in New York speaking only the Irish language—and to their supposed gregariousness—although the Irishman who led Tammany from 1902 to 1924, Charles Francis Murphy, earned the well-deserved nickname of "Silent Charlie" for his closed-mouth style of leadership. Murphy and many other Irish leaders of Tammany achieved their rarefied status in politics not by slapping backs and pouring pints but by devoting themselves to the unglamorous work of forging relationships, listening to constituents, and providing services. They managed their districts, talked to their neighbors, took care of those who needed help, and made sure that voters—*their* voters, to be sure—went to the polls. As a young Tammany leader in Manhattan's grimy Gas House District on the East Side, Charlie Murphy sent cards to voters he knew personally if they hadn't shown up at the polls by late afternoon on Election Day.[2]

Such work required painstaking attention to detail. More than anything else, however, it required an enthusiasm for politics and a keen appreciation of human nature. The founders of the republic believed that democracy required dispassionate analysis and objective disinterest from the electorate. Tammany's Irish leaders knew that victory required public spectacle and passionate self-interest. George Washington Plunkitt, a Tammany district leader, state senator, and serial jobholder, argued that it was the promise of a job that turned ordinary citizens into patriots. Anarchists, he concluded, were former patriots who had been denied government jobs because they couldn't pass the reform movement's civil-service tests.[3]

For the Irish of Tammany and for their supporters, politics was theater, not a solemn civic obligation; politics appealed to self-interest, not to dispassionate analysis. In writing about civic reformer Seth Low, one of Tammany's most vociferous critics in the early twentieth century, muckraking journalist Lincoln Steffens conceded that Low, a one-term mayor of New York City, was not a likable person. "A politician can say 'no' and make a friend, where Mr. Low will lose one by saying 'yes,'" wrote Steffens, who regarded Low as a champion of disinterested, apolitical municipal administration. Steffens argued that Low's cold personality, personal unpopularity, and inability to command the loyalty of allies should not matter. "Why should anybody like him?" Steffens wondered.[4]

Tammany, in its own fashion, prepared the way for modern liberalism as its network of block captains and district leaders encouraged the poor to look to accessible political figures to mediate the capriciousness of laissez-faire capitalism and the contempt of moral reformers. Of course, Tammany did so with the understanding that a favor granted was a favor earned. Tammany's unapologetic embrace of interest, the eagerness with which it traded jobs for votes, and the tactics it employed to enforce discipline flew in the face of elite perceptions of how democracy ought to work. An influential journal, *The Outlook*, complained that Tammany Hall "is not only un-American in its methods, but it is distinctly un-American in its ideals," in part because Tammany was a symbol of "the broad distinction between what may be called Anglo-Saxon ideals of character and public service, and the Celtic ideals of character and public service."[5]

This, in the view of many of Tammany's critics, was an important distinction—the difference between Anglo-Saxon ideals and Celtic ideals. While several recent historians have theorized that Irish-Americans in New York and elsewhere desperately sought entry into a world of white privilege, the city's Irish community and its antagonists in the reform movement saw themselves engaged in a bitter cultural conflict rooted in sharp differences based on race, national origin, religion, and even physical appearance. The *Freeman's Journal*, an Irish-American weekly newspaper published primarily for pro-Tammany readers, condemned those who claimed "an Anglo-Saxon divine right to domination in a land of such various and inextricably mixed races as ours." Tammany's self-appointed role as an advocate for immigrants in the late nineteenth and early twentieth centuries was a direct challenge to the political and cultural hegemony of the city's traditional elites, people such as civic reformer Joseph A. Choate, a lawyer and onetime U.S. ambassador to Great Britain.[6]

During a speech in Carnegie Hall in 1906, Choate announced that, after consulting the works of Charles Darwin, he had decided that Tammany's slate of judicial candidates that year constituted a "mongrel ticket." He went on to warn his audience that those mongrels, if elected, would serve on the bench until 1920, when his listeners would be "celebrating the three hundredth anniversary of the landing of the Pilgrims on Plymouth Rock."[7]

For Tammany and for its foes, the struggle for political and cultural power—indeed, the larger conflict over the meaning of Americanism—was at its heart a battle between the political machine's mongrels and the descendants of the *Mayflower*. An anonymous Tammany critic published a broadside arguing that at the nation's founding, "to be an American was to belong to the very highest type of manhood." But after waves of immigrants, the pamphleteer complained, the nation was home to "stunted illiterate interlopers" intent on stealing "our ballot birthright."[8]

This was a battle that Tammany's Irish voters recognized as a variation on a conflict that, to a greater or lesser extent, drove them out of their native land. Ireland's Catholic majority had long been engaged in cultural and political conflict with an Anglo-Saxon Protestant ruling class that viewed the island's conquered masses as victims of moral failings and character flaws that encouraged vice, laziness, and dependence and rendered them unworthy of liberty.

During the height of the catastrophic potato failure in Ireland in the mid-nineteenth century, the British official in charge of relief efforts, Sir Charles Trevelyan, complained that the "great evil with which we have to contend [is] not the physical evil of the famine, but the moral evil of the selfish, perverse and turbulent character of the people." In New York, political reformers concluded that the ignorant masses who insisted on voting for Tammany were perverse indeed, motivated not by disinterested love of country but by cynical calculation. The editors of *Littell's Living Age*, a New York–based magazine, printed a letter signed by "An American," which complained that the "chief ambition of the Irish in America appears to be to get offices and gain a livelihood at the expense of the taxpayers." In other words, the Irish were looking for a handout.[9]

Public officials, journalists, and prominent clergy in the twin capitals of Anglo-America, New York and London, constructed a transatlantic narrative of Irish degeneracy in the late nineteenth and early twentieth centuries, a narrative arguing that Irish poverty, intemperance, and corruption made them unworthy of charity and unable to rule themselves. Trevelyan's complaints about the "moral evil" of starving Irishmen were echoed in the moralizing of well-meaning Protestant aid organizations in New York, where the poor who applied for aid were subjected to investigation to determine whether they were morally fit.

Critics who saw a continuity of character in the transatlantic Irish experience were not wrong, even if their conclusions were wrongheaded. The attitudes, cultural narratives, and values that informed Tammany's Irish-American politicians and voters can be traced not just to tenements of the Lower East Side but also to the villages of rural Ireland that were home to the bulk of the island's Catholic population and that sent hundreds of thousands of emigrants across the water to New York

City. While most of Tammany Hall's district leaders, petty officeholders, and elected officials never set foot in Ireland, it would seem clear
that for Tammany's voters the New York experience was only half the
story. They or their ancestors brought with them from Ireland a political and cultural framework that helped them interpret power in New
York.[10]

This assertion sounds obvious enough, although it has been ignored
in endless histories of Tammany Hall. And yet scholars of the African
diaspora in the United States have shown how African cultural forms—
from the ring shout to the social importance of mothers to ethnic and
linguistic differences—influenced the speech, religious rituals, kinship
circles, and cultural memories of enslaved African-Americans.[11]

In similar fashion, then, the Irish who dominated Tammany Hall
cannot be seen simply as generic white European immigrants. There
were important particulars to the Irish emigrant experience, particularly after the potato famine, that informed their analysis of power and
privilege and influenced national politics in the early twentieth century
through Tammany Hall. The Tammany Irish certainly saw in their
antagonists in the New York reform movement a continuation of the
prejudice and intolerance inflicted on their ancestors in Ireland.

Even the achievement of prosperity and power in New York could
not flick away the chip on many an Irish-American shoulder. In 1898,
a prominent New York Irish businessman named John Byrne saw in a
friend's failure to win a top judicial appointment the same sinister forces
that, in his view, prevented Irish Catholics from attaining office and
success in Ireland. Byrne complained to Tammany Congressman William Bourke Cockran, an affluent Irish Catholic, that his friend had been
brought down by the same "iron heel of tyranny . . . from which our
ancestors suffered enough."[12]

"Our Celtic fellow citizens are about as remote from us in temperament and constitution as the Chinese," wrote the New York diarist and
lawyer George Templeton Strong. Different, indeed, were the rural Catholic Irish who descended on New York's streets in the mid-nineteenth

century. They were different not simply because they confessed their sins to a priest. They were different because they were Irish, not Anglo-Saxon, at a time when that surely was a difference with a good deal of distinction. They were a poor, starving, rural people with few skills, and they had been subjects of an oppressive colonial system that some of them had routinely challenged through extralegal means.[13]

"Their means of resistance—conspiracy, pretense, foot-dragging, and obfuscation—were the only ones ordinarily available to them, 'weapons of the weak,' like those employed by defeated and colonized peoples everywhere," wrote historian Robert James Scally in his masterful re-creation of Irish townland life. In Tammany Hall, the Irish found a vehicle for expressing their resistance and their grievances, a weapon to wield against those who wished to disenfranchise them or deny them jobs on the public payroll, and, at times, a conspiracy designed to counter the power of privilege exercised in quiet private clubs.[14]

Power, then, was an end worthy of justifying the means to attain it. But under Irish-American rule, Tammany Hall became more than just a center of power and patronage. At the height of its influence, Tammany Hall supported the writing of a new social contract in New York, one that served as a model for a more aggressive role for government in twentieth-century American society.

Tammany's Irish leaders, flawed though so many were, helped create modern government and urban politics. They did so not simply by arranging for jobs, although jobs were needed, not simply by fixing elections, although the ballot was not sacrosanct, and not simply by appealing to voters' worst instincts, although theatric demagoguery was a Tammany staple. They created a new politics by embracing the pluralism of the neighborhoods in which they lived, and by burying, once and for all, the transatlantic Anglo-American idea of how government ought to run.

ONE

"TAMMANY HALL BELONGS TO US"

A s they made their way through the darkening city streets on a late April evening in 1817, members of a private political organization known as Tammany Hall were thinking not of the glories of a New York spring but of an election battle just days away. A man they despised, DeWitt Clinton, was on the verge of winning a special election for New York governor—and, as governor, Clinton surely would be happy to return Tammany's disdain with special enthusiasm, since Tammany had ousted him as the city's mayor in 1815. Tammany was prepared to distribute ballots to voters listing one of their own, Peter Porter, as the only opposition to Clinton, but they very likely knew they had little chance of success.[1]

The Tammany men saw themselves as the proud keepers of true republicanism, men who were very different from the economic elites who traded in paper or profited from the labor of others. Tammany was aligned with the Democratic-Republican Party, the party of Thomas Jefferson, the party of the skilled tradesman. Clinton also was a Democrat-Republican, but the purists at Tammany considered him too aristocratic, too arbitrary, too high and mighty. He reminded them of the Federalists who were on their way to extinction, a party of bankers and merchants who worshipped at the altar of Alexander Hamilton, dead these thirteen years, shot in a duel with Vice President Aaron Burr, the man who helped turn Tammany into a political power. Burr was not a member of the organization, but he recognized its potential as a source of votes and support as he planned his own rise to power in New York at the turn of the nineteenth century.

As they neared their headquarters at the intersection of Nassau and Frankfort Streets, just a short walk from the East River, the Tammany men had another bit of business to discuss privately before their meeting got underway. They were under pressure from the city's growing Irish population to nominate an immigrant from County Cork, Thomas Addis Emmet, for State Assembly. Emmet would have seemed a natural—he was a loyal Democrat-Republican, a true believer in Jeffersonian democracy, and he had served as state attorney general for several months before the Federalists grabbed power in 1813 and kicked him out of office, because that's how politics worked.

But Emmet wouldn't do. He was a Clinton man, and so were most of his fellow Irishmen. Clinton had been good to the Irish. Many of the city's Irish were Catholics—although Emmet was not—and until Clinton intervened on their behalf, Catholics were effectively barred from holding public office in New York thanks to a "test oath" required of all civil authorities. Commonly used throughout the transatlantic Anglo-Protestant world, test oaths were constructed to offend Catholic sensibilities and thus prevent them from holding even minor office. In Ireland, the island's majority population was kept powerless because officeholders were required to swear their belief that the Catholic Mass and the veneration of "the Blessed Virgin Mary and other saints" was "impious and idolatrous." In New York, the test oath included language that essentially required Catholics to renounce their allegiance to the pope. Clinton, a Protestant like Emmet, heard the protests of Catholics and in 1806 helped win abolition of the oath during the first of his three terms as mayor. The Irish repaid him with their votes.[2]

Emmet's friendship with Clinton would have been enough to keep him off Tammany's ticket. But even if he broke with Clinton, he couldn't possibly resolve another issue—he was an immigrant, and Tammany Hall did not look kindly on those born in the Old World. Tammany Hall was about Americanism, about the New World, about the rejection of Europe with all its privilege and pomp. Only a native-born American could serve as an officer of Tammany Hall.

Ironically, the immigrant Emmet was as fervent a republican as any Tammany man. He sought to throw off British rule and establish a republic in Ireland in the late 1790s, but he was arrested and imprisoned for several years before his release and exile to New York. His equally rebellious younger brother, Robert, suffered a far worse fate. Arrested after leading a botched republican revolution in Dublin in 1801, Robert Emmet was convicted of treason and hanged. Such was the fate of so many of Ireland's rebels—dreamers they were, fighting against the massed power of the state, and dying young.

Thomas Addis Emmet was a hero for many in the city's Irish population of about ten thousand, and, coincidentally, he was one of the city's most prominent attorneys. He established his own law practice in 1805, and it soon became one of the city's most respected firms. A century after Emmet's death, an out-of-work politician named Franklin Delano Roosevelt became a partner in the firm, which was renamed Emmet, Marvin and Roosevelt. When FDR found himself gainfully employed in the White House some years later, he hired Emmet's great-great-grandson, famed playwright Robert Emmet Sherwood, as a presidential speechwriter.

Tammany saw Emmet not as an attractive personality and potential vote-getter but as an annoyance. The Irish could protest all they wanted, but his name certainly would not appear on the organization's ballot, no more than DeWitt Clinton's would. That much was clear as the Tammany men filed into their meeting room, where they were treated to a shocking sight.

The Irish got inside the hall first—some two hundred of them, many from the Irishtown district near St. Peter's Roman Catholic Church on Barclay Street. They sat in places reserved for Tammany members, and they had no plans to move until Tammany agreed to nominate Thomas Addis Emmet for the State Assembly. At their head were two other Irish political exiles, a physician named William James MacNeven, a native of County Galway, and William Sampson, a lawyer from County Derry. Like Emmet, both men had risked their lives and liberty by seeking for Ireland what the Americans and the French had won for themselves—a republic. They were not about to retreat in the presence of Tammany Hall's legions.

So all hell broke loose in Tammany Hall. MacNeven attempted to give a speech but was shouted down when a Tammany man yelled, "Go home"—presumably back to Galway. Another Irishman proclaimed: "There is a party who have refused to place any Irishman on the ticket. That party must be opposed." Opposed it was, with fists and furniture. An eyewitness to the melee was inspired to flights of sarcastic poetry in the *New York Evening Post*:

> *At length, O hard to tell! The natives yield,*
> *The stubborn Irish keep the dear-bought field.*
> *O! for a Homer's muse, who could rehearse*
> *The politicians' gallant deeds in verse.*

Homer's muse never did show up, but the mayor did, and the Irish discreetly withdrew while Tammany's wounded were looked after.[3]

By then, the Irish had made their point. They had left behind a country where they were routinely denied access to power. They were not about to let that happen again.

Several days later, DeWitt Clinton, champion of New York's Irish, overwhelmingly defeated Tammany's man in the governor's race.

· · ·

The organization known officially as the Society of St. Tammany or Columbian Order, founded in New York City in 1788, took its name from a chief of the Lenni-Lenape tribe, Tamanend, who, legend had it, greeted William Penn when he landed in the New World in 1682. Tamanend, or Tammany, was credited with the peaceful interaction between natives and newcomers in the colony of Pennsylvania. The chief died before the turn of the eighteenth century, but he lived on in place names (there is a parish called St. Tammany in Louisiana), public memory (the colonies of Pennsylvania and Maryland celebrated a holiday in his honor), and in the consciousness of the members of New York's Tammany Society. The chief's ascension to the communion of saints was declared not by a clerical authority but by popular acclamation. American colonists saw him as an idealized, indeed saintly, representation of the continent's native population. Writing about the cult of Tamanend in Philadelphia, John Adams told his wife, Abigail, "The people here have sainted him and keep his day."[4]

Tammany societies were established throughout the new nation, but none had the staying power of New York's. The New York society included another sainted figure from the continent's past, Christopher Columbus, as part of its formal name. In 1792, members of the Society of St. Tammany or Columbian Order led New York's celebration of the three-hundredth anniversary of Columbus's transatlantic voyage, incorporating the Italian sea captain into a pantheon of democratic heroes that included Thomas Paine, the Marquis de Lafayette, and George Washington, all of whom were toasted during the society's celebrations. Eventually, however, members of the society, the public, journalists, and historians dropped the reference to Columbus, and the organization became known simply as the Tammany Society. Their meeting place was called, naturally, Tammany Hall.[5]

One of the society's founders, an artisan named William Mooney, envisioned the organization as a fraternal club dedicated to "the true and genuine principles of republicanism," a counterweight to organizations harboring aristocratic pretensions. Mooney and the society's founders adopted symbols and language from native Americans who, in their imagination, were the true repositories of equality and egalitarianism. The Tammany Society's "grand sachem" presided over a council of lesser elders, called "sachems," while rank-and-file members were known as "braves." The society's headquarters was known informally as "the Wigwam," a reference that would continue into the twentieth century.[6]

It was Aaron Burr, a Mooney associate, who helped transform the organization into a political machine. Tammany members acted as agents of the Democratic-Republican Party in 1800, supporting Thomas Jefferson in that year's closely contested presidential election.

When the Tammany Society applied for a charter from the state of New York in 1805, it described its mission as "affording relief to the indigent and the distressed." Critics pointed out that politics was no place for a state-chartered charity, leading the Tammany Society to establish a separate political organization, the General Committee of the Democratic-Republican Party (later shortened to the Democratic Party), with smaller committees established through the city's wards. The general committee became better known by its meeting place, Tammany Hall.[7]

For the better part of the next century and a half, the Tammany Society and Tammany Hall technically were separate organizations housed in the same building, but the separation was, for the most part, a fiction. The political operation was open to all voters wishing to register in the party, while the society's membership was much more exclusive. The society's leaders controlled the party's general committee and regulated access to its building, barring competing factions. The society's leader, the grand sachem, eventually became little more than a ceremonial figure. The real political power rested in the party's boss, selected by the party's general committee.

. . .

Tammany's feud with New York's Governor Clinton made for colorful political battles, but it was a far more substantial issue that allowed Tammany to become the dominant political faction in New York City beginning in the 1820s, when the nation moved to broaden democracy with new voting rights for white males. As the self-conscious voice of the common man, Tammany successfully supported measures to expand the right to vote beyond a minority of white male property owners. That radical notion did not meet with universal approval. One critic dismissed Tammany as a "noisy rabble." A skeptical writer wondered whether Tammany had thought through its support for expanding suffrage. "Would you admit the populace, the patroon's footman, to vote?" he asked. Tammany had a ready answer for that query.[8]

New York dropped most property-owning requirements for suffrage in 1821 and ended them entirely by 1826, meaning that virtually all white males over the age of twenty-one could vote. Black adult males could, too, provided they owned property. Tammany threw a party to celebrate the occasion. A new, exuberant, and chaotic democratic spirit transformed political culture throughout the infant republic, bringing an end to the long line of Virginia planters and New England aristocrats who dominated the presidency from George Washington to John Quincy Adams. Tammany was part of this new democratic age, incorporating into its evolving ideology a deep suspicion of economic monopolies that symbolized concentrated wealth and power.

In the end, however, Tammany never did support Thomas Addis Emmet for elected office. But when he died in late 1827 at the age of sixty-five, many of the men who broke up the Tammany meeting in 1817 returned to the Hall for a much more restrained occasion, a public memorial for the lawyer-immigrant attended by "naturalized citizens of Irish birth and parentage." Dr. MacNeven, who had been among the leaders of the attempted Irish coup, delivered a heartfelt eulogy to his fellow rebel and exile. "Twenty years ago, as several here will remember, strong prejudices against the emigrants from Ireland prevailed widely through this city, and even reached some of the best men in the community," MacNeven said. But that was all over, he announced. Through his embrace of American republicanism, equality, and liberty, Thomas Addis Emmet had helped to change New York's views of the Irish.[9]

Time would show that MacNeven's assessment was far too optimistic. But Tammany's leaders, at least, had begun to put aside their doubts about the newcomers in their midst, if only because they could add and so understood that the Irish formed a sizable and growing bloc of votes. In 1828, Tammany took full advantage of the expanded rolls of voters, turning out huge numbers to benefit the presidential candidacy of a man who came to symbolize the new democratic age: Andrew Jackson, the son of Irish immigrants.

. . .

Many working men in New York did not see Tammany as its leaders wished they would. Tammany celebrated the birth anniversary of the great republican rabble-rouser Thomas Paine every year with a fine festival of drinking. But for an emerging political faction known as the Workingmen's Party, Tammany was not nearly radical enough. Tammany responded to growing signs of worker discontent with legislation abolishing debtors' prisons, but the city remained a roiling, rollicking test case of just how far Jacksonian democracy would go. A partial answer was given in 1836 when Tammany's leaders barred the doors of their meeting hall to workers protesting a crackdown on fledgling union organizing.

A leader of the workingmen's movement, Irish native Mike Walsh, threw down the gauntlet during a speech in the Hall in 1841. Walsh, a journalist who published *The Subterranean*, a newspaper designed to stir up labor agitation, had to shout over cheers and jeers as he told Tammany's leaders: "I wish you to distinctly understand me when I tell you that Tammany Hall belongs to us—we are the only honest, virtuous portion of the Democratic Party, and I wish you also to distinctly understand that we are determined to keep possession of it until you are able to dispossess us."[10]

Walsh and the workingmen's movement represented a serious challenge to the social and political status quo in New York, a challenge that inspired Tammany to bring on a tough former riverboat gambler named

Isaiah Ryders to recruit gang members who could match Walsh's mus-
cle on Election Day. But another struggle for power, this one three thousand miles away, captured the attention of the city's Irish community
even as Tammany fought for political supremacy in the narrow lanes of
downtown New York.

A charismatic middle-class lawyer named Daniel O'Connell was rallying Ireland's Catholic population as no political leader had ever done
before, to the astonishment of the island's Protestant-only civil leaders.
His goal was the removal of the test oath from British politics—the very
same barrier to Catholic participation in government that New York had
so recently abolished. He called it "Catholic emancipation."

New York's Irish-Catholic immigrants mobilized in support of the
O'Connell campaign, for they well remembered the grievances of the land
they had left behind. How could they have forgotten, when the grievances
were not all that different in New York? Dr. MacNeven founded a group
called the Association of the Friends of Ireland, which dispatched two
hundred pounds to O'Connell's Dublin headquarters in early 1829.[11]

Members of another emigrant society, the O'Connellite Association of New York, opened their meetings with toasts that spoke to their
insistence that they could be both Irish and American—they drank to
the president of the United States, Andrew Jackson, and to the emerging
hero of the Irish diaspora, Daniel O'Connell.[12]

For the Irish in New York, politics always was a transatlantic
enterprise.

TWO

MASS POLITICS

Shrewd and pragmatic, Daniel O'Connell was a prototype for future generations of Tammany Hall politicians—except that, unlike the greatest Tammany boss of all, Charlie Murphy, nobody would ever call Daniel O'Connell "silent." Indeed, he was garrulous in two languages, Irish and English, and his voice boomed like a foghorn in either tongue. He addressed mass meetings of hundreds of thousands and could make himself heard. Or so it was said. His voice was so powerful, one farmer said, "You could hear it a mile off as if it were coming from honey."[1]

O'Connell was curly haired, stocky, and larger than life, with a gift for demagoguery and an appreciation for public spectacle. He rose well before dawn and retired late at night, balancing a prosperous law practice in the southern Irish province of Munster with a boisterous family life—he and his wife were parents of five children—and an exhausting public career. He dominated Irish politics from the early 1820s to the late 1840s, presiding over a complex, highly disciplined organization that capitalized on the cultural and political alienation of the island's majority population. For generations of Irish emigrants to the United States, their political touchstone, their point of reference, their political hero, was not George Washington, Thomas Jefferson, or even Andrew Jackson. For them, Daniel O'Connell was their liberator, the embodiment of a political culture that embraced popular mobilization, public spectacle, intense solidarity, and defiance of an established order.

Joseph Tumulty, an Irish-American attorney who served as President Woodrow Wilson's private secretary, wrote that he was inspired to pursue politics in part because of stories he heard in his father's grocery store in Jersey City, where his Irish-American neighbors gathered to talk politics. Tumulty wrote that his old uncle, an Irish immigrant named Jimmie Kelter, regularly recounted stories of attending the House of Commons and hearing Daniel O'Connell "denounce England's attitude of injustice. . . . " Tumulty was a native-born American, but through the memories of his immigrant relatives and neighbors, his political consciousness was rooted in the Irish political experience in the homeland.[2]

Daniel O'Connell was born in 1775 in the western reaches of County Kerry, where his family managed to hold onto its land through careful evasion of Britain's punitive laws against Catholics. O'Connell attended a Catholic Church–run college in France and witnessed firsthand the bloody aftermath of the French Revolution. Particularly frightening for the devout young Irishman was the revolution's harsh anticlerical, anti-Church rhetoric. As violence mounted near the University of Douay, where O'Connell and his brother were studying, a menacing-looking Frenchman spotted O'Connell and several other students wandering off campus. "Voilà les jeunes Jesuits!" the Frenchman shouted. ("There are the young Jesuits!") O'Connell and his companions raced back to the safety of the university. Months later, the revolutionary government shut down the university, and O'Connell left France on January 21, 1793—the day King Louis XVI was beheaded. Of his time in France, O'Connell later recalled: "I was always in terror lest the scoundrels cut our throats."[3]

The violence left an indelible impression on the young Irishman. The causes he would later embrace were carefully calibrated to manage expectations and avoid deadly confrontations. His place in European history rests on his ability to achieve dramatic social and political change through peaceful, constitutional methods and shrewd dealmaking.

In 1823 O'Connell formed his first mass-based organization, the Catholic Association, to agitate for Catholic Emancipation, the right of Catholics to occupy elected and high appointed offices in Ireland and throughout the United Kingdom through abolition of the test oath. For the vast majority of Ireland's Catholics—who made up 80 percent of the island's more than six million people—the right to hold a seat in the House of Commons or an administrative post in Dublin meant very little, but O'Connell brilliantly framed the issue as a symbol of mass Catholic exclusion and Protestant oppression. The Catholic Association, he vowed, would deal with "practical and not abstract questions," including the "many grievances under which the poor and unprotected Catholic peasant smarted."[4]

The Catholic Association was transformed from pressure group to disciplined political movement through the ingenious use of subscriptions, which offered even the poorest tenant farmer an opportunity to become invested in the association. For a mere penny a month, ordinary Irish people could become associate members of the Catholic association, run for and by fellow Catholics. By 1828, the association had three million associate memberships, while some fifteen thousand more affluent Catholics paid an annual fee of one pound sterling.[5]

Many of those who joined the movement brought more than their pennies—they brought their votes, because Irish-Catholic men who owned or leased property worth forty shillings or more had been given the franchise in 1793. Traditionally, freeholders who leased property voted for their landlords or their agents, because they declared their votes publicly—there was no secret ballot at the time—and it was hardly prudent to cast a public vote against the landlord's interest. Tenants were expected to vote as their landlords directed them. The democratic process in Ireland was little more than an empty ritual for some two hundred thousand Irish Catholic freeholders in the 1820s. Contested elections were rare, but when they took place, they often became violent or corrupt.[6]

O'Connell's mobilization in the 1820s did more than change the dynamics of electoral politics in Ireland. It sought to create a place for Catholics in public life in the United Kingdom, undermining the state's self-image as a Protestant nation. "In Ireland, where a little while ago a Protestant shoeblack would have grinned with contempt at the titled head of the most ancient Catholic family, the tables are completely turned," lamented *The Times* of London.[7]

Daniel O'Connell and the Catholic Association provided a foundational experience for hundreds of thousands of Irish people who were destined to flee their starving homeland in the 1840s and cross the Atlantic to find a political climate not unlike the one they had left behind. Equally important, the Catholic Emancipation movement unfolded in the face of an aggressive Protestant evangelization effort that spanned the Atlantic Ocean. Even as the Catholic Association began its campaign for equal rights, evangelical Irish Protestants mobilized the rhetoric of reform and education in an effort to convert the island's Catholics to Protestantism, which would have made the very notion of Catholic Emancipation moot.

The evangelizers in Ireland wanted to change flaws in the Irish character—perceived to be laziness, ignorance, superstition, dependence, and fondness for alcohol—which they attributed to Catholicism. "If [the Irish] people were Protestants, they would be free from spiritual tyranny; they would be accessible to instruction and civilization," wrote an anonymous writer in *Blackwood's Magazine*.[8]

Because they were not free of "spiritual tyranny," Catholics were considered incapable of understanding Anglo-Protestant ideas of liberty. In the 1820s, a Protestant clergyman named Richard Warner issued a popular pamphlet arguing that Catholics throughout the United Kingdom should not be given rights equal to those of Protestants because they were "not to be trusted" and thus should not enjoy "equal participation of political power." It was "insolent" to think otherwise.[9]

For the transatlantic Anglo-Protestant community in the nineteenth and early twentieth centuries, the Irish presented a challenge to cultural, political, and economic norms such as laissez-faire economics, property rights, civic virtue, Anglo-Saxon supremacy, and, of course, Protestantism itself. The evangelical Protestant campaign in Ireland in the 1820s was rooted in larger moral reform campaigns that were sweeping mainland Britain and the United States during the first quarter of the nineteenth century. In the United States, the movement gave impetus to an emerging moral critique of slavery, especially in New England. In Ireland, evangelicals concluded that Catholics were, in the words of a Protestant pamphleteer, "the vassals of papal tyranny" and were "languishing in the lowest intellectual debasement"—not because they had been dispossessed and virtually segregated from civic life in their native land but because they continued to follow the tenets of a faith that was incompatible with Anglo-Protestant ideas of liberty.[10]

The classroom became a key battleground in this cultural war. A publicly funded private organization called the Kildare Place Society (KPS), named for its location in Dublin, was charged with building ostensibly nondenominational schools throughout the island. Inevitably, however, the schools became a source of cultural conflict as the evangelical movement and O'Connell's fledgling efforts to achieve Catholic emancipation developed side by side in the early 1820s. One of O'Connell's shrewdest political lieutenants, a middle-class Catholic lawyer named Thomas Wyse, noted that the KPS schools "were imperceptibly converted into sectarian decoys."[11]

Wyse sought to take advantage of growing Catholic unease with the island's Protestant evangelizers. The typical Irish Catholic, Wyse wrote, "could not conceive it possible that the same men who were so anxious to exclude him from all enjoyment of the rights of a citizen could really feel much anxiety about his education or his soul." A countywide parliamentary election in Waterford in 1826 offered a splendid opportunity to mobilize Catholic freeholders on behalf of a candidate pledged to support Catholic Emancipation in the House of Commons. Such a candidate, of course, would have to be Protestant, because Catholics remained effectively barred from holding a seat in the Commons as long as members were required to take the anti-Catholic test oath. Wyse regarded the incumbent MP, Lord George Beresford, as "an exceedingly friendly and kind man," but he nevertheless recruited another landlord, Henry Villiers Stuart, to run an insurgent campaign as the candidate of the Catholic Emancipation movement. To support the Stuart candidacy, Wyse put together the first authentic Irish political machine, built on defiance of and resistance to the dominant culture.[12]

Under Wyse's direction, the Stuart campaign committee dispatched agents to assist dozens of freeholders with cash and other benefits in return for their electoral support, a method of operation that became familiar to reformers and voters alike in the streets of New York. While Waterford was but one election in a single Irish county, the tactics and strategies deployed there were replicated in a string of parliamentary elections throughout Ireland over the ensuing two years, transforming the Catholic Association into a powerful, grassroots political organization that taught the Catholic Irish the power of popular politics and the mechanics of mass organization. Wyse broke down the countywide election into a series of smaller elections at the barony level—roughly the equivalent of a ward in New York—recruiting two agents to work each barony and report back to the central committee about local conditions and concerns. Some agents were selected because they spoke Irish and so could converse with many freeholders in the native language.

The mobilization inspired the Irish-Catholic peasantry as no political campaign had ever done before. Several tenants sent their landlord a petition that progressed rapidly from deference to defiance, all but announcing the group's intention to vote as it pleased. "Tenants of a kind and considerate landlord, we are fully impressed with the duties which we owe him, and are ready at all times to fulfill these obligations with all the diligence . . . in our power," the petition read. "But . . . if we are your Tenants, we are also the Electors of a free state, and entrusted with the Elective Franchise not for the exclusive benefit of the landlord but for our own benefit and that of our fellow Countrymen." As Catholics, they said, they supported Emancipation. "Any candidate therefore who will not give a pledge to vote for that measure must in our minds be considered an unfit person to sit in Parliament."[13]

Not everybody was so brave. "Patriotism may fill a man's heart but [it] can not fill the belly," one freeholder told a Stuart supporter named Henry Winston Barron. Many freeholders feared the consequences of voting against the interests of their landlords, and some asked for money or favors in return for voting for Stuart. One such freeholder, a man named Anthony Heale, told the committee that after he announced his intention to vote for Stuart, he no longer received work "from the merchants who always employed him." A publican named John Power told Wyse that agents from the Stuart committee promised him "the profit of two barrels of Beer every week" if he allowed the agents to meet in the pub. But now, he said, "my Landlord threatens to turn me out of my house" and he was "reduced to Extreme Poverty." He asked Wyse, as "an Honourable Gentleman," to "do something on my behalf." Illiterate, Power signed the letter with his mark after dictating it to a friend or associate.[14]

Wyse's agents traveled the county ceaselessly, delivering correspondence to and from the central committee, traveling with prominent supporters to attend meetings with freeholders, and keeping tabs on public opinion. Writers churned out propaganda in the form of broadsides and poetry, much of which presented Ireland's Catholics not simply as oppressed but as slaves, a constant theme in Irish and Irish-American discourse.[15]

The freeholders of County Waterford went to the polls beginning on June 22, 1826. It was a colorful and raucous event but remarkably free of violence. Freeholders from at least three estates presented themselves at the courthouse in Waterford City wearing pink-and-green cockades, a visible sign of support for Stuart. The pro-Emancipation Stuart was declared the winner on June 28, polling 1,357 votes to Beresford's 527.[16]

The liberal *Dublin Evening Post* cheered: "The county has risen as one man, and intolerance has been beaten to the ground and trodden into extinction." Beresford himself was bewildered, the victim of forces beyond his control and his comprehension. "When I was a boy," he wrote, "the Irish people meant the Protestants; now it means the Roman Catholics."[17]

Success in Waterford led to a string of similar victories for pro-Emancipation candidates throughout the island, deeply unsettling Britain's Protestant establishment. The Catholic Association expanded its mission beyond the nuts and bolts of political organizations. Its relief committee took on the functions of an unofficial social-welfare agency for the island's majority population. For example, it authorized payment of six pounds, ten shillings, to the widow of a man killed by a police officer and fifteen pounds for a Westmeath man named James Connell who claimed to be "without house or home" after voting for a pro-Emancipation candidate. An agent in Waterford named Pat Hayden proposed that supporters "be placed at permanent employment" instead of receiving cash payments. Finding jobs, Hayden argued, was a more efficient method of protecting O'Connell's supporters than simply supplying them with relief payments.[18]

The O'Connell movement's successes taught the Irish that political power could be seized through organization and mobilization. It also showed that institutions like the Catholic Association could be a source of relief and protection. In Ireland before the late 1820s, the Catholic peasantry usually turned not to middle-class politicians like O'Connell and Wyse for relief and protection but to violent secret societies whose members assaulted and even murdered landlords, crippled livestock, and carried out other resistance against the Anglo-Protestant social and political structure. The association offered an alternative means of resisting injustice through democratic mobilization, shrewd campaign tactics, and an organization that threatened the established order from within.

Two years after the Catholic Association's victories in 1826, O'Connell offered himself as a candidate for Parliament from County Clare. The Catholic Association's political machine geared up for a potentially historic election, spending thousands of pounds and deploying agents and organizers to Clare to rally the Catholic freeholders. One of the association's more enthusiastic agents, James O'Gorman Mahon, reportedly roused people from their beds to deliver late-night appeals on O'Connell's behalf. O'Connell himself left Dublin for Clare in late June amid a spectacle worthy of Tammany at its most theatrical. Clad in green and riding in a fine coach, O'Connell made the two-day journey from the Anglicized East to the Gaelic West to the cheers of thousands along the way. Nearly forty thousand banner-waving supporters watched O'Connell's formal nomination for the House of Commons seat during a ceremony in the town of Ennis.[19]

After five days of polling, O'Connell received slightly more than two thousand votes, while his opponent, a moderate Protestant landlord named William Vesey Fitzgerald, polled fewer than a thousand. O'Connell became the first Catholic elected to the House of Commons since the Reformation.

The British government grudgingly agreed to remove the hated test oath, to the dismay of many British and Irish conservatives who fervently believed in Anglo-Protestant supremacy. The Irish on both sides of the Atlantic greeted news of Catholic Emancipation with celebrations. The New York *Irish Shield* praised O'Connell for having "snatched the rusty key of the temple of Liberty from the tenacious grasp of gloomy Intolerance, without slaying her guards." But the O'Connell victory was by no means complete—the grasp of the powerful was strong indeed. O'Connell did not so much as snatch the key to the temple of liberty as he did borrow it.[20]

In return for granting Catholic Emancipation, the British administration changed the rules and rewrote the law. O'Connell's most ardent supporters, the forty-shilling freeholders, were stripped of their franchise as part of the price of Emancipation. The property qualification for voting was raised to ten pounds sterling, reducing the number of Irish freeholders from two hundred sixteen thousand to thirty-seven thousand. O'Connell had said he would not accept Emancipation if it were "coupled with any conditions that would tend to deprive the forty-shilling freeholders of the elective franchise." Faced with a choice between principled idealism and a practical path to power, however, O'Connell agreed to a political deal rather than remain on the outside.[21]

The British government manipulated the rules in another way before allowing O'Connell to take his seat. It insisted that O'Connell take the test oath before entering the Commons because he was elected before the oath was abolished. It was a particularly vindictive maneuver, one that surely did little to inspire reverence for the rule of law among the Irish. Rather than take the oath, O'Connell submitted himself to voters again and was elected without opposition on July 29, 1829.

Many in Britain believed that the Catholic Association's victory would lead to revolution in Ireland, but that was not the intention of the movement's leaders. Like so many Irish politicians on both sides of the Atlantic, Thomas Wyse sought to achieve practical change from within rather than pursue abstract ideals from outside. "My principles are already before you," he told a crowd in County Tipperary when he stood for election himself in 1830. "I am an enemy to revolution, and therefore a friend to reform; opposed to anarchy and confusion, therefore hostile to abuses of all kinds." To that end, Wyse created a network of local political organizations, called Liberal Clubs, that would create, in his words, "precision, constancy, unanimity, and uniformity." This highly disciplined, centralized control of local politics, with its emphasis on unity and order, would become a hallmark of Tammany Hall under Irish-American leadership.[22]

Wyse's genius for organization and his emphasis on pragmatic results rather than utopian ideals established the framework for the sort of organization that the Irish would embrace once they arrived in New York. The Catholic Association's victories were a credit to O'Connell's charisma and eloquence, but they also required discipline, order, and organization. As Thomas Wyse understood, the hard work of political organization often is far removed from the color and sound of rallies and meetings. Tammany Hall, like the Catholic Association, understood the importance of spectacle. But its greatest strength was organization.

. . .

In early 1840, Daniel O'Connell welcomed an Irish-born visitor from New York City to his office in London, where he was tending to public business as a member of the House of Commons. John Hughes, a forty-three-year-old man with a strong chin, sharply drawn nose, and expansive forehead, was a native of County Tyrone, a highly contested borderland between Protestant settlers and Catholic natives like the Hughes family. O'Connell may have had a gift for articulating Catholic political and cultural alienation, but Hughes had experienced it first-hand, and he made little attempt to hide the scars. Writing of his early childhood, Hughes noted with characteristic irony that for five days—the first five days of his life—he was "on social and civil equality with the most favored subjects of the British Empire." But then he was baptized a Catholic and so was relegated to second-class citizenship. He emigrated to the United States in 1817, when he was twenty years old, hoping to find a respite from what he called the "hereditary degradation" of Catholics in his native land.[23]

He found work first as a laborer in a stone quarry in Pennsylvania and then as a gardener on the grounds of Mount Saint Mary's Catholic Seminary in Emmitsburg, Maryland. He caught the attention of a French-born priest named Jean Dubois, who noticed that the young Irishman often skipped meals to catch up on his private reading. Dubois arranged for Hughes to be admitted to the seminary, and Hughes was ordained a priest in 1826.

By the time of his meeting with O'Connell, Hughes was a bishop in New York, serving alongside his aging and frail mentor, Jean Dubois. It was hardly a secret that the younger and feistier Hughes was the true leader of New York's mostly Irish Catholics, even though Dubois technically was the senior man in the diocese. Hughes was outspoken, aggressive, and political to his very marrow, although he spared little in excoriating those who accused him of acting more like a boss than a bishop.

Hughes's many critics called him "Dagger John," a reference to the little cross that he and other Catholic clergy scrawled next to their signatures on official correspondence. David Hales, editor of the *Journal of Commerce* newspaper, charged that Hughes's cross actually *was* a dagger aimed at the identity and culture of Protestant New York. So he became "Dagger John." The menacing nickname only added to the bishop's larger-than-life image, but it also symbolized fears that Hughes might command his impoverished immigrant flock to violent political action—fears that Hughes was happy to stoke.

The bishop's high profile, his insistence that Catholicism was compatible with American ideals, and his eagerness to confront hostile politicians and journalists made him a favorite target of those who saw him as little more than an agent of foreign popery. Walt Whitman called him a "mitred hypocrite," while former New York City mayor Philip Hone called him a "generalissimo." He was admired for his intellect, although some critics believed his focus was too narrow. The noted writer and Catholic convert Orestes Brownson, a contemporary of Hughes, complained of the bishop's "habit of taking practical views of all questions."[24]

O'Connell, too, was a pragmatist, but both he and Hughes shared an unshakable conviction about the righteousness of Catholic claims to civil and political equality in the Anglo-Protestant world. Both men, operating on opposite sides of the Atlantic, saw Anglo-Protestant evangelicalism as a threat to Irish-Catholic culture, values, and identity. The greatest threat of all came in the form of schools that claimed to be nonsectarian but, in their view, subtly undermined the faith of Irish-Catholic children.

The two men discussed O'Connell's views of American slavery—he was one of the Atlantic world's most formidable abolitionists, to the dismay of some Irish-Americans—and an attack on O'Connell's wife printed in the *New York Herald*. If they discussed their mutual interest in Catholic education and their mutual suspicion of public schools,

Hughes made no record of it in his letters back to New York. But after leaving O'Connell, Hughes traveled to Ireland and saw firsthand the tremendous growth of Catholic schools in the years since O'Connell's election to Parliament. The Kildare Place Society and other Protestant-dominated school societies collapsed after Catholics broke the Protestant monopoly on public office, replaced by a system of government-funded schools that were under the effective control of local clergy. Hughes concluded, perhaps not surprisingly, that the schools were well run and worthy of emulation. He had never seen "such order" in a classroom, he wrote.[25]

Hughes's trip to Ireland and his visit with O'Connell could not have been more timely, for when the bishop returned to New York in July 1840, he found his fellow Catholics embroiled in a bitter political controversy over culture, identity, and education, a controversy that would have sounded so very familiar to the transatlantic traveler.

. . .

In early 1840, Governor William Seward of New York saw a political opportunity. He believed that he and his fellow Whigs could make inroads with New York City's growing immigrant community on an issue that was dividing newcomers as well as natives: public education. Democrats in Tammany Hall had been straddling the issue, unsure where the debate might lead. Seward knew that thousands of Catholic children remained outside of the public school system, their parents suspicious of the Public School Society, the private, theoretically nonsectarian organization that ran the schools. The society's trustees may have been sincere, but their notion of nonsectarian education was imbued with Protestant assumptions and attitudes, as evident in their selection of the King James Bible for students' lessons. Textbooks contained disparaging phrases about Catholics—a geography text, for example, asserted that "superstition prevails not only at Rome but in all the states of the Church." Children were taught Protestant hymns and prayers. Textbooks routinely referred to Catholics as "papists," a derogatory term especially popular among Irish Protestants. Another book warned that if Irish immigration continued, "our country might be appropriately styled the common sewer of Ireland."[26]

For Irish Catholics with memories of religious oppression in Ireland, the presence of Protestantism in public schools, even in generic form, conveyed cultural disrespect. Catholic New Yorkers demanded in vain that their children be allowed to read from the Douay Bible, which included notes and commentary to help interpret the readings, but the Public School Society refused. Governor Seward, a political rarity in that he was an opponent of slavery who also sympathized with the plight of the Irish, proposed the establishment of publicly funded schools in which the "children of foreigners . . . may be instructed by teachers speaking the same language with themselves and professing the same faith." Too often, he said, immigrant children were "deprived of the advantages of our system of public education in consequence of the prejudices arising from difference of language or religion."[27]

Seward's proposed solution was, in essence, precisely the way the British government responded to Catholic dissatisfaction with the Kildare Place Society schools. If it worked in Ireland, Seward may have figured, it could work in New York. This revolutionary concession to Irish-Catholic concerns came not from Tammany but from Seward's Whig Party.

Catholic leaders wasted little time in applying for public funding from the city's Common Council. The Public School Society, sensing a threat to its monopoly control over education, moved with equal alacrity, joining with some of the city's leading Protestant clergymen in pleading with members of the Common Council, each of whom served as an ex officio member of the PSS, to put aside the Catholic petition.

The city's political leaders must have noticed that Catholic leaders were not entirely united behind Seward's proposal. The *Catholic Register*, the voice of the Catholic hierarchy in New York, favored Seward's plan, arguing that public schools already were sectarian, so Catholic schools were as deserving of public money as Protestant schools disguised as nonsectarian. But another Catholic journal, the *Truth Teller*, opposed the acceptance of public money for Catholic schools—mainly, it seems, because they were suspicious of Seward and his fellow Whigs. The Catholic community appeared to be divided, powerless, and, perhaps worst of all, disorderly. The Board of Assistant Aldermen overwhelmingly rejected the Catholic petition for government funds, voting 16–1 against the proposal.

"Dagger John" Hughes returned to New York from Ireland shortly after the vote. The bishop was quick to notice that his flock had not spoken with one voice on this critical issue. That would not do. Order was soon restored. He wrote directly to the governor, who soon became a personal friend as well as a political ally. "My people are divided," he wrote, "and my Sacred Office requires that I should be a father to all."[28]

Hughes's strategy for achieving unity among the city's approximately seventy thousand Catholics soon became clear—he would not cooperate with the Public School Society. In his view, the PSS was no different from the sectarian organizations that had dominated Irish education until fierce Catholic resistance broke their power. John Hughes had definite ideas about the issues he and his fellow Irish-Catholic immigrants faced in New York. They might have sailed three thousand miles from their homeland, but the enemy hadn't changed—the enemy still was the moralizing reformer, the civic elitist, the high-church Protestant who believed that Catholics had to shed their superstitions and their cultural identity before they could be politically and socially redeemed. "We are, in truth, placed in the same situation as the Catholics were by the Kildare [Place] Society in Ireland," Hughes told his fellow New York Irish in 1841.[29]

In the face of such hostility, order and discipline were all-important—the Irish knew that better than most. Their songs and poetry were filled with laments for rebellions lost and lives snuffed out because of treachery, bad luck, confusion, disorder in the face of the enemy. Daniel Patrick Moynihan pointed out that the principle of boss rule under the Irish, whether in politics or in the Catholic Church, "was not tyranny, but order." Bishop Hughes once wrote that he wanted Catholics "to become educated, and as a consequence, orderly."[30]

Members of the Public School Society asked for a meeting with Hughes to discuss revisions of the offending textbooks. Hughes curtly replied that he was too busy—his "many and incessant duties" left him with no "sufficient leisure for this purpose." He was busy, indeed, for he was about to embark on a political campaign designed to preserve a space for religious minorities to define and protect their own culture.[31]

Over the next several months, Hughes led an extraordinary public effort to defeat the Public School Society and the civic leaders who supported it. In doing so, he identified a genuine grievance rooted in an Irish memory of religious and cultural domination in Ireland. The Public School Society was portrayed as the equivalent of the Kildare Place Society; its mission was the same—to separate the Irish from their faith and culture and so make them more obedient citizens of the Protestant republic. Hughes confided his strategy to an unnamed fellow priest, saying that he planned "to detach" Catholic children "from the dangerous connexion and influence of the public schools."[32]

Throughout the summer of 1840 and into the fall, Hughes rallied the city's Catholics against the public schools by portraying New York's civic elites in terms that his listeners would easily understand and resent. "In England," he said at a meeting on September 21, "there is an officer who is designated the 'Keeper of the King's Conscience,' and the Trustees of the Public School Society are becoming the guardians of the consciences of both the Catholics and Protestants." He argued that if the city refused to fund Catholic schools, "let it be branded on the flag of America that Catholics were denied and deprived of equal rights." And he portrayed the Public School Society as elitist and undemocratic. The society, he said, "was not at any time from its origin the representative of the state, but merely a private corporation" made up of some of the city's wealthiest citizens. In fact, of the thirty-four members of the PSS executive board, twenty-three were financiers.[33]

Behind the scenes, Governor Seward encouraged Hughes to pursue his aggressive campaign against the PSS. "I need not assure you of my sympathy in regard to the ultimate object of your efforts, the education of the poor," Seward told Hughes. "I content myself therefore with saying that it will afford me great pleasure to consult with you freely on the subject whenever it fits your convenience." Seward added that Hughes would "have what support is in my power."[34]

With Seward's tacit encouragement, Hughes and his allies again petitioned the Common Council for funds to expand Catholic schools, leading the city legislature to convene two days of public hearings in late October 1840 to consider the matter. The proceedings promised to be tense enough, but when Hughes decided that he would deliver the case for funding himself, rather than rely on a lawyer, the stakes—and public interest—grew enormously. Some of Hughes's own supporters were concerned that the bishop was taking too big a risk, exposing himself too publicly to his critics. Hughes said he was prepared to "bear insult from morning till night." And he was ready to reply in kind.[35]

No Catholic cleric of Hughes's standing and reputation had ever before addressed the legislature of New York City or so publicly challenged his critics. The Common Council chambers were filled to capacity on the afternoon of October 29, 1840, when the bishop, surrounded by a phalanx of priests, arrived at City Hall for the first day of hearings. Awaiting him were not only the council's aldermen and assistant aldermen but also hundreds of ordinary New Yorkers, many of whom had never laid eyes on a Catholic priest, never mind a bishop. If they expected him to resemble some imagined picture of the Antichrist, complete with horns and a tail, they were disappointed. His physical presence was not nearly as imposing as his larger-than-life image as an officer in the pope's army of invasion.

Hughes addressed the council for nearly three hours, until the autumn afternoon gave way to the chill of evening. His Ulster accent, with its ascending cadence taking the edge off even his sternest declarative sentences, marked him as an outsider, a foreigner, as did his very aura as a supposed agent of international popery. It was, therefore, critical that he frame his argument not on religious grounds but as a matter of secular justice. And so he did. "We do not apply [for funding] as a religious body," he said. "We apply in the identical capacity in which we are taxed—as citizens of the commonwealth, without an encroachment on principle or the violation of any man's conscience."[36]

Opposing Hughes was Hiram Ketchum, a noted anti-Catholic lawyer recruited by an outspoken Protestant supremacist, Reverend William Craig Brownlee, who often insisted that the "great toe" of the pope was "already on our shores" and threatening to stamp out American liberties. Ketchum delivered a bombastic speech of more than two hours, testing the patience of listeners as the night dragged on toward ten o'clock. Noting Hughes's request that Catholic children be allowed to read the Douay version of the Bible, rather than the King James version, Ketchum played the papist card by asking why a "foreign Potentate" should decide "whether the Bible should be read in our common schools." Ketchum wondered whether the pope would allow the Declaration of Independence or the Constitution to be read in the city's public schools. Reporters noticed that Hughes smiled during Ketchum's performance. He may have been thinking that he could not have chosen a clumsier antagonist.[37]

The following day, an even larger crowd gathered to hear Hughes do battle with several Protestant ministers who opposed the Catholic position. Hughes framed his argument as particularly American and republican, presenting himself as a guardian of the nation's values no less zealous than his native-born antagonists. "Now, in our schools, I would teach . . . that when the young tree of American liberty was planted, it was watered with Catholic blood, and that therefore we have as much right to everything common in this country as others," he said. "We are a portion of this community," he added. "We desire to be nothing greater than any other portion; we are not content to be made less."[38]

Hughes's performance won him the grudging respect of foes and the undisputed leadership of his flock, marking him as far more than a spiritual leader in the nation's most important city. The *Catholic Miscellany,* based in South Carolina, described Hughes "not as a priest or a theologian" but as an "earnest advocate of a great civil and religious right." The secular New York dailies, invariably hostile to the Catholic claim, conceded that Hughes was a formidable antagonist. "No one could hear him without painful regret that such powers of mind . . . and such apparent sincerity of purpose were trammeled with a fake system of religion," wrote the *New York Observer.*[39]

Members of the Board of Aldermen were somewhat less impressed. They voted overwhelmingly against the Catholic appeal for a share of school funds. The bishop publicly denounced the "petty array of bigotry" in the Common Council and decided to take his campaign to Albany, home of his ally, Seward. In doing so, Dagger John Hughes became an overt political boss—plotting strategy, making alliances, and mobilizing voters. Ironically, Seward's fellow Whigs believed that Hughes was working on behalf of Tammany Democrats, the dominant political party in New York City but not yet the advocate of immigrants that it would become. Seward himself denied the charge. "From one end of the state to the other, the complaint rings that Bishop Hughes and his clergy have excited the Catholics against us," Seward wrote to his fellow Whigs. "I know this to be untrue, totally untrue." Hughes, the governor wrote, was "my friend. I honor, respect, and confide in him."[40]

.   .   .

The city's Catholics, following Hughes's lead, established a special committee that organized meetings at the parish level designed to pressure the state legislature into acting on Governor Seward's words. Lawmakers asked one of Seward's top aides, John Spencer, to investigate the Catholic demands. As Spencer was doing so, New York voters went to the polls for a round of municipal elections. Tammany Democrats easily captured the mayor's office and control of the Common Council, but the lone alderman who had supported the Catholic petition for public funding, Daniel Pentz, was defeated for reelection. Bishop Hughes's new newspaper, the *Freeman's Journal*, contended that Pentz was the victim of anti-Catholic bigotry.[41]

In late April, after the municipal elections in New York, Spencer released his report on the city's school controversy. It was a stunning blow for the Public School Society. Spencer agreed with Catholic claims that the society's notion of nonsectarianism was, in fact, a form of Protestantism. He assailed the PSS for appalling enrollment figures—the result, he said, of the society's refusal to accommodate the values of parents. The Spencer report recommended a new, decentralized system of ward-based public schools under the control of elected trustees. It also recommended that Catholic schools that educated poor children (nearly all of them did) receive public money while remaining under the control of Catholic authorities.

The Spencer report was a landmark challenge to Anglo-Protestant cultural power in New York City. The issues Spencer raised were the very issues Hughes had raised, issues that called into question the right of a majority population to dictate the terms of citizenship, cultural authority, and civic engagement in a diverse, pluralistic society. The state legislature, concerned about Catholic sensibilities but also fearing nativist backlash, decided in May 1841 to postpone consideration of a school reform bill until the new year—well after the fall's state legislative elections.

Hughes chose this moment to intervene in politics as no Catholic clergyman had done before and none has since. On October 29, 1841, he announced the formation of a separate Catholic political party, dubbed the "Carroll Hall ticket" for the venue in which Hughes made his announcement. The bishop did nothing to hide his prominent role as the de facto chairman and organizer of the Carroll Hall ticket. In fact, after insisting that it was "not my province to mingle in politics," he publicly announced the names of candidates who had his personal approval.

"We have now resolved to give our suffrage in favor of no man who is an enemy to us . . . and to support every friend we can find among men of all political parties," he told a crowd of supporters. "You have often voted for others, and they did not vote for you, but now you are determined to uphold with your own votes, your own rights." On Election Day, he told the audience: "Go, like free men, with dignity and calmness, entertaining due respect for your fellow citizens and their opinions, and deposit your votes." Hughes's listeners waved their hats, stomped their feet, and shouted themselves hoarse as the bishop finished this remarkably overt intervention in a tightly contested election.[42]

The Carroll Hall ticket was a curious amalgam. Of the thirteen State Assembly candidates Hughes endorsed, ten already were on the ballot as candidates of the Democratic Party, and of those ten, seven told the *New York Evening Post* that they supported the Public School Society, even though Hughes insisted that they supported the Spencer report's recommendations. Three State Assembly candidates and two State Senate candidates ran exclusively on the Carroll Hall ticket. One of them was the radical union organizer Mike Walsh, an Irish-Protestant immigrant who regarded the city's reformers as "a fanatical hypocritical set of imbecile humbugs."[43]

Hughes's intervention provoked a furious reaction from the city's leading newspapers. Pro-Whig papers insisted that Hughes was a tool of Tammany Hall; Democratic papers argued that the bishop was plotting with Seward and the Whigs against Tammany Democrats. It's hardly a wonder the newspapers were confused—when one of the city's leading nativists, Samuel Morse, and the anti-Catholic *Journal of Commerce* endorsed a ticket of their own to oppose Hughes and Carroll Hall, three of the presumably nativist candidates on the Morse–*Journal* ticket also had Hughes's endorsement! Some candidates apparently found much to admire in both the Hughes and the Morse positions.

The legislative elections of 1841 were a Democratic triumph, as they captured both houses of the legislature from Seward's Whigs. All ten Democratic State Assembly candidates endorsed by Carroll Hall won, but a more meaningful result came in the three Assembly districts in which Hughes's candidates ran separate campaigns and proved to be spoilers, splitting the Democrats and allowing Whigs to prevail. The message was clear: Irish Catholics could hold the balance of power between the Whigs and the Democrats. Tammany Hall had tried to evade the public school issue until now, but the election of 1841 put an end to the Hall's straddling. The city's Whigs, on the other hand, moved in the other direction, appalled by the spectacle of a Catholic bishop functioning as a de facto political boss, even if that boss happened to be friendly with the Whig governor, Seward.

In the opening weeks of the new legislative session, the chairman of the Assembly's schools committee, William Maclay, a Democrat from New York City, introduced a new school-reform bill that portrayed the Public School Society as an unaccountable private monopoly that had lost the public's confidence. He proposed that the school system be run on a ward level, as the Spencer report had recommended, accountable to locally elected trustees and other ward-based officials. There was, however, no mention of religious instruction in publicly funded district schools. The wording was intentionally agnostic, so to speak. It neither mandated nor barred religious instruction.

The Maclay bill passed the State Assembly thanks to the overwhelming support of Democrats. Bishop Hughes, who met with Maclay prior to the vote, was delighted with the result, even though the bill did not achieve his goal of public funding for Catholic schools. He told Seward that he was willing to give the new system "a fair trial."[44]

When the bill seemed stalled in the State Senate in April 1842, Hughes made preparations to field another independent Catholic political ticket, this one in the city's looming elections for mayor and the Common Council that same month. Catholic candidates promised to wage a campaign against any incumbents who supported the "aristocratic" and "anti-republican" principles of the Public School Society—the notion of Irish Catholics defining what was "republican" and what was not would have struck critics as incomprehensible.[45]

Democrats understood the threat Hughes posed, but opposition to the bill was so intense that supporters agreed to a painful compromise: The Senate version of the bill contained new language that prohibited sectarian religious instruction in public schools. The original wording had been studiously vague on the subject of religion, but the Senate version removed any middle ground. With the modified language, the bill passed the legislature, and the Public School Society's monopoly passed into history. New York City's Catholic leaders celebrated the defeat of an "oligarchy" based on "anti-republican principles," language that emphasized that the city's mostly immigrant Catholics were on the side of bedrock American values, while its antagonists were the stewards of an outdated aristocracy.[46]

A portion of the city's electorate did not share the Catholics' joy or their analysis of the Public School Society. Walt Whitman, writing in the journal *Aurora*, complained that passage of the Maclay bill would allow the "teaching of Catholic superstition." He was disappointed that his fellow Democrats had caved in to Hughes and the "filthy Irish rabble" he led. Two days after passage of the Maclay bill, when voters went to the polls to choose a mayor and aldermen, gangs rampaged through the heavily Irish Sixth Ward and then moved on to assail Hughes's residence adjacent to the old St. Patrick's Cathedral on Mulberry Street. Little damage was done, but the message was unmistakable. [47]

John Hughes did not achieve his immediate object, but, in a sense, the campaign for public funding was a means to a larger political and cultural end. Hughes contended that the nation's founding ideals created a place for minority groups who had the right to reject the values of a dominant culture if they found them offensive. He used the language of liberty to argue with his antagonists; he used the power of memory to unify the Irish portion of his flock. This mobilization, like that of O'Connell's in the 1820s, demonstrated the power of mass politics even in the face of more powerful cultural and political forces.

John Hughes was, in fact, much more than a local spiritual leader— he was the voice of politically engaged American Catholicism. He was not a member of Tammany Hall. But he was, to be sure, the boss.

. . .

Before John Hughes arrived in New York, the Irish lacked a commanding, unifying political voice around which to rally in the face of a hostile civic culture. The Roman Catholic Diocese of New York was fragmented and loosely administered before the 1840s. Hughes changed all that, replacing anarchy with a tightly organized hierarchy that foreshadowed the style and discipline of Tammany Hall. After Hughes became bishop in his own right when Jean Dubois retired due to ill health, power was centralized in Hughes's office, lay trustees at the parish level were made irrelevant, dependable clerics were recruited from Ireland to serve as foot soldiers in Hughes's expansion plans, and a new newspaper, the *Freeman's Journal*, was founded to serve as a print pulpit for the bishop.

With his skepticism of reformers, including abolitionists, whose ideals and theories seemed to promise heaven on earth, Hughes also set a pattern for Tammany Hall. Hughes's religious training taught him that perfection was impossible on earth. The Catholic Church, he said in 1852, had "little confidence in theoretical systems which assume that great or enduring benefit is to result from the sudden or unexpected excitements, even of a religious kind . . . by which the pace of society is to be preternaturally quickened in the path of universal progress." Social experiments, he added, too often were prescribed by "new doctors who turned out to have been only quacks." Tammany's aversion to radical politics, especially socialism, could be traced to Hughes's suspicion of those who promised to achieve moral purity and civic perfection in the form of a well-administered city government.[48]

John Hughes rose to prominence not only because he demanded equal justice for Catholics but also because he defied the popular linkage of Americanism with Protestantism. When one of his longtime antagonists, lawyer Hiram Ketchum, insisted that the United States was a Protestant country, Hughes issued a stinging reply that must have shocked non-Catholic New Yorkers. "That a great majority of the inhabitants of this country are not Catholic, I admit," he said. "But that it is a Protestant country, or a Catholic country, or a Jewish country, or a Christian country in a sense that would give any sect or combination of sects the right to oppress any other sect, I utterly deny."[49]

Hughes saw all minority religions, not just Catholics, as vulnerable to an oppressive dominant culture, and he advised his flock to align with other minority groups rather than assimilate the dominant culture's values. "If the Jew is oppressed," he told his fellow Catholics, "then stand by the Jew." New York's Irish Catholics certainly did not always heed that advice, but Hughes's exhortation spoke to his vision of a society that included those who were not Anglo-Saxon and Protestant. "There is no such thing as a predominant religion," he said, "and the small minority is entitled to the same protection as the greatest majority."[50]

.   .   .

There were approximately eighty thousand Catholics in New York City in 1844, an increase of some forty-five thousand since 1830. About two-thirds were Irish. Protestants in New York and elsewhere believed that American society was doomed as the foundation stone of Plymouth Rock eroded with the crash of each immigrant wave. Evangelical groups with titles that would have sounded familiar to Irish-Catholic immigrants, like the American Tract Society, sprang up in hopes of converting the immigrant Catholics to Protestantism, just as tract societies sought to convert Irish Catholics in Ireland to the state religion of Protestant Britain. A U.S. senator from New Jersey, Theodore Frelinghuysen, descendant of one of his state's oldest families, saw no future for people like him in the new America of the 1840s. "The tide is constantly swelling and breaking over us," he said, speaking of his fellow Protestants. "We cannot repel it now."[51]

Not everybody was willing to concede the cultural and political field to immigrants. In New York, noted publisher James Harper campaigned for mayor in 1844 as the candidate of the American Republican Party, an avowedly anti-immigrant political faction that emerged in the 1840s, not long after Dagger John Hughes successfully challenged the Public School Society. Harper was a reformer, a member of the city's mercantile elite, and a committed anti-Catholic nativist. In 1836, his family's publishing house, Harper Brothers, had secretly printed the memoirs of a French-Canadian woman who told of all manner of sexual depravities in a Catholic convent. The inflammatory tract, *Awful Disclosures of Maria Monk*, prompted a fresh round of nativist outrage against the city's growing Catholic population. The tale was quickly proven to be a hoax, but that did not prevent sales of *Maria Monk* from reaching three hundred thousand, a spectacular publishing success.

Harper and his supporters were far more determined than Senator Frelinghuysen to fight back against the un-American hordes. The American Republican Party demanded laws barring immigrants from holding public office and extending the naturalization process to twenty-one years, meaning that immigrants would have to wait that long to become citizens and, thus, voters. The party's executive committee published a long tirade against "foreign influence" in the United States, stating that "these aliens and adopted citizens" cared "little or nothing for the purity and permanency of our institutions." The "masses that flood our country," the committee stated, were determined to commit "rash, blind and anti-American acts." For that reason, the party pledged that it would "not appoint to any office . . . any person who is not an American by birth."[52]

Harper cloaked his nativist rhetoric with the language of a business-minded reformer who vowed to bring efficiency and competence to City Hall. Not for the last time did the language of political reform and the rhetoric of nativism blend seamlessly into a single platform.

Dagger John Hughes—not Tammany Hall, and certainly not the Whig Party—emerged as the immigrants' champion in the face of aggressive nativism. Hughes bombarded antagonists like Harper and William Stone, editor of the anti-Catholic *Commercial Advertiser* newspaper, with long letters arguing that the promise of the United States was not reserved for one religious denomination. The bishop asserted that, rather than intriguing against the traditions of the United States, he and his fellow Catholics embraced the nation's ideals. "My feelings and habits and thoughts have been so much identified with all that is American that I had almost forgotten I was a foreigner, until recent circumstances have brought it too painfully to my recollection," he told Harper. In one of a series of letters to the influential Stone, Hughes continued to argue that in a nation like the United States, place of birth was immaterial—he described himself as "an American who knows and prizes the rights secured by the American Constitution."[53]

Harper captured the mayoralty in 1844, to the astonishment of the Democratic and Whig Parties. In mid-May of that year, just weeks before Harper was scheduled to take office, Bishop Hughes was summoned to City Hall to meet with the city's outgoing mayor, Robert Morris, a veteran leader of Tammany Hall. Morris was deeply concerned about the possibility of violence in the streets. Nativists already had set fire to Catholic churches in Philadelphia, and there were rumors that mobs from the City of Brotherly Love might march north to attack Catholics in New York.

Hughes had responded to those rumors with a threat of his own. If "a single Catholic Church is burned in New York," he announced, New York would "become a second Moscow." Hughes's reference to Russia's capital, nearly destroyed by fire in 1812 during the Napoleonic Wars, was not lost on the city's nervous political and mercantile leaders.[54]

Mayor Morris thought it prudent to take the measure of the man who was so outspoken on behalf of the city's largest immigrant group. Even if Hughes had blunted the threat from Philadelphia, Morris knew that Harper's supporters were planning a potentially explosive rally near City Hall to mark the incoming mayor's inauguration. Morris desperately wished to know how Hughes's fellow Irish Catholics might react to such a demonstration. It was a sign of Tammany Hall's isolation from the city's immigrant population in 1844 that Morris was obliged to consult with Hughes about the temper of Catholic opinion, rather than call on Tammany's own intelligence-gathering operation.

The mayor, an affluent Protestant like most of the city's political leaders, opened his meeting with Hughes with a question. Acknowledging the church burnings in Philadelphia, Morris asked the bishop whether he was concerned about similar incidents in New York. "Are you afraid that some of your churches will be burned?" he asked.

No, responded Hughes. "I am afraid that some of *yours* will be burned."[55]

Morris's reaction is unrecorded, but Hughes's calmly worded threat no doubt made its way from City Hall to the streets. The planned nativist rally near City Hall was canceled soon after the mayor's meeting with Hughes. No churches of any denomination were set alight in New York.

Dagger John Hughes's confrontational style and demands for a more inclusive urban political culture made him the first effective political boss of the New York Irish. He also provided Tammany Hall's future leaders with one of their core beliefs: New York contained multitudes, and those multitudes deserved a share of political power rather than lectures in Americanism. Hughes's embrace of pluralism was summed up in a letter he wrote to Mayor Harper shortly after the avowed nativist took office. "I even now can remember my reflections on first beholding the American flag," Hughes wrote. "It never crossed my mind that a time might come when that flag, the emblem of . . . freedom . . . should be divided by apportioning its stars to the citizens of native birth and its stripes only as the portion of the naturalized foreigner."[56]

James Harper served only one term of a single year. He left office in the middle of 1845, pronouncing himself satisfied with his reforms, which included the beginnings of a professional police force.

Weeks after Harper left office in 1845, a mysterious blight appeared in the potato fields of Ireland. The staple crop of the Irish people turned black and inedible. Starving Irish soon began to stumble ashore on the East Side of Manhattan, impoverished and embittered, the victims, John Hughes said, not of an act of God but the cruelty of man. The city, and Tammany Hall, would never be the same.

THREE

THE GREAT HUNGER

T he fall of 1845 brought frightening news to New York's Irish
community: Ireland's potato crop had failed, literally overnight.
The *New York Tribune* reported the failure in an anxious tone. "We regret
to have to state that we have had communications from more than one
well-informed correspondent, announcing . . . the appearance of what is
called 'cholera' in the potatoes in Ireland," the paper's editors noted. The
Tribune account quoted a farmer who reported that his potato crop had
turned black and slimy in a matter of hours. Other reports noted that a
sickening odor lingered over the blasted fields.[1]

The potato was one of many crops harvested on Irish soil, but it
was the one crop on which nearly half the island's eight million people
depended for their daily existence. Adult male farmers and landless farm
laborers consumed as much as fourteen pounds of potatoes a day; the
other crops they tended were used to pay the rent. Irish-Americans in
New York knew better than their fellow citizens that a prolonged crop
failure would be catastrophic. And so it was.[2]

The potato failed again in 1846, and again, and again, year after
year, until 1852. Newspapers in New York carried terrifying reports of

the horror unfolding in Ireland, but Irish New Yorkers heard about the hunger firsthand from their starving fellow countrymen arriving by the thousands. By the time the potato was restored in 1852, a million people were dead and another two million were across the sea or on their way to England, to Canada, to Australia, and, of course, to the United States. Huge swaths of the island were virtually depopulated. Farmlands that once provided sustenance for millions were converted to grazing pastures for livestock. Cabins that once were home to peasant families were pulled down, their tenants either dead, evicted, or simply vanished. A census of Ireland in 1840 counted more than eight million people. By 1850, the number was 6.5 million, and by 1910, it was under five million. The Irish nation scattered across the Atlantic world and beyond, carrying among its possessions the searing, bitter memories of hunger and deprivation in the midst of plenty, memories that would permanently and unalterably color its narrative of grievance and exile, memories that were destined to inform Irish identity and their view of the world.[3]

Or not. The question of whether the Great Famine produced what the sociologist Maurice Halbwachs called a "collective memory" among the Irish—emigrants as well as those who remained in their native land—remains contested. But there is no question that a bumper crop of bitterness and rage was harvested from the island's blackened potato fields. Famine survivors absorbed a new and fundamental lesson about power: Those who possess it will never be helpless, and those who are denied it are doomed to starvation and exile when resources become scarce.[4]

In his last speech in the House of Commons, a dying Daniel O'Connell, his once-powerful voice reduced to a whisper, told his colleagues in early 1847 that "Ireland is in your power. If you do not save her, she cannot save herself." The Irish people themselves understood how powerless they were, and how much their survival depended on the powerful. "The Potatoe crop is much worse than the last," wrote James Prendergast, a farmer in County Kerry, in 1846. "We expect good measures from the British parliament this year but we [must] wait to know the issue." Prendergast's expectations were dashed, and he would not survive the famine. His children emigrated to the United States.[5]

This sense of powerlessness in the face of disaster traumatized the Irish on both sides of the Atlantic. When faced with the ultimate sense of powerlessness—they could not feed themselves—they found government to be aloof, unsympathetic, and judgmental. They had expected more. A group of local relief administrators criticized the government's response in a letter to Prime Minister John Russell in 1847, insisting that starvation "could have been easily prevented by a liberal policy on the part of Her Majesty's government." Whether or not the British could have done more to prevent mass starvation, whether they should have halted exports of food from the island while its population starved, remains a matter of academic debate all these years later. In a cultural sense, the argument is beside the point; the Irish were convinced that the authorities could have done more and did not.[6]

When the children and grandchildren of the Famine achieved power in the United States, they would hold onto it and keep it from their enemies, even if that meant defying what Daniel Patrick Moynihan called "Yankee proprieties." Reformers and civic elites who sought to bring down urban machines and their immigrant constituents—whether through criminal prosecutions, outright disenfranchisement, or moralistic reform campaigns—unwittingly invoked in Irish-American politicians and their constituents Famine memories of powerlessness, of state power mobilized on behalf of the propertied and the privileged.[7]

From the perspective of New York politics and Tammany Hall, one assertion is inarguable: The Great Famine immigration marked the beginning of the end of old New York, a city governed by Anglo-Protestant patricians and mercantile elites. That is not to say nativists and old-stock families simply surrendered their cultural and political power once Famine ships began docking along Manhattan's East Side waterfront. Quite the opposite. A powerful anti-immigrant movement capitalized on the fear and loathing of the starving Irish in the 1850s. But try though they might, the anti-immigrant campaigners in New York could not counter the power of sheer numbers, for the Famine marked a demographic tipping point in the struggle over power and identity between new Irish-Catholic immigrants and native-stock New Yorkers. The island's population was 371,000 in 1845. It grew to 630,000 in ten years as the hunger took hold in Ireland. By the time the Famine wave receded in the mid-1850s, more than one in four New Yorkers was a native of Ireland, and 52 percent of the city's residents were foreign-born.[8]

The new Irish, the starving Irish, would not have to storm Tammany Hall to demand respect. The door would be open upon their arrival.

.   .   .

The hunger did not affect all of Ireland, or all classes of Irish people, the same way. The island's western counties, where traditional Gaelic culture stubbornly defied the forces of modernization and Anglicization, were hit especially hard. Until the Famine, they had been able to resist Victorian Britain's moral reformers, who regarded their way of life as not simply premodern but morally inferior, requiring not a more equitable distribution of resources but reform of the peasantry's character. A newspaper in Ulster, Ireland's northernmost province, argued that the Famine did not affect the heavily Protestant areas of the island because "we are a painstaking, industrious, laborious people who desire to work and pay our just debts, and the blessing of the Almighty is upon our labour. If the people of the South had been equally industrious with those of the North, they would not have so much misery upon them."[9]

The immediate cause of Ireland's misery was *Phytophthora infestans*, a deadly fungus exported to Ireland from the New World, just as the potato itself had been. But even as the starving and dying were underway throughout Ireland, British administrators and politicians sought to pinpoint what they saw as the calamity's true cause—the character, or lack thereof, of the Irish people. Sir Charles Trevelyan, the British civil servant placed in charge of administering public-works projects and other relief efforts during the first two years of hunger, insisted that the catastrophe was a reflection of Ireland's collective moral failings, "the judgment of God on an indolent . . . people."[10]

The British government did not simply throw up its collective hands, even if God's judgment was involved. Government soup kitchens fed three million people a day in the summer of 1847, an extraordinary administrative and logistical effort. By the end of the year, however, London shifted the burden of paying for relief to Irish landlords, in essence leaving the Irish to devise their own solution to the catastrophe because, in Trevelyan's words, local ratepayers "know how to discriminate between the different claims for relief."[11]

Trevelyan, like many other Victorian politicians, was intent on establishing the moral worthiness of those who applied for government assistance, which is why he believed local ratepayers were in the best position to judge who was worthy of charity—and who was not. Victorian economic policy bore the influence of a handful of economists who also were Protestant clerics, most prominently Thomas Malthus and Nassau Senior. They viewed laissez-faire economics as more than a system to promote commerce. From their perspective, the market, uninhibited by artificial regulations, encouraged virtue among the lower classes and served as a framework for determining the difference between the worthy and the unworthy poor.

Those precepts determined Trevelyan's course of action during the Famine, but he was not alone in his moralistic approach to the catastrophe. Charles Wood, Britain's chancellor of the exchequer during most of the Famine years, asserted that the true cause of "helplessness" among the Irish was their "habit of depending on government. . . . If we are to select the destitute, pay them, feed them and find money from hence, we shall have the whole population of Ireland upon us soon enough." A new publication called *The Economist* insisted that government interference in the distribution of food would only transfer resources "from the more meritorious to the less."[12]

British policymakers feared that efforts to assist the starving might make them even more dependent on government charity. It was important, they believed, that government policy should encourage self-reliance. Relief projects, Trevelyan wrote, should be "so unattractive as to furnish no motive to ask for it, except in the absence of every other means of subsistence."[13]

Those who were granted outdoor relief—that is, labor on some form of public works—generally toiled up to ten hours a day without a meal break. Other starving Irish people reported to workhouses, fearsome places of death and disease. In a single week in 1848, fourteen hundred people died in the workhouses, out of a total workhouse population in Ireland of about one hundred twenty thousand. While these deaths were regrettable, policymakers believed some good would come of the suffering. Eventually, Trevelyan hoped, Ireland would "begin to understand that the proper business of a Government is to enable private individuals of every rank and profession in life to carry on their several occupations with freedom and safety," interfering as little as possible with "the business of the land-owner, merchant, money-lender, or any other function of social life."[14]

As they dispersed across the Atlantic world, Famine emigrants reached a very different conclusion about "the proper business of a Government." When they were starving, the government told them they lacked character; when government offered aid, it did so with reluctance. When survivors and their children built new lives in New York and elsewhere, they made it clear through their votes and their actions that they regarded those who provided jobs and influence as their friends and those who offered disdain and moral uplift as their enemies.

. . .

Bishop John Hughes was among the first on either side of the Atlantic to suggest that starvation in Ireland was the result not of an absence of food but of flawed economic dogma. In a remarkable speech in Lower Manhattan's Broadway Tabernacle on March 20, 1847, Hughes declared that the potato crop's failure should not have led to "so frightful a consequence" because it was "but one species of the endless varieties of food" grown on the island. The problem, Hughes said, was not to be found in Ireland's potato fields but in the ideology of a political and economic system that placed profits and the privileges of commerce ahead of human needs.

"The soil has produced its usual tribute for the support of those by whom it has been cultivated, but political economy found the Irish people too poor to pay for the harvest of their own labor and has exported it to a better market, leaving them to die of famine or to live on alms," he said. "And this same political economy authorizes the provision merchant, even amidst the desolation, to keep his doors locked and his sacks of corn tied up within, waiting for a better price, whilst he himself is, perhaps, at his desk, describing the wretchedness of the people."

Hughes conceded his church's traditional belief in the "sacredness of the rights of property" but argued that "the rights of life are dearer and higher than those of property, and in a general famine like the present, there is no law of Heaven, nor of nature, that forbids a starving man to seize on bread wherever he can find it." He acknowledged that some saw God's hand in the catastrophe—he asked them "not to blaspheme Providence by calling this God's famine." The catastrophe, he insisted, was man-made. The state should take action to "guard the lives of its members against being sacrificed by famine."[15]

In linking starvation in Ireland to the British government's devotion to laissez-faire economics, John Hughes launched a broader assault on the priorities of the transatlantic world's political and mercantile elites. Hughes's analysis of the Famine quickly made its way to Ireland, where it won the approval of a group of political dissidents in Dublin called Young Ireland. The bishop's lecture was reprinted in Young Ireland's journal, *The Nation*, in early May, touching off an intense political debate in Ireland about the true causes of the ongoing death and displacement. In seeking a political explanation for the Famine, John Hughes helped to create a debate over land ownership, political economy, and distribution of resources in Ireland itself.

. . .

The tens of thousands of Irish who settled in New York during and just after the Great Famine were different, even when compared with their fellow immigrants of an earlier generation. Between 80 and 90 percent of the newcomers were farm laborers or servants with few skills and no assets; only about 10 percent were skilled artisans. Only twenty years earlier, in 1826, 48 percent of Irish immigrants had been skilled workers. More than half of Famine immigrants were from regions where Irish speakers were a majority of the population. And nearly all the new immigrants brought with them the embittering experience of mass starvation and, in many cases, mass eviction.[16]

The Famine immigration led to profound changes in New York's civic and political life. After trying to please nativists and immigrants alike in the early 1840s, Tammany Hall's leaders recognized the power of numbers and the inevitability of a shift in power in the city, abandoning for good the machine's occasional flirtations with nativism. The city's old mercantilist and cultural elites responded to Tammany's embrace of these strangers with reform movements that sought to portray professional politicians as inherently corrupt and the voters who supported them as unworthy of the franchise. Inevitably, these Protestant-dominated reform movements associated corruption with Catholicism. Walt Whitman echoed their complaints. "Shall these dregs of foreign filth—refuse of convents—scullions from Austrian monasteries—be permitted to dictate what Tammany must do?" Whitman asked in 1842. Increasingly, the answer to Whitman's question was "yes."[17]

Famine immigrants transformed New York into the capital of a transatlantic Irish diaspora. New York City accounted for an astonishing 12 percent of all Irish immigrants in the United States during the Famine years of 1845 to 1851. Huge sections of the city became virtual extensions of Irish townlands and villages—four wards along the East River from the Battery to Grand Street were more than a third Irish-born in 1855. So was the famed Sixth Ward, home to African-Americans as well as the immigrant Irish.[18]

The city became the base of operations for Irish revolutionary organizations and immigrant aid associations, the seat of the profoundly Irish Catholic Church in the United States, and a center of political and cultural debate about Irish identity in America. Bishop Hughes and a cadre of immigrant journalists and political polemicists developed a political interpretation of the Famine that called into question Anglo-American economic dogma and established an ideological framework for the urban liberals who would rise to power in Tammany Hall during the Progressive Era. Indeed, if Progressivism can be defined as (among other things) a rejection of laissez-faire economics, Irish America's interpretation of the Famine might well serve as a starting point in the development of that critique, long before the excesses of the Gilded Age.[19]

The Great Famine and its aftermath produced other long-term changes to New York's civic life. By the opening decade of the twentieth century, as men born in the shadow of Famine exile assumed positions of power in City Hall and in Albany, New York's civic leadership was vastly different from the elite-led structure of the early nineteenth century. Famine exiles helped to create a political culture that was more populist and more representative of the city, a culture personified by immigrant and immigrant-stock political figures who rose to prominence through Tammany in the Progressive Era and who helped pass groundbreaking social legislation that challenged and then defeated the laissez-faire approach used by British authorities while Ireland starved.[20]

There is no question that the Famine cast a long shadow over the New York Irish. Memories of hunger and want were regularly invoked in New York's Irish-American weekly newspapers. Editors published poems and stories that reminded readers of all they had suffered during the Famine, creating a memory that surely was passed from immigrant parent to native-born child into the twentieth century. In 1887, as the transatlantic Anglo-Protestant world celebrated Queen Victoria's fiftieth anniversary on the throne, thousands of Irish New Yorkers gathered in Cooper Union to remember victims of the Famine. The great hall was decorated in black bunting and other symbols of mourning as speakers denounced Victoria as a symbol of British neglect during Ireland's catastrophe. Speaking of those who died of hunger and disease, the event's chairman said, "It is our duty tonight to remember who they were, and how they died, and recall the despotism that either extirpated them or drove them into famine's graves."[21]

Many years later, the Irish in Ireland took note of the persistence of Famine memories in places like New York. "The Irish in America live in 1846," noted T. P. O'Connor, an Irish member of the House of Commons, in 1918. Mothers and grandmothers, O'Connor asserted, kept alive memories of the Famine and its injustice, so that "there is only one permanent factor in the minds of men of Irish blood [in America] and that is the famine and emigration of 1846."[22]

Al Smith's mother left Ireland just before the famine, so she would not have experienced the catastrophe firsthand. But Smith developed a view of political power that challenged the assumptions of the transatlantic free-trader who believed the government had no role to play in ameliorating the inequities of the market. There were, Smith said, two distinct approaches to the use of state power. "One group believes that the Constitution and statute law is intended only for the protection of property and money," he said. "The other group believes that law in a democracy is not a divine principle but exists for the greatest good to the greatest number and for meeting the needs of present day society . . . That is the theory I hold. . . ."[23]

It is hard, however, to find evidence of Famine memories in the rhetoric of mainstream political leaders like Smith and his mentor, Charles Murphy (whose father fled the Famine in 1848), or even politicians who were Famine immigrants themselves, including a Tammany lawyer and judge named Richard O'Gorman. No Tammany politician of note followed the course of two of the city's most-noted Irish immigrant journalists, Jeremiah O'Donovan Rossa, who wrote about his father's agonizing death by starvation in Skibbereen, County Cork, and John

Mitchel, who wrote a fiery polemic accusing the British of deliberately starving the Irish.

Murphy, Smith, O'Gorman, and other Tammany figures never drew on an explicit memory of starvation or oppression to explain a vote, a point of view, or a policy position. But public silence does not necessarily indicate the absence of a personal narrative or memory. After all, Murphy, Smith, and other Tammany politicians in the early twentieth century also were silent about their impoverished childhoods in New York, although their backgrounds certainly influenced their support for such progressive reforms as workers' compensation, minimum wage, and pensions. These conspicuous silences may suggest that the memory of deprivation—whether through a lack of food in Ireland or a lack of resources on the Lower East Side—was simply too painful and best left unspoken.[24]

Contemporary observers of the Famine-era immigrants understood that the experience of loss and the humiliation of exile were bound to affect the immigrants' worldview. In an editorial bearing the headline "Ireland in America," the *New York Times* took note that the Irish who had come to the city since the Famine were different from those who had come earlier. Previous immigrants, the paper said, retained affection for the land they left behind. The Famine immigrants, however, had no warm memories to keep them company in their new land. "When men are driven away by unjust laws—by starvation and the fear of death— when they are forced to snatch their wives and children and take them three thousand miles across the sea to save them from the jaws of famine, while they see plenty and luxury all around them—their memories of home become motives of hatred, and will feed the fires which time cannot quench."[25]

Time surely did not quench the fires that burned in New York's Irish community. Colonel Michael Corcoran, a Famine immigrant from County Donegal and commanding officer of the famed 69th Regiment, New York Volunteers, refused to allow his men to march in a parade honoring the visit of the Prince of Wales in 1860. The prince was the son of Queen Victoria, often referred to as "the Famine queen" in Irish folklore. (Corcoran was court-martialed for his defiance but was allowed to return to duty after the Civil War began.) Thomas Francis Meagher, who took command of the 69th after Corcoran died in 1863, referred to the Irish as a "famine-exterminated race" during a lecture in New York in 1868, prompting a prolonged ovation. Irish-American journalist Patrick Ford, a Famine immigrant who founded the influential *Irish World* newspaper in New York in 1870, frequently called on Famine memories to mobilize the Irish community's support for trade unions, radical politics, and anticolonialism. Ford's coverage of a famine in India in 1877, for example, linked the Irish and Indians as victims of British imperialism. "Ireland and India—what a similarity in their destinies," he wrote. "And both their destinies brought about by the robber oligarchy of Great Britain!"[26]

Ford's anti-British sentiments were not unusual in post-Famine Irish-American culture, but his reference to a "robber oligarchy" reflected a broader critique of power among the New York Irish. References to victimization, exploitation, and social injustice rooted in the Famine became commonplace in the *Irish World* and in Irish-dominated trade unions during the Gilded Age and into the Progressive Era. Leonora O'Reilly, a founder of the Women's Trade Union League and the daughter of Irish immigrants, noted in 1910 that a critic of hers had never been "face to face with hunger or eviction."[27]

By the early twentieth century, this Irish populist critique of social and economic inequality, rooted in firsthand experience rather than abstract theory, was a vital part of Irish-American political consciousness. Even the well-off and utterly respectable Tammany Congressman William Bourke Cockran emerged as a critic of monopoly power and the abuses of big business in the late Gilded Age and the early Progressive Era. "It is high time that the people awoke to this fact that the speculator is abroad in the land, that ingenious men . . . are seizing control of all the institutions of trade and commerce," he said.[28]

The place of hunger in Irish-American memory has been invoked or teased out of some rather unlikely cultural artifacts, demonstrating the enduring power of hidden Famine memories. Novelist Thomas Flanagan suggested that Irish-American film director John Ford consciously invoked Famine imagery in his adaptation of John Steinbeck's *The Grapes of Wrath*. In the 1930s novel and film *Gone With the Wind*, Katie Scarlett O'Hara, daughter of Irish-Catholic immigrants who lived, somewhat improbably, on a plantation in Civil War–era Georgia, vowed that she would never be hungry again—even if she had to steal, cheat, or kill. Novelist William Kennedy observed that for the Irish who controlled politics in his home city of Albany, New York, "starvation . . . was immorality"—not graft, or vice, or ballot-stuffing, or intemperance, or any of the other issues that preoccupied reformers.[29]

Anxieties about the very basics of life—food on the table, a roof over the house—were evident in the Famine generation's embrace of secure public employment rather than riskier ventures in the boom-and-bust private economy. To be sure, most Irish-Americans in New York were privately employed, typically as unskilled laborers on construction sites and domestics who tended to the needs of upper-middle-class families. But in popular culture and memory, the stereotype of an Irish police officer or firefighter resonates even today, and for good reason—the Irish dominated these jobs in New York City and other urban centers in the late nineteenth and early twentieth centuries.

"The first thing I learned was that to be a cop or a fireman meant that you would never get laid off, and that to be a construction worker, even in the high-paying skilled trades, was not quite as good because there were always layoffs when the construction boom ebbed, and, most important, because they did not have the twenty-year pension," wrote Irish-American novelist Dennis Smith, who spent nearly twenty years as a firefighter in the Bronx in the 1950s and '60s. Within a quarter-century of New York's conversion from a volunteer fire department to a paid service in 1865, nearly three hundred of the city's approximately one thousand professional firefighters were Irish-born, and if native-born members with Irish last names were included, the department's roster for 1888 was more than 75 percent Irish.[30]

The Irish also developed a quick and strong presence in other government jobs. In 1860, three hundred nine Irish immigrants served in the New York Police Department, compared with eighty-four German immigrants. Twenty percent of the city's public school teachers were Irish women in 1870. The *New York Times* reported in 1869 that Tammany Hall arranged for government jobs for seven hundred fifty-four Irish immigrants, but only forty-six such jobs went to German immigrants. There's no doubt that the Irish were more active in city politics and so were in a better position to take advantage of Tammany patronage. But it would also seem true that the Irish were more eager for the security of those jobs, while Germans, who generally were more skilled and more entrepreneurial than the Irish, were less inclined to seek government employment. For the Irish peasant transplanted in New York, fear of joblessness replaced fear of eviction. The solution was the very institution that had facilitated eviction in Ireland but that offered protection in New York: the government.[31]

In the winter of 1850, at the height of the Famine, Irish-American leaders, including Bishop John Hughes and Congressman Mike Walsh, a onetime leader of the radical workingmen's movement, joined Whig Governor William Seward and abolitionist editor Horace Greeley in calling for broad land reform in the United States, another implicit sign of the Irish community's reaction to hunger and eviction in Ireland. During a Tammany Hall rally attended by all four men, resolutions were passed demanding a ban on the purchase of public land by non-residents, an end to the "land monopoly," and the creation of a more democratic nation "in which every citizen is a free holder."[32]

While the anti-rent and land-reform movements in New York dissipated, the very articulation of these radical demands—uniting an Irish-born Catholic bishop with an Irish-born Protestant union organizer—spoke to the growth of Irish political consciousness in New York. The Famine inspired a broader understanding in New

York's Irish community of other forces at work in a commercializing society, forces that seemed to place economic dogma over the well-being—indeed, the very lives—of the poor.

.   .   .

Anxieties about the character of the poor, especially the Irish-Catholic poor, spanned the Atlantic, as New York's Famine immigrants quickly discovered. The newcomers landed just in time for an economic downturn in New York, which prompted the city's self-styled reformers to demand a reduction in government spending. "Retrenchment is the twin of reform," argued one of the city's leading civic leaders, Peter Cooper. He and many future Tammany foes associated political reform not just with traditional good-government causes like ballot access but also with demands for smaller government and lower taxes. That message certainly appealed to the city's elites, but it lacked a certain resonance with those who benefited from government spending—a group that included, of course, many Irish Catholics. In an article describing the plight of New York's poor during the winter of 1855, the *New York Times* quoted a German-American woman who complained that the "Irish drew all the public assistance, and got all they wanted, and she could obtain nothing."[33]

Coincidentally, the Famine Irish arrived in New York just as the city's trade-union movement began to find its voice again after years of relative quiet. An umbrella organization known as the New York Industrial Congress emerged as an important force in local politics, threatening Tammany's hold on labor's loyalties at a time when the organization was in disarray and willing to cut deals with the city's financial elites, leading to the nomination and election of a Wall Street Democrat, William Havemeyer, as mayor in 1853. (It was Havemeyer's second election to the mayoralty—he unseated the nativist James Harper in 1845.) A reform-minded Common Council cut municipal taxes by 20 percent, but, not surprisingly, the measure did nothing to alleviate the distress of the city's unemployed and its ever-growing population of unskilled Famine Irish.

The Irish quickly became an important presence in the labor move-ment's demonstrations during the mid-1850s, when protest rallies attracted tens of thousands of workers and jobless to the city's public spaces. At one such rally in Tompkins Square Park in the fall of 1857, an Irish speaker was on hand to translate speeches into the language of the Irish poor. The *New York Evening Post* took note of the Irish presence at the demonstration, mocking a speaker named Maguire by mimicking his accent in print form: "We niver will sase while there's a man in the land that nades employment," the paper quoted Maguire, poking fun not simply at his accent but also at his earnest declaration of assistance for the jobless.[34]

The city's leading newspapers and reform organizations shared with Charles Trevelyan a loathing for any suggestion that government ought to play a role in shaping, or softening, market forces. The *Evening Post* insisted that the government was under no obligation "to find people employment or food." Despots followed such a "monstrous" course, the paper argued, but "our republican system of government professes to leave every channel of industry open." The *New York Times* contended that society's "less fortunate brethren" could not demand government relief "as a right." Instead, the paper's editors argued, relief should be administered as the "moral obligation" of the wealthy.[35]

These restrictive views on the power of government put the city's top editors in conflict with a favorite of New York's Irish immigrant community, Fernando Wood, a colorful, ethically challenged Tammany Hall demagogue who was elected mayor three times in the 1850s. A tall man with elegant taste and an aristocratic bearing, Wood did not have a great deal in common with his loyal Irish constituents. Although born into humble circumstances, he was a wealthy man—he estimated his worth to be $250,000 in 1858—and he lived in comfort uptown, a world away from the slums that were home to his most ardent admirers.[36]

Although Wood was a Tammany man through and through, he unexpectedly set reformers' hearts aflame during his first few months as mayor in 1855 when he improved public transportation and fought plans to shrink the size of Central Park, then under construction. But he also took inordinate interest in staffing the Municipal Police Department, leading critics to charge that he favored immigrant hires over the native-born, and Democrats over Whigs and Republicans. Wood's insistence on total control over law enforcement led the state to disband the municipal police force in the early summer of 1857, replacing it with the state-controlled Metropolitan Police Department. Wood and his officers, however, refused to acknowledge the new police force, a situation that was bound to end badly. And so it did.

On July 16, 1857, Daniel Conover, an appointee of Governor John King, showed up at City Hall for his first day of work as city street commissioner, only to learn that Mayor Wood had appointed another man, Charles Devlin, to the post. Wood was not about to allow King to impose a commissioner as well as a police force on the city. Wood's Municipals eagerly carried out the mayor's orders to remove Conover from the building. The would-be commissioner promptly swore out a warrant for the mayor's arrest, but when a captain of the Metropolitan force attempted to remove Wood from City Hall, the Municipals charged to the mayor's defense. The Metropolitans then rallied to their captain. The result was a bloody riot between the two police departments inside and on the steps of City Hall. More than fifty officers were injured, one severely, during half an hour of intense skull-cracking. Several units of the New York National Guard marched to the scene to restore order and to make good on the warrant for Wood's arrest. He submitted peacefully but issued a defiant declaration from his jail cell, referring to the governor's police force and his would-be street commissioner as "usurpers" of "municipal rights."[37]

No demagoguery could hide the city's disgrace, and Wood's Municipals were formally disbanded months later by court order. But the riot represented a larger battle for power and influence in New York. Politicians from all parties practiced skull-cracking, bribe-taking, influence-peddling politics that resembled the tactics of the city's infamous gangs, with names like the Dead Rabbits and the Bowery B'hoys. In 1852, the

Whig Party, the main opposition to Tammany Democrats until the rise of the Republican Party, printed eighty thousand fraudulent ballots in an attempt to steal local elections, including a mayoral race. Tammany regularly employed legions of toughs to intimidate and even arrest unfriendly voters. A Tammany sheriff, Jimmy O'Brien, hired as many as two thousand deputies to make their menacing presence known on Election Day. Caleb S. Woodhull, a distinguished attorney, onetime Whig mayor, and the ancestor of an old New York family, made $10,000 on a corrupt ferry-franchise deal in the early 1850s.

Politics in the 1850s in New York was a crooked and violent enterprise. No party and no candidate had a monopoly on the use of intimidation at the polls and the acceptance of rewards for delivering contracts. Even so, no politician could match Fernando Wood for sheer audacity.

He dominated Tammany Hall after his first election as mayor, but just as the Democratic Party nationally was coming apart over the Kansas–Nebraska Act, the emergence of the Free Soil Party, and the emerging challenge of the new Republican Party, Tammany, too, was riven with dissent. Wood saw the organization as his personal machine, alienating other Democrats who were cut off from patronage and other spoils. Wood went his own way, splitting with the organization to create his own faction, Mozart Hall, which briefly challenged Tammany for dominance in the late 1850s.

Fernando Wood was a man who made enemies with ease, and with little apparent regret. He was a double-dealer who managed the neat— albeit morally reprehensible—trick of posing as a friend of immigrants in the mid-1850s while secretly joining the Know Nothings, a vicious anti-immigrant group whose members were trained to answer questions about their activities with a simple phrase, "I know nothing." Wood's ethical and moral failings did not end there. He sympathized with Southern slaveholders, and when war divided North from South, he sought—unsuccessfully—to declare New York a free city, aligned with neither side. His critics had no shortage of material with which to assail him.[38]

But the Irish loved him. In the cellars and saloons of downtown Manhattan, Famine Irish immigrants cared little about the cost of municipal government or the tax burden of the rich or even, sadly, the plight of Southern slaves. If Wood did indeed favor the immigrant over the native-born—at least after his short, secret dalliance with the Know Nothings—the Famine Irish could hardly be blamed for expressing their gratitude, even when it was delivered early and often in the rough-house politics of 1850s New York.

There was, however, much more to the Irish embrace of Wood than jobs, important though they were in the 1850s. Wood was the antithesis of the moralizing British administrators who had presided over the catastrophe that so embittered Famine survivors. From his earliest days as mayor, he advocated an activist municipal government at a time when the city's commercial and intellectual elites viewed assistance to the poor as "bounties for highwaymen," as an 1857 headline in the *New York Evening Post* put it. He championed government assistance for the poor and hungry during a deep recession in 1857, and he considered it government's responsibility to provide work for the unemployed and, even more ambitiously, higher education for the children of the poor. Wood proposed the creation of a free public university so that "the poor man, as well as the rich" could send his children to college.[39]

Whether Wood acted out of genuine sympathy for the poor is hard to know—he was a slippery fellow. But that hardly mattered to his Irish constituents. What mattered was the sound of a sympathetic voice—and the almost hysterical cry of critics who sounded very much like their brethren across the Atlantic. The *Irish News*, another periodical on the Irish-American community's expanding newsstand, stated its case for government action in terms that recent immigrants were sure to understand. "When famine stares fifty thousand workmen in the face, when their wives and little ones cry to them for bread, it is not time to be laying down state maxims of economy, quoting Adam Smith or any other politico-economical old fogy." The invocation of famine and the reference to Adam Smith, the British economist whose work was treated with religious reverence in Victorian Britain, shows that the Irish in New York saw a connection between their plight in Ireland and the conditions—and antagonists—they faced in New York.[40]

"Mr. Wood is greatly indebted as a politician to what are called by social philosophers the 'dangerous classes,'" wrote the *Evening Post* in 1857 after the mayor proposed that the city borrow money to purchase fifty thousand pounds each of flour, cornmeal, and potatoes to give to the city's army of unemployed workers in exchange for their labor on public-works projects. The mayor justified the request by noting that it was October, and winter was approaching. If the city did nothing, "want, destitution, and starvation will pervade the homes of the working men," he said, adding that the poor did not have the means to "avoid or endure reverses." Then, turning to language that would sound familiar to members of the workingmen's movement, Wood added: "Truly it may be said that in New York those who produce everything get nothing, and those who produce nothing get everything."[41]

Criticism of Wood became increasingly shrill after this admittedly demagogic speech. John Van Buren, son of former president Martin Van Buren and an important power in New York politics, charged that Wood was attempting to "array the poor against the rich." The *Evening Post* said that government was not under "any obligation to find people employment or food." The Association for Improving the Condition of the Poor, a private charity, asserted that "foreigners" were scheming to obtain government handouts. The association was the outgrowth of a Protestant evangelical organization called the New York City Tract Society, a group very much like the Bible societies in Ireland that sought to improve the condition of the Irish poor by leading them away from Catholicism. The association was intent on distinguishing between the "worthless" poor and the "modest and deserving" poor, in the words of Robert H. Hartley, the group's executive secretary. Those who wished the association's help were required to allow staff, or "visitors," from the organization to inspect their homes and investigate their private lives and habits.[42]

These moralistic views of the poor, framed by an unshakable belief in the intellectual and even physical inferiority of Catholics, were variations on the arguments of Charles Trevelyan and other Famine administrators who believed that government had no role in ameliorating the natural law of the marketplace, and that the poor often had only themselves to blame for their plight. Fernando Wood surely was a scoundrel and arguably a traitor, given his overt pro-slaveholder sympathies (although under Wood's administration, African-Americans obtained licenses as carters after trying and failing to win city approval under previous mayors). But his advocacy for the poor and his insistence on an active government role to help the unemployed were both humane and progressive, and they foreshadowed the actions and rhetoric of Tammany's Irish-American leaders in the decades to come. As the first mayor elected after the surge of Famine immigrants transformed the city's demographics, Wood became an important figure in the development of an evolving Irish-American political consciousness rooted in the Famine experience.

The Irish remained among Wood's most loyal supporters in all three of his successful mayoral campaigns (1854, 1856, and 1859). In the heavily Irish Sixth Ward, home of the notorious Five Points slum, Wood polled 2,107 votes in the 1856 mayoral election. All other opponents combined polled only 724 votes. Wood's popularity was no doubt enhanced when he bolted Tammany after a group of civic elites, including Samuel Tilden, a wealthy railroad lawyer, and August Belmont, a banker, joined the society. They and their fellow merchants, bankers, and professionals opposed Wood's radical solutions to joblessness and poverty. The new powers at Tammany conspired to bring about the mayor's defeat in a special election just weeks after Wood proposed spending public money on food for the poor. On the eve of that election in December 1857, Congressman Daniel Sickles—a Tammany member and future Civil War general—told President James Buchanan that "the best men in our party" wished to "get rid of Wood" and put in his place a more "reliable" mayor. The Irish vote followed Wood (except in Tammany's home base in the Sixth Ward) in his vain bid to hold onto his office, an indication that the Irish were more than capable of straying from Tammany on ideological grounds—a lesson Tammany would have to learn and then relearn in the decades to come. Indeed, the Irish again supported Wood when he successfully won back his old office in 1859 while running on an anti-Tammany ticket.[43]

Wood's popularity among the Irish in New York was a product of the singular circumstances of the 1850s, a time when tens of thousands of Irish immigrants were recovering from a catastrophe they came to see as a symbol of political powerlessness, official neglect, and callous moralism. It should hardly be a surprise that they rallied behind a mayor who, while tremendously flawed and cynical, appeared to sympathize with their plight and, perhaps not coincidentally, seemed to delight in enraging the city's moralizing elites.

CIVIL WAR

He was shrewd, ambitious, and ruthless, qualities that served him well as he rose from a tough city kid to a place of honor as the foreman of one of the city's best-known volunteer fire companies, Engine Company 6. For William M. Tweed—and for many other young men in New York in the years before the Civil War—the firehouse was a finishing school in the fine art of local politics, for it was there that he learned how to command, how to cultivate alliances, and how to manipulate the system. As the elected leader of his company, Foreman Tweed had a built-in base of supporters as he contemplated bigger and better things. That base only grew larger as he became a neighborhood legend—a magnificent sight with his red shirt and formidable physical presence—swaggering through the streets ahead of his company's engine, shouting from a speaking trumpet as his men raced to the rescue of their neighbors, and defending his company's honor and turf when competing companies were foolish enough to race Tweed's men to a fire. Bill Tweed was a young man in a hurry, and Tammany Hall noticed.

His career path took an unexpected and potentially damaging turn in the summer of 1850, when he and his men in Engine 6 were accused of attacking another engine company with "boxes, barrels and missiles of various kinds," according to an official report. It was hard to know at times whether New York's volunteer fire companies lived to fight fires or to fight each other. Individual companies were often affiliated with rival street gangs, but even if they weren't, each company saw others as rivals for the honor of dousing a fire. Tweed's Engine 6 was especially aggressive in the defense of its honor.

The head of the department, Chief Engineer Alfred Carson, saw these rivalries as an embarrassment, not to mention a hazard to life and property. He decided that Tweed should be "forever expelled" from the city's fire service because of the disgrace he brought to the department. This was a potential disaster for Tweed, for banishment from the firehouse would have put an end to his informal politicking and his neighborhood celebrity. Undaunted, Tweed contacted his friends on the Common Council's Committee for the Fire Department. The aldermen, a sympathetic lot, were known to put their sympathies in service to the highest bidder, earning the nickname "the forty thieves." By one means or another, Tweed persuaded them to reduce his banishment from forever—no small sentence—to three months. Chief Engineer Carson could hardly contain his anger, accusing one alderman of accepting "sundry golden trinkets" from Tweed and condemning the entire proceeding as a "black and infamous transaction."[1]

Carson's public display of disapproval did little to inspire the aldermen to reconsider. Tweed quickly returned to the fire service, and his standing in the community was revived. He and the lads from Engine 6 were invited to the White House to meet President Millard Fillmore a year after the foreman's short hiatus from the department, and, in 1852, twenty-nine-year-old Bill Tweed was elected to the Common Council's Board of Aldermen. The political organization he joined, Tammany Hall, soon adopted Engine 6's mascot for its own—a tiger. The Tammany tiger would go on to become one of the organization's indelible images.

Tweed, a big man with a dark brown beard and blue eyes, seemed destined for civic leadership. He was better educated than his old friends from Cherry Street, for his artisan father had found the money to send him to boarding school in New Jersey for a year. Tweed's sheer size set him apart—he was a growing young man who eventually topped out at more than three hundred pounds—but he was surprisingly nimble on the dance floor, to the delight of his child bride, who was seventeen when she wed twenty-one-year-old Bill in 1844. And he had a deep appreciation for his moment in the history of New York City. Although he was a native-born Scots Presbyterian, Tweed gained power and influence in accordance with his physical size thanks to his courting of the city's immigrants, especially the Catholic Irish, at a time when immigrants needed all the help they could get. A new and virulent nativism, more potent than the wave that elected James Harper as mayor in 1844, was beginning to take shape in New York life in the early 1850s as Famine immigrants settled into their new lives. Tweed himself dabbled in nativism briefly, but he came to embrace the cause of the city's immigrant population and its treasure trove of votes.

A new, diverse, chaotic, and—for many—alien community was taking shape in the streets of downtown Manhattan and in other cities with large immigrant populations. And in no city was this demographic revolution greeted with celebrations of difference and pleas for tolerance. Tweed's friend and ally, Abraham Oakey Hall, a Harvard Law graduate whose pince-nez, quick wit, and theatrical pretensions (he dabbled in writing for the stage) made him an irresistible character in New York politics, could not help but notice that many of his fellow citizens resented the city's transformation. New York's "rich old men," he said, pined for a simpler time when New York lacked "boulevards . . . museums, lyceums, free libraries, and zoological gardens." They simply didn't realize, Hall said, "that New York is no longer a series of straggling villages."[2]

Some of those rich old men—and some who were neither rich nor old—gathered themselves into a new and secretive organization called the Order of the Star Spangled Banner. They and others like them became better known as Know Nothings, and they became an electoral sensation in many Northern states as the country drifted toward civil war in the mid-1850s.

Outright nativism never truly disappeared from New York life even after James Harper was defeated for reelection and the American Republican Party faded as an independent faction in city politics in the late 1840s. Nativists targeted the Democratic city comptroller for defeat in 1849, and while he won anyway, his vote tally trailed that of other Democrats. Bishop John Hughes's old ally, William Seward, kept a careful watch over the movement, especially since many of his fellow Whigs were collaborating with the nativists. One of Seward's correspondents noted in 1852 that the Order of the Star Spangled Banner was a force "by no means to be overlooked."[3]

That assessment was, if anything, an understatement. The membership rolls of nativist organizations nationwide grew by the tens of thousands between 1852 and 1854, one of the most astonishing mass mobilizations in U.S. political history. The timing was hardly a coincidence, for the Know Nothing movement capitalized on the arrival of hundreds of thousands of poor, unskilled Famine Irish whose faith, customs, and culture changed the face of Northern cities and challenged the assumptions of those who saw the United States as an Anglo-Protestant nation. Catholic spokesmen, including Dagger John Hughes, hardly went out of their way to reassure the anxieties of the nation's majority population. One of the bishop's more prominent lectures, given at the height of Famine immigration, was entitled "The Decline of Protestantism and Its Causes."

Nativism explicitly sought to keep immigrants far from the levers of power. But nativist reaction had a softer side as well, expressed in the proliferation of Anglo-Protestant charitable groups such as the Children's Aid Society, the Ladies' Home Missionary Society, and the Association for Improving the Condition of the Poor, all of which were created in reaction to the huge influx of immigrants who were poor, unskilled, intemperate, and otherwise not in conformance with Anglo-Protestant norms.

These organizations certainly were earnest enough, but their efforts at amelioration were steeped in Anglo-Protestant cultural attitudes that would have seemed familiar to any Irish-Catholic immigrant. The Ladies' Home Missionary Society, for example, was affiliated with the Methodist Church, and its first priority was evangelization, because the journey out of poverty required that the poor put aside religious tenets that were holding them back. When the society announced plans to use public funds to build a new mission in the notorious Five Points neighborhood, Catholic spokesmen objected because of the group's overt evangelizing mission. The *New York Times* wondered why Catholics would not allow the missionaries "the chance of making a possible convert to their faith" in exchange for "the unquestioned good they have done."[4]

Immigrants who held onto their old-world ways explicitly challenged the assertion of nativists who insisted that the United States was not simply a white republic but a Protestant republic, an Anglo-Saxon republic, and a thrifty, sober republic. Drink, then, became another one of the evils that nativists associated with Catholic immigrants and, therefore, with their advocates in Tammany. The Irish fondness for whiskey, or *uisge baugh* ("the water of life," in Irish), and the German affection for beer seemed to be further evidence that the new arrivals were morally unfit for citizenship in a republic of virtue. The *New York Tribune* complained that "ninety percent of the rum holes" in some neighborhoods "are kept by foreigners."[5]

Not surprisingly, James Harper was a prominent member of a temperance movement in New York City called the Washingtonians—nativism and temperance had much in common. In a dry run of the nation's most successful antialcohol movement, Prohibition, a dozen states passed temperance legislation seeking to regulate or prohibit the sale and use of alcohol in the early 1850s.

The temperance movement made great strides in New York, leading in 1854 to the passage of state legislation dubbed "An Act for the Suppression of Intemperance," designed to prohibit the consumption of alcohol. The bill was based on a law passed in Maine in 1849, and its supporters had some reason to expect that Democratic Governor Horatio Seymour would sign it. After all, during his 1852 gubernatorial campaign, he told members of the New York State Temperance Alliance that he believed in "the importance and necessity of suppressing the evils of intemperance," although he managed to evade the alliance's direct question—would he sign a bill that would "prohibit the sale of intoxicating liquors"? Candidate Seymour gravely noted that, if elected, his "high and responsible duties" as governor would require him to be "free to act upon every question . . . according to my convictions of duty at the time."[6]

The time came in the early spring of 1854, when the temperance bill—actually, an outright prohibition bill—landed on Seymour's desk after winning overwhelming approval in the State Assembly (where it passed by a 76–27 vote) and somewhat less enthusiastic approval in the State Senate (18–10 in favor). At stake was more than just the right to drink, or the right to regulate potentially destructive personal behavior. The saloon was, along with the volunteer fire company, a center of immigrant political life. Tammany's ward-level politicians and their constituents met face-to-face in saloons. More to the point, saloons served as polling places on Election Day in many immigrant neighborhoods. Temperance advocates and elite reformers saw in the saloon the very antithesis of the moralistic, disinterested civic order that, in their view, the founders intended. The crusade for temperance, then, was more than a case of moral uplift, more than an assertion of cultural superiority. It was a direct assault on immigrant political power.[7]

Governor Seymour, under pressure from his allies in Tammany, vetoed the bill, arguing that "experience shows that temperance, like other virtues, is not produced by law-makers." Laws seeking to regulate morality, he wrote, would inevitably "provoke resistance where they are designed to enforce obedience."[8]

Seymour's veto outraged the city's moral reformers, who firmly believed in the power of government to legislate morality—at least, that is, the morality of newcomers. "This great cause is the cause of virtue, of morality, of religion, of social progress, of humanity itself," the bill's supporters wrote. "A single man has stood between the will of the people, clearly expressed, and the accomplishments of their purpose on this subject."[9]

Tammany Hall's governing body, the General Committee, convened a special meeting in late June of 1854 to prepare for an energetic campaign against the Know Nothings in the coming statewide and municipal elections. The committee passed a resolution defining the campaign as part of a larger struggle between immigrants and those who sought to deprive the foreign-born of their rights and their culture. The committee's resolution reads like boilerplate pandering today, but in the heyday of Know Nothing power in the Northern United States, it was an expression of high-minded principle.

The "greatness and glory of this republic have been materially advanced by the industry, energy, and patriotism of a large portion of its citizens of foreign birth," the resolution read, adding that it was "the glory and pride of old Tammany Hall" that it discriminated against nobody "on account of birth or religion." The committee's resolutions received prominent notice in the *Freeman's Journal*, the widely read weekly newspaper geared toward the city's Irish Catholics. The paper's headline referred to the committee's action as a "repudiation of the Know Nothings."[10]

The Know Nothings founded a new electoral vehicle, the American Party, to promote their anti-immigrant agenda of longer naturalization periods (which would delay citizenship and, thus, the right to vote for up to twenty-one years), temperance, moral reform, and restrictions on immigration. There were fifty thousand card-carrying Know Nothings in the United States in the spring of 1854. By October, as voters prepared to go to the polls in New York, Massachusetts, and other states with significant immigrant populations, more than a million people joined the Know Nothing rolls.[11]

Faced with a national uprising against immigrants, New York's

Irish community took understandable comfort in Tammany's pledge to defend the rights of the foreign-born and uphold religious freedom—the temperance-nativist linkage of morality, virtue, and religion surely carried more than an echo of the Protestant supremacist rhetoric with which Irish Catholics were so familiar. But Tammany could not provide a vigorous defense against the Know Nothing onslaught. The Democratic Party in New York was bitterly split over the Kansas–Nebraska Act, which allowed residents of the two territories to vote on whether to become slave or free states, and the larger question of slavery's expansion in the West. Emblematic of these passionate divisions in society, culture, and politics, two Democrats ran for governor in 1854. They were Horatio Seymour, the incumbent, who ran as Tammany's candidate, and Greene C. Brosnan, who represented the so-called hardshell Democrats, a faction that sought to punish other Democrats who strayed from the party line to support the Free Soil Party's efforts to keep slavery out of new territories.

The dying Whig Party nominated the author of the temperance bill, Myron Clark, and the Know Nothings rallied behind their own candidate, Daniel Ullman, a lawyer and frequent office-seeker. He argued that America's assortment of "castes, races, and nationalities" threatened the nation's future unless they became part of "one great homogenous American race."[12]

For Irish-Catholic spokesmen in the city's ethnic press, a "homogenous" America was an Anglo-Saxon America, a Protestant America. Those who spoke of homogeneity in America invariably sounded like those who sought the conversion of Catholics in Ireland. Anglo-Saxons, wrote the editors of the *Freeman's Journal*, "believe in their own divine right and mission to set the world straight" and that all other groups in the New World owed their rights and privileges to the " 'praying and prayerful men' who landed first on Plymouth Rock." The editors of the *Irish World*, writing several years later, described "the Anglo-Saxon race . . . in England and in America" as "our traditional enemies," and featured a poem entitled "I Am Not an Anglo-Saxon."

Out upon the very name . . .
It tells of wrong and outrage,
Of slavery and crime . . .
O! I'm not an Anglo-Saxon,
I am Irish blood and bone.[13]

These Irish-Catholic newspapers offered a counterpoint to the dominant narrative of the American experience that emphasized Puritans and Pilgrims and an assumed supremacy of Anglo-Saxon values. The Irish, with the support of Tammany, asserted a more expansive view of the American experience, one that included the stories of those whose hyphenated identities were just as legitimate, just as American, as the Anglo-Saxon's.

In the elections of 1854, however, the narrow view of American identity prevailed; in fact, it delivered a smashing, almost catastrophic assault on those, like Tammany's leaders, who spoke up for the immigrant and for a more pluralistic society. In New York, the temperance advocate Clark prevailed in an ugly four-way race in which the Know Nothing candidate, Ullman, recorded about a quarter of all votes cast. It was at the local level, however, where Know Nothing power was most on display. Four Know Nothing congressional candidates captured seats from New York, and several Whigs prevailed thanks to secret deals with Know Nothings.

The Know Nothing victories in New York were significant, but they were a political pittance compared with the movement's success in Massachusetts. There, the Know Nothing Party won every one of the commonwealth's eleven congressional seats, and the party's gubernatorial candidate won with more than 60 percent of the vote.

The Know Nothing whirlwind swept through Manhattan even in areas where Tammany seemed strongest. Perhaps sensing electoral disaster, or perhaps simply bored in Washington, freshman Congressman William Tweed did not run for reelection in 1854 after winning a seat in 1852. In a four-way race to succeed Tweed in New York's 5th congressional district, the cofounder of the Know Nothing movement, Thomas Whitney, stunned the two established parties and became one of sixty-two Know Nothing candidates to win seats in the House beginning in 1855. While the Democrats retained a majority in the House, despite having lost seventy-one seats in 1854, the Know Nothings were the second largest party in the House from 1855 to 1856.

As he contemplated the end of his short tenure in Washington, Tweed was nearly disconsolate, not for himself but for his party. The Know Nothing movement seemed on the verge of even greater power as its winning candidates took office following the 1854 elections. "Our only hope this fall," Tweed wrote of a fellow Democrat in early 1855, "is in having the [Know Nothings] fight among themselves. Otherwise we are a used up party for the present."[14]

Tweed decided that the Know Nothings "must be beaten at all hazards." Even as he prepared his departure from office, the soon-to-be-former congressman kept careful watch over the disbursal of federal patronage in his district to make sure jobs did not fall into the wrong hands. An ally of Tweed named James Murphy occupied the patronage-rich position of postmaster in the city of Williamsburg on Long Island, which was part of Tweed's congressional district. Murphy, at Tweed's urging, had appointed a man named Newcombe as a letter carrier, but the congressman now had disturbing intelligence about his choice. Tweed told Murphy that he had "heard stories" that Newcombe was a closet Know Nothing.

"I think you had better see if [Newcombe] is not one of the K.Ns & if he is I would advise his dismissal," Tweed wrote. If the Know Nothings were to be beaten, Tweed knew that Tammany had to use all means at its disposal, especially the spoils system. He urged Murphy to be "careful" about firing Newcombe, urging him to find a good reason "for his removal." If Murphy couldn't find a cover story for the suspected Know Nothing's dismissal, Tweed suggested that he contact a mutual friend who, he added darkly, "can furnish you one."[15]

Within a few months of Tweed's departure from Washington, Tammany's John Kelly, the lone Catholic member of the House of Representatives, rose to deliver a speech that required no shortage of nerve. The chamber, after all, was now a hotbed of nativism thanks to the Know Nothing victories in 1854—not to mention the Whigs and Republicans who were elected with Know Nothing support. Kelly was the son of Irish immigrants and a mason by trade. Photographs taken later in his life show him stuffed into a respectable three-piece suit but displaying rough-hewn hands that told of another life lived far away from places of influence. Like so many ambitious sons of the downtown wards of Manhattan, Kelly was introduced to politics at the local volunteer firehouse, where he may have impressed minor Tammany officials with his oratorical gifts—he was a self-trained actor who enjoyed performing Shakespearean roles in local theaters.

Kelly dropped out of school at a young age when his father died—the loss of fathers at a young age would haunt the childhoods of many future Tammany figures—and while he later returned to the classroom, he had no degree or formal academic training. He seemingly was out of his element in Congress. But on July 28, 1856, his fellow New Yorker, Thomas Whitney, cofounder of the Know Nothing movement, took to the House floor to assail the Catholic Church as a menace to republican government and civil liberties. Most "of the Papists—I do not say Catholics— in this country are foreign-born, and . . . they carry with them to the ballot-box the anti-American influences, prejudices, and superstitions of their church," he said. Catholics simply were not fit for citizenship upon their arrival on American shores—the longer they waited for naturalization and the right to vote, the healthier the republic would be.[16]

Kelly decided that he could no longer remain silent in the company of his more learned colleagues. On August 9, Kelly replied to Whitney in a long address that, he said, would "vindicate the constitutional rights and liberties of every American citizen, whether Protestant or Catholic." Responding not only to Whitney but also to those who were sent to Congress in the nativist surge of 1854, Kelly warned that, "in a government like ours, the rights of no class, however humble they may be, can be assailed without endangering the rights of all. The persecutor of today, when religious intolerance has fairly started on its disastrous course, will inevitably become the victim of tomorrow."[17]

Kelly continued to speak out against Know Nothingism, but his career in the House was short and otherwise undistinguished. After two terms, he left Capitol Hill for a job closer to home as sheriff of New York County. But his speech against intolerance, given in a legislative chamber filled with newly empowered Know Nothings, was a milestone in the nation's fractious debate over culture and identity—not because he was the only advocate for immigrants (he was not) but because he was the sole Irish Catholic in the chamber, and the son of immigrants himself. The speech was ignored in the city's press, but New York City's Irish-Catholic community printed it in booklet form and distributed it to the city's immigrant neighborhoods.

The debate over the worthiness of immigrants—which, in the context of 1856, meant Irish Catholics—was not nearly as passionate and poisonous as the ongoing argument over slavery. But on the streets of many Northern cities, it was an everyday reality for the people Kelly represented.

The Know Nothings disappeared almost as quickly as they rose to prominence, in part because events, including the Dred Scott decision in 1857, moved the more combustible issue of slavery closer to the forefront of national politics. Northern Know Nothings abhorred slavery just as much as they despised Catholics. Many found the new Republican Party to be congenial to both views.

.   .   .

With a temperance advocate as governor and a third of the state legislature in the hands of Know Nothings, New York quickly implemented the prohibition legislation that the ousted Tammany governor, Seymour, had vetoed in 1854. Among those who hailed the bill's success was the great abolitionist preacher Henry Ward Beecher, who spoke at a mass rally of fellow prohibitionists in the Metropolitan Theater on Broadway. Beecher said that if temperance could carry the day in New York City, it surely could triumph anywhere. But Tammany still had an ally in power. Fernando Wood owed his office in large part to the votes of working men who found comfort in whiskey and beer. To the outrage of the temperance crowd, Wood announced that the city's police officers simply would not enforce the new prohibition law. It was, he argued, unconstitutional—a judgment that the courts would validate months later. He was shrewd enough to seize on a fatal flaw in the legislation— the bill made all other liquor legislation moot, but it did not take effect until July 4, about two months after it was passed. Wood threw open the saloon doors on Sunday, arguing that until July 4 there no longer was a legal ban on liquor sales on the Christian Sabbath.

Wood's actions certainly made him a popular fellow in the wards of Lower Manhattan, but they were a sign of something deeper as well. In his defiance of temperance, Wood strengthened the bonds between Tammany and its immigrant constituents as they confronted the growing forces of nativism. Tammany, Wood, and the city's dominant immigrant group, Irish Catholics, became ever more closely associated with moral evils—whether the evil was drink, bloc voting, self-interested politics, or, to be sure, slavery.

· · ·

Tammany Hall leaders like Wood and other Northern Democrats have been rightly called to task for their overt pro-slavery sentiments or their studied agnosticism on the subject. Republicans and abolitionists, however, have escaped the scorn of history for their alliances with overt nativism. For example, the Reverend Edward Beecher, a member of the celebrated abolitionist family, authored a tract entitled *The Papal Conspiracy Exposed and Protestantism Defended in the Light of Reason, History, and Scripture* during the height of antebellum nativism. The Beechers were powerful advocates for abolition. They also were intensely anti-immigrant and anti-Catholic. Historian David Potter noted decades ago that it has been "psychologically difficult" for historians "to cope with the fact that anti-slavery, which they tend to idealize, and nativism, which they scorn, should have operated in partnership." But this insight is critical to understanding how and why Irish-Americans in New York acted and voted as they did in the years just before the Civil War.[18]

During his speech on the House floor in 1856, John Kelly called out abolitionists for their attitudes toward Catholics, particularly their complaints that Catholic clergymen acted as politicians rather than as ministers. Protestant clergy, Kelly noted, were "said to be at the head of the abolition party in the North, and some of them . . . I see sitting as legislators before me now." But, as he surveyed the House floor, Kelly noted: "I look around me in vain for a representative of the Catholic clergy here."[19]

Irish-American hostility toward nativism, or anything that hinted at nativism, was visceral and instantaneous. New York's Irish-American newspapers patrolled the city's political culture for signs of nativism or abolitionist hypocrisy, and their forays were rarely in vain. Horace Greeley's *New York Tribune*, one of the antebellum era's most powerful abolitionist organs, breathlessly reported on a possible "Catholic conspiracy" against the city's public schools in 1858. The paper went on to list the names of public school teachers in the heavily Irish 4th, 7th, and 14th wards—Mary A. Mahoney, Mary A. O'Brien, Mary S. McDermott, Mary B. Dolan, and three dozen others with similarly Gaelic surnames and suspiciously Catholic first names. "The foregoing names," the paper's correspondent wrote, "are given as a sample to show the sort of instructors placed over our school children, and who are expected to educate them for the responsibilities of American citizenship."[20]

While an abolitionist organ like the *Tribune* freely cast doubts on the ability of Irish-Catholic women to administer a proper American education, Tammany Hall was happy to provide those women— and, of course, their male counterparts—with the jobs and favors that came with power. It was no wonder, then, that the connection between Tammany Democrats and the Irish community grew stronger as nativism took hold, not just as a potent third party in the mid-1850s but also as a powerful faction in the fledgling Republican Party.

As the Irish reorganized their lives and re-created a sense of community in a city that must have been both tremendously alien and profoundly familiar, they defiantly held onto qualities that, in the eyes of native-born Protestant New Yorkers, made them suspect and something other than American. They reorganized their lives through the Catholic Church, Tammany Hall, and organized labor—institutions that so many elites found disreputable at best, criminal at worst. They developed their own ideas of civic morality that challenged the Protestant framework of disinterest, temperance, Sabbatarianism, and laissez-faire economics. And they insisted on retaining a portion of their Old World identity in their settlement patterns, their continued interest in Irish affairs, and in their expectations from government.

Expressions of Irish cultural and political grievance took many forms, but one of the most prominent was a rejection of the abolitionist movement. Some historians have interpreted Irish antiabolitionist sentiment as evidence that Irish immigrants wished to be accepted as white people, entitled to the rights and privileges set aside for fellow citizens of a white republic. According to this view, the Irish refused to make common cause with African-Americans, another oppressed minority group, and instead sought to establish their bona fides as white people by joining in the oppression of blacks and otherwise seeking to prove themselves worthy of white-skin privilege.[21]

Irish-American hostility toward abolition certainly is curious in light of their hero worship of Daniel O'Connell, one of the Atlantic world's most eloquent critics of American slavery. But O'Connell's own rhetoric helps to explain why the Irish in America came to resent the moral prodding of Anglo-Protestant abolitionists. For it was O'Connell who described oppression in Ireland as a form of slavery, and who often referred to the Catholic Irish as slaves.[22]

He was not alone. The language and imagery of slavery was constantly invoked to describe the plight of the Irish in Ireland as they struggled against Anglo-Protestant oppression. The popular nineteenth-century Irish poet Thomas Moore frequently drew on the language of enslavement in describing his fellow countrymen and their plight:

> *The nations have fallen, and thou still art young*
> *Thy sun is but rising, when others are set;*
> *And tho' slavery's cloud o'er thy morning hath hung*
> *The full noon of freedom shall beam round thee yet.*

One of Moore's best-known works, "The Minstrel Boy," narrates the death of an Irish warrior who, in his final act, tears the strings of a harp he carried into battle, rendering it useless:

> *Thy songs were made for the pure and free,*
> *They shall never sound in slavery.*[23]

The Irish were not unique in seeing themselves as little better off than slaves. Frederick Douglass visited Ireland on the eve of the Famine and was shocked to see living conditions on the island. "Men and women, married and single, old and young, lie down together, in much the same degradation as the American slaves," he wrote, although he later added that while the "Irishman is poor . . . he is not a slave. . . . He is still the master of his own body."[24]

Unlike slaves in the American South, however, the Irish found themselves without advocates in the Atlantic world, their plight ignored and their degradation worsened by the very people who condemned slaveholding. One of O'Connell's aides, Richard Sheil, complained as early as 1824 that "the philanthropists of England pity the state of the African and yet were insensible to the condition of the Irish peasant."[25]

Once in the United States, Irish immigrants continued to invoke the language of enslavement to describe their former condition in Ireland. The efforts of the Protestant-led Five Points Mission to remove poor or neglected Irish-Catholic children from their families and place them with Protestant families in the Midwest inspired comparisons with Southern slavery. The *Irish-American* newspaper carried a sensational report in November 1863 that Irish-Catholic children swept from the streets of New York were being offered "for sale" to Protestant families in Indiana. The paper blamed the "canting admirers of African ebony" for this outrage, linking abolitionists with the most heinous sort of anti-Irish activity. The same newspaper attacked an Irish landlord and abo-litionist named James Haughton for speaking out against slavery in the United States, arguing that, as a landlord, Haughton "has white slaves in Ireland as uneducated and uncivilized as the colored race he wants to extend his sympathy to."[26]

The harsh living conditions of impoverished Irish immigrants did little to soothe the sense of resentment and grievance that many felt after fleeing the Famine. The *Irish World* newspaper referred to the Irish in the United States and in Ireland as "the best abused people in the world," a characterization that reflects the narrow mindset of many Irish-Americans who must have taken great pains to avoid reflecting on the indescribable horrors visited upon Africans and actual native Americans.[27]

It surely is a sad irony of history that the Irish narrative of their own perceived enslavement did not translate into sympathy for the enslave-ment of Africans—Daniel O'Connell aside. O'Connell once explained to Dagger John Hughes that he had no choice but to be an abolitionist, because he "was born a slave myself." His followers in America, how-ever, saw matters quite differently. They saw the face of their enslaver in the abolitionist preacher, reformer, and politician. Indeed, some Irish-Americans began to emphasize the transatlantic nature of abolition-ism, arguing that British and American Protestants were in league not simply to end slavery but also to deprive Irish Catholics of politi-cal power. The *Irish-American* condemned what it saw as a conspiracy between "British philanthropists" and "certain insane abolitionists of this country."[28]

In the Irish worldview, any combination between British elites and American abolitionists could only have dire consequences for Irish-Catholic immigrants. The Irish collective memory of Ireland, recounted in editorials and poetry in the Irish-American press, reminded them that they were exiles from a land where power had raised up one group, Protestants, at the expense of another, Catholics. What had happened in Ireland through patronage and discriminatory laws could happen again in the United States if the same hostile forces came into power. The Irish looked to Democrats to protect them not simply from the competition of free black labor but also from the power of a hostile Republican Party aligned with Know Nothings who were determined to strip them of patronage and influence.[29]

Irish-American skepticism of abolitionists blinded them to the moral imperative of the antislavery movement. When the *Freeman's Journal* argued against the candidacy of Abraham Lincoln in 1860, the paper's editors asserted that "it is not the business" of politics "to settle moral questions" like slavery. New York's Irish neighborhoods simmered with resentment—of abolitionists, of the slaves they championed, and of the growing Republican Party—as the nation moved ever closer to a catastrophic conflict over slavery and the meaning of democracy. The Irish had no shortage of grievances with their adopted country, but none even approached the magnitude of the horrors to which slaves were subjected. Few if any of their leaders conceded this obvious point. Instead, spokesmen such as John Mitchel, an Irish political exile who escaped the prison colony of Van Diemen's Land (Tasmania) after his conviction on treason charges, expressed a yearning to settle on a plantation and own his own slaves. Mitchel founded a militantly anti-British newspaper in New York in the 1850s, but he moved to the South several years later. There he found people more in agreement with his view that slavery was a benefit to blacks and whites alike. Two of his sons died fighting for the Confederacy.[30]

. . .

The residents of Charleston, South Carolina, were fast asleep in the pre-dawn hours of April 12, 1861, when the thunder of an exploding mor-tar shell signaled the beginning of civil war. More than thirty hours and three thousand rounds later, the federal garrison in Fort Sumter in Charleston Harbor surrendered to South Carolina troops under the command of General P. G. T. Beauregard. Americans now were at war—officially—with other Americans.

Irish-Americans rallied to the Union cause after Sumter fell. By war's end, one hundred and fifty thousand natives of Ireland—thousands of them from New York—had answered Lincoln's call to defend the Union, regardless of their skepticism of abolitionists. More than fifty Irish immi-grants from New York won the Medal of Honor for their bravery, easily the largest total of any immigrant group. The volunteers from New York marched through the streets of Manhattan on their way to transports that took them to small towns in the South, places with such names as Chancellorsville, Antietam, and Fredericksburg. They joined outfits like the Irish Brigade, commanded by the Irish-born Michael Corcoran, and quickly gained a reputation for bravery and determination, charging into battle with the cry of *Faugh a ballagh*—an Irish phrase meaning "Clear the way." One of the brigade's regiments, the 69th New York militia, caught the attention of an opposing commander who could not help but respect the troops' courage under fire. Robert E. Lee called them "The Fighting 69th."

Tammany followed suit, authorizing its own regiment to join the swelling ranks of blue. Its commander, Michael Kennedy, was among the war's earliest casualties, falling at the first Battle of Bull Run. Tammany candidates for local office during the war were uniformly pro-Union—no hedging, no equivocation, no attempt to blame Republicans for the war. But Tammany did not speak for all New York Democrats, includ-ing Mayor Fernando Wood, who was now the head of his own break-away political faction. Before the attack on Fort Sumter, Wood proposed that the city consider neutrality in the event of civil war. He beat a hasty and temporary retreat after Sumter fell, but when he campaigned for a new term in 1862, the mayor cast his lot with other so-called Peace Democrats. The war, he charged, was little more than a plot to sacrifice the lives of poor white people to benefit Southern blacks. Tammany's official news organ, the *Leader*, charged that Wood was "heart and soul with the armed traitors of the South." In 1862, Wood lost his reelection bid to a Republican.[31]

By early 1863, however, many of the young men who so eagerly volunteered for Lincoln's army two years earlier were dead or maimed, and for what? The Southern rebels still were in the field, and, indeed, they had penetrated Pennsylvania. Fernando Wood staged public rallies to protest "war for the negro" after Lincoln transformed the conflict with his Emancipation Proclamation. Even the news of a great victory at Gettysburg did little to inspire New Yorkers who regarded the battle's enormous casualty list—more than twenty-three thousand dead and wounded on the Union side—to be as significant as the outcome itself. The enthusiasm of 1861 gave way to the grim reality of industrial warfare, and in New York, Wood and other Democratic politicians denounced the war as a poor man's battle, one that would benefit only blacks.[32]

· · ·

On July 11, 1863, federal authorities in New York began the task of implementing the nation's controversial new conscription law, which the Lincoln administration saw as the only option for filling the Union Army's dwindling ranks. Few believed the draft would be popular, especially in New York, but there was little public sign of dissent as men wearing blindfolds pulled sheets of paper containing names of reluctant soldiers from a large spinning wheel. The following day was July 12—well remembered in Irish lore as the anniversary of the Battle of the Boyne in Ireland in 1690, when the Protestant King William III defeated the Catholic King James II. It was a day when Irish Protestants throughout the Atlantic world marched in the streets to remember King Billy and to remind Irish Catholics of who had power and who did not.

That morning, the Sunday newspapers were filled with long columns of type listing the names of the new conscripts. Many of the names were Irish; most were from poor neighborhoods. The law allowed draftees to avoid service if they paid the government $300 or found a substitute. For most New Yorkers, the sum might as well have been $3 million. The war-weary *New York Herald* complained that the draft was patently unfair because "the rich could avoid it" while "the poor man . . . was compelled to go to war." With the draft set to resume on Monday morning, there was a growing sense of resentment and anger in the downtown wards.[33]

As morning broke on July 13, and preparations began to resume the draft, great crowds of men and women, workers and boys, immigrants and native-born marched uptown toward the federal provost marshal's office of the 9th congressional district, near Third Avenue and Forty-Seventh Street. Even before the first name was pulled from the wheel, the crowd claimed its first victim, Superintendent of Police John A. Kennedy. He was an Irishman, but an Irish Protestant, an Orangeman. Perhaps that was why Kennedy, who also was a member of the Republican-created Metropolitan Police Department, was beaten to a pulp. His life was spared when a low-level Tammany man named Johnny Ward intervened with the crowd.

Kennedy was lucky; hundreds of others were not. Mobs took over the city for four days—burning, looting, and lynching in a rage that still seems inexplicable. Not all the rioters were Irish, but by all accounts most were. So were many of the police and soldiers called into the streets to suppress what amounted to an all-out rebellion in the Union's most important city. Mobs attacked the homes of abolitionists, the offices of Republican newspapers, an orphanage for young black children. Any symbol of Republican power, any advocate for the enslaved, any black man, woman, or child who ventured into the street reminded the rioters of every grievance, every slight, every injustice that they imagined or brooded upon or witnessed firsthand.

The blood lust truly was frightening, even in the midst of a war notable for its everyday carnage. A black man was strung up on Madison Street and left there to die. The home of the postmaster—an appointee of the federal Republican administration—was torched and burned to the ground. Two black children were shot to death on Thompson Street. An army officer named Henry O'Brien ordered his men to use cannon fire to disperse the mobs, leading to the deaths of a woman and her child. The following day, the mob extracted its terrible revenge: O'Brien was attacked near his home, and, over the next six hours, was beaten and tortured by men and women alike, dragged through the streets while still alive, and tortured again until, at last, he died.[34]

• • •

New York was spinning out of control. Former congressman Bill Tweed, recently named the city's deputy street commissioner—a post that allowed him extraordinary control over the distribution of contracts and jobs—was a conspicuous presence during the worst of the violence as he gathered information, witnessed the carnage, and reported back to beleaguered civil authorities. His size and celebrity must have made his presence known even amid the chaos and disorder, but he was either courageous enough to put aside concerns about his safety or confident enough that the crowds would not turn on a Tammany man.

Tweed worked with the Republican mayor, George Opdyke, to convene an emergency meeting of the Democratic-controlled Common Council. He told the mayor that he was not safe in City Hall, that he needed to retreat to a place where he could be better protected. The point was driven home when mobs intent on destruction, if not worse, gathered outside the mayor's residence on Fifth Avenue. One of Tweed's Tammany allies, a judge, showed up and begged the crowd to leave the mayor alone. Amazingly, they did.

The violence came to an end after four days, when Union soldiers arrived on the scene fresh from Gettysburg and the federal government suspended the draft in New York indefinitely.

As bodies still lay in the street, decaying in the early summer heat, New Yorkers worried about what would come next. The federal government made it clear that conscription would be enforced again in August, raising the specter of a return to murderous disorder. Some of Tammany's more distinguished members argued for a direct appeal to Lincoln and to the courts to abolish the draft as unconstitutional. Samuel Tilden, an affluent attorney, was convinced that the constitutional argument was a winner.

Tweed had a different idea. He and his allies proposed a simple, practical measure designed to address what they perceived to be the mob's core grievance: The city would borrow funds to pay the $300 exemption for those who wished to avoid the draft, and pay bounties to substitutes willing to take the places of the exempted men. The initial payments would come from a $3 million bond issue, which a special agency, the County Substitute and Relief Committee, would supervise and disburse. Of the four committee members, three were from Tammany, including Tweed.

It was an audacious plan from any number of perspectives, not least of which was fiscal. The eventual cost of borrowing funds to purchase exemptions and pay out bounties exceeded $14 million, including interest. The Tammany-controlled council passed the required legislation several times, each time leading to a veto from a horrified Mayor Opdyke until the council finally put the program into place over his objections. The mayor, a member of the Association for Improving the Condition of the Poor, was among those who believed that government benefits ought to flow only to those whose behavior and morals were deemed worthy of charity. Tammany's program, he complained, "would afford great opportunities for abuse," in part because of its size. It was, he said, "too unwieldy for the investigation of particular cases."[35]

It was without question a gigantic and expensive program. But when the draft resumed in New York, there were no riots. Tammany bought peace, and, after the violence of July, who could say that the cost was too high? As a practical matter, too, the organization mediated the injustice of the draft law—not, as Tilden wished, by launching a quixotic legal campaign on constitutional grounds, but through the most direct means possible: offering nearly every poor potential conscript an equal footing with affluent draft evaders. It was not elegant, but it was effective.

. . .

A week after New York's antidraft violence ended, Dagger John Hughes, frail and gnarled by rheumatism and just months from death, told his old friend William Seward, now Abraham Lincoln's secretary of state, that "some misguided people" believed not that "black labor" would be made "equal to white labor," but that "black labor shall have local patronage over that of the white man." Those fears may well have been misguided, but the city's Irish Catholics knew that they stood to lose government patronage when Republicans were in office. The party's reform initiatives, with their overtly antiurban, anti-immigrant overtones, offered the Irish a glimpse of where they stood with the Republican Party's amalgam of abolitionists and nativists.[36]

The *Irish World* would later complain that in the Republican-dominated Congress of 1871, there were just two Irish-Americans among the 252 members of the House of Representatives and just one U.S. senator. "The negroes, who form but a tenth of the population, have 5 representatives in Congress," the paper noted, acknowledging fears that the Irish would lose their hard-won access to power under Republican rule. But the *World*'s editors did not find competition between blacks and the Irish as a zero-sum game. Of the number of blacks in Congress, the paper wrote: "This is not too many for the negroes, but see the inequality between them and us."[37]

As the war finally drew to a close in 1865, Tweed and Tammany were on the verge of ensuring that the Irish need not worry about losing access to patronage. Tammany emerged from the conflict with a sterling reputation for loyalty—the Tammany regiment fought with conspicuous bravery, and Secretary of War Edwin Stanton praised the organization's bounty program for helping to fill out the ranks of Union blue when the war's outcome hung in the balance. Tweed and Tammany were poised to take full advantage of the coming of the Gilded Age, as were the industrialists and financiers who would soon make their fortunes in New York's postwar boom.

．．．

The nation's Democrats assembled in a house that Tweed built—the Tammany Society's brand-new headquarters on Fourteenth Street—for their national convention in 1868. Tweed and Tammany were in their glory, and with good reason. Not only did the Democrats choose their ornate new building for their first presidential convention since the war's end, but amid the chaos and dealmaking, a Tammany ally, Horatio Seymour, emerged from the smoke-filled rooms as the party's presidential nominee to face Ulysses Grant. Seymour, the New York governor who had vetoed temperance legislation in 1854, proved to be little more than a sacrificial lamb, the first of a long roster of failed Democratic presidential candidates in the late nineteenth century.

Tweed focused Tammany's energies on matters closer to home, and with much greater effect. Thanks in part to his strong pro-Union stance during the war, his credibility as a kingmaker was without question. Already the chairman of the General Committee of Tammany Hall, he was elected to the State Senate in 1867 and was named grand sachem of the Tammany Society in 1869. That power allowed him to virtually handpick Tammany candidates for key municipal offices. In 1868, as Seymour ran his vain race against U. S. Grant, Tweed supported New York Mayor John Hoffman to succeed Seymour as governor. When Hoffman won, thanks to the votes of thousands of newly naturalized citizens in Manhattan's downtown wards, he threw Tammany's support behind the mayoral candidacy of Abraham Oakey Hall, the district attorney for New York County who had prosecuted some of the anti-draft rioters in 1863. Hall, Tweed felt, was a bit of a lightweight in the two-fisted world of New York politics. "All he needs," said Tweed, "is ballast."[38]

Tweed was happy to have the new mayor preside over civic ceremonies and parades, which Hall did with great flair, while he extended his personal empire. He formed a crucial political alliance with Comptroller Richard Connolly, the city's chief financial officer and a man known popularly as "Slippery Dick," giving Tweed almost complete power over New York politics. Even Samuel Tilden, the upper-crust railroad lawyer and ambitious Tammany insider, considered it prudent to answer any summons from Tweed, such as the one that arrived on his desk in late 1868. "I wish to see you on important business," Tweed wrote, instructing Tilden to stop by his office at 237 Broadway near City Hall—but taking care to leave the business unstated. Tweed also sent his local operatives to see Tilden on Democratic Party business. If Tilden, who fancied himself a reformer, objected, he must have kept it to himself.[39]

But Tweed's ambitions went beyond the everyday needs of a mass political organization. He branched out into the city's booming private sector, aligning himself with two of Wall Street's most brazen buccaneers, James Fisk and Jay Gould, as they successfully wrested control of the Erie Railroad from Cornelius Vanderbilt. Tweed's partnership with Fisk and Gould meant that he was in a position to cash in on everything from government contracts to insider trading. But to make his power absolutely complete, Tweed had one more move to make, and he showed that he was as light on his feet as he had been years earlier, before the lavish dinners with Fisk and Gould and the late nights in his Fifth Avenue mansion took their toll on his body. He needed a new charter for New York City, one that would return to city officials the powers that the Republicans in Albany took away before the Civil War.

It would be no easy task, even for Tweed. Upstate legislators despised the city, but they also rather enjoyed the bribes they received from time to time in exchange for voting in the city's interests. If they surrendered their enormous power over the city's police and fire departments and other agencies, Tweed and his friends would have no reason to bring wads of cash with them to Albany.

As chairman of the State Senate's Committee on Municipal Affairs, Tweed was not without traditional influence. But persuading his colleagues to cede their control over the city required more than collegial horse-trading and even bare-knuckle threats. It required cash. Opponents of the new charter spent freely, and so did Tweed, although only Tweed earned the disapproval of history for this corruption. The proposed charter gave the mayor the right to appoint four people to a new oversight board with no input required from the Common Council. The new board would have absolute power over the city's finances. Tweed knew that Mayor Hall would be delighted to defer to Tammany's wisdom in the selection of the board's members.

What's more, the charter gave the mayor power to appoint commissioners, which seemed like a simple matter of justice. Why, after all, should upstaters in Albany have that power? But, once appointed, the commissioners could not be fired—they would fill out their terms regardless of the mayor's desires. Under the guise of returning power to City Hall, the charter actually provided Tweed with the opportunity to put his allies in powerful positions, knowing that, once installed, they could not be removed.

The charter eventually passed, but not before Tweed and his allies handed over hundreds of thousands in bribes. If it was a corrupt business, well, some reformers in New York were less interested in the process than in the results. The new Tweed charter was welcomed in the city as a genuine reform. It certainly streamlined the chaotic budget process—four men, not a committee of a legislature, were in charge of the city's finances. It was all very efficient, very businesslike.

Peter Cooper, one of the city's great industrialists and the voice of the reform movement, signaled his approval of both the charter and of Tweed himself. The *New York Sun* soon afterward suggested that the city erect a statue of Tweed, until the man himself intervened. "Statues," he wrote, "are not erected to living men, but to those who have ended their careers." Tweed was in the prime of life, and of his career. Statues could wait.[40]

The mayor was quick to make use of the broad new powers Tweed had arranged for him. He needed a new commissioner of public works, and he knew exactly who would fit the bill. State Senator William Tweed, chairman of the General Committee of Tammany Hall and grand sachem of the Tammany Society, received a letter from the mayor requesting that he assume control of the Public Works Department. Hundreds of jobs and millions in contracts would be at Tweed's disposal. Naturally, the senator was delighted to accept the mayor's kind offer.

People started calling Tweed by a new name: "Boss."

FIVE

A TAMMANY RIOT

The fateful year of 1871 began with a parade, with no less a figure than Boss Tweed at its head, the grandest of grand marshals. But the parade's true honorees were five Irish political exiles, freshly arrived from Her Majesty's most notorious prisons and prepared to resume their agitation on Ireland's behalf in New York. The exiles' arrival in late January touched off a race like few others in New York's raucous political history, for it literally was a race.

With the exiles docked off Staten Island awaiting clearance from quarantine officials, a Tammany-sponsored boat churned through New York Harbor in hopes of overtaking a Republican boat that somehow had gotten a head start from the docks of Lower Manhattan. Each boat carried an Irishman with an impressive political title and an official greeting from high-ranking officials. The Republicans sent Thomas Murphy, who was President Ulysses Grant's choice to hold the patronage-rich job of collector of the Port of New York. His mission: Beat Tammany to the punch, welcome the exiles on behalf of the Grant administration, persuade them to come ashore on the Republican cutter, and win the gratitude of the Irish community. It was not such a quixotic mission:

The Irish in New York certainly were loyal Democrats in local elections, where Tammany was dominant, but on a national level, Republicans had reason to believe they might make inroads with a group that had fought for the Union with such conspicuous bravery.

In the Tammany boat, anxiously peering west toward The Narrows, was a Famine immigrant named Richard O'Gorman, now a judge. He carried with him a message of welcome to the city from none other than State Senator William Tweed. If he didn't beat the Republicans, there would be hell to pay.

The exiles had just finished a card game on the deck of the SS *Cuba*, and one of them, Jeremiah O'Donovan Rossa, was seven pounds richer for the experience, after having told his traveling companions that he had never played a card game in his life. Nobody seemed to mind—after serving years in prison for their role in an abortive rebellion in Ireland, they were free men.[1]

The Republican cutter arrived at the *Cuba* first, allowing Murphy to tell the startled former prisoners that the president of the United States was pleased to welcome them to their new home. A furious O'Gorman soon burst into the cabin and demanded to speak to the Irishmen on behalf of the city of New York. Murphy, O'Gorman, and their aides began to scuffle, verbally and otherwise, to the astonishment and disgust of their audience. Somebody warned the exiles against "Tammany tricksters." In the end, the bewildered Irishmen told both parties to leave—they'd make their own arrangements. They arrived in Manhattan the following day in a nonpartisan Cunard tugboat. Three thousand people, including Boss Tweed, greeted them at their hotel.[2]

The Republicans might have won the race for first impressions, but Tweed had power the Republicans couldn't match. He raised more than $25,000 and announced that Tammany would honor the new arrivals with a fine parade, with the aldermen and assistant aldermen and the Irish emigrant societies and, in the parade's final group, a unit of black citizens. This final touch inspired the *New York Times* to wonder why any black New Yorker would participate in a parade of Tammany Irish.

"Let them remember the Colored Orphan Asylum," the editors said, referring to the infamous torching of an orphanage during the anti-draft riots. Tammany had had nothing to do with the atrocious assault, although rioting Irish-Americans certainly were to blame.[3]

Two of the exiles who marched with Tammany, Tweed, the aldermen, the Irish organizations, and "the colored societies" would go on to become conspicuous political figures in the transatlantic Irish community. Rossa was the driving force behind a campaign of terrorism exported from New York to London in the 1880s, when Irish and Irish-American nationalists bombed Scotland Yard, Parliament, and the London underground rail system. John Devoy became the chief organizer of Irish-American nationalist politics from the 1870s until his death in Atlantic City in 1928, shifting his alliances between Republicans and Tammany Democrats as he sought to win American political support for Irish independence movements. During the last quarter-century of his life, Devoy was aligned with a prominent Tammany judge, Daniel Cohalan, who helped him raise money for a rebellion in Dublin in 1916.

The political maneuvering between O'Gorman and Murphy on board the *Cuba* was noteworthy because it showed that both major political parties actively competed for the Irish-American vote in New York even as late as 1871, when Boss Tweed and Tammany were thought to have had complete influence over the Irish. "As for the Irish, they have gone in a drove—as they always do—for the regular Democratic ticket," wrote the *New York Times* in 1856. "They will probably never do anything else, as long as they remain Irish, and it takes at least two generations to convert them into Americans."[4]

Relations between Tammany and the Irish, however, were far more complicated than the *Times* realized. The relationship was subject to constant negotiation, and voters were not afraid to walk away from the bargaining table when Tammany overindulged in shady practices or was unable to deliver promised services. The *Irish World* newspaper complained in 1874 that the "Republican Party has treated the negroes as *men*; the Democratic party has treated the Irish as *niggers*."[5]

Earning and keeping the Irish vote was more than simply a matter of naturalizing immigrants and sending them on their way into the
alien streets of New York. It required constant attention. Tweed organized picnics for children, made sure that the Catholic Church was taken
care of in state charitable appropriations, and gave voice to the Irish
community's aspirations for the land they left behind. For critics, these
were empty gestures, the worst sort of politics. After all, the picnics
did not provide a solution to childhood poverty; charitable contributions
simply stabilized an unjust society; and parades did nothing to bring
about revolution in Ireland.

Still, these were signs of respect, if not affection. And the Irish
noticed.

· · ·

The arrival of the five Irish exiles in early 1871 marked the beginning
of the most tumultuous year in Tammany's history. Riots, murderous
violence, and shocking allegations of extraordinary corruption would,
by year's end, reveal yet again the extent of the Irish-American community's alienation from mainstream society and would forever link Tammany with the grossest sort of political chicanery.

The beginning of the end for Tweed began to unfold even as the
boss looked absolutely unassailable. Tweed and his allies continued to
put the finishing touches on their schemes to control the city's budget.
They put into place another official entity, the Board of Audit, consisting of Mayor Hall, Comptroller Richard Connolly, and Tweed himself.
The board unilaterally decided to collect all outstanding bills that were
payable to the county Board of Supervisors, a move that seemed like a
good-government reform. After all, what could be more businesslike
than collecting payments for outstanding bills? The collections ran into
the tens of millions, especially after Tweed and his coconspirators added
a 50 percent markup, which was divided among Tweed, Connolly, Hall,
Tammany strategist Peter Sweeny, and lower-echelon clerks who knew
about the payment padding.

The great raid on the public treasury was underway. Tweed and his friends raked in millions as they took their cuts from inflated bills for public-works projects, including construction of a grand new courthouse on Chambers Street, just behind City Hall, and the continued construction of Central Park. The city borrowed tens of millions, rather than raise taxes, to finance its construction projects. Holders of city bonds, including some of the great financial institutions of Europe, had little reason to suspect that the city's books were cooked. Debts owed by New York—both the city and New York County—rose from $36 million in 1869 to $73 million in 1871. Money raised from bond issues paid contractors, who then paid off the politicians, including the man who supervised the city's finances, Comptroller Connolly.[6]

The involvement of Tweed and his allies—collectively known as "the Ring"—in the city's finances was hardly a secret. The *New York Times* regularly called attention to the probability of corruption, making up in invective what it lacked in solid evidence. New York's reformers finally were beginning to understand how Tweed had hoodwinked them with the new city charter. A group of civic elites met in Cooper Union in the spring of 1871 to hear orations from the likes of onetime abolitionist Henry Ward Beecher, who, along with other speakers, waxed indignant over Tammany's leaders and voters. Tammany could not have chosen better enemies—Beecher represented all that Tammany's core constituency, the Irish, resented about reformers, and, in any case, the reformers took no action other than to applaud the fine words they heard from the podium. Several days later, the New York Council of the Union League, another reform-minded civic organization, passed a resolution that, among other things, deplored the "ruffianism" of Tammany.[7]

Tweed might have smiled over all this indignation. As usual, Tammany's critics appeared to be foaming at the mouth, making charges with no hard evidence, and doing nothing but strengthening the bonds between the organization and its voters. Tammany's friends in the press, many of them bought off, offered a very different picture of the boss. A piece in the *New York Sun*, with more than a little exaggeration, dubbed him a "model public officer" in an article that recounted the boss's quick work in resolving a drainage issue deemed to be a public health hazard on the East Side. But the criticisms were taking their toll in other centers of power: Bondholders were becoming increasingly worried about the size of the city's debt and its ability to make good on those debts. The *Times* claimed that bond issues were among "the means by which our Tammany politicians . . . get their customary 'rake.' "[8]

On July 8, 1871, the *Times* published a fascinating but not especially sensational story about enormous rents the city was paying for facilities linked to Tweed and his friends—including a portion of Tammany Hall. The facilities were said to be armories. In fact, they were nothing of the kind, especially not the upper floor of Tammany Hall, for which Tweed charged the city a rental fee of $36,000 a year. The boss apparently added a zero to the market-rate rental for such a facility.

The *Times* story was a good deal more serious than the usual windy condemnations of Tammany's methods. The paper had hard facts, thanks to the efforts of a shocked city auditor, Matthew O'Rourke, who provided the *Times* with figures he had copied from the city's books. The story stated unequivocally that money from the high rents was "divided among the thieves of the Ring and the miserable tools who provide their dirty work." Among those who read the story with interest was a former Tweed ally, Jimmy O'Brien, the onetime sheriff known for flooding voting places on Election Day with tough-looking "assistants" who kept an eye on Tammany's foes. He had fallen afoul of the boss several years earlier and lost his lucrative job as a result. O'Brien, too, had incriminating documents, and they told a story that went far beyond inflated rents for nonexistent armories. O'Brien was soon on his way to the *Times* newsroom.[9]

. . .

Tweed and Tammany had other matters to worry about as the city's political class absorbed the *Times*'s accusations. A story about overpriced leases certainly was damaging, but it was hardly a death blow.

Tammany could shrug it off, perhaps even buy off the *Times*. (An offer was made; George Jones, owner of the *Times*, turned down millions.)

The more immediate problem was a looming anniversary—July 12. For Protestant Irishmen in the United States and in Ireland, July 12 was a day to celebrate supremacy over Irish Catholics with parades, songs, revelry, and, if the occasion demanded it, violence. These celebrations reminded the Protestant Irish of the heady days of July 12, 1690, when King William's victory at the Battle of the Boyne ensured the future of a Protestant monarchy in Britain. Irish Protestants who belonged to the Orange Order—an anti-Catholic fraternity named in honor of William of Orange—annually commemorated the battle with parades and music designed to remind Irish Catholics that while they had numbers, Protestants had power.[10]

Of course, the ancient battle meant little to most Americans who weren't Irish. America was the New World, a place where the rivalries and bitterness of the Old World were left behind—or so the narrative had it. Irish Catholics regularly were reminded that their Old World loyalty to the pope made them less American, less capable of living up to the republican ideals of the nation's antimonarchist founders. Irish Protestants, however, were free to march through the city's streets on July 12 to celebrate a military victory by a long-dead British king.

The city's Irish Catholics had a difficult time understanding why authorities allowed this display of religious supremacy to take place, especially in a city where, it was said, Tammany Hall was under the thumb of Irish-Catholic voters (or vice versa). During the parade in 1870, violence between Catholic protesters and Protestant marchers had led to the deaths of five people. The *New York Tribune* pointed an accusatory finger at Tammany Hall and Tweed, asserting that they represented the "ruffians who have committed this crime." Other newspapers echoed the *Tribune*, blaming Irish Catholics and Tammany for the riot. The city's Irish newspapers, on the other hand, lashed out at the marchers as un-American, literally. The *Irish-American* newspaper charged (without providing evidence) that the British government had helped to found and finance Orange lodges in New York, so it was the Protestant Orangeman, not the Catholic Irishman, whose loyalty to the United States and republican institutions was suspect.[11]

As another July 12 approached, city officials had reason to believe that the violence of the previous year could be repeated. Irish-Catholic objections to the parade inspired ringing denunciations in the city's secular press. Letters to the editors of the *Times*, the *Sun*, the *Herald*, and other newspapers warned of Jesuit conspiracies to deny native-born Americans of their liberties, efforts that required vigorous opposition from "one grand Vigilance Committee" that should "take this matter into their own hands. It should have been done long ago." The threats of violence, the assertions of Catholic conspiracies, the accusation of a plot against republican liberties—all would have sounded frighteningly familiar to the city's Irish Catholics. Pro-Orange factions circulated a broadside that insisted that the "claims of Roman Catholicism are incompatible with civil and religious liberty," an almost word-for-word adaptation of the arguments used against Daniel O'Connell's Catholic Emancipation movement of the late 1820s.[12]

Irish Catholics countered that they, in fact, were the defenders of American ideals, and their intolerant opponents were the real threats to republicanism and democracy. An Irish-American interviewed by the *New York Herald* argued that the Orangemen were not a religious faction but "Englishmen," and it was the duty of "American citizens" to "put them down."[13]

Tweed understood how close to the edge the city was. But there was a solution—the parade's organizers had applied for a required permit, as any group would have. What if the permit were taken away? Tweed couldn't do that, but Police Superintendent James Kelso certainly could. The boss and the mayor persuaded him that allowing a march down the West Side and into Greenwich Village would lead to bloodshed and disorder, perhaps even a radical coup against the governing order. Kelso got the message.

On July 10, with the parade due to step off in less than forty-eight hours, Kelso issued an order to his officers granting them power to keep the streets clear and to prevent any public processions on July 12. Mayor Hall, after consultations with Tweed and other Tammany figures, issued a letter to the Orangemen declaring that he found it "singular" that they would wish to celebrate "a foreign event occurring nearly two hundred years ago, and with which American citizens cannot actively sympathize."[14]

Kelso's directive, known as General Order no. 57, immediately inspired an uproar among Irish Protestants as well as the city's business community and some of New York's leading newspapers. The *Times* complained that the city "is absolutely in the hands of Irish Catholics," while the *Tribune* contended that the police superintendent, the mayor, and Tammany Hall had surrendered "to the mob."[15]

Inside the high-ceilinged halls of the city's Produce Exchange, where businessmen traded and speculated on the price of grain and other food-stuff, well-dressed men lined up to sign a petition protesting the parade ban. One respectable-looking businessman approached Superintendent Kelso at Police Headquarters.

"Did you issue that order, Mr. Superintendent?" the visitor asked.

"Yes, sir," Kelso replied.

"Well, God damn you, Sir, you deserve to be shot."[16]

Kelso's men quickly intervened, and no shots were fired. But through-out the city, invective only slightly less passionate was directed at both the superintendent and the mayor. Governor John Hoffman could not help but note that powerful New Yorkers saw the Orange parade as a matter of civil rights—and a test of who controlled the city's streets. The *New York Tribune* reported gravely that, in "the palaces of the Protestant aristocracy, in the little by-streets where Methodists congregate, all day sad hearts were brooding over what they naturally consider a blow at religious liberty." Hoffman rushed down the Hudson from Albany to Manhattan on July 11 and met immediately with Tweed and Hall. The meetings did not go well. As the bells of New York chimed midnight and July 12 officially began, Hoffman countermanded the city's order and declared that the Orangemen would be free to parade through the streets of New York. Several regiments of state militia were ordered to assemble in the city's armories in preparation for the day's festivities.[17]

Some two hundred marchers, protected by five hundred militia and police officers, assembled on Eighth Avenue and Twenty-Ninth Street that morning. Officers spread word of armed men roaming the rooftops of nearby buildings, waiting for the parade to pass by. Ambulances were deployed behind the marchers and their protective screen of troops and police, just in case.

As the marchers assembled into tidy lines for the journey down-town, one of the parade's organizers reminded them that the parade commemorated a "conquest over all our enemies." Those enemies—the city's Irish Catholics—were beginning to gather by the scores in nearby streets. American flags and banners bearing a likeness of King William himself flapped lazily in the languid summer breeze. The march's fife-and-drum corps played only American music rather than traditional Protestant Irish tunes designed to intimidate Catholics. The message was unmistakable: The Orangemen were the true Americans, and the American tradition of liberty included the Protestant victory over Catholics won on July 12, 1690, on the banks of the River Boyne.[18]

Catholic spectators on nearby rooftops and in the streets disagreed. As the march began, one leather-lunged dissenter called the Orangemen "infernal Englishmen." It wasn't long before brickbats began to fly, indiscriminately hitting marchers as well as troops. The Seventh Regiment of the New York National Guard led the way forward. One of the young men in the unit's ranks was the city's most famous political cartoonist, Thomas Nast, a German immigrant who despised Tweed, Tammany, and the Irish who supported them. As he and other militia-men tried to clear a path for the parade, a shot or two rang out, adding to the chaos, but nobody was hit—at least one discharge was likely acci-dental. As the main body of Orangemen moved toward Twenty-Sixth Street—just a few blocks from the parade's starting point—panicked troops opened fire on what they believed to be snipers in a tenement apartment house. The parade came under a furious counterattack from Catholic protesters, who picked off troops with well-aimed stones. The march continued.[19]

As the Orangemen reached Twenty-Third Street, where the column was supposed to turn east, troops from the 84th Regiment fired a fusillade into the waiting crowd. Mounted police charged into the crowds, cracking skulls. The streets quickly were covered with bodies, cobblestones, and shards of broken glass.

In no more than a few minutes, scores of people were dead or injured. The official tally found that sixty-two civilians were killed and a hundred wounded. Twenty-eight of the dead and forty-two of the wounded were natives of Ireland. Three militiamen and two police officers also were killed. Newspaper accounts of the violence described the sight of blood, brain matter, and chunks of flesh in the streets, in the nearby shops, and on windowsills. Amazingly, the parade continued.

In the Irish-American weeklies, the violence of July 12, 1871, was portrayed as yet another outrage perpetrated on Irish Catholics by Protestants and their enablers in positions of political and cultural authority. The *Irish World* newspaper reversed the lead rules separating its columns, creating a black, mourning effect on its pages. The paper condemned what it called "the Hoffman massacre," blaming the governor for caving in to Protestant prejudice. The paper's illustrations clearly were designed to portray the violence as part of a continuing narrative of transatlantic oppression of Irish Catholics. One drawing showed a triumphant Orangeman carrying a banner reading "King William" and stepping past two dead children and a grieving mother. Another depicted soldiers firing their muskets point-blank at a crowd of unarmed civilians, an image guaranteed to play on folk memories of one-sided rebellions in Ireland. The *Irish World*'s editor called the violence "the most atrocious murder ever done by official authority" in New York history.[20]

The city's mainstream press, however, had a very different reaction, with very different illustrations. The *New York Observer* said the violence was carried out "in the interest of Romanism," while the *New York Sun* referred to Irish Catholics as "barbarous assailants." Thomas Nast offered his interpretation in *Harper's Weekly* two weeks later. He drew the feminine figure Columbia with her right hand carrying a whip (labeled "law") and her left hand on the throat of an apelike Irishman. The caption read: "Bravo! Bravo!" For the rest of the summer—indeed, for the rest of his career—Nast continued his depiction of Irish Catholics as thuggish, drunken apes whose religious and political leaders posed a violent threat to the city's social and civic order.[21]

The intensity of anti-Catholic, anti-Irish commentary from the likes of Nast and the city's newspapers showed that nativism had not disappeared or become less respectable. A police official named Henry Smith even expressed regret that more civilians weren't killed. The *New York Tribune* referred to the violence as "the Tammany riot," asserting that such "frightful scenes" would continue as long as Tammany "depends for its existence upon the votes of the ignorant and vicious." A letter published in the *New York Herald* argued that the city was "governed too much by foreign influence. This should not be. Let Americans govern America. Let the offices be held by American-born citizens." A Presbyterian minister named David Gregg hailed the militiamen who fired on the Catholic crowds as "American patriots," telling members of his congregation that if they had been on Eighth Avenue that afternoon, they would have heard "rifles . . . ringing out salutes to religious freedom, and proclaiming death to religious tyranny and prejudice."[22]

For Irish Catholics raised on a narrative of grievance and violent oppression at the hands of Protestant enemies, efforts to justify and even celebrate the Orange Day killings showed that they remained vulnerable despite their growing political clout. For some, the memory of the carnage never faded—half a century later, as he approached his final days, Tammany fixture George Washington Plunkitt often told stories of witnessing the massacre and caring for the wounded and dying as they lay in the street. The *Times* campaign against Tammany and Tweed, along with Nast's offensive caricatures, furthered the notion of a growing political backlash against the influence of the city's immigrant-based institutions. In an editorial entitled "The Church of Aggression," the *Times* warned that Catholics had gained "a political power that is dangerous to our future" and were seeking "the control of our schools and our charities."[23]

As the city recovered from the shock of more political violence in its streets, the *Times* delivered another blow to Tweed—and to his Irish-Catholic allies.

. . .

On July 22, 1871, the *New York Times* published a long, sensational account of monumental corruption in city government. Tweed's onetime ally Jimmy O'Brien had slipped copies of the city's books to the newspaper's top editors. The books told a story of theft that even Tweed's harshest critics could not have imagined. There was enough material in the books for a series of stories, and that's precisely how the *Times* presented its revelations. Day after day in late July brought new tales of incredible fraud—nearly $3 million for furniture and half a million for carpets to outfit the new courthouse behind City Hall, hundreds of thousands of dollars for "repairs" and "alterations" paid to a firm with ties to Tweed. A carpenter named George Miller received more than $350,000 for a month's work. By way of comparison, total construction costs for the new Tammany Hall building in the mid-1860s came to about $300,000, and that sum was considered extravagant.[24]

Within days of the disclosures, the city found itself locked out of the bond market. Financial houses made it clear that the city's political leadership would have to change before New York could once again borrow money. Some of the city's most respected citizens banded together to form a group that called itself the Committee of Seventy. Disgusted with the results of mass politics, the committee set out to cleanse city government of the likes of Tweed and Tammany, who owed their power to the votes of immigrants and their children. The committee drew its inspiration in part from the goading words of E. L. Godkin, editor of

The Nation, a self-conscious voice of reform politics. Godkin blamed the city's plight on the "ignorant Irish voting element"—an interesting charge, considering that Godkin himself was an Irish immigrant. But he was a Protestant, and he surely believed he had nothing in common with the "ignorant" Irish-Catholic voters who were ruining the city. It was time, he said, for the city's better elements to make their voices heard, for "the Anglo-Saxon race" was not inclined to stand idly by while it was "robbed."[25]

The committee agreed, although it stayed away from Godkin's charged language. The group's seventy self-appointed reformers issued a special plea to New Yorkers who presumably shared Godkin's disgust. "At least one-third of the best classes of our people are habitually absent from the polls," the committee announced in late September. It was time they took an interest in civic affairs, the committee stated, because the "forces of evil" were "active, crafty and resolute."[26]

Actually, not all of the committee's enemies were so resolute. "Slippery Dick" Connolly, Tweed's ally, surrendered to pressure from reformers and agreed to appoint Andrew Green, a friend of Democratic Party state chairman Samuel Tilden, as his assistant in the comptroller's office. Tilden made it clear that Green would henceforth make all key decisions, and that Connolly, the elected comptroller, would function as little more than a figurehead. Connolly went along with the plan, hoping that playing nice with Tilden and his friends might serve him well as the crisis worsened. At this critical juncture, men like Tilden began to dismantle the city's elected government, replacing it with reliable fellow elites like Green, who could be trusted to restore the city's credit and to purify City Hall of patronage and politics.

As Tilden and the Committee of Seventy made their move, Thomas Nast created a series of vivid pictures in *Harper's Weekly* that played off the revelations in the *Times* and captured the sentiments of those like Godkin who believed that the city could no longer cater to the interests of Irish-Catholic voters. In late September, Nast upped the ante with a crude though vivid cartoon showing bishops as alligators preparing to attack innocent American children on the shores of New York. In the background was a rendering of Tammany Hall made to look like St. Peter's Basilica in Vatican City, with a banner showing an Irish harp flying from a flagpole. From a cliff above the beach, Boss Tweed and his friends hurled young children down toward the bishop-alligators.

Just as offensive, although not as crude, was an essay that accompanied Nast's drawing. In it, journalist Eugene Lawrence dragged up school controversies of the past—an issue that seemed to belong to another era—to argue against the presence of Catholics on school boards and other elected bodies. In Lawrence's view, the Catholic presence in city politics had led to the city's "treasury rifled; our credit shaken . . . our schools decaying, our teachers cowering before their Catholic masters. . . . the interests of the city neglected, its honorable reputation gone."[27]

As Nast continued his crusade and the city's print outlets followed the *Times*'s lead in demanding drastic changes in city government, Tweed and his fellow state legislators were in the midst of a brutal reelection campaign. To the astonishment of his growing number of critics, Tweed retained his hold on the city's Democratic machine and on his mostly Irish constituents. He drew cheers when he appeared in Tammany Hall for a campaign rally in late September and condemned the "vilifications" and "malignant attacks appearing in the daily papers." Reformers could only shake their heads in disgust, concluding, as Godkin did, that Tammany's ignorant voters were a blight on democracy. It did not seem to occur to them that Tweed's supporters saw him as a necessary ally at a time when the city's opinion-makers and would-be leaders were turning to the pages of *Harper's Weekly* for Thomas Nast's latest portrayal of the Irish menace.[28]

An unlikely reformer rose to challenge Tweed's State Senate seat: Jeremiah O'Donovan Rossa, one of the Irish exiles who had arrived in New York earlier in the year. Rossa, of course, had been in New York less than a year, so his candidacy might have inspired cries of fraud from critics who regularly complained about the speed with which Tammany naturalized the city's immigrants. But Rossa ran as an anti-Tammany candidate. Reformers chose to overlook his quick path to citizenship. The *Times* criticized "groundless" charges that Rossa was not a citizen and so was ineligible for election.[29]

Rossa was handed what must have seemed like a clinching argument on October 28, about a week before Election Day, when Boss Tweed was placed under arrest by a fellow Tammany man, Matthew Brennan, a onetime comptroller whom Tweed had disposed of in order to put the more reliable Richard Connolly in charge of the city's books. Brennan, now a sheriff thanks to Tweed's support, informed the boss of his arrest, accepted a $1 million bond for Tweed's bail, and departed. It was all so very civilized.

But days later, Tweed defeated Rossa to win reelection to the State Senate. Rossa charged that Tammany stole the election, but if it did, it was small comfort. Elsewhere the organization was routed from power—an anti-Tammany slate of Democrats called Apollo Hall captured every one of the fifteen aldermanic contests, and four of five State Senate races (all except Tweed's district). The reform Democrats and a resurgent Republican Party combined to win fourteen of twenty-one State Assembly seats—Samuel Tilden was among the victorious anti-Tammany Assembly candidates. Defeat at the polls led to further embarrassments: Connolly was arrested, Mayor Hall was charged with corruption (although, in the end, never convicted), and Peter Sweeny, the grand strategist of Tammany Hall, fled the country. By year's end, members of the General Committee of Tammany Hall understood that their boss had become a pariah, even if he remained popular with his constituents. They voted to remove Tweed as grand sachem and expelled him from the society. His coconspirators suffered the same fate. In Tweed's place, Tammany chose John Kelly, an Irish-Catholic son of immigrants, to salvage what remained of the organization's reputation.

The disgraced Tweed was found guilty on corruption charges in 1873 and died in prison in 1878 at the age of fifty-five. Before his death, Tweed testified before a special committee of the Board of Aldermen, publicly admitting to his crimes but assailing his critics when he believed they were simply posturing.

If he thought his confession would rescue his reputation, he could not have been more wrong. He remains, in popular image, the face of urban corruption—the face, indeed, of the institution he made famous, Tammany Hall.

His departure, however, marked a turning point in the organization's history.

SIX

TAMMANY'S IRISH RECONSTRUCTION

He was called "Honest John," and by all accounts the title was not given as an ironic joke. Quiet, shrewd, and deeply religious, John Kelly was a natural choice to lead Tammany Hall's rescue mission after the fall of Tweed. Not that Kelly's assignment would be easy, for the Tweed scandals promised to be—and, in fact, turned out to be—a burden that Tammany would never be able to shed. The organization was in utter disarray, and Tweed's formidable figure continued to cast a bleak shadow over its headquarters. Even after he was arrested and expelled, Tweed didn't go away—although he tried his best. Granted occasional opportunities to venture out of Ludlow Street Prison, where he awaited a new trial on corruption charges, Tweed managed to escape his guards (and his own family, whom he was visiting) in late 1875. He fled to New Jersey, then to Cuba, and then to Spain, but it was all in vain. American authorities tracked him down a year after his flight, and Spanish officials were happy to turn him over to U.S. custody. He returned to prison and shortly afterward began to tell his side of the story to the aldermanic committee.

So, even after his fall, Tweed remained in the news, a target of ridicule and contempt, while Honest John Kelly sought to persuade New York Yorkers that Tammany Hall had learned its lessons and no longer served as a power base for a corrupt few. But doing so required more than simply asserting Tammany's honesty in long-winded speeches. It required dramatic action. Kelly, a shrewd politician, understood that symbolic gestures would never satisfy Tammany's ferocious critics. He needed the assistance of the very men who drove Tweed from power.

To a certain sort of political moralist, to a certain kind of crusading journalist, Tammany Hall and, indeed, popular democracy itself were beyond redemption. Tammany-style politics attracted all sorts of disreputable types, people such as John Morrissey, an athlete and horse-racing enthusiast who used his celebrity to win election to Congress in 1866. The *New York Tribune* wondered: "How can a decent citizen vote for a prize-fighter and gambling-house keeper" like Morrissey?[1]

Even worse were the legions of neighborhood politicians inevitably referred to as "henchmen" in anti-Tammany newspapers. The lowest life form of all was the voter: ignorant, alien, dependent on government, and susceptible to Tammany's cynical manipulation. In American cities, wrote the reformer Andrew D. White, "a crowd of illiterate peasants, freshly raked from Irish bogs, or Bohemian mines, or Italian robber nests, may exercise virtual control." The results were all too plain, in White's view. As a rule, voters were "not alive even to their own most direct interests." It is not clear how White, writing from his perch in Ithaca, New York, where he served as president of Cornell University, was able to ascertain the best interests of illiterate peasants. But, like so many reformers, he was certain that he knew what was best for them, even if *they* didn't.[2]

Even before the Tweed scandal, reformers were beginning to talk about the need for men of property to rescue democracy from the ignorant and the poor—people who had no appreciation of the burden of taxation. In 1867, a group of civic-minded business leaders and reformers called the New York Citizens Association proposed the creation of a new City Council consisting of men who owned property valued at more than $20,000. Voting would be restricted to property owners whose holdings were worth more than $5,000. Reformers like Peter Cooper believed this was the only way to attract a better sort of person to politics.

He spoke for many, including the poet of the common man, Walt Whitman, who warned of the "appalling dangers of universal suffrage." White and other reformers made the argument that city government had nothing to do with politics. It became a familiar argument—there is no Republican or Democratic way to pick up the garbage—but many civic reformers in the Gilded Age were not concerned simply with the efficient delivery of services. They despised politics, at least at the municipal level—where, not coincidentally, the poor and immigrants outnumbered and generally outvoted the more privileged. Cities in Europe, White argued, were corporations governed in businesslike fashion, while in the United States, local government was hostage to mass politics. The result? A city where "the vote of a single tenement house, managed by a professional politician, will neutralize the vote of an entire street of well-to-do citizens." Tammany would not have disputed that assessment. Indeed, it would have considered White's complaint a point of pride.[3]

. . .

But not all of the city's mercantile elites shared the pessimistic views of Whitman and White. Rather than withdraw to the comfort of mere criticism or engage in the difficult work of sustaining a new faction within the Democratic Party, they chose to work with John Kelly in rebuilding Tammany. They included the likes of attorney Samuel Tilden and financier August Belmont, who had joined Tammany in the late 1850s, along with industrialist Abram Hewitt, Charles O'Conor (a prominent lawyer who prosecuted Tweed), and former governor Horatio Seymour, who had enjoyed Tammany's backing but who joined the Committee of Seventy to oppose Tweed's power grabs. Tilden, Belmont, and O'Conor were elected to serve on Tammany's governing body.

For John Kelly, a child born to Irish-Catholic immigrants in one of the city's poorest neighborhoods, this alliance with some of the city's most privileged men was no small coup. The new boss was a boxer of some renown as a youth and a volunteer firefighter—hardly the sort of person who generally did business with Tilden and Belmont. But Kelly understood that Tammany could redeem itself only if it were purged of the excesses of the Tweed era, and only if members of the city's business community were invested, literally and figuratively, in municipal government.

For their part, business leaders and reformers like Tilden understood that they could exercise control over Tammany—and thus, over city politics—only if they acknowledged the power of the organization's most fervent constituency, Irish Catholics. So Kelly became the first in Tammany's long line of Irish-Catholic bosses, and men of privilege like Tilden and his colleagues were, in essence, given the keys to Tammany's headquarters.

The joining together of uptown and downtown, of the interests of the few and the interests of the many, was bound to get complicated. For the moment, however, Kelly had little time to think about how he might keep together this unlikely coalition. Tammany Hall may have been rescued from disgrace, but it still had powerful enemies. As a political leader, Kelly's job was to make sure those enemies—Anglo-Protestant reformers, dissident Democrats, upstate Republicans—were kept away from the levers of power.

• • •

At an early age, John Kelly learned a fundamental reality of life in the immigrant slums of New York: Fathers often died young, and when they did, their widows and children were on their own. Kelly's immigrant father died when John was eight, in 1830. He later took a job as an office boy in the newsroom of the *New York Herald* to help support his family, putting an end to his formal education but not to his ambition. He learned the mason's trade and opened his own business while in his early twenties. He must have been a diligent worker, for he expanded his business quickly, but he was not entirely consumed with work. He found time for Shakespeare, and in the evenings he took to the stage as the leading man in amateur productions of the bard's tragedies. Young men with a gift for public speech-making invariably caught the eye of Tammany, and John Kelly was soon on his way to a life in politics. He was elected an alderman in his early thirties, and was sent to Congress in the Know Nothing year of 1854. There he gained notoriety for his speech in defense of Catholic liberties and loyalty. Later he became sheriff, a job known to make poor men rich because they were entitled to keep fees they collected. Kelly collected debts against the city with great efficiency, and he moved his family uptown in 1860 after only two years on the job.

That happy family was shattered in 1866 when Kelly's wife and young son died of tuberculosis, leaving him a widower with two daughters to raise. He quit politics, at least for a short time—in part because he had doubts about Tweed's leadership, in part because his own health was poor. He must have made his reservations about Tweed known, for in 1868 a group of reformers paid him a visit and urged him to run against Tammany's candidate for mayor, Abraham Oakey Hall. Kelly found the prospect intriguing, agreed to enter the race as the anti-Tammany candidate, but then had second thoughts. He withdrew from the race and sailed to Europe with his daughters. It was, politically speaking, an opportune departure. Kelly was out of the country while Tweed and company had their way with the city's treasury. He returned just as "the Ring" collapsed. He might have been a Tammany man, but nobody could say that Honest John Kelly was a mere stand-in for the disgraced Tweed.

Almost nobody, that is. The *New York Times*, reveling in the role it had played in bringing down Tweed and Tammany, saw Kelly's succession not as a turning point but as more of the same. Kelly, with his beard and stocky physique and past associations with fire companies, was nothing more than a slightly smaller version of the man now in Ludlow

Street Prison. Although the paper at first praised Kelly for bringing in reformers and ridding the organization of Tweed's allies, editors quickly changed their minds. The newspaper, no doubt echoing the thoughts of the city's reformers, objected to the tough Irish-American politicians who, they said, had Kelly's ear. "A revolution that left such men . . . at the helm" was hardly a change for the better, the paper argued.[4]

.   .   .

Kelly's first order of business, once he consolidated his power with the help and acquiescence of people such as Tilden, was to impose Catholic-style organization and discipline within Tammany's disorderly ranks. He was familiar with the institution, for not only was he a churchgoing Catholic, but his second wife, whom he had married in 1876, was the niece of Dagger John Hughes's successor, Cardinal John McCloskey. The union did little to dim criticism that Tammany served as an adjunct of the Catholic Church—or vice versa. The satirical magazine *Puck* portrayed Kelly in the robes of a clergyman and the pope as a scheming Tammany politico.[5]

Like John Hughes, Kelly decided that the organization he led had too many moving parts, too many freelancers handing out patronage and favors, too many dissidents who felt free to challenge the organization's hold on the Democratic Party. Tammany, in fact, needed a pope; Kelly was prepared to bring his flock into line.

Methodically, he stripped the power of patronage from the organization's equivalent of parish priests, its low-level operatives who looked after a block, a building, a ward, or a State Assembly district. These anonymous workers were the eyes and ears of the organization, the men who knew faces and names and, most important, situations—who needed help paying the rent, whose son couldn't make bail, whose widow had fallen on hard times. They had grown accustomed to handing out patronage on their own, without coordinating with Tammany Hall.

These local power brokers were known generically as ward heelers, a term of uncertain origin but one that was not necessarily meant as a compliment—although perhaps it was meant as one in the neighborhoods they served. Irish-American historian Daniel Cassidy noted that the word *heeler* may have been derived from the Irish word *elitheoir*, meaning an advocate or petitioner. Kelly was content to have the ward heelers act as advocates, but he was determined to keep control of Tammany's patronage out of their hands. Power was centralized in Tammany Hall itself, where Kelly could be found at all hours of the day or night.[6]

Kelly closely monitored the efforts and loyalty of the organization's midlevel leaders at the Assembly district and ward level. Each Assembly district, which was the basic unit of political geography, had its own leader who presided over a series of committees in each ward, which was a smaller political unit. Wards were further subdivided into election districts, and each ED had a leader as well. For example, the 1st Assembly district, which ran from the tip of Manhattan and north along the East River to Canal Street, contained four wards (the First, Second, Third, and Fifth Wards) and twenty-four election districts. Local leaders at the ward, election district, and block level reported to Assembly district leaders, who were members of Tammany's Executive Committee, answerable directly to Kelly. Four thousand members of Tammany Hall's General Committee, its basic unit of governance, were chosen by enrolled Democrats in party primary elections, which the Hall's Executive Committee did its best to control.[7]

John Kelly expected order from this vast apparatus. Leaders who did not turn out the vote were unceremoniously removed. Trustworthy, competent district leaders were placed in charge of distributing jobs—the precise number was determined in Tammany Hall and was based on performance on Election Day—and some were invited to join Kelly's inner circle of advisers.

Journalist William L. Riordon captured a sense of how this all worked in his compilation of the sayings of longtime Tammany fixture George Washington Plunkitt, published in the early twentieth century. Riordon tagged along with Plunkitt, who was a district leader, on a day that began with a knock on the door at 2 a.m.—a local bartender had been arrested and needed bail money—and ended at midnight after a late-night appearance at a wedding. Hours earlier, at 7 p.m., Plunkitt had met at district headquarters with his election district captains. "Each captain," Riordon wrote, "submitted a list of all the voters in his district, reported on their attitude toward Tammany, suggested who might be won over and how they could be won, told who were in need, and who were in trouble of any kind and the best way to reach them." Plunkitt took notes, issued his orders, and moved on to a church fair, where he bought ice cream for the local children.[8]

Such a sprawling organization required money—for campaigns, for influence, and for administration. Tammany's foes generally had unlimited access to private wealth, but Tammany's key supporters were hardly in a position to underwrite their political protectors. Kelly put into practice the adage that to whom much is given, much is expected. Those who were given his blessing and Tammany's nomination were expected to contribute a portion of their earnings to the organization's campaign treasury. Kelly didn't invent political kickbacks, but, as with everything else he did as boss, he made sure the flow of money from candidates and officeholders was steady and systematic.

John Kelly, it has been said, inherited a mob and transformed it into an army. He needed every soldier he could find, for enemies from within and without the Democratic Party were gathered around him, emboldened and determined. These enemies included reformers who refused to follow Tilden inside the belly of the beast, Republicans in Albany who were preparing to reassert control over the city, ferociously independent German organizations that steered clear of Irish-dominated Tammany, and a succession of Democratic factions that sought to replace Tammany as the city's legitimate party apparatus.

Discipline and loyalty were not the only weapons in Kelly's arsenal. He and Tammany both were remarkably patient, calculating that their most dangerous antagonists would soon give up the prosaic business of political organization and return to the sidelines, where they could observe, criticize, lecture, and otherwise congratulate themselves on their righteous purity.

．　．　．

Tammany's experiment in cross-class collaboration seemed doomed to failure early on, as the organization continued to perform penance for Tweed's sins. Kelly and Tilden were unable to unite the party for the national and local elections of 1872, leading to a splintering of the Democratic vote and yet another battering at the polls. Republicans had nominated the chairman of the Committee of Seventy, William Havemeyer, a sixty-seven-year-old banker and two-time mayor who once upon a time was a Tammany Democrat and the man who thwarted the Know Nothing James Harper's reelection bid in 1845. As Election Day approached, Havemeyer's supporters staged a rally on Wall Street to show off the candidate's business support. "The Stock Exchange and Gold Exchange were almost deserted by their members, and transactions in stocks during the period of the meeting were materially lessened," the *Times* noted approvingly.[9]

Voters dealt Tammany another seemingly lethal defeat, electing not only Havemeyer but also a Republican governor, John Adams Dix. The GOP's presidential candidate, incumbent Ulysses S. Grant, won the state even though a New Yorker, Horace Greeley, opposed him. Republicans retained control of the state legislature and dominated the state's congressional caucus. For all of Kelly's vaunted discipline and for all of Tilden's eminent respectability, Tammany seemed destined for irrelevancy in the closing months of 1872, as Dix and Havemeyer prepared to take office. Patrick Ford, editor of the increasingly influential *Irish World* newspaper, told readers that Tammany was pummeled in the elections of 1872 because they were "identified with" Catholicism. The *New York Times* surveyed the results of 1872 and rejoiced that the city would no longer "be tyrannized" by "our esteemed friends from the Emerald Isle. This is going to be an American city once more—not simply a larger kind of Dublin."[10]

Just over a year had passed since armed troops opened fire on the city's "esteemed friends from the Emerald Isle." The government of the city and the state were now in the hands of hostile forces. It was John Kelly's task to win back power, or see Tammany fade into irrelevance.

. . .

Despite the stereotype of Tammany as a free-spending raider of the public treasury, John Kelly shared with reformers a profound skepticism of government spending and debt. The Tweed scandals left a legacy of fiscal conservatism both within and outside the organization. Kelly noted in a letter in 1875 that the people had little faith "in the present management of our Governmental finances." Samuel Tilden, Kelly's partner in the reconstruction of Tammany, spoke for his fellow Swallowtail Democrats—named for the formal clothes they wore—when he told Kelly that the nation needed to return to the Jeffersonian idea of small, limited government. "What the country now needs, in order to save it, is a revival of the Jefferson democracy," Tilden told Kelly. "He [Jefferson] repressed the meddling of government in the concerns of private business. . . . The reformatory work of Mr. Jefferson in 1800 must now be repeated."[11]

Kelly's leadership of Tammany was contingent on his ability to please the likes of Tilden, Belmont, and the other Swallowtails who were interested in low taxation, efficient government services, and reductions in the city's debt, while not losing sight of the expectations of his fellow Irish-Americans who looked to Tammany as a friend in need when times were tough. Upstate Republicans sought to make Kelly's task more difficult in the spring of 1873 when they imposed a new city charter designed to dilute the city's ability to govern itself. The mayor's office was weakened, and the Board of Assistant Aldermen—a rich source of elective office patronage—was abolished. A new one-house City Council would have only limited power over the city's budget. The new source of financial power was the Board of Estimate and Apportionment, an unelected body. Local politics, the backbone of Tammany rule, was watered down in a provision calling for the election of six council members on an at-large basis, meaning they would be selected citywide, not from individual wards—the heart of Tammany's organizational strength. If the right sort of people were elected citywide, they could function as a check on Tammany's ward-based power in the new council.

The reformers' narrative of urban corruption, ignorant immigrants, and scheming Democratic bosses—in other words, the Tweed narrative—began to fall apart not long after passage of the new city charter. A new series of political scandals shocked the nation, but this time the villains were associated with Republicans, specifically, the administration of Ulysses S. Grant, and big businesses. The Crédit Mobilier bribery scheme implicated high-ranking Republicans, members of Congress, and one of the era's corporate titans, the Union Pacific Railroad. New York Republicans could no longer assume the moral high ground on the subject of government efficiency and disinterest. Indeed, the scandal rivaled anything Tweed cooked up while plotting with Sweeny and Connolly in Tammany Hall—although, of the era's many notorious malefactors, Tweed was one of the few who went to prison.

As Republicans and big business went on the defensive, Mayor Havemeyer made good on his campaign promise to reform the city's finances, slashing spending on public-works projects even after the city's economy collapsed in the wake of the Panic of 1873, one of the nineteenth century's worst recessions. Brought on by reckless speculation in railroad stocks and the collapse of the Philadelphia-based financial firm of Jay Cooke & Company, the recession led to the closing of thousands of factories, banks, and businesses, in turn leading to a national unemployment rate of nearly 20 percent. In New York conditions were even more dire: About a quarter of the city's workforce was unemployed. Jobless men wandered the city's streets, sleeping under streetlights and huddling together in public parks during the long northern winters. "On some days," the *New York Times* noted, "the main thoroughfares seem absolutely blockaded with beggars in all sorts of disguises. . . . Here and there one meets a petitioner who might be a highway man if the night were dark and the street unfrequented."[12]

Hard times persisted, month after month, year after year, through the mid-1870s. Workers throughout the country became more restive as government and business leaders stood aside to let market forces play out without interference. In Chicago, outraged voters elected a mayor and a majority of City Council candidates who ran on an independent People's Party line, threatening the city's political order. Labor unrest in the coalfields of northeastern Pennsylvania, blamed on an Irish secret society called the Molly Maguires, led to violent strikes, murders, and the mass execution of ten miners on a single date in 1877.

In New York, Tammany's constituents joined in calls for more active government intervention on behalf of the unemployed, staging huge protests in Tompkins Square Park to demand a loosening of the city's purse strings. Mayor Havemeyer urged the poor to do as his father did—save their money rather than spend their nights in "beer shops and theaters." The press supported the mayor's tough stand, arguing, as editors had in Fernando Wood's day, that government had no business interfering in the natural law of the marketplace.[13]

The police broke up the Tompkins Square rallies, to the mayor's delight, but his political problems were only just beginning. The number of families receiving a rudimentary form of public assistance from the city increased fivefold, from five thousand to twenty-five thousand, in less than a year. The mayor nevertheless concluded that the important issue was not deprivation but the city's balance sheet. He ordered a suspension of so-called outdoor relief, that is, small cash payments to impoverished families—a move that, combined with the mayor's cuts to public-works projects, deepened the discontent in the city's immigrant wards.

When Havemeyer ran for reelection in 1874, he fought a lonely battle. The reform movement that seemed so ascendant just two years earlier had tired of the boring business of governance. The Committee of Seventy simply disbanded, abandoning its former chairman in the midst of his campaign. Members dispersed to the more rewarding pursuits of commerce or the righteous purity of civic associations. Meanwhile, former congressman John Morrissey, an emerging power in Tammany, gave voice to the anger and frustration of the unemployed, charging that the mayor's austerity program was costing the city between thirty and forty thousand jobs. Morrissey was an Irish immigrant who made a fortune as one of the founders of a racetrack and spa in the upstate town of Saratoga Springs, but he never lost the hard edge of a onetime prize-fighter. When another politician made a derogatory remark about John Kelly in a barroom, Morrissey reverted to his former profession, leaving his antagonist with a swollen nose and two black eyes. "Those who are skilled in such affairs say he will not be able to appear in public for some days," the *New York Times* reported.[14]

To oppose the friendless Havemeyer, Tammany ran an utterly respectable diamond merchant named William Wickham. Morrissey and other Tammany figures pounded away at the city's inaction in the face of the deepening economic crisis, leading the *Times* to complain that "Tammany orators have been spreading Communistic ideas during the campaign," which the paper's editors feared would lead to greater "demands by the unemployed on the City authorities for work." For Gilded Age reformers in New York and elsewhere, such demands carried with them a whiff of the sort of radicalism that had overtaken the coalfields in Pennsylvania and the municipal offices in Chicago. New York's civic elites shared the Gilded Age reform agenda of low taxation, limited government, and, increasingly, a brooding skepticism about the virtues of popular democracy.[15]

John Kelly's Tammany, however, was not a People's Party and surely not a part of the Molly Maguires conspiracy. In supporting Wickham for mayor and the very eminent Samuel J. Tilden as its candidate for governor in 1874, Tammany managed to be both a stabilizing force and an advocate for the alienated and unemployed. It proved to be a shrewd combination. Both of Tammany's men were elected, unseating the two Republican-reform candidates whose twin victories in 1872 had seemed to signal a return to the rule of true Americans in New York.

. . .

After Tilden took over as governor, his ally Kelly quietly became a power in state politics. He was not afraid to remind the new governor that Tammany's wishes ought to be respected. In May 1875, he instructed Tilden not to sign several pieces of legislation until they spoke in person about the bills' merits. And he continued to exhibit a post-Tweed obsession with the cost of government, a trait not always associated with Tammany bosses. Kelly once sent an urgent telegram to an ally in Albany, insisting that a prospective bridge project—a potential source of patronage and employment—should be funded in a "clearly comprehensible" way. Otherwise, he added, "we will be censured. It would be very improper to give unlimited power to spend money."[16]

Kelly became Tilden's political and personal confidante as the new governor struggled with persistent hard times. Public discontent was not restricted to New York City—upstate farmers, like farmers around the country, were struggling with debt as credit dried up and crop prices fell. "May God spare you," Kelly wrote to Tilden. "Most men would have become disheartened at the many repulses."[17]

But early on in Tilden's tenure, a political observer writing in the *New York Times* predicted trouble between the two. Kelly, the anonymous writer asserted, wanted the governor to remove incumbent New York City Comptroller Andrew Green, who had succeeded the infamous Slippery Dick Connolly as keeper of the city's finances during the Tweed scandal. Green steadfastly refused to go along with demands for increased public-works spending to create work for the city's jobless, contending that it was more important to keep taxes low. Kelly was nearly as skeptical of government spending as Green was, but, unlike the comptroller—who was appointed, not elected—Kelly's power ultimately rested on voter approval. And many of Tammany's voters were either jobless or living on the margins. The *Times* saw a bitter fight in the making, arguing that Tilden had the support of "honest" men and taxpayers, while mere "politicians . . . wish the Kelly people success."[18]

Tilden, who had power over key city appointments thanks to post-Tweed limitations on home rule, refused to support a bill to remove Green. Just as the *Times* had predicted, Kelly broke with Tilden on the eve of the governor's presidential campaign in 1876. Tilden went on to win the Democratic nomination but lost the presidency to Republican Rutherford B. Hayes, despite winning the most popular votes. The Tilden–Hayes election was one of the closest and most controversial in U.S. history—the counting of contested votes in Florida, Louisiana, Oregon, and South Carolina went on for weeks, until a special commission awarded all the outstanding electoral votes to Hayes. Democrats were outraged, but they extracted a promise from Republicans to remove federal troops from the South and let the former Confederate states run their own affairs—which meant the return of white supremacy in the region. Tilden, who had given up his gubernatorial reelection bid to run for president, was a mere spectator to these machinations. Broken in spirit, he left New York for Europe to brood over his loss.

· · ·

Even as Tilden crossed the Atlantic, one of his most controversial actions as governor was about to dominate political debate in New York and around the nation. In early 1875, Tilden had asked twelve prominent citizens, including journalist E. L. Godkin, to serve on a commission to study the problems of urban governance. The Commission to Devise a Plan for the Government of Cities in the State of New York, which the press mercifully shortened to the Tilden Commission, began its deliberations in the long shadow of the Tweed scandals and in the midst of continued concerns over Irish-Catholic political influence in the city. In northern cities brimming with newcomers from Europe, powerful voices were beginning to argue that the problems of urban government could be resolved if the vote were restricted to those who owned property or paid taxes. "Universal suffrage can only mean in plain English the government of ignorance and vice—it means a European, and especially Celtic, proletariat on the Atlantic coast, an African proletariat on the

shores of the Gulf [of Mexico], and a Chinese proletariat on the Pacific,"
asserted Boston's Charles Francis Adams Jr., grandson of John Quincy
Adams. Elites like Adams saw power slipping from their hands into the
grasp of strangers—Irish, Africans, Chinese—whose votes threatened
not just the political status quo but the nation's culture and self-image
as a white, Anglo-Saxon, Protestant nation.[19]

Property qualifications, of course, had been all but eliminated in
most states during the exuberant age of Andrew Jackson, but critics
like Charles Adams and others were prepared to declare Jacksonian
democracy a failed experiment. Famed historian Francis Parkman dismissed the "flattering illusion that one man is essentially about as good
as another" and argued that in the hands of immigrants, the right to
vote led to nothing but "mischief." The New York Citizens Association, a
reform group of prominent citizens founded by Peter Cooper, joined the
debate, asserting that "it is not safe to place the execution of the laws in
the hands of the classes against which they are principally enforced."[20]

Critics of universal male suffrage realized that their position seemed
at odds with the American narrative of democratic progress. "Thirty or
forty years ago it was considered the rankest heresy to doubt that a government based on universal suffrage was the wisest and best that could
be devised," wrote reformer Jonathan Baxter Harrison in the *Atlantic
Monthly*. "Such is not now the case." Complaints about the expansion of
voting rights, Harrison added, could be heard "at the top of our society,
among some of the most intelligent, the most thoughtful, and the most
patriotic men."[21]

To justify new limits on the franchise, at least at the municipal
level, civic elites argued that cities—where the bulk of the immigrant
poor lived—were not subject to the same rules as state and national
governments. As creations of the state, cities were more like private
corporations and so should be governed, as private corporations were,
by stockholders, in this case, property owners and taxpayers. Yale
University President Theodore Dwight Woolsey captured the reformers' argument in a phrase: "None who do not own property should

vote for representatives who lay taxes on property." Such a measure, he eagerly noted, would mean that "the mass of city proletarians ought to be excluded from the polls where tax levying councilmen or officers are elected."[22]

The Tilden Commission's members already were inclined to view Tammany's voters as the source of New York's various political ills. Godkin, through his journalism, was on record about the unworthiness of Irish-Catholic voters. Other commission members included lawyer Simon Sterne, who had delivered a lecture against universal suffrage in London in 1865; Republican lawyer William Evarts, a future U.S. senator, attorney general, and secretary of state; and Edward Cooper, son of suffrage critic and longtime reformer Peter Cooper. They were not interested in investigating the causes of poor governance in New York City because they already knew what was wrong—the poor man's vote counted the same as the rich man's.

The Tilden Commission announced its findings in March 1877. Not surprisingly, the commissioners concluded that universal male suffrage was not, in fact, such a good idea after all. They proposed the passage of a state constitutional amendment limiting the popular vote in local elections to taxpayers who owned property valued at more than $500 or who paid an annual rent of $250 or more. Those taxpayers would choose a new board of finance that would oversee the city's treasury, leaving other elected officials with little control over how the city spent its money.[23]

One of the commissioners, Sterne, argued that his fellow civic elites had an "almost solemn duty" to take away the votes of the poor. At least one historian recently estimated that the measure would have denied suffrage rights to half of the city's three hundred thousand male voters.[24]

The *Irish World* newspaper greeted the commission's recommendations with a one-word headline: "Disfranchisement." In an Irish context, "disfranchisement" was fixed to a very particular memory. After Daniel O'Connell's election in 1828, the British increased the property threshold for voting rights in Ireland (with O'Connell's reluctant approval) from forty shillings to ten pounds, thus disenfranchising tens of thousands of poor Irish freeholders whose support for O'Connell so disturbed the social and political order in the United Kingdom.[25]

Elite opinion hailed the commission's work. Business and trade groups, including the city's Chamber of Commerce, supported the measure, as did an ambitious young Republican named Theodore Roosevelt. Some New Yorkers saw a similarity between their plight, as hostages to the votes of the poor and immigrants, and that of Southern whites, faced with the new reality of black men in political and civic life. "[White Southerners] have . . . an ignorant class to deal with, as we have here," wrote the weekly financial journal *Commercial and Financial Chronicle*. The problem, in both cases, was the power of suffrage.[26]

A Republican majority in the state legislature passed the proposed amendment in 1877, but that was not the final word. A constitutional amendment in New York required passage by two consecutive legislative sessions, and legislative elections were scheduled for the fall of 1877.

The interval between votes allowed Tammany to stand and fight. It had no choice, really, for the amendment was intended to deprive Tammany of its power by stripping its chief supporters of their votes. As Tammany organized a massive campaign against the amendment in the fall of 1877, and as Kelly shrewdly reasserted power over the state Democratic Party, Tammany's language and arguments underwent a conspicuous change. Rather than revisit the usual themes of anti-Catholic or anti-Irish grievances (although there was some of that as well), Tammany organizers deployed the language of class warfare to whip up opposition to the amendment. The Swallowtail Democrats must have cringed when they heard speakers denouncing the amendment as a plan to create "an oligarchy of wealth."[27]

The city's newspapers objected to Tammany's interpretation of the proposed restrictions. The *New York Tribune* attacked Tammany for telling the poor that the amendment would turn over government to "an oligarchy of landlords and bond-holders." The paper held up for special scorn "tipsy statesmen" who "discuss politics over their gin and bitters."

John Kelly's cross-class coalition, which had allowed the Swallowtails to mingle with the Five Pointers (or their slightly more upwardly mobile friends) at Tammany Hall, began to fray as Tammany's rhetoric became more confrontational. Many, but not all, Swallowtails left Tammany and started a new faction, Irving Hall.[28]

Tammany may have downplayed ethnic and religious grievances during the fight over suffrage, but supporters of the restrictions did not. The *Times* complained that Tammany's control over the city's treasury relied upon "the mass vote of the ignorant and the vicious, and upon the support gained by political hints dropped in front of Roman Catholic altars." The roster of those who supported the Tilden Commission's proposed reordering of the electorate—Republican reformers, hostile newspaper editors, and civic moralists—once again resembled the Anglo-Protestant oligarchy that had rendered Irish Catholics powerless in Ireland.[29]

Tammany successfully transformed the legislative elections of 1877 in New York City into a partial referendum on the Tilden Commission—not just its recommendation, but its very makeup, comprising as it did longtime critics of universal suffrage as well as prominent Republicans like William Evarts, who had no small stake in suppressing the reliably Democratic vote in the city.

The city's press was nearly unanimous in its support for candidates who promised to vote for the amendment. "The evils of municipal misgovernment are so great," wrote the *Evening Post*, "that citizens who bear the burden may demand a chance to give an opinion on any carefully and intelligently contrived measure of relief." The *Times* published a piece entitled "Facts for Working Men" which argued that "demagogues raise the cry" of disenfranchisement, but these "professional politicians and idlers" truly did not have the interests of "the working men" at heart.[30]

Tammany's voters disagreed. As Election Day neared, the *Irish-American* newspaper denounced the plan as "an attempt to confer exclusive privileges upon the few who are fortunate in owning property." Thousands turned up at a Tammany rally on October 29 to add their voices in opposition to the proposed amendment. As Tammany's sachems, ward heelers, and constituents filed into the Hall's meeting room from busy Fourteenth Street, they saw a huge banner hanging from the rafters: "The Republicans say let the property, not the man, vote." The opening speaker, Augustus Schell, immediately launched into an attack on the suffrage amendment, accusing Tammany's foes of trying to "rob" the poor of their right to vote.[31]

The Hall passed a resolution charging that the wealthy sought to seize control of popular politics and thwart the will of the people— including men who had so recently fought for the Union cause. Any party that supported such a scheme, Tammany's resolution stated, deserved "eternal infamy."[32]

The heated rhetoric and mass mobilization worked. Tammany's candidates won sixteen of twenty-one State Assembly seats from the city, leaving just two in Republican hands and three associated with Irving Hall, the dissident Democratic faction. Kelly could not help himself as he delivered a chip-on-the-shoulder victory speech to Tammany stalwarts after the votes were counted on Election Night. Mocking critics who called on voters to dispatch Tammany to the political hereafter, Kelly asked: "Try to drive Tammany Hall out of this community?" The idea was ridiculous. "Why, you might as well try to drive out the government." For Kelly, for the hundreds of political operatives in the city's immigrant neighborhoods, and for thousands of immigrants whose votes meant the difference between holding power and being powerless, Tammany was indistinguishable from government itself. For John Kelly, that association was a source of pride. For reformers, that was precisely the problem.[33]

When the Tilden Commission's amendment came up for a second vote in the spring of 1878, it failed miserably. Tammany Democrats did not control the legislature—Republicans did—but supporters of the amendment were more than capable of interpreting the previous fall's election returns, however skeptical they were of the democratic process in New York City. The movement to limit the franchise to the city's wealthy came to an abrupt end.

Abrupt, but not unlamented. The *Times* still was complaining about universal suffrage in 1880, as Tammany Hall prepared to support an Irish-Catholic immigrant for mayor. The paper noted, correctly, that the Democratic Party in the South engaged in "cheating and intimidating the ignorant negro voters," but in the North, the party counted on "the adhesion of voters beside whom the negro is an educated, virtuous, and law-abiding citizen." The Democrats, the paper asserted, could succeed nationally only by repressing "the vote of the plantation negro" while protecting "the vote of the citizen who is not the negro's peer from the slums of New York."[34]

Several years later, a Protestant clergyman named Joseph Hartwell published a thirty-page pamphlet entitled *Romanism in Politics: What It Costs—Tammany Hall the Stronghold of Rome.* In the course of complaints about Jesuits and "imported voters" ruining "the United States of Protestant America," the minister argued that the city needed "leaders" like "a William of Orange," the man in whose name the Orange Day parade took place in 1871.[35]

That was just the sort of thing the city's Irish-Catholic voters feared most.

.   .   .

As the city's two Democratic factions—Tammany Hall and Irving Hall—prepared for the 1880 mayoral campaign, both understood that their divisions would surely lead to electoral disaster. But finding a candidate who would please both the aging Swallowtails of Irving Hall, who equated civic virtue with wealth, and John Kelly, who understood that Tammany's power required access to patronage, seemed impossible. The two factions went through the motions of compiling separate wish lists of candidates to succeed reform-minded Mayor Edward Cooper, who, in the manner of many reformers, decided that he had had enough of practical politics after just two years in office.

Kelly no doubt recognized many of the names on Irving Hall's list, and it is easy to imagine this stubborn, battle-scarred veteran grunting at his desk in Tammany Hall as he glanced through names of earnest reformers from uptown, men with little practical experience in governing a city of multiple tongues, faiths, interests, and agendas. One name on the list, however, would have prompted a smile, if Honest John were so inclined. If not a smile, then surely a sparkle in his eyes.

Victory.

Somewhere on Irving Hall's list of acceptable mayoral candidates was the name of William Russell Grace, respectable business leader and philanthropist. Curiously, he was not a member of Irving Hall, nor had he been particularly active in civic affairs until this very year, when he tried to persuade the national Democratic Party to nominate a friend of his, Judge Calvin Pratt, for the presidency. It was not a particularly effective campaign, but Grace's political acumen didn't matter to the Swallowtails. He was wealthy, and that suggested civic virtue.

But he was Catholic. And an Irish immigrant. New York had never before elected an Irish-Catholic mayor. The very idea seemed absurd in many sections of elite opinion—the readers of *Harper's Weekly* and *Puck* continued to chuckle over cartoons featuring outlandish caricatures of Irish-Americans and Catholic bishops. Kelly nevertheless sensed the arrival of a moment when there were more of "us" than there were of "them." While immigration from Ireland had slowed since the peak Famine years, about 17 percent of New York's 1.2 million people had been born in Ireland, a figure that does not include the native-born adult male children and grandchildren of immigrants. Perhaps with that demographic reality in mind, Grace received the support of both Democratic factions, but it was hard to know which one was more bewildered—Irving Hall, which put forward Grace's name without knowing much about him, or Tammany Hall, which had to poach an Irish-Catholic candidate from the swells at Irving Hall.

To be sure, William R. Grace was not a typical immigrant from Ireland. He made a fortune after starting a shipping firm, W. R. Grace &

Company, in South America. When he finally settled in New York, he took up residence with the city's uptown elites. He was a wealthy man, a devout Catholic, and a confidante of the city's Catholic archbishop, Cardinal John McCloskey. Through His Eminence, he had had some dealings with the cardinal's nephew-by-marriage—Honest John Kelly.

If Grace's life story represented a new chapter of the Irish-Catholic narrative in America, some parts of it would have sounded familiar to the Irish who lived south of Fourteenth Street. Born in what is now County Laois in the Irish midlands in 1832, Grace was old enough to remember Daniel O'Connell and some of his younger allies who agitated against British rule in Ireland in the 1830s and early '40s. "His earnest, devoted [and] intelligent patriotism has ever been held in reverence by me," Grace wrote of O'Connell many years later.[36]

He also was old enough to retain firsthand memories of the Famine. While the Grace family did not suffer as so many others did, evidence of the catastrophe was all around them. Gaunt men worked on a road adjacent to the Grace family's farm, others worked on the property itself. Grace's father owned his own land and leased two other large plots, but as death and disease took hold of the Irish countryside, the family left their land and moved to Dublin, where young Grace attended school—but not for long. He ran away to sea in 1846 at the age of fourteen, fleeing a country where mass death and exile were only just beginning.

All these years later, the wealthy William R. Grace certainly had more in common with Swallowtail Democrats than he did with Tammany's legions. His credentials as a businessman and philanthropist should have impressed elite opinion-makers who saw wealth as evidence of political independence and disinterest. But Grace's religion mattered a good deal more than his political independence and his uptown respectability. The election turned on a single issue: the would-be mayor's Catholicism.

During the course of an ugly campaign even by nineteenth-century standards, newspapers and reformers questioned Grace's citizenship, his true loyalty, and his general fitness for office. At a late October meeting of anti-Tammany forces in Cooper Union, Elihu Root—future U.S. senator, secretary of war, secretary of state, and Nobel Peace Prize–winner—warned listeners that Grace's election threatened the "fundamental principle of our Republic that Church and State shall be separate. . . . " After Root's speech, two Protestant ministers, the Reverend Stephen H. Tyng Jr. and the Reverend John P. Newman, delivered speeches on behalf of Grace's opponent, a Republican named William Dowd, with Tyng conjuring the ghost of Archbishop John Hughes in arguing that Grace, as a Catholic, would undermine public schools just as Hughes had, while Newman suggested that New York under Catholic rule was doomed to suffer the fate of Spain, a nation kept illiterate under the rule of Catholics.

Another speaker, Lawson N. Fuller, built on the clerics' arguments, noting: "The Irish and Germans and the Scandinavians are placed in the public schools, have the dirt washed off them, and are turned out refined American citizens. They lose their identity as they should." Immigrants like the would-be mayor could become American, in Fuller's view, only by transforming their identity and shedding their Old World customs.

Faced with the possibility that New York might elect an immigrant from Ireland as its first Catholic mayor, the *Tribune* questioned the legality of Grace's naturalization in 1867, at a time when Tammany under Tweed was churning out naturalized citizens with assembly-line efficiency. The paper was forced to back down when the Grace campaign produced proper documentation, but editors remained unconvinced and continued to question the candidate's citizenship. It was a commentary on the city's Democrats, the *Tribune*'s editors wrote, that they were "running a man for Mayor of the greatest city on the Continent about whom old and well-informed residents ask whether he is even a citizen!"[37]

As the election neared, the anti-Catholic hysteria grew even more shrill. The *New York Herald* declared: "This is a Protestant country and the American people are a Protestant people." The *Tribune* dragged up a decade-old accusation that Grace had made a fortune by taking out large insurance policies on ships he knew were not seaworthy.[38]

On the Sunday before Election Day, the city's most-prominent Protestant preachers urged their congregations to stop Grace and the papal conspiracy he represented. "The Roman hierarchy," declared Reverend W. F. Hatfield of Washington Square Methodist Church, "should be dealt such a blow at this time that its encroaching power in this city will be destroyed." Reverend Newman told his congregation in the Central Methodist Episcopal Church on Fourteenth Street that they ought to oppose "the Democratic candidate for Mayor." The congregants burst into applause, to the satisfaction, no doubt, of a prominent Republican seated in the front pew—former president Ulysses S. Grant.[39]

Later that night, as Grant and his fellow worshippers reflected on the day's sermons warning against the influence of priests in politics, a crowd of some seven hundred Jews assembled in a hall on Third Street on the Lower East Side to denounce the anti-Irish, anti-Catholic assaults on Grace. A series of prominent speakers, including former judge Albert Cardozo, warned that if Grace were rejected on religious grounds, Jews could expect the same sort of treatment. Cardozo was not a perfect spokesman, for he was aligned with Tammany and had been forced to resign his judgeship several years earlier in the aftermath of the Tweed investigation. But his point and the point of other speakers was clear—the vitriol directed at Grace because of his religion was, in Cardozo's words, "contrary to the spirit of this country and its institutions."[40]

Tens of thousands of Jews were moving into Tammany territory on the Lower East Side, transforming entire neighborhoods. The 4th Assembly district, which bordered the East River north of the great bridge under construction between Manhattan and Brooklyn, was on its way to becoming overwhelmingly Jewish. Within its one hundred sixty-six acres lived more than seventy thousand people, making it one of the most crowded neighborhoods in the city. It was also the home turf of John Ahearn, one of Tammany's best-known district leaders. As Orchard Street became crowded with pushcarts, and as the sights and sounds outside the tenement houses changed in ways that would have shocked the old immigrants from County Cork, Ahearn and his Irish allies held court in the local Tammany clubhouse every Monday and Thursday night to hear the complaints and pleas of immigrants not far removed from the shtetls of Central and Eastern Europe. "To where besides the Tammany clubhouse could a white-bearded, eighty-year-old patriarch go for assistance. . . . Unable to speak or write a word of English, he would seek out our Irish leader," recalled Louis Eisenstein, the son of Jewish immigrants who grew up in Ahearn's district and who later became a prominent Tammany figure himself. Ahearn and Tammany received their thanks on Election Day.[41]

Candidate Grace might have won over some of the new immigrants south of Fourteenth Street, but many people above that traditional dividing line still had a hard time conceiving of a Catholic in City Hall. On the morning of Election Day, the *New York Times* made one final assault. Under the headline "Reasons for Rejecting Grace," the paper's editors argued that Grace was a mere puppet of Kelly, as incapable of independent action as Tammany's voters were. Grace, the paper reminded readers, was "a comparatively unknown man, an Irish Catholic . . . whose record in private business is covered with suspicion." Voters had a choice not between a Democrat and a Republican, or a Tammany man and an anti-Tammany man, but between "an Irish Catholic" and "an American Protestant with a long and honorable record." The commentary didn't even mention Grace's opponent by name. It didn't matter. He was, after all, an American Protestant.[42]

While the votes were being counted hours later, it seemed clear that the righteous pronouncements of clergymen and journalists alike had helped turn the tide in William Dowd's favor. When the early returns were reported back to Tammany, Kelly, the brooding puppetmaster, found himself facing yet another catastrophe. Dowd had a significant lead. Kelly's gamble apparently had failed; New York was not ready to elect a Catholic chief magistrate. As Kelly and his advisers kept mournful watch over the returns in Tammany Hall, Grace slipped into bed in his townhouse on Thirty-Third Street, presuming he had lost.

Late returns—too late for some of the morning papers, which proclaimed Dowd the winner—changed Grace's fortunes, and those of Tammany. New York elected its first Irish-Catholic immigrant mayor by about three thousand votes, a shockingly thin margin. By contrast, Tammany's previous victorious mayoral candidate, William Wickham, had won the 1874 election by nearly thirty-five thousand votes.

It was a victory all the same, and in the Irish neighborhoods of downtown New York, the election of a Famine immigrant who prospered in the New World was greeted with political hosannas.

SEVEN

CHALLENGING THE GILDED AGE

On a hot October evening in 1881, John Kelly and hundreds of supporters poured into Tammany Hall from the dancing shadows of gas-lit Fourteenth Street to announce a formal alliance between Tammany and a new independent civic organization called the Anti-Monopoly League. It was a highly unlikely combination, but then again, Kelly was no stranger to reconciling seemingly disparate interest groups. He had rescued Tammany after Tweed's downfall by joining together uptown and downtown, Fifth Avenue and the Bowery. If he could manage that, there was no reason to think he couldn't manage what might seem an even more audacious scheme: bringing together reform-minded businessmen and ward politicians in common pursuit of a traditional Tammany position—opposition to monopolies.

Civic organizations generally were the gathering places of reformers and civic elites who saw in Tammany everything that they despised about partisan politics. Tammany embraced transactional politics, the notion that voters—even those born elsewhere with only the vaguest understanding of American politics—had a keen sense of their own interest and would act accordingly. The independent civic organizations sought to uphold the ideal of a republic of disinterest, a place where the best men were empowered to identify the common good and proceed without having to step into the gutter of partisan politics. The Irish sang songs about neighborhood politics, like this ditty entitled "Two Aldermen from Tyrone."

> *We are two solid men and well known in the state*
> *Our political influence, sure it is great;*
> *In the Seventh and Tenth Wards we are first candidates,*
> *And our names in the paper in big letters you will see.*[1]

Members of reform organizations were not inclined to compose music to celebrate their involvement in politics, but if they did, the resulting dirge would have done little to lift the spirits of most voters. Mark Twain spoke for many of these self-consciously independent reformers when he complained that most American voters were like sheep: "We wait to see how the drove is going, and then we go with the drove."[2]

So it surely was with some trepidation that members of the Anti-Monopoly League filed into raucous Tammany Hall on this October evening. The league was part of a growing national reaction to the depredations of the age's robber barons, men like Tweed's old business partner Jay Gould, who swallowed up railroads and then moved into communications through a hostile takeover of Western Union, the nation's largest telegraph company. The league's leaders were, by and large, independent wholesalers who rightly feared the power of monopoly control over transportation and, with Gould's takeover of Western Union, of information. The wholesalers had to get their goods to market, and increasingly they needed access to information about prices, markets, and orders. They had no interest in seeing these resources in the hands of a few.

Among the league's most prominent members was none other than Lawson N. Fuller, who had spoken during William Grace's mayoral campaign about the need to rinse immigrant children of their Old

World ways. Fuller and other prominent league members saw their organization as an instrument to oppose "public corruption and corporate aggression." They were aghast when one of the league's founders, an upstate wholesaler named F. B. Thurber, proposed an alliance with John Kelly's Tammany, but Thurber proved to be persuasive.

Tammany's willingness to march into the Gilded Age's class politics no doubt caught many by surprise, including the antimonopolists themselves. As he addressed his new allies in Tammany Hall, Thurber acknowledged that many of his fellow antimonopolists had warned him that Tammany had no real interest in challenging the power of great corporate titans like Gould, John D. Rockefeller, the Vanderbilt family, and others. Rather, Thurber said, his friends believed Tammany was interested merely in power, not principle. With Kelly's supporters roaring their approval, Thurber announced that he rejected the doubts of other antimonopolists: "I say all honor to Tammany Hall."[3]

Thurber surely liked what he heard from Tammany's stage. Kelly himself spoke for half an hour, accusing both parties—Democrats as well as Republicans—of refusing to confront the growth of business monopolies because "they were frightened by the great power wielded by the corporations." He called on Democrats locally and nationally to support only those candidates who pledged "to legislate for the whole people . . . and not for the corporations which have come into power within the last few years."[4]

Of course, the dewy-eyed antimonopoly advocates, unaccustomed as they were to the flexibility of practical politics, might well have missed the broad rhetorical wink Kelly delivered during his stem-winder. Despite Kelly's populist rhetoric, Tammany certainly was not about to storm the barricades of capitalism, nor was it about to cut ties to aldermen and state legislators who took into account the needs and wants of railroad moguls and captains of industry. Nevertheless, Kelly's speech signaled what the *New York Times* called a "new war cry" for Tammany. Long before Theodore Roosevelt busted his first trust, Tammany Hall at least was sounding the alarm about the power of huge corporations at a time when the era's robber barons were transforming Manhattan into the corporate headquarters of the Gilded Age.[5]

Tammany's alliance with antimonopoly reformers came just months after the organization elected one of the city's wealthiest men, Grace, as mayor. Grace was no Rockefeller in terms of cash value and cultural power, but neither was he a critic of the era's growing inequality between rich and poor. Not long after taking the oath of office as the city's top elected official, Grace visited the elite Lotus Club, where he reassured some of the city's leading citizens that although he was Catholic, he did not bear the marks of the Antichrist. He won them over completely when he successfully challenged Tammany's control over the city's street-cleaning department, long a source of patronage for Tammany and of complaints from business leaders. Grace's actions led to a break with Kelly within weeks of the new mayor taking office. Not long thereafter, Kelly moved Tammany into an alliance with the antimonopolists. Grace, for his part, encouraged the growth of yet another dissident Democratic faction, called the County Democracy, which he believed could "unite all the Conservative elements" of the Democratic Party.[6]

Kelly's critique of corporate power might have surprised his former allies among the Swallowtails, but the signs of a transformation had been evident years earlier. The *Times* noticed a change of emphasis as early as 1877, when it complained that Kelly, then the city's comptroller, was "not an advocate of reducing salaries" for city workers. Taxpayers, the paper concluded, "can expect no quarter at [Kelly's] hands."[7]

They were not alone. Jay Gould, accustomed to favorable treatment from Tweed's Tammany, found out that there was more than a little bite in John Kelly's populist bark. After Gould consolidated his hold on Manhattan's elevated railways in the early 1880s, he doubled the price of a ride to ten cents, although the fare during rush hours remained at five cents. Gould's unpopularity and his unchallenged grip on the city's rail system made him a natural target for Tammany's new antimonopoly mission. A Kelly-controlled state convention in 1882 denounced the fare hikes and committed Tammany to bringing prices back down to five cents at all times, an aggressive assertion of government prerogative at the height of the Gilded Age. In early 1883, Tammany legislators in the State Assembly and State Senate helped to pass a bill requiring a rollback of fares, despite the heated objections of the powerful Gould and dozens of his fellow capitalist buccaneers. Among those who supported the bill was an eager young Republican assemblyman with a droopy mustache, Theodore Roosevelt. With his Harvard degree and polish, Roosevelt was portrayed in the *New York World* as "chief of the dudes" who inhabited the well-born Republican caucus in the State Assembly. He had little but contempt for bills that he believed set class against class, but, like members of the Anti-Monopoly League, he was alarmed as the era's great industrialists grew more powerful and seemingly unaccountable.[8]

The fare-rollback bill then went to the desk of Grover Cleveland, freshly elected as New York's governor after gaining a reputation as an antimachine mayor of Buffalo. Cleveland was an emerging hero of reformers—including dissident Republicans dubbed "mugwumps" (a word derived from the Algonquian language, roughly meaning a sanctimonious big shot)—who saw him as a bastion of the sort of nonpartisan, disinterested government they longed to achieve. They also saw him as a defender of the unregulated marketplace, a critical position at a time of economic unrest. Belief in the transatlantic dogma of laissez-faire economics was so ingrained in American politics and society that the president of the Massachusetts Institute of Technology, Francis Walker, wrote that it was "not . . . the test of economic orthodoxy, merely. It was used to decide whether a man was an economist at all."[9]

As if to prove his free-market bona fides, Cleveland promptly and forcefully vetoed the Tammany fare rollback, arguing that it violated the state constitution's protections of private property. Kelly could not round up the broader support he needed to override the veto— Roosevelt, for his part, reversed his position and refused to override, announcing that he was ashamed of his previous vote—and so the bill failed. Another populist bill, this one designed to legislate a twelve-hour day for overworked railway conductors, also passed with Tammany's support but fell victim to another Cleveland veto. Mugwumps and conservative Democrats were mightily impressed. There was talk of Cleveland as a presidential candidate-in-waiting.

Tammany and the governor were hardly allies to begin with (even though Kelly offered Cleveland his nominal support in the 1882 gubernatorial race). But after the veto of the fare rollback and other measures, they were implacable enemies. Most observers at the time attributed the feud to the governor's stalwart defense of the public payroll against Kelly's raids. But the conflict was much more complicated. Cleveland was a conspicuous defender of the economic status quo. And while Tammany may not have posed a radical threat to the laissez-faire economics of the 1880s, Kelly's army of district leaders and other hyperlocal operatives encouraged constituents to look to politicians—to the shadow government that was Tammany Hall—as mediators and advocates who could soften the blows of the free-market economy. Men such as George Washington Plunkitt, who made himself available to his constituents at any time, day or night, and Barney Martin, a Famine immigrant whose saloon on West Twenty-Third Street and Sixth Avenue served as an informal job-placement center and political clubhouse, were hardly rabble-rousers or radicals. In their own way, however, they subverted the Gilded Age consensus that government ought to play little or no role in the marketplace—the very dogma that had guided British policymakers in Ireland during the Famine. Every time they found a job for an unemployed immigrant, every time they arranged for a delivery of coal to a struggling widow, they did more than win a vote. Wittingly or not, they challenged the transatlantic Anglo-Protestant culture of rugged individualism and minimalist government. And they offered a sharp contrast to the Swallowtail Democrat or liberal reformer obsessed with low taxation and the morality of the marketplace.

While Tammany's alliance with the Anti-Monopoly League never developed into a true political partnership, individual Tammany members continued to sound the alarm over concentrated wealth throughout the 1880s. State Senator Thomas Grady, known (and often mocked) as Tammany's best orator, consistently voted in favor of antimonopoly laws and regulations during Cleveland's tenure as governor, leading Cleveland to demand that Tammany withdraw its support for his reelection. (Kelly did, reluctantly.) In an exhaustive analysis of the legislature's voting records, the Anti-Monopoly League found that Grady had cast more votes in support of antimonopoly positions in 1883 than any other senator save two (out of twenty-eight). While Cleveland was winning admirers for his opposition to Tammany's supposed depredations, the Anti-Monopoly League declared that the eminently respectable Chauncey Depew—Yale graduate, Skull and Bones member, and general counsel of the New York Central Railroad—"has probably done more than any other man in this state to corrupt legislation." Depew, a Republican, went on to become a two-term U.S. senator at the turn of the twentieth century. In his memoirs, Depew wrote that Cleveland had "more political courage . . . than almost any man who ever held great responsible positions." He "defied Tammany Hall."[10]

• • •

The conflict between the governor and Tammany became the dominant story of the 1884 presidential election as Grover Cleveland emerged as a leading candidate for the Democratic nomination. As the national Democrats assembled for their convention in Chicago in the summer of 1884, Kelly mobilized Tammany's two best orators, a young Irish immigrant named William Bourke Cockran and the organization's reigning master of the spoken word, Thomas Grady, to assail Cleveland with every combination of epithets they could wring from the English language. They did so with enthusiasm. Addressing his fellow Democrats from the convention stage, Grady portrayed Cleveland as an enemy of labor and a friend of monopolies, a charge that once again reflected Tammany's leftward movement in the 1880s. Grady conjured the ghost of Cleveland's veto of the five-cent fare, telling delegates unfamiliar with the issue why it was important. "It meant that when the workingman on Sunday takes his wife and his two or three children to the elevated railroad depot to go from . . . the tenement district to the suburbs, there to have the only holiday vouchsafed him during the week, he should pay twenty cents instead of forty cents," he said. As Cleveland supporters heckled in the aisles, Grady predicted that Cleveland would lose his home state "not because of any Irish question, not because of any Catholic question, but because of this anti-monopoly question."[11]

Cockran followed Grady with a display of irony and wit that would one day capture the attention of his future friend and oratorical protégé, Winston S. Churchill. Cockran, a well-educated lawyer and patron of the arts, portrayed himself as a friend of Cleveland. "Gentlemen, there is no person in this hall who feels more kindly to [Cleveland]," he insisted, adding that he was, in fact, so "warm a friend" of the governor that he did not wish Cleveland's "promotion to an office for which I do not believe he has the mental qualifications." Continuing to assess his dear friend Cleveland, he told delegates: "We have been told that the mantle of Tilden has fallen upon the shoulders of Cleveland. Gentlemen, when the mantle that fits the shoulders of a giant falls on those of a dwarf, the result is disastrous to the dwarf."[12]

Cockran's irony was not lost on a Cleveland supporter from Wisconsin, who sought to silence the Tammany orator with points of order and appeals to the convention chairman. When the delegate, retired Union general Edward Bragg, got his chance to deliver a riposte to Grady and Cockran, he uttered a line that history has remembered fondly. The young men of Wisconsin, Bragg said, loved and respected Grover Cleveland, "not only for himself, for his character, for his integrity and judgment and iron will, but they love him most for the enemies he has made." The line stung. Grady, seated with his fellow delegates, bellowed from the floor: "Mr. Chairman, on behalf of his enemies I reciprocate that sentiment, and we are proud of the compliment." Grady was ruled out of order by the convention chair and by most historical accounts that view Bragg's indignant putdown as a direct hit on the corrupt machinations of evil Tammany. Rarely is it noted, however, that Grady's argument (less so Cockran's) was based not on religious or ethnic appeals but on social justice, with Tammany's spokesman serving as the voice, however flawed, of New York's workers and the fledgling critics of the Gilded Age's economic order.[13]

During the weeks after Cleveland's nomination, New York buzzed with rumors that Kelly and Tammany might support former governor and congressman Benjamin Butler of Massachusetts, who mounted a quixotic third-party presidential campaign as the candidate of the Greenback and Anti-Monopoly Parties. Butler, a onetime Union general and an avowed opponent of slavery, was widely despised in Brahmin Boston as an economic rabble-rouser because he supported greater regulation of business and the implementation of a federal income tax. He was popular with the Irish in Boston and in New York, although he was not Irish himself, suggesting that issues beyond ethnicity factored into Irish-American voting patterns.

Kelly gave some thought to bolting the party, but eventually he fell in line and announced Tammany's support for Cleveland in early September. But Tammany did little to get out the vote for Cleveland, and it nearly cost him the presidency. He defeated Republican James Blaine thanks to New York's thirty-six electoral votes—but he won those votes by a margin of just 1,149 popular votes in his home state.

For Kelly and Tammany, the elections of 1884 proved a double catastrophe. Not only was Cleveland promoted to the White House, but their onetime friend, now an open and adamant enemy, William R. Grace, captured a new two-year term as mayor on the County Democracy ticket. Tammany and John Kelly faced a daunting prospect: Democrats were in power all right, but not Tammany Democrats. And, despite their rhetoric, Tammany's foes were not above engaging in the sort of bare-knuckle politics they themselves had so often criticized.

.   .   .

The presence of Tammany enemies in both the White House and City Hall meant that patronage, that disreputable practice of using access to power as a means to provide work for political operatives and favors to constituents, would dry up, and that critics like Cleveland and Grace would hire their allies and call it a merit system.

For Irish-Americans in New York, however, the scramble for political offices was becoming less important than the economic disparities of the Gilded Age. As great palaces rose along upper Fifth Avenue and Central Park to house the Vanderbilts, the Rockefellers, and the Morgans, the tenements below Fourteenth Street grew more crowded. Labor unrest in the late 1870s led to deep concerns among New York's wealthy about their own safety and that of the social order they represented. The shadows of the draft riot and the Orange Day riot were never far from the city's collective memory—it was no coincidence that some of the city's wealthiest families, including the notoriously anti-Catholic Harpers, helped to fund a new armory on Park Avenue on the Upper East Side.

A bold new Irish-American critique of the era's inequities was apparent in the conspicuously Gaelic leadership of the Knights of Labor, the country's largest labor union, and in Irish-American support for a new antilandlord campaign in Ireland. With the energy and danger of anti-Catholic nativists seemingly spent by the early 1880s, the city's Irish community could afford to discuss the ends, rather than simply the means, of holding political power. New York became the center of political activity and debate in the transatlantic Irish world. Patrick Ford, editor of the *Irish World*, and John Devoy, head of the Irish nationalist movement in New York, mobilized the Irish community behind radical land-reform efforts in Ireland championed by Michael Davitt, a onetime Irish rebel, and Charles Stewart Parnell, an austere Anglo-Protestant member of the House of Commons whose mother had been born in the United States.

Their challenge to the power of landlords inspired a social revolution in Ireland with implications for Irish-American industrial workers in New York, as Ford frequently pointed out in the pages of the *Irish World*, which added the title *Industrial Liberator* to its masthead at around this time. During the late 1870s and early 1880s, Devoy, Ford,

Davitt, and Parnell built support among Irish-Americans for aggressive antilandlord agitation in Ireland. They reached a consensus on the radical idea of land redistribution and peasant ownership of the land on which they worked—ideas that challenged the very structure of British rule in Ireland. Patrick Ford sent economist Henry George to Ireland to witness the antilandlord campaign and to frame the agitation as part of a wider Atlantic-world struggle between labor and capital. Ford's newspaper employed a columnist who wrote under the pen name of "Transatlantic."[14]

Parnell traveled to New York in early 1880 to raise funds and, with the help of Kelly and several Irish-dominated labor unions, he founded a new antilandlord organization in New York called the American Land League. The league borrowed its organizational strategy from Tammany, establishing a strong, centralized leadership and points of contact at the ward level in New York. Within a year, the league had raised more than $500,000 (in 1882 dollars) to fund Parnell's antilandlord campaign in Ireland. Tammany continued to raise funds and hold mass meetings on Parnell's behalf throughout the decade, leading the *Times* to note that the Hall was "outdoing itself . . . in behalf of the Parnell fund."[15]

The mass support for Parnell showed that the Irish community in New York was prepared for a radical new departure in achieving social justice—and demonstrated yet again its deep and continued connection to Ireland. Teachers in St. James Parochial School on the Lower East Side introduced students to a poem entitled "The Song of the Shirt," by a socially conscious English poet named Thomas Hood. Many decades later, one of those students at St. James, Alfred E. Smith, would recall the poem's sympathy for exploited women working in the needle trades.

> *With fingers weary and worn,*
> *With eyelids heavy and red,*
> *A woman sat in unwomanly rags,*
> *Plying her needle and thread—*
> *Stitch! Stitch! Stitch!*

John Kelly, sensing the growing discontent among Tammany's key voting bloc, ramped up his own populist rhetoric. New York, he said, was governed "by the railroads, rich corporations, and great monopolies," leaving Tammany Hall as "the only rallying point around which the masses may concentrate for the perpetuation of democratic principles."[16]

Tammany, however, had competition on its left. The Central Labor Union, one of the city's most important organizations of workers in the late nineteenth century, was founded after several New York unions came together to advocate for land reform in Ireland. Catholic social thought in the United States also was beginning to move to the left during this time of labor strife and management suppression of workers' movements. Despite the presence of a new archconservative bishop, Michael Corrigan, in St. Patrick's Cathedral, Catholic prelates like Bishop John Ireland of St. Paul, Minnesota, and Cardinal James Gibbons of Baltimore urged the American Church to take up the cause of its working-class flock.[17]

With Catholics in prominent positions in the labor movement, the liberal prelates argued, it was imperative that the Church understand the conditions that had led to worker discontent. Corrigan and other bishops pushed for a formal Vatican condemnation of the heavily Catholic Knights of Labor and of Henry George's agitations in Ireland, but Gibbons successfully argued against such a statement, especially at a time when "land grabbers are stealing thousands of acres of land with impunity." The voice of American laissez-faire liberalism, The Nation's E. L. Godkin, condemned the cardinal's sympathy for working-class discontent, accusing the prelate of "partaking freely of the labor beverage."[18]

Tammany and the Catholic Church both adjusted their ideological bearings as their core voters and believers moved to the left in the mid-1880s. But John Kelly no longer was strong enough to keep a firm hand on the tiller. The double defeats of 1884 had left him a broken man, physically as well as politically. Once a constant presence in Tammany Hall, he now rarely left his apartment on West Sixty-Ninth Street, leaving the daily business of running the machine in the hands of an Irish immigrant and onetime gang leader named Richard Croker.

Like Tweed and Kelly, Croker sported a full beard and a physique that did not invite challenge. As an up-and-coming Tammany leader, he exercised his right to vote seventeen times in a single day during an election for constable in 1865. Nobody said a word.

As Kelly began to fail, Croker left little doubt about where he stood in the matter of succession. He set up shop in Kelly's office, behind Kelly's desk, in Kelly's chair, while the old boss spent his final days in his uptown apartment. Tammany sachems who might have entertained ideas of somebody other than Richard Croker as the organization's next boss took one glance at the menacing figure in Kelly's old chair and returned to their districts to think other thoughts. Kelly died on June 1, 1886, after a long and debilitating illness. On the day of his funeral, June 5, thousands gathered outside his home to pay tribute to the man who had rescued Tammany and then transformed it. A reporter noted that the mourners included any number of high and low city officials, but most impressive was the turnout of working men. These "hard-fisted laboring men," the reporter noted, "never asked for more than a mere living and . . . had obtained that through Mr. Kelly's influence and power. These men exhibited more honest grief over Mr. Kelly's death than was displayed by all in the rest of the crowds."[19]

The following day, Richard Croker took up residence behind a desk that was no longer Honest John's. Now it was Richard Croker's desk. There was no further discussion. Tammany now had its first immigrant boss.

EIGHT

❖⇒◎⇐❖

TO HELL WITH REFORM

R ichard Croker's parents made the journey from Ireland to New
York in 1846, the second year of the Famine and the third year
of young Richard's life. They were not the typical starving exiles from
the Emerald Isle, for they were Protestants, and Croker's father was the
scion of an old landholding family. But Eyre Coote Croker, a veterinary
surgeon and a blacksmith, had fallen on hard times just as so many poorer
Catholic tenant farmers had when the potato failed. Croker packed up
his family and sailed to New York to start anew. They settled for a time
in a shantytown along the western edge of Central Park, where it was
not uncommon to hear Irish spoken, but they eventually moved south
to East Twenty-Sixth Street, near the gas plants that would give their
name to the neighborhood, the Gas House District.

Richard Croker grew up in the rough-and-tumble world of antebellum New York, in a neighborhood where leadership required powerful
fists and a willingness to put them to use. He came to the attention of
Tammany's local talent scouts not through his subtle understanding of
the Federalist Papers, nor for his facility with the English language. He

was brought into politics because he packed a mighty punch, as Tammany learned when young Croker pummeled a noted street fighter, Dickie Lynch, at a favorite Tammany picnic ground called Jones Wood on Manhattan's East Side. Croker was elected to the Board of Aldermen in 1868 and was put to efficient use in the early 1870s as one of Tammany's more dependable "repeaters"—that is, someone who could be counted on to cast multiple ballots on Election Day.

As he matured, other attributes recommended him to people like Honest John Kelly. Croker was a tireless worker, and his loyalty was beyond question. Kelly promoted him within the organization even after Croker was linked to the murder of a Tammany critic in 1874. (The trial ended in a hung jury, although it seemed likely that Croker was not guilty.) Croker repaid the boss during Kelly's final months of life, visiting him frequently and offering comfort at a time when Tammany was alienated from the White House and City Hall. Lonely and broken, the dying Kelly could at least take some comfort in Croker's presence. And Croker eagerly absorbed the lessons Kelly chose to pass on as his life, and his control over Tammany, slipped away.

Croker inherited an organization that had survived serious challenges to its dominance from other Democratic factions through hard discipline and artful maneuver. But as he settled into Honest John's old office in the Hall, Croker was confronted with two new threats to Tammany's dominance.

Assessing one of those threats required just a short walk south from Tammany Hall, where the old neighborhoods south of Fourteenth Street were changing in ways Croker's fellow County Cork natives barely recognized. Pogroms and poverty were driving Russian Jews and southern Italians across the Atlantic to the crowded cities where the Irish had settled four decades earlier. Those who had viewed the Irish as a threat to the nation's political and cultural heritage were equally swift to condemn this new invasion. The *New York Tribune*, which gave voice to anxieties about Irish teachers in the public schools in the 1850s, soon warned of an invasion of "pauper Jews." New native groups with names such as the Loyal Men of American Liberty and the United Order of Native Americans recruited thousands in the cities of the Northeast and Midwest to defend pure Anglo-Saxon Americanism. Members of a national organization, the American Protective Association, took an oath promising that they would avoid hiring Catholics and would never vote for one.[1]

Tammany's power base of the Lower East Side, the home of tens of thousands of Irish immigrants in the middle of the nineteenth century, was well on its way to becoming the center of Jewish life in the United States. New York was home to about sixty thousand Jews in 1870. That figure grew to nearly three hundred thousand over the next thirty years, with most settling in the wards south of Fourteenth Street. The newcomers from Central and Eastern Europe brought with them traditions, culture, and customs that were very different from those of the German Jews familiar to Tammany's Irish leaders.

Italians were a minute presence in New York in the middle of the nineteenth century. By the mid-1880s, the Italian-born population grew to about twelve thousand. Within two decades, the Italian-American population—including first- and second-generation Italians—reached a quarter of a million.

All the while, the number of Irish-born New Yorkers declined, from 295,000 in 1890 to 275,000 in 1900. That number, which obviously did not include the children and grandchildren of immigrants, was destined to grow smaller as emigration from Ireland slowed—in part because the island's population was half of what it had been in 1840. There were fewer Irish leaving because so many already had left. As Richard Croker took over Tammany, it was clear that the face of immigrant New York was changing, drastically. The young, single Italian men who settled near the old Five Points neighborhood, the Yiddish-speaking families who patronized the pushcarts of Hester Street—this was the *new* New York. Its narratives were different from the Irish narrative; its attitudes toward politics and political authority were formed in the shtetls of Russia and the olive groves of Calabria. Tammany's Irish-born leader faced the task of adapting to the needs of this new population or risk losing the newcomers to the other new threat to Tammany's power—organized labor.[2]

Even as John Kelly's body was being placed in a crypt in the old St. Patrick's Cathedral on Mulberry Street, New York's labor movement was preparing to mount an independent mayoral campaign in the 1886 election, directly challenging Tammany's claim on working-class loyalties. The number of labor unions in the city had skyrocketed from about a dozen to more than two hundred in just four years (1882 to 1886), a reflection of growing national discontent with the Gilded Age's excesses. Workers by the hundreds of thousands across the country walked off their jobs in the early 1880s to demand better working conditions and higher wages, leading to accusations that immigrant socialists and anarchists were to blame for union militancy. But discontent was evident among newcomer and native-born alike. Two hundred thousand workers struck the giant Union Pacific and Missouri Pacific Railroads, owned by New York's Jay Gould. Textile workers, miners, even cowboys in Texas walked off their jobs rather than submit to the status quo. Industrialists hired strikebreakers and private detectives to subvert the unions, leading Gould to boast that he could hire half the working class to kill the other half.

In New York, the city's largest union, the Central Labor Union, reached across the Atlantic to borrow a controversial new tactic from the Irish Land League. The league had captured the attention of the transatlantic world in the early 1880s when it embarked on a campaign of social and economic ostracism against landlords and their agents. The tactic contributed a new word to the English language when the Irish Land League targeted an unpopular land agent in County Mayo named Charles Boycott.

The CLU quickly organized its own boycotts against employers and products, including a brewer who fired four workers without cause and a shoemaking shop where twenty-five unionized workers—all young women—were dismissed. The boycotting campaign worked so successfully that New York's courts outlawed the practice, arguing that it was an unconstitutional conspiracy. More than a hundred workers were indicted in New York for organizing boycotts, a development cheered in many of the city's newspapers. A *New York Times* headline insisted that "Boycotting Must Go" because "An American Community Will Not Tolerate It."[3]

Labor's favorite son in New York was the radical economist Henry George, a brilliant and irascible voice of protest against the inequalities of the Gilded Age. As the mayoral nominee of a new, union-backed party called the United Labor Party, George posed a very real threat to Tammany's alliance with the city's Irish-American working class, for he was something of a folk hero thanks to his sensational coverage of Ireland's land war in the early 1880s in the *Irish World* newspaper. British authorities arrested George twice during his assignment in Ireland, transforming him from a mere observer of the agitation to a martyr for the cause of oppressed Ireland—a transformation that only increased his popularity in New York City's Irish community. But George's appeal in New York went beyond Old World grievances and spoke to a rising sentiment among Irish-Americans and other working-class groups that the Gilded Age was a rigged game, that the promise of New World success was giving way to Old World privilege, decadence, and social stratification.

.   .   .

Henry George was neither Irish nor Catholic; indeed, he was descended from an Anglo-Protestant evangelical tradition that did not always see eye-to-eye with Irish-Catholic culture. He was new to New York in the early 1880s, having moved from San Francisco, where he wrote in relative obscurity for years. But George was no newcomer to Irish and Irish-American politics. Even before Patrick Ford sent him to Ireland to cover the land war, George had taken a keen interest in the cause of the Irish peasantry. Unlike so many other Anglo-Protestant evangelicals, George viewed Irish poverty not as a reflection of papal superstition or congenital laziness but as the inevitable result of oppression and injustice.

In 1879, shortly after completing the book that made him famous, *Progress and Poverty*, George wrote an essay examining the inequities of landlordism in Ireland. The work captured Ford's attention, and through Ford's promotional efforts, George came to the attention of Irish-Americans like Father Edward McGlynn, the forty-nine-year-old son of Irish immigrants and pastor of St. Stephen's Church on Manhattan's East Side.

McGlynn was not a child of poverty. Although his father died young, he was a prosperous contractor who was able to provide for his wife and ten children even after his death. But as a priest working in a poor parish on the East Side, McGlynn bore witness to the reality of Gilded Age capitalism. He wrote of a "never-ending procession of men, women, and children" who came to his door "begging not so much for alms as for employment; not asking for food, but for my influence and letters of recommendation, and personally appealing to me to obtain for them an opportunity for working for their daily bread." Why was it, he asked himself, that the "poor shall be constantly becoming poorer in all our large cities. . . ."[4]

He found his answers in George's book, which advocated a single tax on property and which, more generally, assailed the age's inequitable distribution of wealth. McGlynn met George in 1882, and the two men became fast friends and correspondents. McGlynn was not shy about preaching from the gospel according to George, earning a reputation as a radical priest and, among his parishioners, the nickname *soggarth aroon* (Irish for "precious priest"). The sobriquet spoke of the bond between McGlynn and his poor flock—it also was evidence of the persistence not just of Irish tradition but of the Irish language itself in Gilded Age New York.

Richard Croker was canny enough to recognize the power of Henry George's message as the mayoral election of 1886 neared. Croker needed a candidate who could speak to labor's concerns while not alienating the party's dwindling but still-powerful Swallowtails, shaken as they were by the startling increase in strikes and boycotts in New York and, even worse, a bomb blast in Chicago's Haymarket Square that killed nearly a dozen people during a confrontation between workers and police on May 4, 1886. A split between Tammany and the party's business elites surely would lead to victory by either George, a true radical capable of inciting further labor trouble in the city, or—perhaps just as bad—the unpredictable Theodore Roosevelt, who returned to politics after a brief retirement following the death of his wife, Alice, in 1884. Roosevelt had the backing of the Republican Party and most of Wall Street as both recoiled over the possibility of Henry George as mayor.

In his first major test as Tammany's new leader, Croker found a middle ground that was becoming a defining characteristic of the organization and its Irish-American leadership. His choice for the Democratic mayoral nomination was former congressman Abram Hewitt, a Tammany man who moved in circles that were beyond the reach of the rough-and-tumble Croker and Tammany's rank and file. He was related by marriage to the impeccable Cooper family, he was wealthy, and he was a fixture in Gilded Age society.

Hewitt was not, however, entirely out of touch with the issues that had propelled Henry George from obscure economist to legitimate mayoral candidate in just a few years. Hewitt didn't necessarily regard unions as the vanguard of communism. His support for unions was limited, to be sure—there would be no effective union presence in the iron foundries that were the source of his wealth. But he urged his fellow industrialists to accept the legitimacy of craft unions, at least those that were limited in size and ambition, and to consider profit-sharing schemes with their workers. Hewitt practiced some of what he preached—his plants did not shut down or slow down when times were hard, so his workers were spared mass layoffs and salary cuts.

The *New York Times* could not conceal its relief when Croker threw his support behind Hewitt's mayoral candidacy during a mass meeting at Tammany in early October. Beneath a headline reading "Tammany

Takes the Lead," the newspaper cast aside its practiced skepticism of the organization's motives to quote approvingly the words of the irrepressible orator William Bourke Cockran, so often dismissed as just another of Tammany's windbags. Hewitt, Cockran pointedly noted, was a friend of working people—after all, five thousand people worked for Hewitt, and they never had cause to go on strike.[5]

Whether or not Hewitt truly was a benevolent capitalist was beside the point. In portraying its candidate as a friend of labor as well as a successful industrialist, Tammany sought to acknowledge the grievances of its working-class constituents and to steer them away from the dangerous Henry George. Like the Catholic Association of Daniel O'Connell's day, Tammany Hall did not reach for the unattainable, for the perfect. The graveyards of Ireland were filled with dreamers. The Irish leaders of Tammany Hall were not about to make that same mistake.

Father McGlynn was not so cautious, publicly proclaiming his support for George in the mayoral campaign. His superior, Archbishop Michael Corrigan, was mortified. "I have read with great regret a printed circular in which you and several others call a political mass meeting to be held in this city," Corrigan wrote to McGlynn, referring to a planned George rally in late October. "As Your bishop, I now forbid you in the most positive manner to attend the proposed meeting." McGlynn ignored the archbishop and eventually was excommunicated from the Catholic Church.[6]

Hewitt ran as the candidate of a united Democratic Party, but his victory over George was uncomfortably close. He polled 90,552 votes to George's 68,110, with Roosevelt taking 60,435 in a highly competitive race that some historians believe Tammany stole. But the usual press guardians of the electoral process did not utter a peep about any alleged underhanded Tammany tactics.

George's extraordinary showing, accomplished without an established party mechanism and despite the vocal opposition of the city's civic, religious, and intellectual elites, seemed to signal a new kind of class-based politics in New York, and perhaps even throughout the United

States. In London, Friedrich Engels took time from editing the works of his late partner, Karl Marx, to hail the turnout for George as "epoch-making." The city's vested interests understood that Hewitt's victory was a close-run thing, and, ironically, they had Tammany to thank for George's defeat. (Hewitt served just a single two-year term, losing Tammany's backing when he proved to be a latter-day nativist. "America should be governed by Americans," he declared. The immigrant boss Croker lost little time in replacing him with a protégé, Hugh Grant, son of Irish immigrants.)[7]

In the days and weeks after George's close call, Richard Croker did not spend his time awaiting thanks from the city's leading editors, merchants, and bankers for keeping a radical out of City Hall. Instead, he buried himself inside a story narrated in numbers—the number of votes Tammany won, and didn't win, in its traditional strongholds; the number of votes George won in districts that were home to the city's newcomers, especially Jewish voters whom George had actively courted. For a practiced professional like Croker, the tedious columns of numbers from Election Day told fascinating stories that eluded so many amateurs in his business. They told him about the shocking defection of Catholic voters to Henry George—historians Edwin G. Burrows and Mike Wallace estimate that five-sixths of George's support came from Catholics who clearly paid little heed to the preferences of their spiritual leader, Archbishop Corrigan. And they told him a story about organization—Tammany's own area of expertise. The George campaign, through the efforts of the city's labor movement and Patrick Ford's *Irish World* newspaper, had organized clubs that served as clearinghouses and gathering spots for George's army of supporters. Croker saw the results, and responded in kind.[8]

The saloons that had served Tammany so well as a source of intelligence and a place for back-room dealmaking gave way to a well-organized network of respectable clubhouses in each of the city's Assembly districts. In keeping with Tammany tradition, the clubs often took their names from Native American lore, such as the Delaware Club on East

Seventy-First Street (which was led by a child of the Famine, Thomas J. Dunn, for many years) and the Narragansett Club on West Fifty-Fourth Street (whose most famous member was the Tammany philosopher George Washington Plunkitt).

Clubhouses became the physical articulation of Tammany's ad-hoc ideology of service and social welfare. The clubhouse system strengthened the role of district leaders such as John Ahearn and Thomas Foley on the Lower East Side and Thomas McManus in the Hell's Kitchen section of the West Side. The network over which they presided was remarkably similar to the system of Liberal Clubs that Thomas Wyse had founded in Ireland after the Catholic Emancipation campaign in the late 1820s. Wyse described the clubs as part of a "well-digested system of political tactics, emanating from a single point, and extending in circle upon circle, until it shall embrace the entire nation." The clubs, in Wyse's view, were necessary because the passions of mass meetings and campaigns were soon spent and forgotten. A permanent network, he argued, was required to win and hold political power.[9]

The clubhouse system in New York allowed Tammany to achieve undisputed dominance over Democratic Party politics. The strong challenges from dissident Democrats were crushed by 1890, in part thanks to the powerful influence of the clubhouses, which served as providers of social services, employment, judicial review, and entertainment throughout the city. The clubhouse was where those in need of coal, a meal, a job, or a political favor met with district leaders, who were the public and often highly popular faces of Tammany Hall.

"Thousands of new citizens and soon-to-be citizens found an impersonal government translated and interpreted here by the personal touch," wrote Tammany operative Louis Eisenstein, whose mostly Jewish neighbors were introduced to New York culture and politics in the clubhouse of the John F. Ahearn Association on Grand Street and East Broadway on the Lower East Side. "The harshness of life in an unfamiliar New World was cushioned for newcomers who could not fill out citizenship papers or meet excessive rent payments and for those in need of jobs or peddlers' licenses."

Of course, these were not entirely philanthropic enterprises. The clubhouse did not represent a branch of municipal government—for government did not provide many constituent-based services at the turn of the twentieth century—but the Democratic Party under the control of Tammany Hall. Favors and services, then, were designed to win the loyalty of those who needed them. This transactional republic continued to infuriate reformers and journalists who saw Tammany not as a supplier of necessary services but as an exploiter of need. But Tammany figures such as Eisenstein asked a pertinent question: "At the turn of the century . . . who else offered aid? Certainly not the stiff, aloof Republicans, [while] the Socialists were too busy preparing for the brave new world of the future to bother with the immediate needs of the present." So families like Eisenstein's turned to Tammany to intervene on their behalf.[10]

Clubs and Tammany-aligned political associations fostered a sense of community and common purpose in neighborhoods that were home to newcomers from Southern and Eastern Europe as well as older immigrant or first-generation Irish-Americans. For example, the Ahearn Association sponsored an annual cruise that took thousands of families from the Lower East Side to bucolic picnic grounds on the banks of the Hudson River. The *New York Times* described the event on July 31, 1893, as the "biggest pleasure party that ever left this city by way of water," noting that some twenty thousand people took part. They started boarding six barges and two steamboats at eight o'clock in the morning, and by eleven o'clock, "they were still coming, married men and women with their whole brood, like young ducklings, along with them, young men and young women, girls of all ages, sizes and descriptions, and the multitudinous, copper-lunged east-side small boy."[11]

The cruise and picnic certainly enhanced John Ahearn's popularity and emphasized Tammany's commitment to spectacle and service, but his success on the Lower East Side—and the success of other midlevel Tammany figures elsewhere—was not simply a matter of bread and circus. As a state senator at the dawn of the Progressive Era, Ahearn supported public pensions for teachers, firefighters, and police officers, and he wrote legislation making it easier for mothers to keep dependent children when their fathers died, disappeared, or were otherwise unable to provide for their families. He represented a district that changed from predominantly Irish to predominantly Jewish during the late nineteenth and early twentieth centuries, but his role and that of his political club remained the same. George Washington Plunkitt noted that Ahearn was as likely to be found in the district's synagogues as he was in his own Catholic parish. Tammany's opponents were simply incapable of this sort of outreach. But for Tammany, it was all in a night's work—and the payoff came when voters went to the polls, where they cast their ballots not so much on the merits of individual candidates but in gratitude for the services provided by their local district leader or one of his subordinates.

"As a district leader, Ahearn exemplified to a high degree the Tammany type in his intense and constant playing of the political game and his devotion to the intimate personal needs of the men and women in his district," the *New York Times* wrote upon Ahearn's death in 1920.[12]

．　．　．

It was the transactional nature of Tammany politics—in which the right to vote became, in part, a means to an end rather than an exercise in civic virtue—that appalled reformers and spurred them to embrace civil-service reform as a way to limit the power of political parties over government hiring. Tammany, not surprisingly, embraced a more pragmatic approach to mass politics. The vote was all many of these people had—and they were unafraid to use it to gain access to power. Those who led reform movements—middle-class professionals, journalists, Protestant clergy—already had access and were unlikely to regard a job in the Public Works Department as some kind of reward. Such notable anti-Tammany critics as E. L. Godkin, Richard Watson Gilder (editor of *Century Magazine*), and George William Curtis (writer, editor, and advocate of civil-service reform) were well situated to spend their time thinking about the ways in which men like themselves could better govern New York. Tammany's constituents did not have such luxuries; if Tammany required their support, Tammany would have to find them work, or contracts, or other kinds of incentives.

"Does the college graduate who talks politics in evening dress at Carnegie Hall . . . know how many votes a ton of coal will bring in?" asked a member of the Bowery's famed Sullivan clan, "Little Tim" Sullivan, cousin of Tammany fixture "Big Tim" Sullivan.[13]

For Gilded Age reformers, Tammany Hall symbolized more than just bad or inefficient government—it symbolized irredeemably evil government. "According to the opposition, the first requisite for admission into Tammany Hall is that you must be a sinner," noted Tammany's Thomas F. Grady. Indeed, Tammany represented a close approximation to the reform movement's former foe, Southern slavery. Arguing in favor of civil-service reform in 1897, one of the age's great reformers, Carl Schurz, asserted that the struggle over civil service reminded him of "the struggle against slavery." Just as the "virtue and wisdom of the American people . . . wiped out the blot of slavery . . . so they will surely at least sweep away the barbarism and corruption of the spoils system." Schurz warned the governor of New York, Frank S. Black, that if he supported a Tammany-backed civil-service bill, which critics saw as an attempt to thwart genuine reform, he would be remembered as "the Buchanan of New York"—a reference, of course, to President James Buchanan and his listless leadership during the pre–Civil War violence in Kansas.[14]

Three decades earlier, when slavery was very much a fresh memory, Thomas Nast drew an image that explicitly linked Tammany to the enslavement of its ignorant followers. Tweed's picture showed an apelike Irishman chained to a post, watched over by one of Tweed's trusted aides, Peter Sweeny. In smaller images surrounding the main picture,

Nast depicted Tammany operatives wielding cat-o'-nine-tails as they drove Irishmen to the polls. Nast titled the image "The Slave Drivers."[15]

If there was a new slave power lurking in Gilded Age New York, however, it was not based in politically connected saloons or in the local political clubhouse—at least not in the view of Tammany's constituents. Instead, it was based in the well-appointed salons of the reform movement, where hostile forces were believed to be plotting to take away the votes, pleasures, and power of the poor through disenfranchisement, temperance, Sabbatarianism, and civil-service reform.

. . .

While Tammany certainly did not have a systematic solution for the problems that faced so many of its constituents, it was hardly blind to their plight. In their own way, Tammany leaders believed that with every job placement, every whispered word to a judge, and even with every drink consumed on Sunday, they were providing no small amount of relief to those who needed it most. But they did not act alone.

Beginning in the 1870s with the arrival of large numbers of Irish-Catholic nuns in New York, Tammany funded the city's growing network of Catholic orphanages, asylums, homes for unwed mothers, and other social services that were constructed in defiance of the worthiness-based criteria established by allegedly nonsectarian charities that nevertheless were imbued with evangelical Anglo-Protestant values. The growth of these government-funded Catholic social service institutions introduced new actors in the city's ongoing political and cultural debate about how best to care for the immigrant poor.

The Children's Law of 1875 required that poor children in need of institutional care be housed in institutions reflecting their religious upbringing, with the city required to pay for the care. The Sisters of Mercy lobbied judges to remand destitute children to their institutions, rather than to non-Catholic private charities. Their efforts were a huge success—a Mercy-run institution for poor boys received $77,000 in city funds in 1880 to look after the welfare of nearly a thousand orphaned or neglected children. But the fledgling alliance between Tammany's male chieftains and the Irish nuns who cared for the Catholic poor was not simply about funding separatism and building institutional empires. Catholic-run institutions insisted on keeping families together—the nuns viewed their services as a temporary remedy for severe distress, not as an opportunity to reorder their clients' values and belief system.[16]

This approach defied the practices of Anglo-Protestant charities, including the Children's Aid Society, which sought to remove children not only from the homes of the poor but, in many cases, from the city altogether. It also contrasted with the approach of some government institutions, such as the state Board of Charities, which were beyond the control of Tammany politicians. The board echoed the transatlantic Anglo-Protestant critique of poverty as evidence of character flaws, particularly when the poor were Irish and Catholic.

In its annual report in 1877, the Board of Charities blamed most "cases of pauperism" on "idleness, improvidence, drunkenness, or other forms of vicious indulgence, which are frequently, if not universally, hereditary in character." Because these problems were hereditary, the board argued, "the sooner [families] can be separated and broken up, the better it will be for the children and for society at large."[17]

Irish-Catholic nuns, empowered with funds from Tammany and other political allies, believed in keeping families together—and away from Protestant influence. Irish political power helped provide the funds for the nuns to carry out their charitable work, which many of New York's civic elites believed was little more than just another handout. Even a charitable woman like Josephine Shaw Lowell, founder of the Charity Organization Society, believed that the provision of services to the poor only encouraged pauperism and other moral defects associated with the city's immigrant wards.

Mrs. Lowell and her organization bitterly opposed the efforts of another organization, the Society for the Prevention of Cruelty to Children (SPCC), to place children temporarily in institutions, many of them operated by Catholic charities, rather than in homes with new, adoptive parents. Not coincidentally, the head of the SPCC was a well-connected lawyer and Tammany ally, Elbridge Gerry, and the SPCC secretary, William Barry, was a noted Tammany operative in the 26th Assembly district. Mrs. Lowell's supporters successfully blocked a Tammany bill, introduced by John F. Ahearn, that would have allowed the SPCC to disburse public funds to needy mothers after their children were returned home from the society's care.

Critics, ever wary of Tammany's motives, argued that the society should not have such broad power over taxpayer money. But the reformers, aligned with an anti-Catholic organization called the National League for the Protection of American Institutions, were rebuffed during a state constitutional convention in 1894, when they sought to ban religious charities from receiving public money.

The NLPAI's president, Reverend James M. King of the Methodist Episcopal Church, complained to the convention that Catholic charitable institutions in the city received $1.1 million in public funds in 1893, while other religious charities received $178,000. Reverend King was followed by a spokesman for the American Patriotic League, who told the convention, according to a news report, that "it was impossible to be a good Catholic and a good citizen at the same time." (Both men spoke on July 11, 1894, the day before the anti-Catholic holiday of July 12, a coincidence that Tammany's Irish-Catholic politicians could not have failed to notice.) Thanks to a coalition of Catholics and Jews, among others, efforts to ban state funding of religious charitable institutions failed.[18]

.   .   .

The conflict between reformers and Tammany politicians during the Gilded Age was not simply a battle between the advocates of good government and the forces of corruption. It was, at its most elemental level, a fight over the meaning of democracy and tolerance in a rapidly changing city, an ideological struggle over the role of government in a modern industrial life, and a debate over the very construction of Americanism in a cosmopolitan, global city. While the reform movement created new "nonpartisan" organizations, including the Citizens Union and the City Reform Club, and continued to draw its members from among the city's Anglo-Saxon Protestant elites (including many Protestant clergymen, who often complained about the political influence of Catholic priests), Tammany reached out to its new neighbors on the Lower East Side and sought to build a more representative civic order.

By the turn of the twentieth century, the Hall's roster of state legislators included not just those with such names as Hugh Dolan and Thomas McManus, but also Edward Rothstein (12th Assembly district), Emanuel Cahn (28th AD), Gotthardt Litthauer (30th AD), Milton Goldsmith (31st AD), and Julius Rosen (32nd AD). Among its aldermen in 1903 were Moritz Tolk (8th district), Leopold Harburger (10th district), Frederick Richter (15th district), and Philip Harnischfeger (39th district). Five of the six new members inducted into Tammany Hall on February 1, 1897, were Simon H. Stern, Edgar Levy, Nathan Straus, Randolph Guggenheimer, and Herbert Merzbach. Several years later, the organization's propaganda arm, *The Tammany Times*, celebrated the promising career of a young new member named Benjamin Goldberger, who had been appointed secretary to Tammany Congressman (and future governor) William Sulzer. Goldberger came to the organization's attention after having organized impressive rallies to support Alfred Dreyfus in 1894, when he was eighteen years old.[19]

The Union League, home to so many reformers and avowed Tammany enemies, including Thomas Nast, formally barred Jews from membership in 1893.

Tammany was slower to bring in Italian immigrants, many of whom were single men who were far less likely than the Irish to file for naturalization and thus be granted the right to vote. Only 10 percent of Irish immigrants had not become citizens in 1900, but more than 50 percent of Italian immigrants had yet to be naturalized. Whether Tammany was purposely negligent or whether many Italians simply resisted the idea of changing their citizenship is difficult to assess. To the average district leader or block captain, however, all that mattered was turnout, or the lack thereof, on Election Day.[20]

For all its outreach to new immigrant communities and voting blocs, few would argue that Tammany under Richard Croker was a model political organization. As Croker installed allies in government, his personal fortunes grew accordingly. He owned stock in companies that did business with the city, including the Manhattan Elevated Railroad Company and the U.S. Fidelity and Casualty Company. Tammany itself tapped into the resources of railroad magnates, contractors, and others who wished to get in on the riches to be had in a city that was growing in every way possible. Officeholders were expected to kick back a portion of their salaries to the organization in exchange for its support. The purveyors of vice, especially in and around the Bowery, had little to fear from Tammany or the police—they were paid to look the other way as brothels and pool halls operated openly in the city's poorest neighborhoods. Suffice it to say that at a time when writer Jacob Riis was exploring the terrible living conditions of the poor in his classic book *How the Other Half Lives*, Tammany had no broad solution to the problems of poverty and inequality during the last fifteen years of the nineteenth century.

Still, as New York became ever more divided between old native-stock Anglo-Saxon Protestants and the immigrant-stock masses concentrated downtown, Tammany stood its ground on protection of immigrants' rights and on access to the ballot box—regardless of race. During Croker's tenure as Tammany boss, the organization's Irish-American leaders actively solicited the votes of African-Americans and sponsored black-run local political organizations, even as their fellow Democrats in the South were presiding over the disenfranchisement of blacks. The *New York Times* noted in 1894 that seven "colored men" were "holders of lucrative positions in this city under Tammany."[21]

The presence of a few African-Americans in a city workforce numbering about twelve thousand cannot be taken as evidence of Tammany's forward thinking on race, especially given the organization's past association with racists like Fernando Wood. But it does indicate Tammany's desire to extend its reach to the city's traditionally Republican black community—and this at a time when Jim Crow laws were being passed in Southern states. The *New York Times* noted in 1893 that the Tammany organization in Manhattan's 8th Assembly district in Greenwich Village paid "great attention" to the "colored voters . . . and the work has borne fruit." Presiding over this outreach was district leader Barney Martin, regularly excoriated in the press and among reformers for his dubious dealings as a saloonkeeper.[22]

Tammany was rarely given credit for these efforts at inclusion. Perhaps its critics saw little to praise—either because they regarded the organization's efforts as little more than self-interest (which it surely was) or because they were not so keen on further diversifying the city's electorate. Tammany's position, in any case, was clear. In a propaganda pamphlet, Tammany's leaders asserted that they believed "there is nothing more dangerous to our country than the indifference of a large class of our citizens who neglect to vote on public questions."

Tammany's critics, however, saw politics as a solemn duty that ought to be left to the enlightened few who regarded themselves as public-spirited guardians of civic order and morals. "It would be a great gain if our people could be made to understand distinctly that the right to life, liberty, and the pursuit of happiness involves, to be sure, the right to good-government, but not the right to take part, either immediately or indirectly, in the management of the state," wrote the *New York Times*. Tammany could not have disagreed more profoundly.[23]

. . .

The success of Henry George's 1886 campaign, the disciplined mobilization of labor unions with a large Irish-Catholic presence, and ongoing Irish-American agitation for social justice in Ireland combined to keep Tammany moving ever so slightly to the left through the final years of the nineteenth century. Tammany successfully sought alliances with leaders of the Central Labor Union and other unions, so by the turn of the twentieth century, Tammany members were among the leaders of unions representing such trades as granite cutters, plasterers, and paperhangers. While the alliance between Tammany and labor was never a perfect fit, Richard Croker was careful to bear in mind the new militancy of his working-class constituents. In late January 1889, as the city prepared for a strike against streetcar companies, Croker advised his protégé, Mayor Hugh Grant, to consider the plight of workers, who offered to take a reduction in their daily pay of between $1.60 and $2 if their workload were reduced.[24]

"There is no doubt in my mind that their request is reasonable as their hours are very long with small pay while their employers are drawing large dividends from their labor," Croker wrote. The strike, led by an Irish-American organizer named James Magee, ended in defeat for the union, but Tammany's refusal to denounce the strike was a sharp contrast to the condemnations issued in the press. The *Times* charged that the strike was "frivolous" and "silly," and that the "foolish" strikers deserved no sympathy from the public.[25]

If Croker's Tammany did not have the big answers to the poverty and exploitation of Gilded Age New York, it at least cultivated a new generation of elected officials who were searching for solutions. In 1893, Tammany sent to Albany several assemblymen who reflected the organization's tentative forays into a more ideological form of politics. Among them were Meyer Joseph Stein of the 20th Assembly district, who supported pensions for public school teachers, Philip Wissig of the 8th district, a native of Germany who wrote legislation regulating the type of manufacturing that could take place in tenement houses, and, most notably, "Big Tim" Sullivan of the 2nd district, who introduced bills regulating the price of gas and lowering the fees that pawnbrokers charged their customers. The state legislative manual for 1893 noted that Sullivan, a child of Irish immigrants and Five Points poverty, authored "some of the greatest and most-important legislation" of the previous session.[26]

These were men whose backgrounds provided them with firsthand knowledge of conditions in the city's immigrant and working-class neighborhoods, and who were challenging the traditional American narrative of rugged individualism and laissez-faire economics that bore little relation to life on the Lower East Side. Thomas Dunn, who was born in Famine Ireland in 1850 and emigrated to New York when he was ten years old, was Croker's handpicked choice as Tammany's district leader in the 20th Assembly district, covering the East Side from Fifty-Ninth Street to Seventy-Third Street. More comfortable behind the scenes, Dunn gave a rare interview to the *New York Times* in 1893, not long after taking charge of the district. The neighborhood, Dunn explained, was "solidly Democratic because it . . . is largely a working people's district. We have little of the brownstone element."[27]

Dunn cultivated his constituents with clambakes and excursions to the wilds of Queens County, which attracted such disparate Tammany officials as State Senator Jacob Cantor, Congressman William Sulzer, and, inevitably, indefatigable State Senator George Washington Plunkitt. Fifteen hundred members of Dunn's political club attended his outing in College Point in 1893 and were entertained by sack races, a baseball game between married men and single men, and a football match between the Irish and the Germans (the Irish won—there were no reports of irregularities). A club member named Michael Conroy brought home mixed results. He won one of the day's foot races. That was the good news. The not-so-good news? The race was reserved for "fat men."[28]

These were community-building exercises as well as party-building events. What's more, with the Irish and the Germans mixing it up on the playing field, in the presence of Jewish, German, and Irish politicians, the club's outings were experiments in toleration and ethnic cooperation at a time of tremendous demographic change in New York. Tammany's own brand of laissez-faire government, applied not to economics but to cultural policy, was born on the playing fields of College Point and other bucolic venues, where the city's ethnic and religious groups—white ethnic and religious groups, to be sure—learned to live and let live, and where they came to understand that the imposition of one group's rules could infringe on the values of another group's.

Dunn, a stonecutter from County Tipperary who made good in business and devoted countless hours to the care and feeding of his constituents, saw voters not as slaves or as ignorant foreigners but as fellow citizens capable of making informed choices. He told the *Times*: "We have a most-intelligent class of voters" in the district—a characterization that Tammany's critics found laughable. The *Times*, suitably impressed, went on to describe Dunn as "one of the most liberal leaders in Tammany Hall."[29]

The Dunn club's successful outing to College Point, with its melting pot of politicians and voters and fun and games, took place just as a coalition of anti-Tammany forces saw an opportunity to overthrow the organization. And they took it.

· · ·

It began with a sermon. Reverend Charles H. Parkhurst was a scholarly Presbyterian minister with a handsome goatee, thinning hair, and round spectacles. His name was virtually unknown beyond his congregation in Madison Square Church, a few blocks but many psychic miles from Tammany Hall's headquarters on Fourteenth Street. He was not a native New Yorker; his formative years were spent in New England, where he worked on a farm and in a grocery store before attending college and moving to the city in 1880.

As Parkhurst strode to the pulpit on the morning of February 14, 1892, New York was the fastest-growing city in the Western World, on the verge of jumping the East River and becoming even more sprawling, even more chaotic, even more symbolic of the age's achievements and inequities. It was also, undeniably, a place that trafficked in vice—in the sale of women's bodies, in games of chance that inevitably exploited the desperate, in secret payments made to those who wrote and upheld the city's laws and regulations.

In his sermon on that Sunday morning, Parkhurst departed from his usual biblical themes to denounce Tammany Hall, the mayor, and anybody else who held power in the city. "They are a lying, perjured, rum-soaked, and libidinous lot," Parkhurst thundered. The city was, in his words, a "Tammany-debauched town." At least one member of his congregation must have been thrilled: Thomas C. Platt, boss of the Republican Party in New York.[30]

The Parkhurst sermon, followed by a sensational investigation of the city's underworld, was a turning point in the reform movement's battle with Richard Croker's Tammany. Under the leadership of State Senator Clarence Lexow, an upstate Republican, the state put together a full-scale investigation of city government. The Lexow Commission's hearings shed light on the unseemly connections between the city's police force and Croker's Tammany, although the outrage heaped upon Tammany may not have been proportionate to the commission's actual findings. The commission's associate counsel, a reformer named Frank Moss, announced his shocking discovery that some political figures wrote letters on behalf of men seeking appointment to the city's police department.

Moss told members of the nonpartisan Good Government Club that he had access to a thousand letters containing testimonials to police candidates who failed the required exam. Of that figure, Moss said, 123 were written on Tammany letterhead. Moss found this an astonishingly high figure. Croker might well have wondered who in the world wrote the remaining 877.

The Parkhurst crusade against prostitution, gambling, drinking, and other forms of corruption came amid renewed doubts in the transatlantic Anglo-Protestant world about the Irish capacity for self-government, or the capacity of Irish-ruled cities like New York to govern themselves without strict oversight at the state level. A Canadian writer, Goldwin Smith, described the baneful effect of the Irish in both Britain and the United States. The Irishman, he wrote in the British journal *The Nineteenth Century*, "uses his vote as a shillelagh . . . his fatal influence threatens with ruin every Anglo-Saxon polity and Anglo-Saxon civilization throughout the world." As evidence, he took note of the Irish influence over American politics: "The [Irish-Catholic] aptitude for municipal self-government . . . has been displayed to the full satisfaction of the taxpayer and of all decent cities in the Irish-ridden cities of the Union."[31]

Similar sentiments were expressed in Britain and New York as home rule, albeit in two very different forms, became a political controversy on both sides of the Atlantic in the late nineteenth century. The Irish in Ireland sought home rule—that is, a limited form of self-government within the British Empire as an alternative to outright independence, which many deemed unachievable. The Tammany Irish in New York City fought an ongoing battle with predominantly Anglo-Protestant Republicans from upstate over Albany's power to intervene in local decisionmaking. In both cases, critics argued that granting home rule— to Ireland, and to Irish-dominated New York City—would lead inevitably to corruption and sectarian Catholic rule, and then to the end of liberty itself.

In the British periodical *Fortnightly*, journalist T. W. Russell argued against self-government for Ireland by pointing to "two cities wholly under the control of the Irish population in America," New York and Boston. He described New York as "a disgrace to the United States" as a result of "the Irish vote." Only the "good sense of the Anglo-Saxon race" protected American liberties from the ravages of universal suffrage and Irish rule. Those who favored home rule for Ireland had no choice, he argued, but to consider what had become of New York and other Irish-dominated cities in America. Americans understood the flaws inherent in the Irish character, wrote Sydney Brooks in *The Monthly Review*, a British journal, which was why New York "has not even a semblance of Home Rule."[32]

Those arguments echoed the thoughts of home-rule opponents in New York who insisted that the state should limit the city's power over expenditures and appointments. The *New York Times* argued that home rule could not work in New York because it was "anything but an American city" thanks to of its high proportion of immigrants. Giving New

Blessed with a golden voice and a theatrical presence, Daniel O'Connell created a new kind of mass politics in Ireland, articulating the grievances of the island's Catholic majority and mobilizing the vote with a disciplined political organization. (*Bettmann/Corbis*)

Known to friend and foe alike as "Dagger John," Archbishop John Hughes organized New York's Irish Catholics behind demands for equal rights and cultural respect. He insisted that he was not a politician, but he certainly acted like one. (*Library of Congress*)

William "Boss" Tweed became an enduring
symbol of political corruption after he and
his allies looted New York's treasury for
personal profit. But he remained popular
among Irish immigrants, who saw his
Tammany Hall as a bulwark against anti-
Catholic nativists. (*Library of Congress*)

Thomas Nast's cartoons helped bring down Boss Tweed, but his illustrations also
reflected an intense hatred for Tammany's Irish-Catholic voters. In this image
published by *Harper's Weekly* in 1871, Nast pictured Catholic bishops as alligators
coming ashore to feast on American children. In the background, Tammany Hall
is pictured as St. Peter's Basilica in Vatican City. Tweed is at the top of a cliff,
watching with approval as children are hurled toward the advancing bishop-
alligators. A public school building nearby has been destroyed, but a stouthearted,
native-born American has come to the rescue of the nation's children. (*Corbis*)

Richard Croker was a child when he and his parents fled starvation and death in Famine-era Ireland. The first immigrant boss of Tammany Hall, Croker tightened discipline and grew wealthy off graft before retiring and returning to his native country. (*Bettmann/Corbis*)

A fire in the Triangle Shirtwaist Factory in 1911 killed more than 140 workers. Here, family members line up to identify the bodies of those who flung themselves out of ninth-story windows to escape the flames. The fire led to demands for workplace reforms around the country. (*Bettmann/Corbis*)

A skeptical press dubbed them the "Tammany Twins." But Robert Wagner, left, and Al Smith, right, helped transform New York politics with their support for progressive social policies and greater government regulation of the private marketplace. (*Bettmann/Corbis*)

Frances Perkins enjoyed working with Tammany figures like "Big Tim" Sullivan and Al Smith during her years as an advocate for social reform in New York. Franklin Roosevelt appointed her secretary of labor, the nation's first woman Cabinet member, in 1933. (*AP Photo*)

When he was a young Tammany district leader, Charles Francis Murphy sent cards to his constituents on Election Day if they hadn't voted by midafternoon. Murphy himself needed no reminder. Here he is shown (center, wearing glasses) casting his ballot during his long reign as Tammany boss. (*Bettmann/Corbis*)

Manhattan's Gas House District got its name because of the enormous gas storage facilities that cast a shadow over the neighborhood's tenement houses. Two of them are visible in this photograph of a busy street scene on the Lower East Side, home to Tammany's most dependable voters. (*AP Photo/Library of Congress*)

As a young state senator, Franklin D. Roosevelt described Charles F. Murphy as a "noxious weed." But in 1917, a chastened Roosevelt posed for this picture with Murphy during an appearance at Tammany Hall on July 4. When Murphy died in 1924, Roosevelt issued a statement praising his onetime nemesis. (*Bettmann/Corbis*)

Edward J. Flynn learned the game of politics from Tammany's Charles Murphy. He grew close to Franklin Roosevelt in the 1920s, and on Election Night in 1932 Flynn (right) joined FDR and James Farley to monitor election returns. Flynn went on to become a key political adviser to the Roosevelt White House. (*Bettmann/Corbis*)

A memorable night for New York: Franklin Roosevelt celebrates his victory in the 1932 presidential election with former governor Al Smith and newly elected Governor Herbert Lehman. Smith later broke with FDR and the New Deal. (*AP Photo*)

Tammany Hall as it looked in 1939, lonely and soon to be forgotten. Within a few years of when this photo was taken, the New York County Democratic Party moved to new headquarters uptown. But the old Tammany building still stands and was designated as a landmark in late 2013. (*AP Photo*)

Yorkers "absolute home rule," the paper continued, "would be to deprive Americans by birth and descent of the small share they yet retain in the control of [city] affairs."[33]

It surely did not pass without notice on either side of the Atlantic that the Irish home-rule movement was financed in part by the New York Irish, who themselves were not to be trusted with home rule for the city they dominated. Tammany, for example, raised more than $18,000 for the Irish home-rule movement in early 1886, including about $1,200 from the predominantly Jewish 8th Assembly district, led by a Tammany operative named Moritz Herzberg.[34]

As these critiques of the Irish capacity for self-government were under discussion, James Bryce, a British writer, member of Parliament, and future ambassador to the United States, published a long study of American politics called *The American Commonwealth*. It was greeted with raptures of praise from New York's Anglo-Protestant reformers, who found in a single phrase from the massive text everything they had been saying and thinking for decades, ever since Tammany Hall had become a vehicle for the empowerment of foreign immigrants. "There is no denying that the government of cities is the one conspicuous failure of the United States," Bryce wrote. For elite urban reformers at the turn of the twentieth century, *The American Commonwealth* was a foundational document in their narrative of corrupt political bosses who presided over urban misgovernment based on the support of unthinking immigrant-stock voters. (Bryce's observations about growing economic inequality in the United States did not receive similar attention from his elite readers.)[35]

Bryce was invited to speak before reform organizations such as the City Club, where he was welcomed not as a mere foreigner but rather a "valued instructor" in American politics. In his preface to the first volume of his work, Bryce acknowledged the guidance and contributions of a veritable who's who of New York reformers: Theodore Roosevelt, Seth Low (the president of Columbia University and future reform mayor of New York), E. L. Godkin of *The Nation*, Henry Villard of the *New York*

Evening Post, and Andrew D. White, the Cornell University president who had complained about city governments ruled by the votes of "illiterate peasants, freshly raked from Irish bogs, or Bohemian mines, or Italian robber nests." There is no evidence that Bryce received input from the "illiterate peasants" who actually ran the nation's municipal governments, but then again, they operated in very different social circles.[36]

A more polemical variation on Bryce's observations about American municipal government, written by Protestant clergyman Joseph Hartwell, asserted that the "government of New York City is an unbroken reign of the worst element of imported voters" and urged "the descendants of the Pilgrim fathers" to resist Jesuit-inspired corruption. Bryce's somewhat more subdued condemnation of political bosses and machines appeared just as the Parnell-led home-rule movement in Ireland was reaching a climax—in the end, it failed—and helped set the stage for Reverend Parkhurst's exposé of Tammany's links to the city's vice industry.[37]

Critics saw a continuum of interest, style, and corruption in Irish political figures, whether they were based in Ireland or in the United States. During the land agitation in Ireland in the 1880s, the *New York Times* charged that some Tammany figures wished to bring Charles Parnell across the Atlantic as Tammany's new boss. "With Parnell at the helm, it was claimed that Tammany would be invincible," the *Times* reported, clearly referring to a group of terrorists known as "the Invincibles" who hacked two British officials to death in Dublin's Phoenix Park in 1881.[38]

In 1914, a critic of home rule in Ireland asserted that Croker's successor as Tammany boss, Charles Francis Murphy, might return to his father's native land to take over a proposed new home-rule government in Ireland. If that happened, the critic vowed, "Charley Murphy will be beaten back to his American stronghold." A British periodical, *The Academy*, argued against home rule for Ireland by asking whether the English people were prepared "to hand over" Ireland to a "party of political rowdies whose exchequer is periodically reimbursed by contributions from the 'hard-earned' dollars of New York 'corner-boys' and Chicago 'bar-tenders'?"[39]

If Anglo-Americans were dubious about the ability of the Irish to rule themselves, the Tammany Irish were equally disdainful of American and British claims that they were suited to rule other people. As American nationalists like Theodore Roosevelt, Albert Beveridge, and many others advocated overseas expansion as part of the Progressive Era's mission to bring Anglo-Saxon civilization to races deemed barbaric or undeveloped, Tammany leaders, no doubt drawing on the Irish narrative of oppression and defeat, argued that there was nothing progressive about imperialism. "Let me explain what I mean by anti-imperialism," said Richard Croker in 1900. "It means opposition to the fashion of shooting down everybody who doesn't speak English. It seems to be the fashion nowadays when a people don't speak English to organize an army and send troops to shoot them down."[40]

Croker's fellow Irish immigrant, Tammany Congressman William Bourke Cockran, protested American expansion in Cuba and the Philippines at an anti-imperialism rally in Manhattan's Academy of Music on Fourteenth Street in 1899. Imperialism, he said, "is a policy which, from its material point of view, is a policy of folly, and from its moral point of view, a policy of infamy." He wondered aloud why it was that "any person who gives out an interview in New York favoring imperialism . . . will find his remarks paraded in all the London newspapers and terms of encomium showered on his head." Cockran saw American expansion as an extension of an Anglo-Saxon imperial project founded in London and put to ruthless use in the land of his birth. He later became involved in Irish nationalist politics and was an outspoken critic of British colonialism, no doubt to the dismay of his friend and frequent correspondent, Winston Churchill.[41]

.   .   .

Reverend Parkhurst's sermon and his subsequent secret investigation of New York's nightlife, which included lurid descriptions of a "dance of nature" performed by five naked prostitutes, linked Tammany to crimes of the flesh, not simply to offenses against the public treasury. In another homily, Parkhurst complained about gambling houses operating just a short distance from his church, including one "furnished with roulette . . . in which there were counted forty-eight young men." The police, he said, were aware of illicit gambling but did nothing about it.

Several months later, the press reported that betting on the outcome of the 1894 mayoral campaign was active "at the downtown exchanges." One financier at the New York Stock Exchange publicly announced that he had wagered $5,000 on the reform movement, whose platform, of course, included promises to close down gambling. The press spotted another intrepid Wall Streeter who made his way around the Stock Exchange floor, "stopping at every group to bet $1,000 or $500" on the reform movement's chances. Tens of thousands were wagered openly on the reform movement's antivice campaign. Reverend Parkhurst managed to contain his shock.[42]

Regardless of the apparent hypocrisy, Parkhurst's crusade had struck a chord, and Tammany paid a price. Croker temporarily relinquished control over Tammany and traveled to Europe, ostensibly to regain his health. Reformers rallied around the candidacy of William Strong, an Ohio-born bank president. Reverend Parkhurst was among Strong's most vocal supporters, announcing at a pro-Strong rally that "this is not a political campaign. It is simply a warfare between that which is right and that which is wrong."[43]

Thanks to the Parkhurst revelations, Strong captured the mayoralty and Republicans seized control of the Board of Aldermen and won a majority (seventeen) of the city's thirty Assembly races. Tammany's humiliation was complete, and there was no shortage of satisfaction among its opponents. Reverend Robert MacArthur, pastor of Calvary Baptist Church on West Fifty-Seventh Street, used his Thanksgiving Day sermon to express his gratitude that with a new administration in City Hall, the flag of the United States would henceforth be protected from "improper association . . . with the little green rag that represents no nation. Ireland has no flag, only the British flag; the green flag represents religious bigotry on one side, national disloyalty on the other." MacArthur had special reason to give thanks in 1894—in his Thanksgiving homily a year earlier, he had called for an "uprising of the people" to create "America for the Americans."[44]

Tammany's legions had warned that if Strong captured City Hall, the taps of New York's saloons would run dry on the only day most workers had off—Sunday. It may have sounded like a demagogic appeal to the worst instincts of Tammany's voters. It also happened to be prophecy. The new mayor appointed a stalwart moral crusader, former assemblyman Theodore Roosevelt, as one of the city's three police commissioners. Roosevelt was candid enough to concede that he "knew nothing of police management," but those who regularly chastised Tammany for appointing unqualified people to high office welcomed Roosevelt's new career path. "For a man of his years, his record has been remarkable," raved the *New York Times*, taking note of Roosevelt's Harvard education.[45]

Among the causes that received his ardent attention as police commissioner was Sunday drinking, a reflection of Roosevelt's intimate and tragic knowledge of the perils of drink—his brother Elliott, a terrible alcoholic, died at the age of thirty-four in 1894. (He left behind a daughter, Eleanor Roosevelt, whose mother had died two years earlier.) Roosevelt zealously cracked down on workingman's saloons that sold alcohol on Sunday despite state laws prohibiting such sales. Roosevelt's boss, Mayor Strong, apparently was not prepared for his new commissioner's enthusiasm: "I found that the Dutchman whom I had appointed meant to turn all New Yorkers into Puritans."[46]

Not surprisingly, saloon owners and patrons resented the Dutchman and his Puritan crusade. U.S. Senator David Hill, a Tammany man, took note of the hypocrisy of Roosevelt's crusade. Liquor sales—and even, according to one judge, soda sales—may have been illegal in saloons on Sunday, but private clubs were exempt from the restriction. "A glass of beer with a few crackers in a humble restaurant is just as much of a poor man's lunch or meal on Sunday as is Mr. Roosevelt's elaborate champagne dinner at the Union League Club on the same day," Senator Hill noted.[47]

Tammany's criticism only seemed to inspire Roosevelt to new heights of zeal. Albany Republicans were delighted to give him a new tool—a state law creating new restrictions on alcohol consumption, and not just on Sunday. Saloonkeepers were banned from offering free lunches to customers and, curiously, from offering drinks to Indians. (Perhaps the upstate lawmakers read too much into the proliferation of Tammany clubs named for Native American tribes.) More ominously, the new law, authored by Republican Senator John Raines, raised the excise tax on the average workingman's saloon from $75 a year to $800. The fee applied to private clubs as well as to downtown grog shops, but most antialcohol crusaders believed the huge tax increase would disproportionately affect the city's saloon culture, connected so intimately with Tammany Hall.

Hotels were given exemptions from the new restrictions, leading to the sort of evasions that the Irish had turned into an art form during the height of anti-Catholic legislation in Ireland. Saloons controlled by the family of Tammany operative Timothy "Big Tim" Sullivan on the Bowery became "hotels," although it would be a brave customer indeed who might consider renting one of the closet-size spaces added to the second floor of Sullivan's places and, soon, to hundreds of other saloons.

The war on drink did nothing to persuade the city's working classes that reformers were anything more than busybodies. Tammany was always happy to accept the reform movement's gift of silver-plated hypocrisy. In his last great struggle with reformers before quitting as Tammany boss for a second and final time, Richard Croker confronted longtime nemesis Frank Moss, an associate of Reverend Parkhurst and an indefatigable attorney on retainer to the reform movement. Moss, acting as lead counsel for another Republican-led state legislative investigation of Tammany, the Mazet Committee, probed Croker's extensive private business dealings to show how he manipulated politics to benefit his own finances.

Wasn't it true, Moss asked, that Tammany-appointed officials hired an auctioneering firm in which Croker had an interest? "Yes, sir," replied Croker, dressed for his grilling in a black frock coat and a black ascot tie. And wasn't it also true that judges whom Croker handpicked for the bench handed out patronage to the real estate firm of Meyer & Croker? "We at least expect [the judges] will be friendly to us," Croker replied.

"Then you are working for your own pocket, are you not?" Moss asked.

"All the time," Croker responded. "Same as you."

Many in the crowded hearing room were aghast. Croker had publicly admitted that he was not, in fact, a disinterested citizen engaged in political work solely for the sake of the public good. Moss himself could hardly believe his ears, asking Croker to restate his view of how politics worked. Croker obliged: "We win and we expect everyone to stand by us," he said.[48]

Croker's acknowledgment that he was working for his pocket became a rallying cry for a generation of anti-Tammany candidates and advocates. During state legislative elections in 1899, city Republicans distributed thousands of campaign postcards bearing a distorted version of Croker's now-infamous quote. "I am working for my pocket all the time," the cards read. It did not occur to Croker's critics that the second part of his answer to Moss—"same as you"—very likely resonated just as loudly in Tammany's strongholds as the first phrase did in the city's brownstone districts and newsrooms. At a time when reformers seemed intent on preventing the poor from enjoying a beer on their only day off, Croker's defiance of one of the city's most ardent reformers gave public voice to the Irish community's grievances and alienation—even though Moss was absolutely right about the unsavory connections between Croker's private dealings and the city's treasury.

.   .   .

Police Commissioner Roosevelt's campaign against Sunday drinking became a laughingstock, but as it did, another threat to Tammany, on a far larger scale, loomed: the expansion of New York City from Manhattan and a portion of today's Bronx (then known simply as "the annexed district") into the gigantic, five-borough City of Greater New York. The merger of the independent city of Brooklyn and the rural counties of Queens and Richmond (Staten Island) with Manhattan and the Bronx created at its birth on January 1, 1898, a city of nearly three and a half million people (compared with just under two million in Tammany's stronghold of Manhattan). The majority of these new New York City residents had no history with Tammany Hall and no loyalty to the organization's vast army of neighborhood operatives, and that was no coincidence. A top city Republican, Edward Lauterbach, took note of Tammany's opposition to the consolidation bill, which was rammed through the legislature by state Republican boss Thomas Platt. Tammany leaders understood, Lauterbach said, that, "in a city of 3.5 million souls . . . the power of Tammany Hall . . . will be absolutely annihilated."[49]

The test of Lauterbach's assertion came in the fall of 1897, when city voters were to choose a mayor for the new metropolis. The reform movement nominated former Brooklyn mayor and Columbia University president Seth Low as the candidate of the new Citizens Union Party, whose founding principle was the "separation of municipal from state and national politics." Low was the quintessential disinterested, nonpartisan candidate, at least in the view of reformers and the new muckraking journalists who believed that politics should have nothing to do with running city government.[50]

The wealthy Low personified the transatlantic ideal of the true amateur, a person devoted to civic affairs in the same way that Britain's gentlemen athletes were devoted to sport—not as a way to make a living but as a hobby. Low got his start in public life as a volunteer for charity organizations in Brooklyn, and he shared with those private, elite-led institutions a moralistic understanding of government's role in ameliorating the needs of its least-served citizens. As Albany put together a new charter for the expanded city of New York, Low, a member of the charter commission, wrote and pushed through a regulation banning the city from providing outdoor relief to the poor, a measure he had put into place when he was mayor of Brooklyn. That provision included a ban on the free distribution of coal, one of the many tricks Tammany used to fool voters into believing that it had their interests at heart.

To oppose Low, Tammany chose an obscure jurist named Robert Van Wyck, figuring that he would offend nobody and would pose no threat to Tammany's lucrative alliances with private companies eager to bid on city franchises. From his listening post in Britain, James Bryce, now considered the sage of American urban government, followed the mayoral campaign closely, noting with approval that Low conducted his campaign as a struggle between "good and evil."[51]

A spokesman for Tammany Hall summed up the stakes in slightly different language. As he addressed a rollicking meeting of about three hundred Democrats in Harlem, the organization's candidate for Manhattan district attorney, Asa Bird Gardiner, recounted what he saw as the various broken promises of Mayor Strong's reform administration. The Police and Fire Departments were demoralized, he said, and the reformers had found no evidence of the widespread corruption they alleged (he prudently made no reference to the corruption that the Lexow Commission had indeed found). "Now don't you forget that," he said to growing cheers, "and when any of these people talk to you about reform, tell them, as I do, 'To hell with reform!' "[52]

The networks Tammany put into place under Croker paid dividends when voters went to the polls to choose between Low and Van Wyck. The clubhouse picnics and cruises, the nights spent attending to the problems of constituents hailing from Odessa, Naples, Budapest, Warsaw—and perhaps even a few from Dublin—proved a formidable match against a reform movement seemingly obsessed with changing the behavior of the city's immigrants and immigrant-stock working class. The inoffensive Robert Van Wyck defeated the reformers without making a single speech in public. For many New Yorkers, Gardiner had said it all.

NINE

AN ADMIRABLE ORGANIZATION?

Nearly every night in the mid-1890s, a lone figure stood under a gas lamp on the corner of Second Avenue and East Twentieth Street, waiting to engage in quiet conversation with neighborhood residents. Charlie Murphy, a solidly built man verging on middle age who grew up not far from this corner of Manhattan's Gas House District, would have been well known to many passersby. He owned a saloon just a few steps away from his listening post, a place that catered to the neighborhood's laborers and dockworkers. He also was a local baseball hero, a gum-chewing catcher on a barnstorming team that had toured upstate New York and caught the attention of professional teams. But by late 1892, Charlie Murphy was known best as a district leader for Tammany Hall, an important neighborhood link to the power and patronage of the city's dominant Democratic Party organization. Tammany's local clubhouse, the Anawanda Club, was based one floor above Murphy's saloon.[1]

In several important ways, Charlie Murphy seemed ill-suited to the job of Tammany ward heeler. Nicknamed "Silent Charlie," he was quiet and reserved in a line of work that seemed to require ebullience and a proverbial gleam in the eye. He was as puritanical as any moral reformer—vice, especially prostitution, offended him—but some of his fellow district leaders and other Tammany colleagues were deeply entangled with illicit rackets. Murphy prized loyalty and discipline, but as a young man he had served as campaign manager for an anti-Tammany Assembly candidate. Although he owned four saloons, he was at most a moderate drinker, hardly the image of a beer-guzzling, back-slapping Irish politico. "Charley Murphy takes a glass of wine at dinner sometimes, but he don't go beyond that," noted Tammany sachem George Washington Plunkitt, a contemporary of Murphy's.[2]

Despite these apparent handicaps, Murphy was a young man on the rise in Richard Croker's organization in the late 1880s and the 1890s. He may have been taciturn and temperate, but he also knew how to get people to the polls, and that talent mattered more than anything else in a political organization whose power rested not on claims to moral or cultural authority but on the perception of mass public approval and the reality of loyal voter turnout. Like other district leaders, Murphy developed a personal loyalty among his constituents in the 18th Assembly district—when they went to the polls, they voted the straight Democratic ticket not necessarily because of the candidates' merits but because of the connection they made with Tammany's local operatives.

Charles Francis Murphy was a political professional, or, to put it another way, he was a professional politician. He had no other hobbies except golf, no other interests outside of his family. Perhaps because he was quiet by nature, Murphy developed the invaluable political gift of listening, and he was known for the attention he devoted to the observations, reports, and complaints of constituents and colleagues alike. "His long suit is asking questions," a journalist wrote in the *New York Times*. "He is an insatiable interrogator." Colleagues understood that Silent Charlie did not issue homilies or public pronouncements. He collected intelligence and acted accordingly, and quietly.[3]

Murphy's political acumen and authentic generosity during the infamous Blizzard of 1888 also marked him as a man of influence in local politics. The historic storm dumped three feet of snow on the city, brought down live electrical wires, and left the city short of supplies, with the poor left to shoulder a disproportionate share of the suffering. Murphy, performing the role expected of a Tammany operative on behalf of his constituents, raised nearly $1,500 in charitable contributions to alleviate conditions in the Gas House District, a sum that accounted for more than a quarter of Tammany's total fundraising effort for the entire city. Murphy delivered the money to one of the neighborhood's civic pillars, St. George's Episcopal Church in the affluent Stuyvesant Square section near Gramercy Park. Reverend George Rainsford, pastor of St. George's, was so appreciative of Murphy's efforts that he singled out the young Irish-Catholic politico in a sermon. "If Tammany had more leaders like Charles F. Murphy, it would be an admirable organization," he told his congregation.[4]

Murphy became Tammany's leader in 1902, after Richard Croker retired and sailed to England in the aftermath of yet another Tammany disaster born of greedy overreach and outright criminality. The Van Wyck administration proved to be just as bad as reformers had feared— not unlike his predecessor, A. Oakey Hall, during the late 1860s, Van Wyck was happy to preside over civic ceremonies while turning a blind eye to the worst aspects of Tammany. The Tammany police chief, William Devery, ignored justified outrage about police cooperation with the vice industry. Croker, dictating patronage and policy despite spending a good deal of his time in England, withdrew the organization's support for a judge, Joseph Daly, who refused to appoint a fellow Tammany man as his clerk.

In Croker's view, Daly, who was up for reelection in 1898, had committed an unforgivable sin. "Justice Daly was elected by Tammany Hall after he was discovered by Tammany Hall, and Tammany Hall had a right to expect proper consideration at his hands," the boss explained. That was the Tammany code in a nutshell, and Croker would have had little reason to think that he was revealing some hidden secret about the organization's modus operandi. But in 1898 the Republican Party in New York nominated Theodore Roosevelt, fresh from his heroics on

San Juan Hill during the Spanish-American War, for governor, and he turned Croker's words into a campaign rallying cry. "My object was to make the people understand that it was Croker, and not the nominal [Democratic] candidate, who was my real opponent, that the choice lay between Crokerism and myself," Roosevelt later wrote. Crokerism suffered a resounding defeat, and Theodore Roosevelt became a national figure, a symbol of the new progressive politics that Republicans, Democrats, and reformers alike would embrace during the first two decades of the twentieth century.[5]

Progressives such as Roosevelt and, later, Democrat Woodrow Wilson, stood for change—change in the relationship between the government and the economy, change in the nation's political system, change in the character and culture of the poor and working classes in the nation's cities. Roosevelt-style progressivism was viewed as the enemy of Crokerism, of the political machines that dominated many of the nation's cities. But Tammany and Crokerism were not one and the same. Charles Murphy would see to that.

Before he could do so, however, Murphy had to repair Tammany's reputation, no small task. Tammany's constituents may have been able to live with Croker's private shakedowns of the rich, but when the boss and his allies sought personal gain from their relationship with an ice company, they knew they would be paying the bill. In those days before refrigeration, ice was a precious commodity, and Tammany sought to cash in with a deal that would have allowed a single supplier, American Ice Company, access to city-operated docks and, thus, monopoly control over this household staple. As an expression of its gratitude, the company provided various officials, including Mayor Van Wyck, with shares of company stock. Details of the Ice Trust scheme were revealed during a legislative investigation of city government, and it resonated with the city's poor far more than any good-government crusade. Tammany, after all, had expended endless hours in righteous denunciation of monopolies, a position that voters accepted as genuine and, indeed, progressive. The scheme exposed Croker as a hypocrite and, in this case at least, as no friend of the poor, who would be forced to pay higher prices for monopoly-supplied ice. Charlie Murphy served as a commissioner with the Department of Docks and Ferries, which ran the docks at the time of the Ice Trust scandal, and was called before investigators to answer questions about his involvement in the scheme. There is little indication that he received Ice Trust bribes, but there's no question that his work on the docks—the gateway to New York's markets—benefited contractors aligned with Tammany.

Adding to the Ice Trust scandal was the seemingly innocuous death of one of Tammany's longtime operatives, Murray Hall, a poker-playing, cigar-smoking, whiskey-drinking member of the General Committee. Hall worked closely with his local district leader, Barney Martin, who found him amusing if a bit short-tempered. He was less than five feet tall, a shabby dresser, and known for driving a hard bargain when he and his wife, who was considerably larger, went to the local marketplace in Greenwich Village. He was a neighborhood character, with a dingy bowler hat and a little black dog whose bark, neighbors said, was as loud as a passing elevated train. Odd though he was, his neighbors in the Village respected him as a Tammany man, and Tammany's men respected him as a diligent worker.

Murray Hall battled cancer for several years but refused to see a doctor, preferring instead to consult a vast collection of medical books in his apartment on Sixth Avenue. Finally, in early December 1900, he sent for a physician, Dr. John A. Burke, who thought it odd that Hall refused to take off his shirt for an examination. Hall simply told him he was feeling better and really didn't require an exam. His condition worsened as the year turned, leading to another house call from a different physician. Too weak to protest, Murray Hall allowed Dr. William Gallagher to examine him. He made two discoveries: Murray Hall was a woman, and she was about to die of breast cancer.

Murray Hall had lived as a man for forty years. Not for a moment had her Tammany colleagues suspected her deception. "Why, he'd line up to the bar and take his whiskey like any veteran and didn't make faces over it, either," recalled one of Hall's longtime friends, Joseph Young, a Tammany district leader. Barney Martin, who was Hall's closest Tammany ally, could barely process the shocking news. "She's dead, the poor fellow," Martin said when he learned of Hall's death and deception. Tammany's men were not alone in their shock: Minnie Hall, the twenty-one-year-old adopted daughter of Murray Hall, learned the truth about her "father" only after Murray's death.

The city's newspapers had a field day with the secret life of a Tammany henchwoman—it was a scandal the likes of which New York had not seen before. Republicans were bemused. Abraham Gruber, a Republican lawyer, announced his support for a bill requiring that "captains in Tammany Hall politics must wear whiskers." Republican State Senator John Raines had a hard time summoning up sympathy for the dead woman. It was no wonder, he complained to Senator Martin, that Tammany rolled up such large majorities in the city "when you can dress up the women to vote."[6]

. . .

The scandals of Croker's final years were too much, even for Tammany's supporters. Seth Low, running for mayor again in 1901 with the combined support of the Citizens Union and the Republican Party, made a special effort to appeal to traditional Tammany constituencies, especially in heavily Jewish neighborhoods that tended to vote Democratic but were not as culturally connected to Tammany as the Irish were. Low and his allies on what was called the Fusion ticket—a combination of independent reformers and Republicans—shrewdly dropped traditional reform platitudes, including those concerning the sacredness of Sunday, and focused instead on the spread of vice and the revelations of Croker's corruption. Rather than sermonize, Low told his audiences that "this fight is your fight," implicitly giving voters credit for recognizing their interest in good government. The anti-Tammany press picked up on this kinder, gentler face of reform: *The Outlook*, a weekly periodical, noted that it was "a common blunder, but an egregious one, to imagine that virtue is to be assumed in the brownstone . . . and vice in the tenement house," and it went on to praise the anti-Tammany campaign for making that point. In a sense, the change of emphasis in the reform movement's rhetoric marked a cultural (if not political) victory for Tammany. Until the Low campaign of 1901, reformers had addressed their remarks to each other—rarely if ever taking their message directly to voters so many regarded as part of the problem. Low's approach worked because it owed much to Tammany's populism.[7]

The result was another massive repudiation for Tammany, with the Fusion ticket sweeping nearly all municipal offices, including the mayoralty. Low, in his victory speech, demonstrated no small amount of political savvy in declaring that the election's outcome was a vindication of universal suffrage. A quarter-century earlier, reformers had made no secret of their contempt for universal suffrage; now, a reformer's reformer saw wisdom in the will of the people.

As he prepared to take over City Hall, Low continued to remind his fellow elites of the demographic reality of Greater New York. A week before his inauguration, he addressed the annual banquet of the city's New England Society in the Waldorf-Astoria Hotel. The mayor-elect allowed other speakers to wax poetic about the enduring virtues of the Puritans and Pilgrims, from whom many in the audience were descended—or at least said they were. Low chose to speak about the other New York, the one far from the flowers and flags of the great hotel's banquet hall. "I want to remind you that when the votes were counted on election day . . . the greatest gains for good government . . . came from the east side," Low said, referring to the city's immigrant districts. Labor, he added, was "so intelligent," and so was "the American political system that gives to every man his vote." These were sentiments not often heard in the presence of the city's Pilgrims and Puritans.[8]

Once again, Tammany's foes delighted in the organization's inevitable demise and began planning its burial. Thousands gathered outside the Metropolitan Opera House for mock funeral ceremonies, during which an effigy of Richard Croker was cremated with all solemn ceremony. Mark Twain delivered a sarcastic eulogy. "Tammany is dead, and there is wailing in the land," he said. "We shall miss so many familiar faces."[9]

Croker left in a hurry. His successor, Lewis Nixon, resigned after four months on the job. (Nixon was not exactly from the rough-and-tumble school of politics—*The Nation* magazine observed that placing Nixon at the head of Tammany was "as absurd as the appointment of a New England deacon to the command of a pirate ship.") A trio of leaders was appointed to take Nixon's place, but the job was too complicated for three people. After several months of confusion and lethargy, one of the three emerged as the new boss—Charles Francis Murphy. After his election, the commissioner—as Murphy preferred to be called—told a reporter, "I won't do much talking," but he promised he would be at Tammany Hall every day, an implicit contrast to Croker, who ruled Tammany from across the Atlantic during his final few years as boss. "There is," Murphy added, "plenty of work to be done."[10]

.   .   .

Born in 1858 in the Gas House District, which extended from Fourteenth Street to Twenty-Eighth Street on the East Side, Charles Francis Murphy personified a stereotypical Irish-American success story in politics. His parents were Irish immigrants—his father fled during the Famine in 1848—and they lived in one of the district's many tenement houses that surrounded Stuyvesant Square's island of affluence. One of nine children, young Charlie dropped out of school at the age of fourteen, taking a succession of jobs near the East River waterfront before becoming a horsecar driver in the late 1870s. He opened his first saloon in 1880 and soon had enough money to open three more. Murphy's two older brothers already were active in city politics, so Charlie followed their path. His reputation as an athlete—he was not only a good baseball player but also a fine oarsman—and his involvement in the saloon trade allowed Murphy to rise quickly in local politics, to the chagrin of critics who saw Tammany's embrace of sporting men, like the future owner of the New York Yankees, Congressman Jacob Ruppert, and saloon owners as insults to the memory of the nation's founders.

When Tammany bestowed a congressional nomination on Big Tim Sullivan, a product of Five Points poverty who gained local fame when he slugged a prizefighter accused of wife-beating, the *New York Times* fulminated that "anywhere outside a Tammany barroom it would be supposed that Sullivan could be elected to Congress only in a district inhabited by the very scum of the earth." Sullivan, the paper charged, was "simply not fit to be at large in a civilized community." Perhaps, but Big Tim Sullivan wasn't asking to be admitted to civilized society. He was running for Congress.[11]

Despite Murphy's slender academic credentials, tenement upbringing, athletic interests, and saloon ownership, he quickly earned a reputation for running a clean operation in the Gas House District. "One thing that I learned from . . . Charles F. Murphy of Tammany Hall was a firm belief in the strength of clean government," wrote Edward Flynn, who took over the Bronx Democratic Party at Murphy's behest in 1922 and went on to become a key adviser to Franklin D. Roosevelt. "Mr. Murphy did not believe that politics should have anything to do with either gambling or prostitution. He further believed that politicians should have very little or nothing to do with the Police Department or the school system."[12]

Flynn's testimony on Murphy's behalf spoke to the very different ways in which progressive reformers and Tammany liberals defined clean government. For progressives, whether they were Republicans who admired Theodore Roosevelt, Democrats who saw Woodrow Wilson as an ideal reformer, or independents forever in search of a non-partisan hero to deliver them from grimy politics, clean government meant government devoid of patronage, interest, and politics itself. The model, at least at the municipal level, was an apolitical commission-style government implemented in Galveston, Texas, in 1900. Commission governments limited the role of mayors and emphasized the professional expertise, not the political connections, of elected commissioners. For Flynn and his mentor Murphy, clean government meant an end to Tammany's lucrative involvement in gambling, prostitution, and outright bribery. But it did not preclude politics and patronage, and it certainly did not preclude the awarding of contracts to politically connected companies, such as the trucking and contracting firm that one of Murphy's two brothers owned (and in which Charlie was thought to have an interest—a silent interest, of course). Nor did it include support for the Progressive Era's moral and cultural crusades—ranging from temperance legislation to laws barring baseball games on Sunday.

Other high-ranking Tammany figures in the 1890s, including Croker himself, were involved in the very activities that so offended Murphy. But after Murphy took over the Gas House District in 1892, vice was shut down in his jurisdiction. Journalist Arthur Krock recalled that Murphy "would have nothing to do with what he considered immoral things. He was a devout Catholic family man. He would not take money from a whore or a criminal." Not long after taking over as Tammany's sole leader, Murphy replaced a district leader, Martin Engel, who was known for his ties to prostitution and gambling rackets, with an ally of his own, Florence Sullivan (a cousin of Big Tim Sullivan, the Bowery leader). He then ordered an end to Tammany's involvement with the neighborhood's vice trade. Florence Sullivan surely was the right man for the job, for he was more than six feet tall and just as menacing as Big Tim. Florence Sullivan and a few well-chosen friends shut down the brothels using methods they chose to keep to themselves. The police were not notified.[13]

Murphy surprised in other ways as well. He relied on the advice of confidantes who hardly fit the stereotype of Tammany henchmen— James Gerard, a Columbia University graduate and future U.S. ambassador to Germany, served as Tammany's campaign chairman under Murphy, and Francis O'Donnell, an accountant and former assemblyman whom Murphy named as the organization's all-important treasurer. (O'Donnell's appointment, the *New York Times* declared, "marked the passing for all time of Richard Croker as a potent factor in the organization.") Years later, when Tammany's Jimmy Walker became majority leader of the state Senate, he prudently contacted the boss to ask about the organization's patronage requirements.

"You're the leader, aren't you, Senator Jim?" Murphy asked.

A startled Walker answered in the affirmative.

"Use your own judgment," Murphy said. "If it's good, you'll be an asset to the party. If it isn't, well, the sooner we find it out, the better."[14]

Murphy's tenure at the helm of Tammany was the longest in the organization's history, from 1902 until his death in 1924. He was boss during one of the most tumultuous and contested periods of New York history, a time during which muckrakers, reform groups like the Citizens Union, and emerging national figures like Franklin Delano Roosevelt arrayed themselves against Tammany in the name of Progressivism. But during Murphy's long tenure, the narrative of reformer versus boss became much more complicated. Tammany responded aggressively to discontent with laissez-faire capitalism, protected immigrant culture and identity from those who demanded conformity with middle-class definitions of Americanism, and continued to develop a pluralistic counterpoint to the nation's self-image as a Protestant, Anglo-Saxon nation of rugged individuals. Journalist Lincoln Steffens, no friend of machine politics, conceded that "Tammany kindness is real kindness, and will go far. . . ."[15]

That kindness was delivered in the most personal way possible. Charlie Murphy was on his way home from a banquet on a freezing winter night in 1914 when he came upon a roaring tenement fire on the corner of Eighteenth Street and Third Avenue, just a few minutes' walk from his home on Seventeenth Street. A hundred or so tenants shivered in the street while firefighters tried to save what they could. Murphy halted his ride home, arranged for a local restaurant to open so the displaced residents could warm up with coffee and hot food, and demanded that the police and nearby residents force their way into locked-up local shops to get clothes and other supplies. Dozens of residents were directed to Murphy's own home, where they obtained temporary shelter. Murphy paid for the supplies and food out of his own pocket.[16]

But few saw this side of Murphy. He was viewed, and portrayed, as simply the latest in a long line of disreputable bosses for whom politics simply was a route to illicit riches. In 1912, the young reformer Franklin Roosevelt announced that "C. F. Murphy and his kind must, like the noxious weed, be plucked out." Roosevelt, a state senator who was seeking to carve out a reputation as a reformer just like his cousin Theodore, saw Murphy as an easy—and obvious—target for his righteous outrage. Eventually, however, he would come to view C. F. Murphy very differently.[17]

. . .

Seth Low may have had the best of intentions upon entering City Hall on a wave of anti-Tammany disgust, but as he prepared for reelection in 1903, history did not augur well for a repeat of the reform movement's stunning victory in 1901. New York politics was littered with examples of reform administrations that did not earn a second term—a tribute to Tammany's resilience but also testimony to the inability of reformers to understand the concerns of voters. Tammany's George Washington Plunkitt famously described reform movements as "mornin' glories"— they "looked lovely in the mornin' and withered up in a short time, while the regular machines went on flourishin' forever, like fine sturdy oaks."[18]

If reformers seemed will-o'-the-wisp, perhaps that was because of their tenuous connection to the people whose interests they claimed to represent. Of the 2,312 members of the New York Reform Club in 1902, the vast majority, some 1,842, lived more than thirty miles from downtown Manhattan.[19]

The distance between reformers and the bulk of the city's population was measured in more than just miles. Simply put, many reformers did not understand the everyday concerns of voters, or, if they did, they dismissed them as parochial and unworthy of a disinterested, reform-minded government. Richard Welling, who cofounded the New York Reform Club with Theodore Roosevelt in the 1880s, looked back on the reform movement's attempts to win the support of labor leaders in the late nineteenth century with some frustration. In a speech in 1942, he noted that the club had sought to educate the labor leaders in "Tammany misrule" in the 1880s, but the effort to create a cross-class reform movement ultimately failed. "It was a tremendous blow to find all these men preoccupied with wage questions," he noted with evident frustration. "As Bryce has said, the conspicuous example of failure of democracy is the misgovernment of American cities."[20]

Welling's dismissal of "wage questions"—that is, the demands of workers for better pay—was as telling as his reference to James Bryce, the British aristocrat and celebrated observer of American politics. Welling could not understand why working men were more concerned with their wages than with grand proposals for more efficient municipal government—this was not his idea of how disinterested citizens ought to behave. And so he turned to the wisdom of Bryce to explain it all: American cities were poorly run because men who worried about their wages voted accordingly, paying no regard to the purer virtues of republican democracy.

Groups like the New York Reform Club were contemptuous of the sort of politics practiced at the street and tenement level, so they had little understanding of why "wage questions" might seem more important than, say, ballot reform or temperance legislation. But Tammany leaders such as Barbara Porges lived with the people for whom she advocated, and she could report back to Charlie Murphy with firsthand observations of the concerns in her district.

Barbara Porges was the boss of the 2nd Assembly district on the Lower East Side, a Tammany operative who was working the tenements of Orchard Street long before women were granted the right to vote. Her special cause was the neighborhood peddlers, most of them Jewish, who sold their wares from pushcarts. She virtually adopted some of the district's lost souls, including a peddler known only by the product he sold: "Onions." When Onions contracted tuberculosis, Porges raised money—from neighbors, from strangers, from anyone who would contribute—to pay for his fare to the drier air of Colorado. Porges's husband, Max, was a two-term alderman at the turn of the twentieth century, but it was Barbara Porges who ran the district for thirty years.

In 1918, as Porges patrolled the pushcart paradise of Orchard Street, she was approached by an elderly woman with tears in her eyes—she owned a pushcart, she said, but the police insisted that she move away from a nearby corner. Surely Porges could help her. But the cops were right—the old woman had set up shop on the wrong side of the street. "Look the other way," Porges told the police. They did.

"I am a practical politician," she explained. "I've lived and worked [on the Lower East Side] since 1876 and I have used the tried and true Tammany methods." She later added: "I can't make a speech, but I get to the individual, and I get the vote."[21]

Delivering kindness with the expectation of winning a vote was not how disinterested government and virtuous politics were supposed to work. The new reform groups in New York shared with Lincoln Steffens and his fellow muckrakers a belief that municipal government was too important to be left to professional politicians—so many of them Irish Catholics—and that campaigns and elections produced only inefficiency and corruption. Power was best left to disinterested professionals who, in Steffens's words, believed in "the New York theory that municipal government is business, not politics, and that a business man who would manage the city as he would a business corporation would solve for us all our problems."[22]

Charlie Murphy might have concurred with Steffens's assertion that running a government was indeed a business, but he would have turned Steffens's logic against him. If running city government were a business, it should be handled by political professionals, not amateurs like Seth Low, a Steffens favorite. For all his undoubtedly genuine praise for immigrants and workers, when it came to filling his administration Low turned not to the Lower East Side but to his fellow civic and social elites. A third of his forty-six appointments to the city Board of Education, for example, were listed in the *Social Register.*[23]

As his commissioner of charities, Low chose a Philadelphia-born professional reformer named Homer Folks, who supported the reform movement's vain effort to ban government aid to private child-welfare charities at the state Constitutional Convention of 1894. More successfully, he lobbied against state legislation in 1897 that would have given destitute mothers a public pension to help them keep their families together. The bill was written by Tammany's John Ahearn.[24]

Murphy's first test of leadership came in the mayoral election of 1903, when Seth Low sought to achieve something no reformer had yet managed—win a second term as mayor. Murphy demonstrated a touch for the unexpected that left his allies and his antagonists—especially the mayor—astonished. He extended Tammany's endorsement to Low's two running mates, Comptroller Edward M. Grout and Board of Aldermen President Charles F. Fornes, both of whom had run successfully on Low's anti-Tammany Fusion ticket in 1901. The two men were delighted to accept Murphy's offer, leading to cries of outrage from the mayor's allies. The president of the Citizens Union dispatched a letter to Grout expressing his disbelief, noting that, during the 1901 campaign, Grout "had not hesitated to denounce Tammany Hall from the platform in fearless and scathing terms." But that was then and this was 1903, and Tammany was offering its hand. Things changed.[25]

Low and his allies in the Citizens Union tossed both Grout and Fornes off the Fusion ticket just weeks before the election. With Tammany's foes now confused and demoralized, Murphy's candidate for mayor, the very respectable George McClellan, son and namesake of the Civil War general and a longtime Tammany member, easily defeated Low. Murphy monitored the results in Tammany Hall's famed long room, home to the organization's Executive Committee, as district leaders returned from polling places with their results. Although the outcome was clear early on, Murphy's men reported their returns in precise detail. One district leader, John T. Oakley of the 14th district, told Murphy that the vote for McClellan in his district was 2,614—exactly twenty-six votes fewer than he had anticipated. Everybody in the room noticed that McClellan won Murphy's home district with nearly 75 percent of the vote (by comparison, his overall percentage was about 53 percent city-wide). It was that sort of level of detail, that sort of careful gathering of intelligence, that made Murphy a political legend and that, in the end, no reform movement could match.[26]

But there was one Tammany foe who had no need for legions of district leaders and precinct captains, because he was able to get out his message on a scale that even Tammany had to admire. William Randolph Hearst, owner of two popular New York newspapers, the *American* and the *Evening-Journal*, spoke to hundreds of thousands of readers—and potential voters—every day. His newspapers featured crime stories and a full page of comics, including one strip printed in color, *The Yellow Kid.* The kid's hue gave rise to the sort of reporting that critics said was a Hearst trademark—yellow journalism.

Hearst hungered to be more than just another ink-stained wretch, although there were few more powerful positions in New York's civic life than that of a daily newspaper publisher or editor. One publisher, Horace Greeley, ran in vain for president of the United States in 1872. Another, George Jones of the *New York Times*, presided over the newspaper's investigation of Boss Tweed. The *New York Evening Post* was founded by Alexander Hamilton and, through the years, was edited or published by the likes of William Cullen Bryant, E. L. Godkin, Carl Schurz, and Oswald Garrison Villard. No list of influential New Yorkers in the nineteenth century would be complete without those names.

But Hearst didn't want to influence decisions. He wanted to make them. He saw his media properties as a vehicle—a machine—for launching his political ambitions. He used his clout to win election to Congress in 1902 with Tammany's support, and he soon fashioned himself as the voice of the city's working class, despite his life of privilege. When the city's reform movement faded after Low's defeat in 1903, Hearst took up the anti-Tammany banner but pitched it from a very different angle. Rather than emphasize political reform, Hearst adopted a range of populist economic reforms, from public ownership of public utilities to support for labor unions.

Hearst's positions were popular and, needless to say, well publicized. In 1905, he mobilized his own political faction, the Municipal Ownership League, as a third-party challenge to Mayor McClellan's reelection. With his newspapers whipping up public sentiment and playing on the familiar narrative of Tammany as a bastion of criminality, Hearst proved to be an extraordinary opponent. McClellan was reelected with 228,407 votes, barely outpolling Hearst's total of 224,989. A Republican candidate garnered 137,184 votes, meaning that a clear majority rejected Tammany, but McClellan survived the challenge with the extralegal help of big-shouldered pollwatchers below Fourteenth Street. Just as worrisome for Murphy, Hearst cut into Tammany's support in the tenements of the Lower East Side, particularly in predominantly Jewish neighborhoods, and Hearst's Municipal Ownership League tipped control of the Board of Aldermen from Tammany to a combination of Republicans and Hearst supporters. Hearst was to Murphy what Henry George was to Richard Croker—a warning that Tammany was lagging behind the views of its constituents.

Hearst remained a powerful Tammany foe for the better part of the next two decades. Murphy called a truce in 1906, handing Hearst the Democratic Party's nomination for governor but then doing next to nothing to support him. A former occupant of the governor's office, Theodore Roosevelt—now the president of the United States—found the prospect of Hearst sitting behind his former desk appalling. Roosevelt advised Hearst's Republican foe, Charles Evans Hughes, to make a play for the state's Catholic voters. The strategy succeeded, Hughes prevailed, and, for the moment, Tammany was rid of William Randolph Hearst.

. . .

The history of early twentieth-century New York is defined not by a political campaign or an election but by a fire, the terrible blaze that killed 146 workers, mostly young Jewish and Italian women, in the Triangle Shirtwaist Factory on March 25, 1911. For Tammany, for the

labor movement, for the burgeoning campaign for women's rights—
even, some argue, for the nation itself—the Triangle fire has been considered a critical turning point, the tragic inspiration for the creation of
a new social contract that foreshadowed the New Deal, which was put in
place by a man who served in the New York State Senate at the time of
the fire, Franklin D. Roosevelt.

The Triangle fire surely did represent a milestone for Tammany Hall,
for two of its promising young members, Robert Wagner and Al Smith,
led a state investigation that brought together professional reformers,
including a young social worker and lobbyist named Frances Perkins,
and pragmatic politicians in an alliance that would have seemed highly
unlikely only a few years earlier. The leadership of Wagner and Smith—
carried out with the blessing of Murphy—seemed to represent a sudden,
uncharacteristic, and perhaps even opportunistic change of priorities for
Tammany. It wasn't, but it certainly would have seemed so to New York
newspaper readers, who had become accustomed to breathless accounts
of Tammany's evil intentions and Murphy's Croker-like appetite for
plunder and Tweed-like enjoyment of the good life at his favorite restaurant, Delmonico's, where he held court in a private room decorated with
heavy red rugs and mahogany furniture. Hearst's newspapers portrayed
Murphy in prison stripes, an overstuffed convict-in-waiting.

In fact, Murphy and individual members of Tammany had been
moving the organization toward the cause of reform—or, more to the
point, to a new kind of reform shorn of its evangelical moralism—well
before the Triangle fire. Tammany's John Ahearn might have passed
legislation to grant pensions to poor mothers in 1897 were it not for
the opposition of reformers who opposed the distribution of cash indiscriminately to the poor. Tammany continued to turn left in the years
immediately following the close call with Hearst's Municipal Ownership League. Governor Hughes had more trouble with his fellow Republicans than he did with Murphy's Tammany when he sought to create a
public-service commission to regulate utilities in 1907. But Hughes, a
prototypical reformer, blocked New York's ratification of the Sixteenth

Amendment, which authorized a federal income tax. The amendment, widely viewed as one of the era's most progressive achievements, passed the state legislature only after Tammany took control of Albany in 1911, over the fierce objections of some of the state's most prominent residents, including John D. Rockefeller, members of the Morgan family, and Joseph Choate, corporate lawyer, former ambassador to Great Britain, and regular denouncer of Tammany Hall's "mongrel" tickets. Robert Wagner framed the amendment as a truly progressive reform, arguing that the tax would "lighten the burdens of the poor."[27]

Under Murphy's leadership in the second decade of the twentieth century, Tammany redefined reform as a pragmatic, lunch-bucket form of liberalism stripped of the Progressive Era's moral pieties and evangelical roots. Liberated from the defensiveness that marked its rhetoric and actions during much of the nineteenth century, Tammany finally developed a forward-looking agenda that one historian described as "the creation of a quasi-welfare state." Murphy's allies supported and implemented sweeping new social legislation—from workers' compensation to the beginnings of minimum-wage laws to stricter regulation of businesses, making New York a hothouse of progressive reform long before the New Deal.[28]

Some observers simply could not reconcile these actions with their image of Tammany. Journalist M. A. Werner, in his often-cited history of Tammany, was so convinced of the organization's evil that he could see nothing good coming of anyone connected to the organization. According to Werner, Big Tim Sullivan, the powerful Tammany leader who ruled the Bowery as a personal fiefdom, authored one of the nation's first gun-control laws in 1911 not because he was appalled by the growth of gun violence but because he wanted to plant weapons on gangsters and pimps who refused to pay bribes to Tammany. Werner complained that Sullivan's seemingly progressive law prevented "citizens from protecting themselves from thieves. . . . " A century after its passage, Sullivan's Law remains on the books in New York.[29]

Other reformers were more open-minded, and came to understand what Tammany was trying to accomplish. Frances Perkins, who came of age politically in Albany during Murphy's tenure and went on to become the first woman cabinet secretary in U.S. history, once said of Big Tim Sullivan and his cousin Christopher, "If I had been a man serving in the Senate with them, I'm sure I would have had a glass of beer with them and gotten them to tell me what times were like on the old Bowery."[30]

Perkins recognized in Murphy's Tammany a change that her future boss, Franklin Roosevelt, did not perceive until years later. Tammany's support for social-welfare and regulatory legislation in the early twentieth century was, she wrote, "a turning point" in changing "American political attitudes and policies toward social responsibility." Jeremiah Mahoney, the son of Irish immigrants and law partner of Robert Wagner, was drawn to Tammany politics because he believed it could become a vehicle for pragmatic social and economic change. Mahoney said that he and other young protégés of Murphy "made the [Democratic] party a liberal progressive party, and we advocated the cause of the underprivileged [and] the cause of labor."[31]

This new approach certainly was not perfect, as Perkins learned when Murphy at first blocked and then sought to thwart a bill that would have limited the workweek for women and children to fifty-four hours. The legislation never made it out of committee in 1911 because Murphy sought to protect allies who owned candy factories that employed many women and children. A year later, Murphy allowed the measure to come to a vote in the State Senate on the last day of the legislative session, but he saw to it that canneries—factories where vegetables and fruit were placed in cans, sealed, and shipped to stores—were exempt. He believed Perkins and her allies would never agree to the measure, but, after a long talk with Big Tim Sullivan, Perkins decided to accept what she could get—in essence sacrificing several thousand cannery workers for the sake of the four hundred thousand women who worked in other industries.

Sullivan explained why he supported the measure despite Murphy's opposition. "My sister was a poor girl and she went out to work when she was young," he told Perkins. "I feel kinda sorry for them poor girls . . . I'd like to do them a good turn."[32]

Sullivan and his cousin Christopher, also a legislator, left Albany before the vote, believing the deal was done. They were wrong, for Murphy ordered Wagner to kill the measure through parliamentary procedures, outraging other Tammany figures, including Thomas McManus, the bill's sponsor in the Senate. When Perkins found out, she got word to the Sullivan cousins, who rushed back to the chamber in time to outmaneuver Wagner and cast the deciding votes in favor of the bill. McManus was the not-so-quiet hero of the episode, holding the floor with a long speech while the Sullivans rode to the rescue.

Perkins's allies were furious with the compromise, but Perkins, learning quickly from tutors like Big Tim Sullivan, came to the realization that legislation did not pass simply because it was worthy, and that compromise was not necessarily corrupt. The lessons Sullivan imparted to Perkins were timely—Big Tim died a year later, in 1913, after months of mental instability. His body was found on a railroad track in the Bronx.

. . .

Charles F. Murphy certainly was not a purist's idea of a reformer. He retained the right to protect his friends in business even as he unleashed the forces of this new urban liberalism in Albany. Why, then, did he support the sweeping reforms that were about to transform New York politics? Murphy left behind few letters and, in keeping with his nickname, he gave even fewer speeches. Not long before his death, however, he did say that he "encouraged the selection of young men for public office" because they offered "a different viewpoint of what Tammany Hall is and its aims and aspirations." Al Smith believed that Murphy supported expansive social legislation because he "had come up from lowly surroundings." Did his father, a Famine exile, impress on young Charlie the misery of hunger and the failures of government during the Irish Famine? It is certainly possible, although there is no clear evidence suggesting a connection.[33]

One possible explanation for Murphy's actions, other than simply a ploy for votes, generally has been ignored: They may have reflected a growing sense among some American Catholics in public life that the poor, so many of them Catholic immigrants, could not be left to fend for themselves. Murphy was a devout Catholic; his bookshelves at home were lined with works devoted to the history and dogma of his faith. He came of age politically at a time when Catholic liberals such as Cardinal James Gibbons of Baltimore, Bishop John Ireland of Minnesota, and New York's own radical clergyman Edward McGlynn advocated greater Catholic support for issues of social justice, including the right of workers to organize. Bishop Ireland, in fact, argued that Pope Leo XIII's landmark 1891 encyclical on social justice, *Rerum Novarum* ("On New Things"), gave tacit papal approval for specific social-welfare measures, including the eight-hour workday.

Pope Leo, prodded by liberal American bishops, acknowledged the "misery and wretchedness pressing so unjustly on the majority of the working class" and argued that those in "exceeding distress" should be "met by public aid." Jeremiah Mahoney, who described himself as Murphy's most important political adviser later in the boss's life, contended that Leo XIII's encyclical had a "marvelous" impact on young Catholic political leaders who interpreted the document as an argument for decent wages, collective bargaining, and state intervention in the private economy. The new Catholic social teachings clearly had an impact far beyond the parish and the diocese. During his presidential campaign in 1932, candidate Franklin Roosevelt cited Pope Pius XI's encyclical *Quadragesimo Anno* ("After Forty Years," commemorating the anniversary of *Rerum Novarum*), which taught that a just economy "cannot be left to the free competition of forces." The encyclical, Roosevelt told a crowd in Detroit, was "just as radical as I am."[34]

Murphy certainly would not have made so bold a claim for himself, but, as a committed Catholic immersed in the literature of his faith, he would have followed the Church's conversation about social justice following publication of *Rerum Novarum*. He may not have read it, but, being the listener that he was, he no doubt heard about the conversation it inspired. Whether the document affected him as much as it did Mahoney and his young Tammany colleagues is impossible to know. But Murphy began to pay closer attention to those young men filled with the era's sense of change and possibilities. He paid less attention to advisers such as Daniel Cohalan, a lawyer, judge, and covert agent for revolutionaries in Ireland; John Quinn, a distinguished lawyer, patron of the arts, and friend of numerous Irish writers and artists, including William Butler Yeats; and conservative businessman Thomas Fortune Ryan, one of the nation's wealthiest men thanks in part to his control of streetcar franchises.

In their place, Murphy increasingly relied on Al Smith, Robert Wagner, Jeremiah Mahoney, James Foley (who married Murphy's stepdaughter), and other, lesser-known figures in New York government. Dubbed the "war board," these young politicians met regularly, sometimes as often as once a week, to plot legislative strategy, kick around new ideas, and strengthen Tammany's commitment to social reform. "We told [Murphy] that a political party had to become an instrument to serve the people," Mahoney recalled. "We made the party into a liberal progressive party. "[35]

The war board certainly did not invent the new liberalism that was taking hold in many cities with immigrant-based populations, nor did these pragmatic politicians spend a good deal of time studying social problems that most of them knew about from personal experience. But they embraced and implemented the new politics of social change, and they set the stage for Smith's four terms as governor, during which New York gained a reputation for efficient, progressive government—with a Tammany man in charge, no less.

. . .

For Tammany, the key moment in this transformation was not the Tri-angle fire but the opening of the state legislature on January 3, 1911, when the Democratic caucus in the State Senate chose Robert Wagner to become the body's new majority leader. The same day, Al Smith was named the State Assembly's majority leader (second in command to the speaker). Both moves came at Murphy's direction.

The choice of Smith was not particularly controversial. Smith, who stood about five feet, eight inches, with an impressive nose and long neck, was a popular young man of thirty-seven known for his hard work and his loyalty to the organization that promoted him from the streets of the Lower East Side to the corridors of power in Albany. His was the story of so many other Tammany figures—his father died young, forcing Al to quit school at the age of fourteen to help support his Irish-immigrant mother and his younger sister. Smith went to work at the Fulton Fish Market, enduring long hours, hard labor, and overpower-ing smells to make up for the social safety net that simply didn't exist for families like his. Eventually he came to the attention of Tammany district leader Tom Foley, who found him a patronage job in the court system and put him to work for the organization. In 1903, Smith was elected to the State Assembly, where he found himself rubbing shoulders with better-educated, more worldly colleagues who looked askance at the grade-school dropout with an accent that spoke of hard times on the streets of New York. Smith decided to educate himself in his new profession, and he set a precedent in Albany by reading the contents of every piece of legislation to cross his desk. Charlie Murphy approved of the young man, and in 1911 Smith became not only the Assembly's majority leader but chairman of the body's powerful Ways and Means Committee. Through Charlie Murphy, Smith had absolute power over the Assembly's legislative agenda. People noticed.

And they took even greater notice when Murphy chose Wagner, a cerebral, mild-mannered German immigrant from Manhattan's Yorkville neighborhood, to lead the State Senate. By all rights, by hallowed tradition, the Senate's top post should have gone to Thomas Grady, Tammany's old warhorse who had labored without complaint as Senate minority leader for more than a decade when Republicans controlled the body. Members of the majority party—in this case, the Democrats—chose the majority leader, but Murphy's power over the caucus was such that he basically told his fellow Democrats how they should vote. Grady was a throwback to the Tammany of the nineteenth century, the Tammany that Murphy now saw as part of another era. Murphy once said that political parties could not remain static; they had to adapt or they died. Grady represented the past. Wagner, who at age thirty-three was even younger than Smith, represented change. Wagner shared a boardinghouse with Smith—the press called the two of them the "Tammany Twins," but they were not very much alike save in their politics and, not coincidentally, in their hardscrabble childhoods. Although Wagner's family had been intact, he and his siblings were sent to work as teenagers to help pay the bills. Wagner, unlike Smith, could afford the luxury of college and law school, giving him a polish Smith would never have—that was part of Smith's appeal—and adding gravitas to the new power dynamic in Albany.

Through Wagner and Smith, Charlie Murphy's control over Albany was enormous, for the new governor, John Alden Dix, was also a Tammany ally. The anti-Tammany Civic League noted with anxiety that "Murphy was in the saddle and Tammany controlled everything in sight." So when flames ripped through the Triangle Shirtwaist Factory two months after the ascension of Wagner and Smith, Tammany had in place the mechanism, the will, and the power to respond to the public's outrage—and the outrage of its young leaders. Wagner and Smith were named chairman and vice chairman, respectively, of the state Factory Investigating Commission (FIC) appointed in the fire's aftermath. No investigative body in the history of New York politics was given more sweeping powers than the FIC—it issued subpoenas, demanded access to private property (such as factories), hired staff without regard to patronage or politics, conducted public hearings, and sought alliances with advocacy groups, labor unions, and other interested organizations.

Joining the two Tammany politicians who chaired the FIC were social reformers, good-government advocates, and elite profession-als who, by tradition and instinct, generally opposed anything that smacked of urban machine politics. Commission member Frances Per-kins already had signaled her support—indeed, her enthusiasm—for Tammany politicians she saw as potential allies. Joining her were the likes of union leader Samuel Gompers, head of the American Federation of Labor; Abram Elkus, a brilliant lawyer and Woodrow Wilson's future ambassador to the Ottoman Empire; Mary Dreier, a union and suffrage activist; and Belle Israels Moskowitz, a social reformer who would go on to become Al Smith's most trusted and cherished adviser. This com-bination of experts, reformers, and political professionals did more than shed light on appalling conditions in factories around the state. It rec-ommended and saw through to passage more than two dozen bills that expanded the FIC's mandate to include the first steps toward compre-hensive social-welfare reform in New York.[36]

The Factory Investigating Commission's voluminous reports became the foundational document for an alliance between Tammany and prag-matic reformers who were more concerned with practical problems than with saving souls. That alliance required reformers to accept Tamma-ny's terms of engagement with the poor and the alienated, terms that were best articulated by Charlie Murphy's predecessor, Richard Croker, during a long interview with a British journalist, W. T. Stead, in 1897. "If we go down in the gutter," Croker said, "it is because there are men in the gutter, and you have to go down where they are if you are going to do anything with them."[37]

Some reformers could not help but notice how Tammany figures—not just Smith and Wagner but also more complicated characters such as the Bowery's Big Tim Sullivan and West Side leader Thomas McManus—did more than simply advocate for the poor and downtrodden. They were engaged in the lives of the people they represented. They understood their problems, in part because so many Tammany figures were not far removed from the experience of tenement life, the catastrophic loss of a parent (usually a father), and the sense of powerlessness that was partner to poverty. Not long after Frances Perkins arrived in New York in 1910, she went to work in Hartley House, a settlement house on the West Side. She soon found herself dealing with the case of a young boy who was arrested, sent to the infamous "Tombs" jail, and was awaiting trial for an unspecified crime. The boy provided the sole support for his widowed mother and two younger sisters, so the family faced the prospect of economic ruin if the boy were sent to prison. Perkins's settlement-house colleagues, trained in the protocols of professional reform, began an investigation into the family's background before offering assistance. They concluded, in Perkins's words, "that the mother was somewhat less than worthy" of help. Worthiness was the deciding criterion, not only for the settlement-house workers but also for the larger private charities imbued with Anglo-Protestant anxieties about the character of the poor.

Tammany's George Washington Plunkitt said that when residents in his district were burned out of their homes, he personally took care of finding them clothes and temporary shelter, rather than refer them to private charities. Those organizations, he said, "would investigate their case . . . and decide they were worthy of help about the time they are dead from starvation."[38]

Startled and angry at her colleagues' decision, Perkins recalled hearing about the work of the local Tammany leader, Thomas McManus, and his clubhouse, which was nearby on Ninth Avenue. Unannounced and unknown to McManus, Perkins showed up at the clubhouse one day, to the surprise of some low-level Tammany operatives gathered in the club's main room, talking politics. Clouds of tobacco smoke clung to the ceilings, and every now and then one of the McManus team made use of one of the spittoons scattered around the room. When Perkins asked to see McManus, she was ushered into the boss's office without hesitation or even a question.[39]

McManus was known not by his first name but as "The" McManus.

Everybody, including the newspapers, referred to him that way. The title was a testament to the resiliency of Gaelic culture in the streets of New York, for in preconquest Ireland, the chieftains of great tribes were known as "The O'Neill" or "The O'Donnell," or, in this case, "The McManus." Thomas McManus, a plain-speaking, middle-aged man with a receding hairline and a dashing Van Dyck beard, became a power in Tammany Hall in the early twentieth century. Perkins found him surrounded by petitioners, but he put aside his other business when this earnest young woman entered his office. She told him she was there on behalf of a boy who was in trouble. McManus asked whether he lived in the district (the 15th Assembly district). He did. He asked whether Perkins lived in the district. She did. McManus took down the boy's name and told Perkins to return to the club the following afternoon.

She did. The boy, McManus told her, would be released from the Tombs at six o'clock that evening.

"I don't know how he did it," Perkins later said of The McManus's actions. "I'm sure it was irregular." But she concluded that the result, not the process, was what mattered.

Not everybody in the Progressive movement was so open-minded. Perkins once told several of her fellow reformers that if she had the right to vote—this was before passage of women's suffrage—she would be a Democrat.

Her colleagues were shocked that she would consider supporting an organization like Tammany Hall. "Well," said one, "look at the scum of the earth they have."

TEN

✦➤══◉══◀✦

MURPHY'S LAW

Straw hats were all the rage on a humid June day in Baltimore as the nation's Democrats filed into the city's Fifth Regiment Armory for their 1912 national convention. All eyes were on Charles F. Murphy and the eighty-nine New York delegates he controlled as they made their way into a furnace posing as a convention hall. The minute they left the relative comfort of the street for the discomfort of the armory, hats came off, and ties were loosened, and jackets were tossed aside.

This was to be Charlie Murphy's debut as a national political figure, the boss of the largest delegation at the convention and the Democratic leader of a state that had become a political colossus. Democrats had chosen a New Yorker as their presidential nominee in five of the previous nine elections. (What's more, New Yorker Horace Greeley ran as a Liberal Republican in 1872, and another New Yorker, Theodore Roosevelt, won the 1904 presidential election.) New York's forty-five electoral votes were by far the largest prize in the forthcoming presidential election. Pennsylvania was a distant second with thirty-eight electoral votes, while California had just eleven and Florida had six. As the most powerful leader of the most powerful state in the union, Charles Francis

Murphy was a good deal more than the boss of a local political machine. Writing from Baltimore as the convention opened, a *New York Telegram* journalist noted: "Mr. Murphy is a bigger factor here . . . than any Tammany Hall leader has ever been in a National Convention."[1]

Superficially, Murphy's prominence was all about pure political power. He commanded a large bloc of votes, and he made it clear that he was prepared to use his stature—and his votes—to achieve a single practical goal: Block any move to nominate perennial candidate William Jennings Bryan, the rabble-rousing voice of the party's rural populists who had lost the presidential contests of 1896, 1900, and 1908. While Bryan was not a formal candidate in 1912, he harbored hopes for the nomination because neither of the two leading contenders, House Speaker James Beauchamp "Champ" Clark of Missouri and Governor Woodrow Wilson of New Jersey, commanded even a simple majority of delegates, never mind the two-thirds required for nomination. Murphy saw the possibility of a rush to Bryan and was determined to crush it. His control over the state's delegates was absolute because, under state party rules, the delegation voted as a unit. So whichever candidate the majority supported—and Murphy controlled the majority, through their affiliation or alliance with Tammany—would receive all of New York's votes. New York's pro-Wilson delegates, including Franklin Roosevelt, could only grumble about Murphy's power.

On a more fundamental level, however, Murphy's prominence at the 1912 convention symbolized the rise of the Irish urban vote in a party dominated by dusty-dry prairie populists like Bryan—known as "The Great Commoner"—and aloof reformers like Wilson. On those rare occasions when he opened his mouth, Murphy spoke for urban residents—Irish, Italians, Jews, among others—who had transformed politics in many cities but who were relatively voiceless in the national party. He also stood against the strident populism of Bryan, whose famed "Cross of Gold" speech in 1896 condemned the monied interests of the East. Murphy sought cooperation, not confrontation, with Democratic-leaning captains of industry, including streetcar magnate

Thomas Fortune Ryan and financiers J. P. Morgan and August Belmont. Ryan and Belmont were delegates to the convention.

Ideology aside, in Murphy's view there was one simple and undeniable fact about Bryan that made him clearly unacceptable at the 1912 convention. His inability to translate his populist message to a national audience had resulted in three crushing defeats. More to the point for Murphy, Bryan lost New York in all three campaigns. If Bryan appeared at the top of the ticket again in 1912, he could bring down the party's candidates for governor and the state legislature, leading to Republican victories and the end of Tammany's post-Triangle reform agenda.

Murphy put Tammany's national clout to the test early and often in 1912, aligning with other urban bosses to secure the election of New York's Alton B. Parker as the convention's temporary chairman, over Bryan's fierce objections. Parker had lost to fellow New Yorker Theodore Roosevelt in the 1904 presidential election. He also was a Wall Street lawyer, symbolizing Bryan's association of the eastern wing of the party with the nation's bankers and financiers.

Bryan fired back at Tammany and Murphy within minutes of the convention's opening prayer, during which the Roman Catholic bishop of Baltimore, Cardinal James Gibbons, reminded delegates that they were "brothers of the same family." Bryan, a devout Christian fundamentalist, made it clear that his idea of brotherly love did not extend to Tammany and its choice of Parker as temporary chairman. As delegates settled into their seats in the oppressive convention hall, Bryan urged them to rise up against their brothers from New York. The Democratic Party, he said, was "true to the people," and Tammany "cannot frighten it with your Ryans nor buy it with your Belmonts."[2]

The reference to Ryan, a delegate from his native Virginia, and Belmont, a delegate from New York, set the stage for a family squabble over the parameters and meaning of Progressivism in the Democratic Party of 1912. Bryan elaborated on his criticism in newspaper interviews, charging that Tammany's men—the "Belmont–Ryan–Murphy crowd"—were representatives of the same "predatory Wall Street interests" he had been railing about for fifteen years. Asked about this characterization, Murphy told reporters that Bryan had "a right to say what he chooses." As for himself, he added, characteristically: "I have a right to be silent."[3]

On the night of June 28, 1912, with the convention three days old and growing more tense with each passing hour, Bryan again appeared on the armory stage to give what the *New York Times* called "the most sensational speech of his life"—even greater, in the correspondent's view, than the "Cross of Gold" keynote address sixteen years earlier. Bryan certainly was in fine form, snarling and scowling as he accused Belmont, Ryan, and Morgan of plotting to purchase the Democratic nomination for the candidate of their choice. Simmering with rage and passion, returning to the biblical imagery of the speech that made him famous, the Great Commoner proclaimed: "If thy right hand offend thee, cut it off. And if it is necessary to cut off Morgan and Ryan and Belmont to save the Democratic body politic, then cut them off." He proposed a resolution demanding that Belmont and Ryan be expelled from the convention, and that the party renounce any candidate they supported. "Pandemonium," a reporter noted, "does not describe the scene that followed." After heated objections from Virginia's delegates, who argued that Ryan was a duly elected fellow delegate who could not simply be compelled to leave, Bryan withdrew his request for expulsion, but he insisted on a roll-call vote on his proposal to condemn the three men and all they stood for.[4]

The chair called the roll, and state after state—Alabama, Arizona, Arkansas—cast all or nearly all of its votes in favor of Bryan's resolution. Belmont, a longtime party stalwart whose father was chairman of the Democratic National Committee in the 1870s, was seated near Murphy on the convention floor, no doubt grinding his teeth as the "yea" votes piled up. When New York was called, Charles Murphy betrayed not a hint of annoyance. With a smile, he turned to Belmont and said, "August, listen and hear yourself vote yourself out of the convention." Murphy then cast all ninety of New York's votes—including Belmont's—in favor of Bryan's condemnation of the three businessmen associated with Tammany. Murphy was not about to add to the crosses of martyrdom that Bryan carried with such evident enthusiasm. If Bryan were looking for another cause around which to rally his aggrieved brethren, Murphy wouldn't give him the satisfaction.[5]

A Bryan boom never developed, but Murphy's own candidate, Champ Clark, was outmaneuvered when Bryan threw his support to Wilson, sealing victory for the New Jersey governor, who was perceived to be the enemy of immigrant-based urban bosses and the hordes at their command. (For his effort, Bryan would be named Secretary of State under Wilson, but critics found nothing distasteful about this apparent bargain.) Murphy offered no resistance as the Wilson surge unfolded during the convention's forty-ninth ballot. Chattering delegates in the cavernous hall grew quiet when the roll call reached New York and "Silent Charlie" Murphy rose to cast the state's ballots. Murphy seemed startled as conversations came to a halt around him on the convention floor, and delegates shushed those who were unaware of the moment at hand. "New York," Murphy announced, "casts 90 votes for Woodrow Wilson." The hall erupted. Delegates from Texas took off their hats to salute the New Yorkers.[6]

Wilson won the nomination and went on to win a three-way election, besting the Republican incumbent, William Howard Taft, and former president Theodore Roosevelt, who hoped to win disaffected Republicans and Democrats to an independent line, the Progressive Party. On Inauguration Day the following March, Wilson and his wife spent the afternoon reviewing the traditional parade in honor of the new president. A familiar figure—bespectacled, paunchy, and dignified—led the Tammany delegation. Wilson turned to his wife and pointed toward the line of march. "That's Charlie Murphy," said the new president.[7]

Wilson's followers in New York, including William Gibbs McAdoo (his treasury secretary and future son-in-law) and Franklin Roosevelt (soon to be named assistant secretary of the navy), also were watching Murphy. Both saw the Tammany boss as an obstacle to their ambitions in New York. Roosevelt, in fact, had appeared at a gathering of dissident upstate Democrats in the Hotel Astor in Manhattan shortly after the Baltimore convention. He must have been delighted to hear fellow upstater Thomas Mott Osborne deliver a speech worthy of Bryan at his vituperative best. Osborne, who saw himself as the defender of the party's progressive purity, expressed the hope that New York Democrats would one day turn to worthy candidates like Franklin Roosevelt for high office. But such hopes were useless, he said, as long as the party had "stupid, ignorant, and arrogant" leaders like Charlie Murphy.[8]

. . .

For a "stupid leader," Charlie Murphy had a pretty good autumn in 1912. Tammany and the Democratic Party swept the state elections that year, leaving him with absolute control over state politics and government, thanks especially to the election of longtime Tammany Congressman William Sulzer as governor in place of the ineffective John Alden Dix and the promotion of Al Smith to speaker of the State Assembly. Sulzer was not one of Murphy's young lions, but he was an interesting choice all the same. He was popular with the city's growing Jewish population, he had a taste for dramatic outfits and gestures, and he was best known for his facility with words—lots of words.

With Tammany fully in control of state government, its commitment to social justice and reform would be put to the test as the Factory Investigating Commission's recommendations and other reforms made their way through the legislative pipeline. Expectations for authentic change were high, and Tammany delivered. In a single, remarkable legislative session of less than five months in early 1913, the Tammany-controlled New York legislature put into place a series of reforms that laid the groundwork for a new and robust role for state government—not only in regulating the workplace but also in providing a social safety net, particularly for women and children.

The legislature approved a new mandatory workers' compensation bill (introduced by Charles Murphy's son-in-law, James Foley, but vetoed by Governor Sulzer), prohibited the use of child labor in dangerous trades, limited the workday for railroad workers to ten hours, established a minimum wage of $2 a day for workers on state canals, required employers to allow workers at least one day off for every seven, created state-supported college scholarships for poor high school students, strengthened government regulation of workplace safety and of public utilities, and gave the state Labor Department new powers to enforce labor laws. Consumer advocate Florence Kelley called the legislature's accomplishments "extraordinarily radical." Many of these reforms had been discussed or proposed in earlier years, but they were not enacted until Tammany's new generation—the Smiths, the Wagners, the Foleys—dominated the legislature. And that was just the beginning.[9]

An inspired legislature went on to approve the construction of new hydroelectric plants that the state, rather than the private sector, would own and operate. Tammany's Jimmy Walker introduced legislation that tightened government regulation of the fire-insurance industry. Assembly Majority Leader Aaron Levy, who became the state's highest-ranking Jewish politician when Smith moved from majority leader to speaker, authored legislation that forced the New York Stock Exchange to incorporate, making it subject to the state's banking regulations. Tammany legislators also proposed measures to regulate stock speculation, including a bill that forced brokers to provide transaction information to buyers. But Sulzer blocked a Tammany bill that would have doubled the tax on stock transfers, a measure that gave further evidence of an ideology at the core of Tammany's political machinations.

Critics were astonished. The editors of *The Outlook*, a constant Tammany foe, complained that the "character of the Legislature [in 1913] was lower than the New York average, which is none too high," and yet, despite the presence of Tammany leaders in both houses, lawmakers managed to pass progressive measures that were "in advance of any similar State in the Union." The editors were bewildered. It had not occurred to them that leaders such as Smith, Wagner, and even Silent Charlie Murphy might believe in something other than avarice.[10]

Jeremiah Mahoney, a member of Murphy's war board, said that he and other Tammany politicians supported social-welfare legislation because they remembered "the days of adversity" when they were children growing up in Manhattan. Mahoney's father, a police officer, died at a young age, leaving six children and a widow to struggle along in a $25-a-month walk-up on Third Avenue. Mahoney went to work in a hardware factory when he was fourteen years old to help his mother pay for rent and food. Later, while working as a stock boy, he met another poor but ambitious young man—Robert Wagner, his future law partner. Even in his old age, when he had achieved a degree of affluence, Mahoney insisted that he and other Tammany figures never forgot the struggles of their youth and that they had acted accordingly once they were in public life.[11]

In 1915, the Civic League, one of the many good-government reform groups that opposed Tammany, published a pamphlet celebrating "five years of moral victories" in Albany. Included among those victories were a ban on Sunday baseball games, restrictions on racetrack gambling, and opposition to Tammany-backed legislation that would have allowed Jewish peddlers to conduct business on Sundays. The Civic League joined with religion-based organizations such as the New York Sabbath Committee, composed mainly of Protestant clergy, in a years-long crusade to prevent any baseball—amateur or professional—from being played on Sunday. A Tammany judge named Francis X. McQuade fought equally long against the prohibition. "Can you conceive of a law which would make your son a criminal just because he batted a baseball in an open lot on a Sunday afternoon?" he asked.[12]

The Civic League and its religious allies regarded such laws as critical in keeping the Sabbath pure, a virtue they regarded as exceptionally American. One critic said that allowing baseball on Sunday would mark the beginning of "the Germanization of the American Sunday." (Baseball eventually was allowed on Sunday; Judge McQuade went on to become club treasurer of the New York Giants baseball team, a World Series rival of the New York Yankees, owned by former Tammany congressman Jacob Ruppert.)[13]

The Civic League's summary of the reform movement's victories included no mention of the social-welfare and workplace-safety measures that Tammany had implemented after the Triangle Shirtwaist fire. For some self-styled progressives, reforms such as workers' compensation and pensions for struggling families meant nothing if unaccompanied by moral reform as well. The contempt of such reformers for Tammany left them blind to the achievements of Smith, Wagner, and the new urban liberalism they represented.

. . .

The historic legislative session of 1913, remembered in the decades that followed as a landmark in New York politics, took place in the shadow of a forgotten but critical drama that unfolded in Albany even as Wagner and Smith corralled the votes needed to create a new social compact between the state and its citizens. Governor William Sulzer, so long a reliable Tammany man, declared war on Murphy and the organization almost immediately after he took the oath of office, inspiring a raft of headlines and dramatic prose that dominated the front pages of the city's newspapers in the spring and summer of 1913. Sulzer was a persnickety sort, a gruff tobacco-spitter who made some of Tammany's district leaders seem as polished and decorous as their Civic League antagonists. He also harbored ambitions, and he surely noticed that Woodrow Wilson had been elected governor of New Jersey in 1910 with the support of his state's Democratic machine but then gained national prominence by turning on the machine as soon as he was elected.

Sulzer's actions were hardly subtle. He ordered an investigation of state highway contracts, a particular area of vulnerability for Charlie Murphy himself, since his family business, New York Contracting and Trucking Company, certainly benefited from Tammany's clout. Murphy sought to limit the damage by urging Sulzer to appoint a close friend and business associate, James Gaffney, as superintendent of highways. Sulzer refused.

The governor's assertions of independence from Tammany, made both publicly and privately to the state's politically independent reformers, were hardly the act of a man grateful to the organization that had supported him throughout his career. Without Tammany, there was no Governor Sulzer. But others had made similar calculations before and lived to tell the tale. William R. Grace, George McClellan, and even the sitting mayor of New York, William Jay Gaynor, prospered despite their defiance of Tammany's leadership. Sulzer concluded that he could do the same.

In early spring of 1913, Sulzer announced his unequivocal support for a bill authorizing direct primary elections, meaning that party nominations for elected offices from top to bottom would be contested on the ballot, not in conventions or in the back rooms of party clubhouses. Individuals seeking party nominations would be required to file petitions with a minimum number of signatures in order to qualify for the primary ballot. Party funds could not be used to support any candidate who qualified for a primary. All of this was designed as a direct assault on the power of bosses like Murphy, who often handpicked top officials—including Sulzer himself—as the party's candidates.

Direct primaries were a critical part of the reform movement's bipartisan agenda, and they had been discussed—to no avail—for several years in New York. But Sulzer was determined to succeed where others had failed, in part, it was whispered, because he sought to dethrone Charlie Murphy and take his place as the head of the Democratic Party of New York.

Tammany, in the midst of other things, offered up a compromise bill that made it slightly easier for independent candidates to petition for a spot on the ballot. That was as far as Murphy was willing to go. Sulzer vetoed the bill and announced that he would brook no compromise as he launched vitriolic attacks on anyone who opposed him. At one point, he delivered a characteristically bombastic speech in which he referred to his opponents as "unmitigated scoundrels," focusing particular attention on one of them: Charlie Murphy. "One boss in the great State of New York

[is] defying the people, spurning their petitions, trampling their rights, laughing in their faces, and like Tweed in his day brazenly and audaciously saying, 'What are you going to do about it?' . . . Shall it go forth from one end of the country to the other that Mr. Murphy doth feed upon something, forsooth, that he has grown so great that he has more power, that he has more influence than all the other ten millions of people in the State of New York?"[14]

Sulzer's audience in the State Capitol burst into wild applause; among those in attendance, direct from Washington, DC, where he had just assumed duties as assistant secretary of the navy, was former state senator Franklin D. Roosevelt. Sulzer chose to picture Murphy as the sole obstacle to his bill, but that simply wasn't true. Republicans in the legislature were opposed as well, which is why Sulzer referred to the Republican leader in the State Senate, Elon R. Brown, as "an old fossil of the Paleozoic age" and a "poor fellow wholly irresponsible and in his dotage." The governor predicted that his bill would pass. If it didn't, he said, "I don't know anything about politics."[15]

He was right about the last part. The Republican old fossil joined hands with Tammany's Murphy to crush Sulzer's proposal, although they hardly had to twist the arms of legislators. Sulzer managed to alienate all but a few upstate Democrats with his outrageous rhetoric, serial insults, and absolute refusal to compromise.

Then came the whirlwind. Murphy decided that Sulzer had to go. That meant impeachment, which required allegations of criminal conduct. A Tammany-led legislative committee was empaneled to find whatever it could. What it found would have been enough to impeach a bishop, never mind an abrasive, uncompromising, and increasingly unsavory governor. William Sulzer, the committee announced, had not reported thousands of dollars in campaign contributions in 1912, funneling the money to a private account where the cash was used to buy railroad stock. He used other campaign money to speculate on Wall Street while his legislative colleagues debated measures calling for greater regulation of the stock market.

The evidence was clear enough. Sulzer was brought before the Assembly, impeached, and then convicted after a relatively dignified trial in the State Senate. Lieutenant Governor Martin Glynn, a long-time journalist with a reputation as a thoughtful progressive, became the state's first Irish-Catholic chief executive when Sulzer left Albany in disgrace. The press was divided on the drama, with most city papers conceding that Sulzer was guilty as charged, but the anti-Tammany *Evening Post* asserted that whatever Sulzer's offenses, he was "an angel of light compared to Murphy." Impeaching and removing Sulzer for financial shenanigans, just a few years after George Washington Plunkitt famously coined the term *honest graft* to describe how he and other Tammany operatives made small fortunes off government service, seemed like a breathtaking exercise in hypocrisy.[16]

Perhaps it was. But Sulzer was hardly a pure innocent, and his refusal to compromise on an issue near and dear to Murphy's heart was an outright betrayal of the man who had helped make him governor. And Sulzer played politics just as harshly as Murphy did—he threatened to pull patronage from legislators who opposed his direct-primary bill, and he wielded his veto promiscuously to punish his enemies in the legislature, regardless of the legislation's merits.

Nevertheless, the spectacle did not reflect well on Murphy and Tammany, offering the organization's opponents an opening in New York City's municipal elections and in annual State Assembly elections held just months after Sulzer's removal. The city's reformers, showing a new appreciation for the realities of multicultural politics, rallied behind a young Irish Catholic with a revered last name and direct connections to the Wilson White House, a formidable combination. His name was John Purroy Mitchel, and if the reform movement could have put together a dream candidate who could appeal to high-minded civic elites as well as Tammany's core constituents, he surely fit the bill. His grandfather was the famed Irish journalist John Mitchel, known for his pro-Southern views during the Civil War and for his fiery polemic, *The Last Conquest of Ireland (Perhaps)*, which accused the British government of deliberately starving the Irish during the Famine—a book that remains in print 150 years after publication.

John Purroy Mitchel inherited his grandfather's charisma and quarrelsome disposition, but not his religion—the elder Mitchel was a Protestant, but, through intermarriage, his grandson was a Catholic. John Purroy Mitchel was not, however, a Paddy from the Gas House District. He attended Fordham Preparatory School, a prestigious Jesuit institution, and earned a bachelor's degree from Columbia College and a law degree from New York Law School. Mitchel quickly earned a reputation as a young reformer in a hurry—one of many in New York in the early twentieth century. He hurled himself into New York politics before he was 30, and won election as president of the city's Board of Aldermen on a reform ticket in 1909. It was an impressive feat, considering that Tammany captured the mayoralty that year. Mitchel soon became a Woodrow Wilson man, and Wilson's men had their eyes on him and on the unsettled situation in New York after Sulzer's impeachment. Colonel Edward M. House, a key adviser to Wilson, noted in his diary that he and Treasury Secretary William Gibbs McAdoo had a "keen desire to revamp New York City and State," and that would require taking on Tammany.[17]

The first step in the revamping project was the appointment of John Purroy Mitchel as collector of customs for the Port of New York, the most-coveted federal patronage job in the city, with the holder regarded as the eyes and ears of the White House in New York. The press speculated that the White House had even bigger plans for Mitchel, plans that the young man did nothing to discourage. On the very day of his appointment as collector, he told reporters that his new job would be no obstacle if he chose to challenge Tammany in the 1913 mayoral election, just a few months away. "Tammany is afraid that the Wilson Democrats are concocting a scheme to retire Charles F. Murphy from the leadership of the organization by grooming Mr. Mitchel for the Mayoralty race," the *New York Times* reported. And so they were. Mitchel performed the duties of collector for several months before announcing his candidacy for mayor on an independent ticket.[18]

The Mitchel campaign, which brought together Republicans, dissident Democrats, and independents who supported the new Progressive Party, was directed at Murphy personally, and it was conducted with a level of venom that would have done the candidate's grandfather proud. Mitchel rarely mentioned his opponent, Edward McCall, a perfectly honorable chairman of the state Public Service Commission, but when he did, he accused him of being little more than a puppet of Murphy. "Tammany Hall is doomed," he told an audience in the Bronx, "but I shall not rest until I have driven Charles F. Murphy out of political life." Voters, given their first chance to pass judgment on the impeachment of Governor Sulzer, delivered a landslide for Mitchel, who became the city's youngest mayor at the age of thirty-four.[19]

Tammany's rout was so complete that even Murphy's own assembly district, which had been as reliably pro-Tammany as any district in Manhattan, went for Mitchel. Tammany's core voters joined with Tammany's core critics in concluding that Murphy abused his power when he ordered Sulzer's removal. Sulzer himself added to Murphy's humiliations by winning a seat in the State Assembly on the Progressive Party line, which cut deeply into Tammany's vote in Manhattan's Jewish neighborhoods. Meanwhile, more than three dozen Democrats who voted for Sulzer's impeachment lost their reelection bids. Tammany's foes celebrated with characteristically over-the-top rhetoric, pitting their goodness against Tammany's evils. "A medieval organization, brutal, tyrannical and selfish, operating through an arrogant head, can never again control the destinies of this city," declared Mitchel's campaign manager, Robert Adamson. Mitchel's win, he said, along with anti-Tammany victories throughout the city, would "sweep the Tammany of today into the waste heap." A front-page headline in the *New York Tribune* echoed the postelection conventional wisdom: "Patronage Gone, Murphy Must Go."[20]

Reporters descended on Murphy outside Tammany Hall just after noon on the day after the Mitchel rout. His expression gave away nothing. Mayor-elect Mitchel and Assemblyman-elect Sulzer had vowed that Murphy and his organization would soon be consigned to history. What, the reporters asked, did the boss think of that?

"Tammany Hall is still here," he said, cryptic as ever.[21]

. . .

Frances Perkins once observed that John Purroy Mitchel might have fared better with Tammany had he expressed even the slightest nostalgia for the land of his grandfather's birth. The "heart of Tammany," she said, "was devoted to Ireland in those days." Mitchel, however, was a decidedly unsentimental man. Tammany respected his grandfather, who had spent his life raging at the British, but had no use for the grandson, who seemed as aloof and puritanical as any WASP reformer.[22]

Although Perkins didn't mention it, Tammany's Irish-American leaders had good reason to be devoted to Ireland during and immediately after Mitchel's mayoralty. When the nations of Europe marched off to war in late summer of 1914, Irish rebels in Dublin and New York immediately went to work on a complicated transatlantic plot to overthrow British rule in Ireland while Britain was preoccupied with fighting Germany and its allies. With the United States neutral in the Great War (or, as it became known, World War I), New York became the center of a plot involving American money, German arms, and Irish guerrillas. Irish rebel leaders regularly communicated with a Tammany judge, Daniel Cohalan, and an aging exile journalist, John Devoy, who persuaded German diplomats in the United States to cooperate with the planned rebellion. Cohalan and Devoy kept Berlin abreast of Dublin's plans through the German Consulate in New York, an act made possible only because President Wilson refused to commit the United States to either side in the war.

Tammany as a whole tended to matters close to home while Europeans slaughtered each other on the battlefields of northern France.

And while Wilson's neutrality was popular, his lectures against what he called "hyphenated Americanism" surely won him few friends in Tammany. The press noted that Wilson studiously ignored Murphy before and after a speech in New York's Biltmore Hotel when he condemned the "alien sympathies" of those "who loved other countries better than they loved America."[23]

Five months after Wilson's speech, on Easter Monday of 1916, a small group of Irish rebels attacked several buildings in Dublin, including the city's General Post Office, and managed to hold off the British for five days. German aid, arranged through Tammany's Cohalan and his ally Devoy, was paltry and ineffective. The rebellion was crushed. But the futility of the Easter Rising gave way to a narrative of martyrdom as the British executed the rebellion's leaders—many of them poets, writers, and labor leaders—one by one. The firing squads finally were called off, not coincidentally, just before a New York native named Eamon de Valera was scheduled to be shot for leading one of the rebellion's command posts. De Valera, sent to Ireland as a child by his widowed Irish-born mother, was spared in part because the British believed it would be foolish to alienate American public opinion while the war's outcome was hanging in the balance.

Assessing the full extent of Tammany's contribution to the Easter Rebellion and to Ireland's subsequent war of independence, fought from 1919 to 1921, is nearly impossible—indeed, it may not have existed, at least in a formal way. There is no question that Cohalan, a longtime Tammany member, served as a covert agent for the rebels in 1916. Another Tammany judge, Victor Dowling, was a member of a New York organization, *Clan na Gael*, aligned with Ireland's paramilitary force, the Irish Republican Brotherhood. Both men were close to Murphy, but it is difficult to know whether they told Murphy about their activities or whether they decided it best to keep the boss in the dark. There is, however, a piece of tantalizing evidence that Tammany's role in financing Ireland's revolution may have been substantial.

In 1919, the Irish again rose against the British, only this time they were far more successful. The head of the Irish revolutionary government was none other than Eamon de Valera, the very symbol of transatlantic Irish politics. A wanted man in Ireland, he evaded British authorities and sailed to New York, the city of his birth, to raise money for the rebels. During a rally at City Hall on January 18, 1920, de Valera announced a campaign to raise $10 million for the cause in Ireland. Forty thousand New Yorkers volunteered to raise the funds through bond sales. Only Tammany Hall could summon that kind of manpower.

De Valera went on to raise about $6 million, only some of which made its way to Ireland before Britain and the Irish rebels called a truce in 1921. The leader of the Irish rebel army, Michael Collins, led the peace negotiations and signed a compromise treaty after British Prime Minister David Lloyd George threatened to bring renewed war to Ireland. The Irish did not receive complete independence but rather a form of self-government within the British Empire called dominion rule. A portion of the island—six counties in what became Northern Ireland—remained part of the United Kingdom. It was a bitter compromise, one that divided the Irish people between those who were willing to take what they could get and those who held out for perfection in the form of a wholly independent Irish republic.

The legend of Tammany Hall was invoked as Irish political leaders debated the treaty in their parliament, *Dail Eireann,* in early 1921. Michael Collins angrily denounced a parliamentary move by the treaty's opponents, led by de Valera. "We will have no Tammany Hall methods here," Collins said. "Whether you are for the Treaty or whether you are against it, fight without Tammany Hall methods."[24]

Another rebel-turned-politician who had just returned from New York, Harry Boland, responded to the Tammany reference. Looking at his onetime friend and comrade, Boland said he presumed Collins's remark was intended for him, for he was organizing opposition to the treaty. "I will say this, that I don't know anything about Tammany Hall except this, that if [Collins] had a little training in Tammany Hall, and reserved some of his bullying for Lloyd George, we would not be in the position we are in today."

Boland later told a reporter, "Between you and me, Tammany Hall has given more aid to the [rebel] cause than any other single body." Tammany certainly did not advertise this sort of fundraising, but if Charles Murphy, son of a Famine immigrant, either gave his assent to the secret transfer of Tammany funds to the Irish rebels or looked the other way while others did, it surely would add another layer to the transatlantic nature of Irish-American politics—and to the murky narrative of Tammany's finances.[25]

Several months after the treaty debate in Dublin, Murphy made private inquiries about the fate of John J. McKeown, an Irish prisoner of war sentenced to death by a British court martial, even as other prisoners were released. The McKeown case threatened to disrupt the fragile peace process between Ireland and Britain, and while the prisoner had no apparent American connections, Murphy asked Tammany Congressman William Bourke Cockran to see whether he could intervene on behalf "of the unfortunate man." Cockran was skeptical that any American intervention would help, but, in any case, McKeown was freed weeks later.[26]

As Tammany and the Irish in America used their political clout on behalf of Ireland's rebels, many British observers—and their kindred spirits in upper-class New York—could hardly contain their rage. Writing in the *Westminster Review*, journalist J. Cottle Green bemoaned the state of the American republic in a piece entitled "Deterioration of Some American People." Cottle complained that the American experiment was far removed from the days of the "British Pilgrim fathers." Proof of this decline, he wrote, was evident in the large number of "political hangers-on" who "play upon the Irish and other ignorant elements . . . with the object of obtaining money, of creating hatred, stirring up discord and revolutionary feeling towards the mother country, and of subsidizing outrages and midnight murder in Ireland."[27]

For most Tammany voters and for the organization's Irish leaders, the term *mother country* had a very different meaning than it did for

Anglo-American readers of the *Westminster Review*. The writer, how-ever, seemed to be unaware of this. Tammany was not.

· · ·

Despite the catastrophe in New York City and in Assembly races throughout the state in 1913, Tammany forged ahead with reform dur-ing a special lame-duck legislative session in Albany in December. The *New York Times* warned that William Sulzer's successor, Martin Glynn, supported "radical" new laws, including what the *Times* called a "lib-eral workmen's compensation" bill, a direct-primary bill that was more acceptable to Murphy than the Sulzer version, and a call for a new state constitutional convention in 1915. All these reforms easily passed the legislature, which Tammany still dominated until the new one convened. One Tammany ally, John H. McCooey, said that a chastened Murphy was prepared to "give the people all they want and perhaps a bit more." But if Murphy sought simply to please voters in the aftermath of his greatest defeat, he failed miserably. In the fall of 1914, Charles Whitman, a conservative Republican who sought to dismantle much of what the legislature had achieved in 1913, easily defeated Glynn's attempt to win a term in his own right, while another Republican, James Wadsworth, won the state's first popular election for a U.S. Senate seat. The twin losses added to the string of Tammany disasters under Murphy.[28]

Most observers agreed that Tammany continued to pay a price for the impeachment of William Sulzer. But there was another factor at work. Glynn was the first Roman Catholic to become governor of New York, and a Democratic official watching the state on behalf of the White House, Thomas D. McCarthy, detected clear evidence of anti-Catholic bias against Glynn. In a memo to Colonel House, President Wilson's top adviser, McCarthy took note of the activities of a Protes-tant supremacist organization called the Guardians of Liberty, which actively campaigned against Glynn in portions of upstate New York. After examining the vote in Erie County and several other reliably

Democratic upstate counties, McCarthy told House that Glynn "may have lost many votes because he was a Catholic" and that Senate candidate James Gerard, a Murphy ally who also served as Wilson's ambassador to Germany, "suffered greatly by the injection of the religious issue," even though he was not Catholic.[29]

Out of power and out of favor, Tammany Hall might have reconsidered its priorities in light of the catastrophes of 1913 and 1914. Murphy had allowed his young men to support sweeping changes in New York's social contract, and, along the way, they alienated some of the organization's old guard and vested interests. James J. Martin, an aging ally of Richard Croker and the man Theodore Roosevelt replaced as police commissioner, publicly complained about Murphy's "stupid leadership." But when Republicans sought to roll back the achievements of 1913 during Governor Whitman's first term and, especially, during the GOP-controlled Constitutional Convention in 1915, Murphy's young men fought to preserve their hard-won victories.

Al Smith became the star of the Constitutional Convention in opposition, arguing forcefully and successfully against a measure that sought to repeal laws granting privileges to a single "class of individuals," such as widows, disabled workers, and children. The measure was the work of the Republican Party's state chairman, William Barnes, a ripsnorting upstate conservative who embarrassed his more moderate downstate brethren. His proposed amendment would have wiped out all of the Tammany-backed social-welfare legislation passed since the Triangle fire, legislation that had won Tammany no rewards from voters. A soulless, irredeemable political organization might well have concluded that there was no point in resisting the repeal of these measures. Instead, Smith, Wagner, and other Tammany delegates worked with moderate Republicans to mount an offensive against the Barnes proposal. Smith was chosen as the voice of opposition on the convention floor, and with his unmistakable Lower East Side accent, theatrical presence, and palpable sincerity, he dismantled the Barnes plank piece by piece.[30]

"The great curse in poverty lies in the utter hopelessness that goes with it," Smith said. "Having that in mind, I ask you, is it wise, is it prudent . . . to reduce that basic law to the same sharp level of the caveman's claw?" Barnes's proposal failed, not simply because Tammany's delegates opposed it, but because men like Smith were capable of making common cause with moderate Republicans, including the convention's distinguished chairman, Elihu Root, a Nobel Peace Prize–winner and former secretary of state and war. It was all for naught, however, for voters rejected the new constitution in a statewide referendum.[31]

The convention may have failed, but for Tammany the proceedings provided a stage for its rising star, Smith, and for its continued embrace of social change. Smith, in fact, did not simply defend Tammany's reforms at the convention but sought, vainly, to expand on them. He introduced a proposal to establish a minimum wage, and even though it was doomed to failure, it nevertheless was a sign that he, and his sponsors at Tammany, were committed to more aggressive government regulation of the marketplace.

So, despite the electoral disasters, Tammany still was alive, and Murphy still was very much in charge, when Mayor Mitchel sought reelection in 1917 after a term that featured first-rate efficiency and third-rate politics. Aloof from working-class voters, he drew heated criticism when he sought to appoint two members of the Rockefeller Foundation to the city Board of Education. Tammany regrouped behind a redheaded Brooklyn judge named John Hylan, a favorite of publisher William Randolph Hearst; he campaigned as the enemy of special interests and as a staunch advocate for a city-owned (rather than privately owned) subway line. It was a wartime campaign, for the United States had entered the European conflict in April on the Allied side. Mayor Mitchel seized on the war as a campaign issue, questioning the loyalty of Tammany's Robert Wagner, a German immigrant, accusing Hylan and his patron Hearst of harboring pro-German sympathies, and reminding voters of Judge Cohalan's dealings with the German consulate before the United States declared war on Germany and its allies. "I will make this a fight against Hearst, Hylan, and the Hohenzollerns," he said, linking the two New Yorkers with the German ruling family. He also promised to take the fight to "Murphy, Cohalan . . . and all the Tammany brood."[32]

His inflammatory rhetoric did him no honor (although Hearst certainly was skeptical of the war effort). Hylan won with less than 50 percent of the vote, while Mitchel himself had a hard time outpolling a Socialist Party candidate for second place.

Mitchel's loss stunned his progressive allies, but Murphy had a simple explanation for Tammany's revival. Hylan and Tammany, he said, "are progressive and in accordance with the world-wide progressive tendencies of the day." Those words stung, for it was Mitchel—certainly not Hylan—who was perceived as the great young progressive reformer of New York, at least among the uptown and Washington crowd. Embittered by his loss, Mitchel swore off politics for the military, joining the infant air service and winning a commission as a major. He died in 1918 when he fell out of his airplane over Louisiana on a training mission.[33]

Murphy and Tammany had one more step to take before their improbable comeback was complete. A gubernatorial election loomed in 1918, and if Tammany could knock off the two-term incumbent, Charles Whitman, the losses of 1913 and 1914 would become simply bad memories. But Murphy had a critical decision to make. Al Smith, now president of the Board of Aldermen, had emerged as an obvious candidate for statewide office. Smith not only commanded the affections of Tammany's base but he had earned the respect of reformers, the press, and even Republicans. No less an establishment figure than Elihu Root described Smith as "the best informed" delegate at the Constitutional Convention of 1915.[34]

As the political calendar turned and the campaign season of 1918 beckoned, Charlie Murphy hesitated. He had no problem with Smith's record and no doubt about Smith's loyalty. But Murphy was in the business of winning elections, and Smith presented a considerable problem—he was Catholic, and a Catholic had yet to win election to the state's highest office. The recently defeated Martin Glynn had stirred up Protestant supremacy even in Democratic bastions like Erie County when he ran for a term of his own in 1914, and now, four years later, a growing Prohibition movement upstate promised even more trouble for any Tammany candidate, particularly one as enthusiastically "wet" as Al Smith.

So Charlie Murphy hesitated. There was yet another wild card to consider in 1918—the women's vote. Murphy originally opposed women's suffrage, despite the presence of Barbara Porges on Tammany's General Committee, but as he and Tammany recognized reality if not justice, New York passed a pro-suffrage referendum allowing women to vote in state and local elections in 1917. The measure succeeded thanks to a strong pro-ratification vote in Tammany's strongholds in Manhattan, allowing New York to become one of only two states east of the Mississippi (Michigan was the other) to allow women equal voting rights with men in state and local elections.

Was New York ready for an Irish-Catholic governor? An Irish-Catholic governor who opposed the growing Prohibition movement and who had opposed women's suffrage while he was speaker of the Assembly? Charlie Murphy was not looking simply to make a statement in 1918 or to carry out some sort of quixotic crusade, as so many reformers were pleased to do. Like any political professional, he wanted to win. And, by all rights, he had to—losing three straight gubernatorial elections to Charles Whitman, who was hardly the second coming of Theodore Roosevelt, might at long last be his undoing.

Ironically, some reformers were absolutely positive about their choice for governor. And their choice was Al Smith. They were, by and large, veterans of the Factory Investigating Commission: Frances Perkins, the consumer lobbyist; Abram Elkus, newly returned to New York after his stint as ambassador to the Ottoman Empire; social reformers Henry Moskowitz and his bride, Belle Moskowitz. They saw Smith as a man who shared their values and, perhaps even more important, knew how to translate those values into practical legislation.

Murphy, on the other hand, saw Smith as an Irish-Catholic anti-temperance Tammany pol with an accent the likes of which nobody in the villages of Onondaga County had ever heard before. As Murphy deliberated, journalist Edward Staats Luther, a political reporter, decided to offer the boss some unsolicited advice. Smith could win, Luther said. New York was prepared to elect a Catholic as governor. The boss gestured to one of his advisers. "Come on in here," he said, "and listen to a man named Luther trying to convince a man named Murphy that a Catholic can be elected governor of New York State."[35]

Luther's thesis may or may not have influenced Murphy. But in the end, he decided that the time was right. Smith won his blessing and was nominated by virtual acclamation at the Democratic State Convention in Saratoga Springs. The lone holdout was a self-styled reform Democrat and perennial candidate for judicial office, Samuel Seabury, who was entitled to half a vote at the convention. He cast that vote against Smith—the only vote Smith did not receive. "Mr. Smith is the best representative of the worst element of the Democratic Party," Seabury sniffed.[36]

Seabury's fellow reformers had a different view. They organized an independent citizens' committee to elect their favorite Tammany man. The extra effort was absolutely necessary: Smith beat Whitman by about fifteen thousand votes out of nearly two million cast in the 1918 election. The victory was Smith's for sure, but it was Murphy's as well. Tammany men had been elected governor before, but no Irish-Catholic Tammany man had ever gone so far—and he did so, for that matter, with the support of reformers and the city's press.

The victory also belonged to the *new* New York—the New York of tenement houses and gas house districts and saloons and pushcarts, the New York of widows who kept their families together with the help of taxpayers, the New York of ambitious schoolchildren who received college scholarships from the state, the New York of disabled workers and their families who no longer were left to fend for themselves. It was a victory for Catholics who did not believe it was sinful to have a drink or play baseball on Sunday. It was a victory for Jews who sought a fair share of political power. It was a victory for reformers like Frances Perkins and Belle Moskowitz, who recognized long before many of their male counterparts did that Charlie Murphy's Tammany was on the right side of history, even if their methods were, as Perkins put it, "irregular." It was, after all, an irregular world—and Tammany knew it.

Not long after his election, Smith made a familiar journey to Charlie Murphy's vacation home in Good Ground, Long Island, a beach town known today as Hampton Bays. Power had been good to Murphy—his full-time residence on Seventeenth Street was near fashionable Stuyvesant Square, and his estate on Long Island included a nine-hole golf course, allowing Murphy the freedom to indulge in his only hobby. The governor-elect, that ultimate product of the sidewalks of New York, did not trek out to the wilds of the Hamptons simply to walk the fairways with the boss. Rather, Murphy wished to have a clear and candid conversation with his protégé.

"I shall be asking you for things, Al," Murphy said. "But I want to say this to you. You understand these things better than I do. If I ever ask you to do anything which you think would impair your record as a great governor, just tell me so and that will be the end of it."[37]

Murphy had never said anything like that to any of the other mayors and governors who had won high office with his support. But Murphy had bigger plans for Al Smith.

. . .

Charlie Murphy's resurrection was not just a matter of luck. He changed the conversation about his future and that of Tammany with the election of Hylan as mayor and, especially, Smith as governor, and he was content to see his name fade from headlines as Tammany continued to support liberal social and political change in New York. Smith took to Albany the experts, advocates, and good-government reformers who only a generation earlier had seen Tammany as the representation not simply of bad government but of evil. Belle Moskowitz, Smith's closest adviser; Robert Moses, the brilliant planner and builder; and Frances Perkins, his labor commissioner, did not come to Smith via Charlie Murphy. But Al Smith trusted them, and Charlie Murphy trusted Al Smith.

Murphy also encouraged other Tammany figures, especially the voluble Congressman William Bourke Cockran, to engage in political debates that were far removed from Tammany's home turf on Manhattan's East Side. In 1920, Cockran became a national spokesman for global disarmament following the catastrophe of World War I, arguing that "the world must disarm or the world must starve." The issue caught Murphy's attention—no doubt to the surprise of those who saw him as little more than a political puppetmaster—and he and Cockran exchanged a series of letters and phone calls about the issue in the early 1920s. Tammany's delegation to the Democratic National Convention in 1920 pressed fellow Democrats to pass a Cockran-authored plank pledging the party to achieving world peace through disarmament. The measure failed, but Murphy continued to endorse it, in spite of opposition within his own party. "We took the stand that disarmament was the transcendent issue of the world and not alone of this country," said Murphy, months after the 1920 convention. The *New York Times* saw a certain logic to Murphy's position, noting acidly that Tammany already was "responsible for the oldest disarmament measure" in the nation, Sullivan's Law.[38]

Tammany's commitment to progressive social and political reforms reached its high point of articulation at the Democratic State Convention in 1922, when Smith was renominated for governor after having failed to win reelection in 1920. Smith's reemergence was not exactly preordained, for Murphy was said to have been considering William Randolph Hearst for the nomination. Smith would have none of that—Hearst's newspapers had accused Smith of colluding with the dairy industry in keeping milk prices high, leading to the deaths of children. Hearst launched the smear campaign after Smith refused to appoint the publisher's allies as state judges, which led Smith to challenge Hearst to a public debate in Carnegie Hall. The publisher failed to show; Smith debated an empty chair.

Smith not only won the gubernatorial nomination in 1922 but also blocked Murphy's compromise plan to nominate Hearst for the U.S. Senate. Smith told his mentor that if Hearst ran for the Senate, Tammany would have to find another candidate for governor. Murphy backed Smith. Hearst's political ambitions were done, once and for all.

While the Smith–Hearst drama unfolded behind closed doors, the Democratic State Convention's temporary chairman, State Senator Jimmy Walker, opened the proceedings with a gleeful attack on incumbent Governor Nathan Miller for his opposition to an eight-hour workday and a minimum wage for women workers. The platform, written by Jeremiah Mahoney, supported public ownership of bus lines, penal reform, state control over the distribution of hydroelectric power, a continuation of rent regulations put in place during World War I, income-tax exemptions for those earning less than $5,000 a year, and restoration of powers taken away from the state Labor Department during Miller's tenure. One plank did not make it into the final document—a clause that called for stricter government regulation of the New York Stock Exchange. Mahoney desperately wanted it included, but it was removed at the request of Joseph Proskauer, a Wall Street lawyer and key Smith adviser. Mahoney later argued that the plank foreshadowed the New Deal's creation of the Securities and Exchange Commission.[39]

During the 1922 campaign, Smith and Tammany portrayed Miller and the Republicans as reactionaries determined to reverse the progressive reforms that they had fought for and delivered during the previous decade. Their arguments found an audience; Smith captured 1.4 million votes in the fall of 1922 to win a second two-year term as governor. It was the biggest landslide in state history. He went on to serve as governor until 1929; on his watch, New York became a model of progressive government even while Washington turned to the right under successive Republican administrations.

Charles Francis Murphy saw in Al Smith a chance to show the nation that a poor Irish-Catholic child of the Lower East Side was as good as any other American. Not long after Smith returned to Albany as governor in 1923, Murphy began quiet discussions with other Democrats about the possibility of Al Smith as a candidate for president of the United States. Those discussions were well underway on the morning of April 25, 1924, when Murphy died after collapsing in his home on Seventeenth Street, not far from the tenement in which he was born. He was buried three days later. Sixty thousand people stood on Fifth Avenue as his casket was taken from St. Patrick's Cathedral to a waiting hearse for a trip to Calvary Cemetery.[40]

Tammany would never again have a leader with Murphy's vision and his eye for political talent. But many of the politicians whom Murphy sponsored and mentored continued to influence New York politics and culture through the Jazz Age and the Great Depression. And at least one former enemy came to realize that the quiet man from the Gas House District was more than a cartoon figure from a Thomas Nast illustration. "In Mr. Murphy's death, the New York City Democratic organization has lost probably the strongest and wisest leader it has had in generations. . . . He was a genius who kept harmony and at the same time recognized that the world moved on. It is well to remember that he has helped accomplish much in the way of progressive legislation and social welfare in our state." So said Franklin D. Roosevelt, just four months before he braced himself at a podium in Madison Square Garden to nominate a Tammany man for the office of president of the United States.

ELEVEN

FRANK AND AL

Less than a week after he lost his bid for a second term as New York governor, a disappointed but philosophical Al Smith wrote a short note to another New York Democrat who had suffered a historic defeat in the election of November 2, 1920—Franklin D. Roosevelt, the party's vice-presidential candidate that year. "Maybe it is for the best," Smith wrote of his dispiriting loss. "I do not know what I would be able to accomplish here in the next two years standing alone by myself." With Warren G. Harding pledging a return to normalcy after Woodrow Wilson's tumultuous two terms as president, Republicans nationwide swept Democrats from power in 1920—across the Hudson River in New Jersey, only a single Democrat was left standing in a General Assembly of sixty members. "The people of this country, in no uncertain terms, gave responsibility to the Republican party," Smith wrote. "Probably it is but right that they not be handicapped to even the slightest degree."

The following day, no doubt before Smith's letter from Albany arrived, an equally reflective FDR echoed his friend's sentiments. "Now that the smoke has cleared away it all seems in many ways for the better," FDR wrote to Smith. It is hard to imagine, however, that either of

these ambitious men really believed that the electoral disaster somehow was "for the better." In the prime of their careers, they had suffered an ignominious defeat and now faced a highly uncertain future,
as Roosevelt acknowledged in his letter to Smith. The two of them, he
conceded, "will in all probability not run for state office" again.

While Smith seemed to believe, at least in this moment of despair,
that his fellow Democrats should stand aside while Republicans pur-
sued an agenda that was hostile to everything for which he stood, Roosevelt was of quite a different mind. He wanted to build a viable, effective
opposition to the new Republican regime, noting that New York voters
would return to the polls in two years for a new round of state elections. He told Smith that the two of them ought to meet soon to begin
rebuilding their party north of the Bronx, in a region where a heavily
Republican vote doomed Smith's reelection effort and delivered New
York into Harding's column despite the presence of FDR on the national
Democratic ticket. "I feel that you and I have about as broad an insight
into the affairs of upstate as any other two people," Roosevelt wrote. He
promised to get in touch with Smith again, "after I come back from a
little shooting trip."[1]

It is not hard to imagine Smith rolling his eyes as he read about Roosevelt's vacation plans. Smith, a child of the Lower East Side, was not
much for shooting trips or, for that matter, any other kind of diversion
other than the care and feeding of the eccentric menagerie of house pets
he kept in Albany. Self-taught and hardworking, he often thought of his
privileged colleague from Hyde Park as something of a lightweight—"a
little boy," in the words of Roosevelt's devoted political adviser, Louis
McHenry Howe. Smith might well have wondered why FDR seemed
to think they were equally knowledgeable about upstate politics and
party organization matters. After having served as governor, as majority leader and speaker of the State Assembly, and as a delegate to the
state Constitutional Convention, Smith certainly understood New York
state politics as few others did.[2]

Roosevelt, on the other hand, had left Albany for Washington in

1913, only months after beginning his second two-year term in the State Senate. His departure was unlamented, for he made few allies and more than a few enemies during his short career in the legislature. (While presiding over a debate in the State Senate in 1911, Robert Wagner cut off FDR by saying, "Senator Roosevelt has gained his point. What he wants is a headline in the newspapers.") If FDR considered himself Smith's equal on matters such as party organization, he very likely was alone in that judgment.[3]

Tall, impossibly handsome, and even more impossibly ambitious, Franklin Roosevelt entered politics in 1910 at the age of twenty-eight, when he won election to the State Senate as a Democrat in a rural Republican district in Dutchess County. His path to power was eased considerably thanks to the machinations of the local party leaders, who arranged for his appointment to the party's district convention—the very convention that would decide on nominations for State Senate. But after Roosevelt won the general election, he made a point of saying that he owed nothing to those who helped arrange his nomination and subsequent election. As a Democrat in Republican territory, Roosevelt knew that he could hardly do otherwise. But his distaste for traditional partisan politics was more than just an acknowledgment of Dutchess County demographics. His voters were skeptical of cities, especially New York City, and the political organization that represented all that seemed wrong with politics, Tammany Hall. Roosevelt cast himself as a progressive reformer in the tradition of his distant cousin, Theodore Roosevelt, except that TR was a Republican and Franklin was a Democrat.

Cousin Theodore was one of the twentieth century's most accomplished men—a writer, a scientist, an environmentalist, a soldier, a diplomat, a president. In 1910, Franklin Roosevelt was none of the above. But he yearned for more, to the amusement of his colleagues in Albany, who regarded him as a political amateur.

By the electoral disaster of 1920, however, Franklin Roosevelt was more mature and a good deal more partisan than he had been as a freshman state senator. He and Smith already had become friendly before the election, but in the following years Roosevelt went out of his way to court Smith's good opinion. Smith responded in kind, although he still regarded Roosevelt as a lightweight.

But Roosevelt's letter to Smith after their defeats in 1920 reveals that there was a good deal more steel in his character than Smith realized. Unlike Smith, Roosevelt was not prepared to concede the field to the victorious Republicans, and, in fact, he seemed convinced that in New York, the Republican victory would be short-lived. His instincts proved to be correct. The Democratic Party in New York revived quickly during the two-year term of Nathan Miller, who defeated Smith in 1920.

And FDR and Smith did, of course, run for office again. Beginning in 1923, they presided over New York politics for a decade, becoming national figures because of their progressive accomplishments during a time of reaction and laissez-faire politics in Washington. The strategic partnership they formed, the imperfect political friendship they enjoyed, and the coalition they built changed not just New York, not just the Democratic Party, but the very nature of U.S. politics during the height of the American century. Roosevelt and Smith represented a coming together of two traditional antagonists—the elite Protestant reformer and the urban, ethnic Tammany politician—in an alliance that would have been impossible during the height of the Progressive Era, when reformers still saw machine politicians as part of the problem rather than a potential source of change, and when Irish-Catholic machine politicians automatically viewed reformers as dreamy-eyed idealists at best, bigoted nativists at worst. The combination of Tammany Hall's Smith and the reform movement's Roosevelt proved to be electoral magic in New York during the 1920s and served as an important building block in the construction of the New Deal coalition, which dominated U.S. politics from the Great Depression to the 1960s.

Roosevelt's relationship with Smith and, more broadly, his cautious embrace of Tammany Hall in the 1920s is critical to understanding how FDR transformed himself from a prototypical Anglo-Protestant reformer into a patron of some (although not all) urban political machines during his years as president. Likewise, Tammany and Smith offered Roosevelt a chance to remain active in New York politics after his loss in 1920 despite his earlier opposition to the machine.

During those years, Roosevelt paid close attention as Smith built on Tammany's post-Triangle progressive credentials to create historically important relationships with such open-minded progressive reformers as Frances Perkins, Belle Moskowitz, Joseph Proskauer, Herbert Lehman, and Robert Moses—two women, four Jews, and one WASP (Perkins), hardly the traditional talent pool that filled Tammany's ranks and payrolls. Through vehicles like the state's postwar Reconstruction Commission, created in 1919 to devise a more assertive role for state government in twentieth-century society, Smith brought together elite progressives, labor activists, and prominent business leaders as his partners in building a new governing paradigm in Albany. By doing so, Smith obliterated outdated distinctions between progressive reformers and traditional machine politics, welcoming as he did the advice and guidance of outside experts and policy advocates while remaining an unapologetic and indeed staunch son of Tammany Hall.

The work of the Reconstruction Commission, chaired by reformer Abram Elkus, is perhaps as important as the work of the Factory Investigating Commission in understanding Tammany's evolution and the ways in which some progressive reformers found common ground with political leaders like Murphy, Smith, and Wagner. If, as Tammany's Jeremiah Mahoney asserted, the FIC's work marked "the beginning of the liberal program of the Democratic Party," the Reconstruction Commission's agenda sought to expand on that liberal program through more aggressive government action in fields ranging from chronic unemployment to housing to public health.[4]

Coincidentally, Smith's Reconstruction Commission issued its recommendations within months of another report that endorsed similarly progressive goals. In fact, the Catholic bishops' Program of Social Reconstruction was to the left of Smith's commission, endorsing not a minimum wage but a more generous living wage. The bishops also called for government commitment to public housing; comprehensive social insurance covering disabilities, unemployment, and old age; stronger child labor laws; and encouragement of trade unions. The bishops' proposals reflected the new thinking in Catholic social teaching that developed alongside the social-welfare policies put into place by Tammany's conspicuously Catholic leadership. The driving force behind the bishops' program was Monsignor John Ryan, who would go on to earn the nickname of "Monsignor New Deal" in the 1930s. Ryan saw the proposals as an extension of the teachings of Pope Leo XIII, who had inspired the likes of Jeremiah Mahoney and other young Catholic politicians in the early twentieth century.[5]

The goals of both the bishops' program and Smith's commission were at odds with the prevailing postwar mood of the country in general and some New Yorkers in particular. Indeed, as he opened the new session of the State Assembly in January 1919, Republican Speaker Thaddeus Sweet of upstate Oswego County noted that New Yorkers "had heard much . . . Socialistic and Bolshevik propaganda advocating social and civic reforms" in the months since Smith's election in November 1918. To drive home his point, Sweet asserted that "the foremost advocates of socialistic doctrines" happened to be "the most ardent proponents of liquor license," an argument that in essence joined together leftist social reformers and Tammany politicians.[6]

In its statement of principles, Smith's Reconstruction Commission issued a ringing call to arms on behalf of better government, asserting that democracy "does not merely mean periodic elections. It means a government held accountable to the people between elections." The wording and tone were the work of Robert Moses, chief of staff of the commission's retrenchment committee, and they reflected the high-minded sentiments of the reform movement. But it took a Tammany politician, Al Smith, to implement them and to bring together these disparate interests and personalities. When critics charged that the commission's call for expanded government was merely a patronage grab by Tammany, Smith was careful to note that among those who supported the commission's work were prominent Republicans Henry Stimson (FDR's future secretary of war) and former governor and future chief justice of the U.S. Supreme Court Charles Evans Hughes. Referring to Hughes, Smith pointedly noted that "nobody ever accused him of being a member of Tammany Hall." Under Smith's leadership, traditional foes of Tammany-style politics—from individuals like Hughes to organizations like the Citizens Union—found themselves working together with Tammany figures on behalf of proposals that represented the ideals of progressive reformers yet also had the support of machine politicians.[7]

Before Franklin Roosevelt, then, there was Al Smith. The fates of these two men were intertwined through the 1920s. Not only were they involuntarily returned to private life together in 1920, they played important roles in each other's comebacks. Roosevelt publicly urged Smith to run for governor again in 1922, when Smith was inclined to remain in the private sector. Smith returned the favor in 1928, urging—indeed, practically commanding—Roosevelt to put aside doubts about his health and run for governor. Smith, the Irish-Catholic, city-dwelling, beer-drinking voice of immigrant culture, and Roosevelt, the patrician Protestant progressive from rural Dutchess County who was partial to martinis, created a new Democratic Party—urban, ethnic, and tilted in favor of the industrial states of the North—after the disaster of 1920. Smith relied on Roosevelt as a Protestant advocate for a Catholic politician, as the scion of a famous family who was eager to champion the cause of a son of the Lower East Side. (Smith, it must be said, did not always welcome the assistance; it took Joseph Proskauer, one of his aides, to remind Smith that "you're a Bowery mick and [Roosevelt's] a Protestant patrician and he'd take some of the curse off of you.")[8]

Roosevelt, for his part, often relied on Smith for the bridges he built between reformers and Tammany, for his credibility with immigrant-stock voters, for the talented advisers he brought into government, and for his famously exhaustive knowledge of state government. Even after FDR succeeded Smith as governor in 1929, at a point when many historians see the beginnings of tension between the two men, Roosevelt continued to seek out his predecessor's advice. When Smith was on vacation in Florida in 1930, Roosevelt wrote to him about pressing business in Albany. "Let me know when you get back to New York," Roosevelt wrote. "I want to talk to you about lots of things, including the Power bill."[9]

The relationship went beyond politics, as FDR's letter to the vacationing Smith showed. "A few weeks ago," Roosevelt wrote, "when my granddaughter was here, your granddaughter came to the house to spend the afternoon and five minutes after I had joined the party, Mary [Smith's granddaughter] was calling me 'Ganpa.' I felt highly honored and have certainly cut you out." Destined though they were to fight a bitter battle for the 1932 Democratic presidential nomination, Al Smith and Franklin Roosevelt clearly came to appreciate each other during the cultural and political battles of the 1920s—battles that found them on the same side rather than aligned as antagonists, as would have seemed natural a decade earlier. Throughout their relationship, in good times and bad, they addressed each other as "Frank" and "Al." It seems fair to say that none of FDR's Harvard and Hudson Valley friends referred to the squire of Hyde Park as "Frank."[10]

It is nearly impossible to overstate the importance of Al Smith and Tammany Hall in understanding the rise and success of Franklin Roosevelt in New York politics in the 1920s. Roosevelt's unlikely relationships with Tammany, with Murphy, and with urban machines in general were the result of the equally unlikely relationships that Smith formed with progressive reformers in New York even as he retained his bona fides as a Tammany politician. The eagerness with which Smith welcomed advisers such as Robert Moses, Frances Perkins, and Belle Moskowitz—all of whom entered politics as opponents of bosses and machines—anticipated the New Deal marriage of machine politicians like Edward J. Flynn of the Bronx and social-welfare reformers like Harry Hopkins, both of whom were great admirers of Smith.

In showing that the cultural gap between elite reformers and machine politicians could be bridged if both sides acknowledged the good intentions of the other, Smith created political space for FDR to construct spans of his own, albeit from a different starting place. This, however, required a dramatic change in FDR's attitude toward political bosses and his own elitist definitions of reform. FDR's transformation from a "political prig" with no "human sympathy, human interests, human ties" (in the words of a legislative staffer in 1911), to a more empathetic and personable public figure is often attributed to the humbling experience of polio and to the influence of his wife, Eleanor Roosevelt, an indomitable advocate for social justice. But it would seem equally possible that this shrewd, ambitious man learned valuable lessons about politics as he observed the wiles and ways of the down-to-earth, pragmatic, and likable Tammany figures who dominated his home state's political culture during the first two decades of his public life.[11]

Albany boss Daniel O'Connell, namesake of but no relation to the Irish statesman, once said that State Senator Roosevelt "didn't like poor people. He was a patronizing son of a bitch." He eagerly sought to identify himself as a high-minded progressive and friend of the muckrakers, with all their disdain for the messy dealmaking of local government. With great moral righteousness, he publicly blocked a state-funded project in his Dutchess County district because he considered the work unnecessary, a mere piece of political patronage. Tammany's Big Tim Sullivan was aghast. "Frank," he said, "you ought to have your head examined."[12]

Roosevelt's journey from aloof political reformer to emphatic advocate for the jobless and hopeless was, to be sure, a long one, and it is worth recalling that it took place during a time when Tammany politicians in his home state wrote, defended, and then expanded sweeping changes in government's relationship with its citizens and the private economy. In 1911, FDR had wanted no part of the push for a fifty-four-hour-workweek bill, for which Tammany figures Tim Sullivan and The McManus had fought so hard (and which Murphy initially opposed). "No, no," Roosevelt told Frances Perkins when his future labor secretary had asked for his support. "More important things. More important things."[13]

One of those "more important things" in 1911 included a well-publicized campaign to defeat Murphy's handpicked candidate for one of New York's two U.S. Senate seats, William "Blue-Eyed Billy" Sheehan, a lawyer with a less-than-spotless record as a Democratic leader in Buffalo. Legislators still selected U.S. senators in New York in 1911—ratification of the Seventeenth Amendment, which allowed for popular elections for the U.S. Senate, was still two years away. (New York's Tammany-controlled legislature ratified the amendment in January 1913. The measure was sponsored by Tammany's Wagner in the Senate and Tammany's Aaron Levy in the Assembly.) With Democrats firmly in charge of the legislature, there was no question that the next U.S. senator from New York would be a Democrat—and, given Murphy's extensive influence over the party and individual legislators, it seemed evident that he need only identify his choice and direct his fellow Democrats to vote accordingly.

Franklin Roosevelt had other ideas. A brand-new senator with a revered last name and limitless ambition, Roosevelt eagerly assumed the role of defender of civic purity and scourge of Tammany Hall as he rallied dissident Democrats against Murphy's presumed choice. This earned him the admiration of contemporary newspapers and of future historians—one of the latter insisted that FDR was a "champion of Progressivism" in part because of his opposition to Tammany in Albany. Never mind that FDR was all but absent from the truly progressive battle to legislate fewer hours for women and children in New York, a battle that the enemies of traditional Progressivism—Sullivan, McManus, and other urban ethnic politicians—fought and won.[14]

Roosevelt reveled in the attention he received during the weeks-long standoff over Sheehan, as ballot after ballot passed with no candidate getting the required 101 votes for appointment. "There is nothing I love as much as a good fight," he told reporters. "I never had as much fun in my life as I am having right now." The fun went on from midwinter into early spring, when Murphy abruptly switched his support from Sheehan to a judge with an impeccable record, James A. O'Gorman. Roosevelt wanted to keep fighting, but his fellow dissidents lost their appetite after it became obvious that Murphy had played them. O'Gorman, while as pure as any civic reformer, was a Tammany man through and through, and much closer to Murphy than Sheehan ever was. Observers suggested that Murphy had backed Sheehan at first simply out of a personal obligation and that he was more than happy to switch to O'Gorman. The *New York Times* proclaimed Murphy as the "victor" in the long standoff.[15]

FDR continued to occupy himself with "more important things"—as he had put it during his conversation with Frances Perkins—while his colleagues in the legislature grappled with the aftermath of the Triangle Shirtwaist fire. He assured reformers of his support for their efforts to regulate the behavior of urban immigrants who wished to attend baseball games or operate their businesses on Sunday. Reflecting the opinions of his rural upstate district and the anxieties of urban progressives, he supported the Anti-Saloon League's efforts to limit alcoholic beverages. Years later, however, when he was running for governor of New York, FDR chose not to emphasize his battle with Murphy or his support for reformers' cultural causes during his brief time in the legislature. Instead, he portrayed himself as a leader in the fight for a fifty-four-hour workweek, noting that it was "the most radical thing that had ever been talked about." Louis Howe also claimed that FDR was responsible for Tim Sullivan's returning to the Senate to cast the decisive vote in favor of the bill, even though Perkins, an eyewitness, mentions nothing about her future boss's role in the dramatic vote.[16]

Efforts to position Roosevelt as an advocate for the fifty-four-hour workweek indicated how much New York's political landscape changed during Smith's tenure as governor in the 1920s. FDR changed as well. In 1922, not long after being confined to a wheelchair, he wrote a letter to Smith that showed how far he had come as a politician and as a human being since he so rudely dismissed Perkins and her cause in 1911. "You, in your whole public career, have shown a true understanding of the needs and desires of the average American man, woman and child,"

Roosevelt told Smith. "You have in your legislative career and your term as Governor, consistently aided changes in laws and in administration aimed to meet new conditions and a higher standard of living. Your attitude has been one of belief in progress, and you have not opposed measures of relief and improvement merely because they were new. In other words, you have been essentially human, for it is human to want to better conditions and to seek new things. That point of view is what has made America."[17]

The Franklin Roosevelt of 1911 would not—could not—have written such a letter, certainly not to a politician who was the pride and joy of Tammany Hall. The concerns of the "average American man, woman and child" were not his concerns, as his attitude toward workplace reform showed. During the eleven years that separated his confrontation with Perkins over the workweek bill and this 1922 letter to Smith, Franklin Roosevelt had grown to appreciate the practical, human concerns of the ethnic machine politicians and their constituents, and had moved away from the abstract moral politics of the well-born civic reformer. Roosevelt's legendary ability as president to connect with voters, especially urban ethnics, would not have been possible had he continued to emulate the pinched Progressivism of his idol Woodrow Wilson, the ardent foe of hyphenated identity politics, or the high-minded detachment of elite reformers like Seth Low and John Purroy Mitchel.

Tammany, in fact, provided Roosevelt with parables about the use of power—parables he later preached from the Oval Office.

In 1938, during a discussion with Perkins about the possibility of easing immigration restrictions imposed over Tammany's fierce objections in 1924, Roosevelt invoked the memory of one of Perkins's favorite legislators. "Tim Sullivan used to say that the America of the future would be made out of the people who had come over in steerage and who knew in their own hearts and lives the difference between being despised and being accepted and liked," the president said. "Poor old Tim Sullivan never understood . . . modern politics, but he was right about the human heart."[18]

Perkins wrote that FDR's remark about Sullivan, who was involved in all kinds of shady enterprises on the Bowery despite Murphy's disapproval, showed that Roosevelt had "learned" something about politics "from the rough Tammany politicians" for whom he had had nothing but contempt early in his career. As president, Roosevelt recalled that Al Smith's favorite method for settling a problem was by "sitting around a table" and hashing out the details. During the Democratic National Convention in 1944, when FDR was sending mixed signals about keeping Henry Wallace as his vice president, he conjured a memory from Tammany's glory days. He asked two young aides if they had ever heard of Charlie Murphy. They hadn't. FDR explained to them how Murphy kept his own counsel at key moments, how he got away with insisting that conventions, not bosses, chose candidates. "Charlie," a nostalgic Roosevelt said, "was a wise man."[19]

Franklin Roosevelt certainly did not emerge from New York politics during the Progressive Era and the Jazz Age without learning something—about politics, and about human nature—from the street-level Irish-American politicians who had been such a presence in New York during his formative years. The prominent advisory roles that Edward Flynn and James Farley played during FDR's years as governor and president show that he came to understand and appreciate the Irish-American style of practical, grass-roots politics, even as he attracted traditional progressives such as Harry Hopkins, Harold Ickes, Josephus Daniels, and others who would have been hard-pressed to imagine working alongside Tammany types when Woodrow Wilson was in the White House. What's more, Roosevelt developed a memorable working relationship with Tammany's Robert Wagner during the New Deal. Wagner possessed the practical skills necessary to get legislation passed, skills he learned as a protégé of Charles Murphy. "The New Deal," recalled a colleague of Wagner's, "owed as much to Robert Wagner as to Franklin Roosevelt."[20]

Roosevelt's willingness to work with Tammany figures during the 1920s could be seen as a necessary but unappetizing calculation that he made because he could not advance his career without Charlie Murphy's support. Murphy, after all, thwarted FDR's attempt to win the party's U.S. Senate nomination in 1914 when he shrewdly backed Woodrow Wilson's ambassador to Germany and longtime Tammany member James W. Gerard for the post. With Tammany's organizational support, Gerard crushed FDR in the state's first primary election for a U.S. Senate nomination, although Gerard then lost to Republican Charles W. Wadsworth in the general election. Some observers have asserted that FDR eventually "learned to use" the bosses he once opposed, an assertion that would seem to defy the evidence. If FDR figured out how to "use" Charles Murphy, it's hard to see how it benefited him.[21]

FDR's surprising rapprochement with Murphy began on July 4, 1917, when Roosevelt delivered one of the two traditional "long talks" at Tammany's annual Independence Day commemoration. Roosevelt was not the only onetime Tammany critic invited to address the organization— fellow keynoter Charles S. Thomas, a senator from Colorado, once complained that the Democratic Party would prosper only "by a negation of the things for which Tammany stands." But now both Thomas and Roosevelt found themselves exchanging pleasantries with the likes of Thomas McManus and John Ahearn, the very symbols of what Senator Thomas had described as the Democratic Party's "degeneracy."[22]

Roosevelt and Murphy were seated together—no coincidence—and both were dressed similarly in straw hats, bow ties, and light summer suits, although the buttons on Murphy's jacket were working a good deal harder than those on Roosevelt's. Around his shoulders Murphy wore a symbolic gold chain of office, making him look more like a lord mayor in Ireland than a leader of the party of the people. Reporters noted that Murphy and Roosevelt seemed to enjoy each other's company as they sat through a welcoming address—luckily, not another "long talk"—from Tammany's eighty-seven-year-old ceremonial leader, Grand Sachem John R. Voorhis. When it was Roosevelt's turn at the podium, he displayed the charm and bonhomie that had been so absent in his dealings with his colleagues from Tammany five years earlier. He fairly winked at his listeners as he said, slyly, "I am not entirely a stranger to Tammany Hall." He was, he said, invited to the event by an unnamed Tammany man, who told him that "if Tammany could stand to have him, he could stand it to come." The audience got a good laugh[23]

If Roosevelt's unlikely appearance at Tammany Hall was simply a political calculation rather than evidence of a genuine change of heart, his timing was curiously poor and politically perilous. For on that Independence Day in 1917, Charles Francis Murphy, the bane of good-government groups, the Hearst newspapers, and progressives throughout the nation, appeared to be yesterday's man. Newspapers had been speculating for several years that he was on his way out after Tammany continued to suffer voters' retribution in the aftermath of the Sulzer impeachment. Murphy was never so vulnerable and Tammany rarely so demoralized as when FDR paid his first visit to the Hall on July 4, 1917. If his appearance at Murphy's side that day was all about calculation and ambition, FDR seemingly was in the wrong place, at the wrong time, with the wrong people.

On the other hand, it is entirely possible that FDR was in the process of a more profound change of heart toward the bête noire of his famous cousin, his own former self, and so many of his progressive allies in Woodrow Wilson's Washington. FDR's actions after 1917 certainly suggest that he finally realized that, whatever its past flaws, Tammany was on the right side of reform and progressive change, and that Smith and Wagner represented the better angels of the machine's nature. He certainly no longer acted as though Tammany were the enemy, although he supported John Purroy Mitchel's anti-Tammany reelection bid in 1917. He did not recoil in horror when The McManus urged him to run for governor in 1918 (FDR declined the invitation) or when State Senator Jimmy Walker told him that it was "always a pleasure" to hear talk of Roosevelt's future in New York politics.[24]

FDR publicly endorsed Al Smith's candidacy for governor in 1918 in a warm, personal letter in which he offered to speak on Smith's behalf in

New York City in the waning days of the campaign. Smith, in a "Dear Frank" letter of reply, told Roosevelt that his endorsement "made quite a hit with all the men around me," a fair number of whom, it seems safe to say, were Tammany men.[25]

The burgeoning relationship between FDR and Murphy's Tammany continued to mature in 1920, when FDR seconded Smith's favorite-son nomination for president and Murphy approved the party's choice of FDR as its vice-presidential candidate. Murphy certainly was not trying to rid the state of Roosevelt, for he was shrewd enough to know that Republican boss Thomas Platt had tried that strategy with another troublesome Roosevelt in 1900, and it did not work as planned. After his defeat in 1920, FDR worked diligently on behalf of Smith's presidential bids in both 1924 and 1928, when liberal publications such as *The Nation* wondered whether a Catholic politician raised by the Tammany tiger truly could be progressive. "Governor Smith is personally, ecclesiastically, aggressively, irreconcilably Wet, and is ineradicably Tammany-branded, with all the inferences and implications and objectionable consequences which naturally follow from such views and associations," wrote James Cannon Jr. in *The Nation* in July 1928.[26]

Though more in the tradition of *The Nation's* sort of Democrat, Roosevelt offered no apologies for his support for his fellow New Yorker whose faith, affiliations, and culture so disturbed some of the magazine's writers and readers. In fact, in a small book released during the 1928 campaign, Roosevelt argued that Smith was "on the side of the progressives in the fields of legislation and of constitutional law" and that he "made it clear that he based actions on fundamentals and not on temporary expediency."[27]

This crucial change in Roosevelt's political development is treated as little more than a footnote in many biographies, granted far less importance than his stint in the Department of the Navy during the Wilson years. One Roosevelt biographer, Kenneth S. Davis, has argued that FDR's fights with Tammany were consistent with his "liberal-progressive stance," a view that endorses the notion that Tammany and progressive politics were irreconcilable—despite all that Tammany achieved during Roosevelt's formative years in politics.[28]

In fact, when Roosevelt made his peace with Tammany during Woodrow Wilson's second term, it was not the peace of equally exhausted combatants, each willing to concede the other's points in the interest of ceasing hostilities. FDR's appearance at Charles Murphy's side on July 4, 1917, was a victory for Murphy and for the urban liberalism and cultural pluralism that he and Tammany represented in the second decade of the twentieth century. Roosevelt, in the end, came to Tammany. Tammany did not come to him.

That journey shattered the standard narrative that pitted Anglo-Protestant reformers against Irish political bosses and their henchmen. And it moved Roosevelt closer to Tammany's vision of Progressivism, which Big Tim Sullivan summed up when he said, "I never ask a hungry man about his past. I feed him not because he is good, but because he needs food." Traditional reformers, immersed in Anglo-Protestant notions of worthiness rather than simple need, sought to change character and culture as part of a contractlike relationship with the poor and distressed. Tammany, by contrast, fed people simply because they needed food. Ward heelers asked no questions and demanded no behavioral changes of those who required a meal, a job, a favor. The entitlement programs of the New Deal, then, had more in common with Tim Sullivan's methods of amelioration than they did with charities and settlement houses that saw the poor as clients rather than as neighbors. No wonder that some progressives did not recognize their agenda in Franklin Roosevelt's programs.[29]

. . .

Franklin Roosevelt's decision to work with, rather than against, the pragmatic Irish-American machine politicians against whom he had campaigned as a young man was an important turning point in his career. But he would not have had the trust of Tammany or any urban machines had he not jettisoned Progressive Era anxieties over the culture and beliefs of urban immigrants, meaning Catholics and Jews. Those issues remained very much part of the nation's conversation after World War I and FDR's return to New York. The concerns of progressives like Theodore Roosevelt, who feared for the nation's future because of declining birthrates among Anglo-Saxon Protestants, were played out in politics and culture during the Jazz Age, with Tammany serving as a symbol of the power of the new dangerous classes—urban immigrants with alien beliefs and uncertain loyalties, at least in the eyes of many on all sides of the political spectrum.

The Ku Klux Klan, prohibitionists, and the eugenicist movement viewed immigrants and their immediate descendants as a source of social disruption, and the immigrants' advocates, symbolized by Tammany Hall, as a wellspring of corruption. "In the city of New York and elsewhere in the United States," wrote Madison Grant in *The Passing of the Great Race*, a famous lament for the end of Anglo-Saxon Protestant America, "there is a native American aristocracy resting upon layer after layer of immigrants of lower races." Those "lower" races, Grant predicted, would inevitably dominate political power because democracy rewarded "the average man" rather than "the man qualified by birth, education and integrity."[30]

Tammany surely encouraged the process that so depressed the likes of Grant, whose dour reflections on the American condition helped inspire the eugenics movement of the 1920s. Again, Tammany was hardly a flawless agent of assimilation, but its leaders did embrace a form of ethnic diversity among its elected officials. Tammany promoted promising Jewish politicians such as Aaron Levy, and while it was less enthusiastic about Italian newcomers—in part because many were migrants who did not settle down as voters—Salvatore Cotillo, an Italian immigrant, won election to the State Assembly from East Harlem in 1912 with Tammany's support. He later became the first Italian immigrant elected to the State Senate, and, like Al Smith and Robert Wagner, became a force for progressive social-welfare measures, earning not just Tammany's blessing but also the support of organizations like the Citizens Union.[31]

Tammany resisted the Progressive Era's assertion that there was only one acceptable American identity, one that was stripped clean of Old World practices and customs. Instead, its leaders embraced hyphenated Americanism at a time when Theodore Roosevelt and Woodrow Wilson insisted on 100 percent Americanism. Indeed, Irish-American activists in New York noted that progressive concerns about hyphenated identities apparently did not apply to those who spoke favorably about Anglo-Saxon or Anglo-American virtues.[32]

Tammany was equally adamant in opposing neonativist moves to restrict immigration in the early 1920s. Congressman William Bourke Cockran, who occasionally strayed from the Tammany reservation but who also served as the organization's grand sachem from 1905 to 1908, was among the most passionate opponents of immigration restriction in the years following World War I. In a letter to the Hebrew Immigrant Aid Society of America in 1921, Cockran called immigration restriction "a renunciation and an abandonment of the policy which has made this country . . . the greatest agency for civilization in the history of mankind." Restriction supporters, he said, "appealed to that peculiar but sinister spirit of hate and distrust that seems to be sweeping over the world." Responding to critics who complained that immigrants were slow to learn English, Cockran wrote, "Personally, I deem it much more important that a man should be able to work effectively, even though he cannot speak our language, than be fluent in several languages but inefficient in industry."[33]

Cockran was dead when Congress began to consider the National Origins Act of 1924, designed to cut back immigration to 1890 levels and create a racialized quota system that radically curtailed immigration from Southern and Eastern Europe and outright banned newcomers from other areas, including Japan and China. Following on the heels of Prohibition and embodying the spirit of the eugenicist movement, the act was another battle in the era's war on immigrants, their sources of protection and power, their culture, and their places of residence—cities.

New York, once a bastion of nativist and Know Nothing sentiment, became a lonely voice on behalf of tolerance and pluralism as a vote on the bill neared. On March 8, 1924, three thousand New Yorkers jammed into Carnegie Hall to witness a remarkable coming together of reformers, independents, and Tammany Hall members unanimous in their passionate opposition to the proposed restrictions. Rabbi Stephen Wise, one of the city's most prominent Jewish leaders and an outspoken critic of Tammany, shared the Carnegie stage with Congressman John Carew, a Tammany ally, and longtime Tammany members Thomas Churchill and Salvatore Cotillo, both now judges. "Those in Washington who are in favor of the bill," Churchill said, "don't know and don't want the Jew, Italian, Frenchman or Slav. They won't have brunettes. They want blondes."[34]

The city's congressional delegation—from reformers Fiorello La Guardia and Emanuel Celler to Tammany's Royal Copeland, Christopher Sullivan, and John O'Connor—stood firm against the tide of neonativism. Their resistance was in vain: Immigration restriction overwhelmingly passed both houses of Congress. The new law was a demographic time bomb for Tammany and other urban political organizations that were just beginning to assert their power in national politics.

Tammany and Irish-American politicians in general had no time for the cultural anxieties of Anglo-Saxon Protestants who saw immigration as a threat to what the law's sponsor, Indiana Congressman Albert Johnson, called "real Americanization." Edward Flynn, the son of Irish immigrants, saw Anglo-Saxon supremacy as an idea whose time had passed. "It seems to me that we can never have a complete settlement of world conditions until the Anglo-Saxon begins to realize that he is not of a superior race but that all races are equal," Flynn told Eleanor Roosevelt in 1943, at the height of World War II. "Certainly, we are today fighting against the ideology of Hitler in which he sets forth the Aryans as superior people to all others. We do not seem to be consistent when we fight against this doctrine and on the other hand do nothing to try to bring about a better understanding" between the races.[35]

Some racists saw Tammany as a threat to the racial status quo because it embraced pluralism and inclusion. In 1928, the KKK's newspaper, *Fellowship Forum*, printed a picture of a black public official in New York, Ferdinand Morton, standing near his secretary, a white woman who, the paper asserted, was "assigned to him . . . by a Tammany Hall administration."

Morton, a Harvard University graduate, was the head of Tammany's United Colored Democracy at the time. The picture should "nauseate any Anglo-Saxon," the paper argued, adding that Morton was one of three civil-service commissioners—the others, the paper noted, were a Catholic and a Jew—who passed judgment over "the moral, mental, and physical qualifications of each and every person seeking employment in the Tammanyized city government. No white man or woman can possibly enter the civil service of New York City until this triumvirate approves. What chance for poor Protestants to ever get their names on any city payroll?" The implications were clear. From the Klan's perspective, a "Tammanyized" government was one that was blind to Anglo-Saxon racial and religious hierarchies.[36]

Tammany was not, to be sure, ahead of its times in reaching out to African Americans, many of whom voted Republican—the party of Lincoln. Still, Tammany did make some inroads within the city's black community beginning in the 1920s, supporting the breakthrough candidacy of Henri W. Shields, who became the nation's first black Democrat to win a seat in a state legislature when he was elected to the state Assembly in 1922.

．　．　．

In early April 1924, Al Smith received a letter from former president Woodrow Wilson's secretary, Joseph Tumulty, the son of a grocer and product of Jersey City's Irish-American politics. Wilson had just died, and Tumulty wanted Smith to know that the former president had been thinking about him in his final days. Wilson, Tumulty told Smith, spoke favorably "of everything you are seeking to do, and, I might say to you frankly, I felt while talking with him that he was a most responsive audience."[37]

Left unstated was the full extent of Wilson's enthusiasm for Smith. For as Wilson lay dying, Smith was preparing to run for the Democratic nomination for president in 1924. His main opponent was an ambitious U.S. senator from California determined to return the spirit of Wilsonian Progressivism to the White House. He was William Gibbs McAdoo, Wilson's son-in-law.

The Democratic National Convention was scheduled for New York's Madison Square Garden, and if Charlie Murphy had his way, Al Smith would complete his remarkable journey from the Lower East Side to the highest reaches of American politics in front of a hometown crowd. No Catholic had ever won a major-party presidential nomination, but Charlie Murphy believed the time was right. Other city bosses were on board, prepared to take the Democratic Party away from the drawling populists and the elite progressives who had dominated it for so long. The party's base, they believed, had shifted—its voters lived in cities, cultivated hyphenated identities, and worshipped God in ways that would not have met the approval of Puritans and Pilgrims, not to mention the evangelicals who rallied behind the crusades of William Jennings Bryan. As Tumulty sent his note to Smith in early April, the New York governor already was ahead in the early delegate count, with 123 committed delegates—including all of New York's ninety delegates, thanks to Mister Murphy—compared with McAdoo's sixty-five.

At eleven o'clock on the morning of April 25, 1924, Al Smith took a telephone call in his Albany office from General Charles W. Berry, commander of the New York National Guard. Berry had bad news: Charlie Murphy was dead at the age of sixty-five.

Word soon spread to the press corps, and reporters descended on Smith's second-floor office in the Capitol building for comment. The governor broke down, twice, as he tried to compose a tribute to his mentor. "It's awful," he said, making no effort to hide his tears. "No one had a better friend and no man could have had such a friend as he was to me." Smith, dressed in a black top hat and tails, led the funeral procession up the steps of St. Patrick's Cathedral three days later.[38]

Several days before Murphy died, a dogged reporter from the *New York Times*, Richard Barry, turned up at Tammany Hall in a seemingly quixotic effort to persuade the boss to sit for a long interview—it would be his first ever. Murphy seemed intrigued, but, not surprisingly, refused to commit himself. The negotiating sessions at least allowed Barry to sneak in a few questions, including one that took note of the changed ethnic character of Tammany Hall. The organization, Barry noted, seemed less Irish than it had been under Richard Croker. What did Murphy think? "I haven't kept track," Murphy replied. Did Murphy believe Tammany would retain its Irishness as a new generation of leaders came to power? "I don't know," Murphy replied.[39]

He was Silent Charlie to the very end.

. . .

Al Smith moved ahead with his presidential campaign without the man who had made it possible. Others stepped in to fill the void on the Smith campaign—Joseph Proskauer, Belle Moskowitz, and, mostly for show, Franklin Delano Roosevelt, two years removed from learning that he would never again have the use of his legs. Murphy had arranged for Roosevelt to play a prominent role in Smith's campaign, and FDR was more than eager. He personally contacted noted political expert Babe Ruth and asked the Yankee slugger to endorse Smith. Ruth was impressed by Roosevelt's description of Smith's rise from poverty. "No poor boy can go too high in this world to suit me," Ruth wrote. The Babe gave Smith his blessing.[40]

The Democratic Party's divisions were deep and bitter as delegates arrived in Madison Square Garden on Thursday, June 24, for the convention's opening session. The early summer air was wet and hot—Al Smith spent a portion of the day swimming off Long Island, seemingly aloof from the proceedings in the Garden. The battle between Smith and McAdoo figured to be epic, but it was a proposed plank in the convention's platform that dominated early back-room politicking. Smith's allies and other Democrats, most prominently a U.S. senator from Alabama, Oscar Underwood, were pushing a proposal to condemn the Ku Klux Klan by name in the party's platform. McAdoo, a native of Georgia, and his allies, including William Jennings Bryan, were bitterly opposed. But before the convention voted on the proposal, there was the small matter of placing the names of candidates in nomination. This chore required leather lungs, an athlete's stamina, a saint's patience, and an alligator's skin. Smith chose Franklin Delano Roosevelt, a man who had rarely been seen in public since the summer of 1921, when he contracted polio.

At around noon on June 26, 1924, the boisterous crowd in the Garden's rafters grew silent as Franklin Roosevelt began to make his way from his seat with the New York delegation to the speaker's podium, clutching the arm of his son, James, with his left hand and leaning on a crutch in his right hand. As he neared the podium, he took a second crutch from James and propelled himself forward on his own. Sweating profusely, he threw back his head and smiled as he faced the crowd. Nobody noticed how tightly he gripped the podium, how hard it was to keep from toppling over. And then he began, his wonderful, resonant tenor voice filling the hall with praise for a Tammany man, a Roman Catholic, an unabashed drinker, a graduate of the sidewalks of New York. Never, of course, referring to his infirmity or his own courageous struggle to reach this dramatic moment, Roosevelt described Smith as the "guiding hand" behind reforms ranging from stronger workplace regulations to pensions for widowed mothers, workers' compensation, conservation, and rural health programs. "That is progressive!" he said.

"He is," Roosevelt said of Smith, "the 'Happy Warrior' of the political battlefield." The delegates roared their approval. Roosevelt actually hated the Happy Warrior line—a reference to a poem by William Wordsworth—but Smith aide Joseph Proskauer pulled rank and insisted that it remain. It remains the best-remembered line of the speech.[41]

Roosevelt spoke for thirty-four minutes. When he finished, the roar in the Garden was fantastic—cheers, sirens, music from not one but several bands. The name of an Irish-Catholic Tammany man had been officially placed in nomination as a potential candidate for president of the United States by a well-born Protestant reformer. Only in New York.

. . .

Al Smith stood for cities, immigrants, saloons, hyphenated Americans, religious diversity, and new ideas about government's role in society— issues that helped revive the Ku Klux Klan in the South and inspired the pseudoscience of the eugenics movement in the North. As the convention's nominating speeches wrapped up, Smith's allies declared political war on their colleagues from the South—and, it turned out, no small number from other regions of the country—when they pressed their demand that the convention officially condemn the KKK by name in its platform. Senator Underwood of Alabama, a dark-horse contender for the nomination if either Smith or McAdoo faltered, introduced a plank that declared "the organization known as the Ku Klux Klan" to be "un-American." The Klan denounced Underwood as "the Jew, jug, and Jesuit candidate"—the "jug" reference meant to disparage Underwood's opposition to Prohibition [42]

Underwood joined with Tammany and other allies in refusing to accept a compromise. They pushed the issue to a vote, stirring passions and fury the likes of which few conventions had ever witnessed. As the galleries crammed with Tammany supporters alternately cheered and jeered, speaker after speaker rose to support the anti-Klan plank or to defend the Klan as a relatively harmless organization with a few bad actors. Many tried a middle ground. Tammany remained steadfast: The party had to call out the Klan by name.

After hours of debate, the final speaker on the subject was called to the podium. He was the ghost of conventions past, William Jennings Bryan, and he rose in righteous indignation to silence the rambunctious voices of a new Democratic Party, with their bands playing "The Sidewalks of New York," as if to herald a new age of an urban, ethnic, non-Protestant democracy. He demanded an end to the assault on the Klan, arguing against further debate over "three little words." He addressed his fellow Democrats as "Christians," asking them to "stop fighting" and recognize that "we can exterminate Ku Kluxism better by recognizing their honesty and teaching them that they are wrong."[43]

The anti-Klan plank came up for a vote just before midnight on June 28. As police worked the chaotic floor, trying to keep order and to keep fellow Democrats from each other's throats, the roll call proceeded. In the end, after more than two hours of voting, the effort to condemn the Klan by name failed by a single vote. More than half of the votes against the plank came from states in the Midwest and West.

The anti-Klan forces, including Tammany's New York, at least had made a statement: Their candidate, Al Smith, stood against the forces of intolerance. His main opponent, William Gibbs McAdoo, had the support not only of those who refused to condemn the Klan but also of the Klan itself.

The balloting for president began on June 30 and would continue for 103 ballots over the next week. There had never been such a contentious convention. This was more than politics; this was a cultural war carried out by sweating men in suits (there were women delegates, though no prominent women speakers) arguing passionately over the future of their party and of their country.

In the midst of the endless roll calls, William Jennings Bryan once again took center stage, asking for time to address the convention and explain his vote. He held the floor for an hour, extolling the virtues of the party's great leaders—Josephus Daniels of North Carolina, Samuel L. Ralston of Indiana, Thomas J. Walsh of Montana (the convention's presiding officer), and a university president from Florida named A. A. Murphee, whose name inspired audible questions of "Who?" from the delegates on the floor. Bryan did not name Al Smith. But he announced that he would support William Gibbs McAdoo—the architect, he said, of the party's "progressive convention" and "progressive platform." Smith's delegates and the Tammany men in the hall hissed and hollered as Bryan made what proved to be his last convention speech. He took the measure of the Smith delegates, the Tammany types, Catholics most of them, city dwellers, drinkers—the sort of people who played baseball on a Sunday and drank beer afterward in spite of the laws of the Sabbath. "You do not represent the future of this country," he thundered. Bryan would never discover how wrong he was. He died a year later.[44]

The balloting continued after Bryan left the stage—and it continued, and it continued, until the exhausted combatants agreed on a compromise candidate: John Davis of West Virginia, who was nominated on the 103rd ballot. The party left New York bitterly divided, so it came as little surprise that incumbent Calvin Coolidge steamrolled Davis in the general election. But from the ashes of the debacle in the Garden and defeat at the polls rose the beginnings of a new Democratic Party—a party born on the sidewalks of New York in 1924.

· · ·

In the four years between Smith's defeat in Madison Square Garden and the 1928 Democratic National Convention in Houston, his administration in Albany continued to bring together downtown and uptown as no other governor had ever done before. He approved the ambitious and costly plans of Robert Moses to build state parks from Montauk Point to the Adirondacks to Niagara Falls, and to construct a network of highways, parkways, tunnels, and bridges that reimagined New York's transportation network for the twentieth century. To win public support for the bond issues required to build state parks, Smith mobilized Tammany's "us against them" rhetoric, portraying opponents as wealthy elites with access to sprawling golf courses (Charlie Murphy might have smiled, quietly, in his grave) who wished to restrict access to open space for everyone else. Moses, with his Yale pedigree and his PhD from Columbia University, served as Smith's able liaison to groups such as the Citizens Union, whose members rarely met an Ivy Leaguer they didn't love.

Smith's vision of a more expansive state government was financed through borrowing—in some cases, through considerable borrowing. Smith put his personal popularity on the line in 1925 as he urged voters to pass a $100 million bond issue to pay for construction of mental-health facilities, schools, prisons, and other public-works projects. The state's workers' compensation program and the Labor Department were strengthened, new resources were devoted to public-health facilities, and state support for schools continued to increase—from $7 million a year in Smith's first year in office to $70 million in 1928.

Smith did not see the need to apologize for the higher cost of government. In fact, he was proud of the salary raises granted to everyone "from the governor himself down to the woman who cleans the Capitol. . . . The office boy who got three dollars a week before [World War I] now gets twelve," Smith wrote in 1929. But Smith was hardly a spendthrift. His demands for efficiency led to a drastic reorganization of state government, including the elimination of redundant or overlapping agencies, centralization, and greater accountability. He considered administrative reorganization—a good-government issue if ever there was one—to be his greatest achievement, and a model for the nation. That allowed him to cut state taxes by 25 percent in 1924, even as the state continued to expand its services to children, the poor, the disabled, and even the imprisoned.[45]

Behind the scenes, as New York continued to defy the conservative mood in Calvin Coolidge's Washington, Smith's allies prepared the groundwork for another effort to win the Democratic presidential nomination. The governor's popularity remained strong in the North, but formidable obstacles remained—the divisions of the 1924 convention continued to roil the nation as well as the party. Thousands of hooded Klansmen paraded in Washington in August 1925 to display their power as well as their opposition to the new forces in the Democratic Party. The Klan's imperial wizard, Hiram Wesley Evans, announced that the Klan opposed the granting of "political power to any Roman Catholic"—the reference to Smith was clear—because they were aliens of dubious loyalty. Evans saw the Democratic Party split between the "native, American-minded, Protestant, 'Dry,'" and the "Catholic, boss-ruled 'wet' . . . Eastern Democracy, with priests instead of conscience."[46]

Those sentiments were not restricted to Klan members or white supremacists in the South. They existed not only in Smith's home state but also in the very city he so loved. Reverend Edwin D. Bailey, pastor of the Prospect Heights Presbyterian Church in Brooklyn, warned his congregation that the party of "rum, Romanism and rebellion now rules at Albany and is headed for Washington." Describing Smith as a "Roman Catholic Tammanyite Governor," the cleric argued that "with a Roman Catholic president in power, Rome will become the winner and America will be run by Rome."[47]

The persistence of anti-Catholicism and reflexive anti-Tammany sentiments made the tireless efforts of a certain Protestant advocate for Smith all the more important. For in the years between 1924 and 1928, Franklin Roosevelt continued to play a critical role as a bridge between Smith and the broader Democratic Party, which was still trying to stitch together the bloody wounds suffered in Madison Square Garden.

Roosevelt and his devoted aide Louis Howe no doubt saw opportunity for themselves in their work on Smith's behalf. Howe saw FDR occupying Al Smith's office some day, perhaps as early as 1932, and the White House shortly thereafter, never mind the man's shriveled legs. And Roosevelt himself placed no limits on his ambition—he did not accept and would never accept his disability as a bar to higher office. In the field of presidential politics, Roman Catholicism was a disability. But polio? Not a chance.

Roosevelt kept in touch with Democrats from around the nation, trying to assure skeptics that Smith was not the man portrayed in anti-Catholic jeremiads and other hostile outlets. (A book prepared for the 1928 campaign bore the unsubtle title *Al Smith's Tammany Hall: Champion Political Vampire*.) After a visit to Hyde Park from a top-ranking Democrat from Utah, Roosevelt assured Smith that if he wanted that state's delegates, "you can have them . . . in 1928." What's more, FDR said, his informant was certain that Smith would carry Utah in the general election. With that optimistic assessment, FDR turned to local politics, urging Smith to accept the recommendation made by a local Democratic county committee for a treasurer candidate in upstate Cattaraugus County. The irony was not lost on the onetime reformer who turned up his nose at the subject of political patronage. "I smile a little," Roosevelt wrote, "at my earnest pleadings with you to be regular." Smith, too, may have smiled a little at the thought of the great reformer Roosevelt begging a Tammany man to follow the party line, to be regular, to be a solid man.[48]

Some of Smith's supporters in Tammany were eager to confront critics in hostile regions of the country—even advocating a national organization based on the Tammany model. But FDR delivered a blunt warning against these ham-handed tactics. "I am convinced that some of your friends are, without your knowledge and consent, giving you aggressive publicity in the south and west, where such publicity is at the present time harmful," Roosevelt told Smith in late 1926. Smith's allies, he added, were "giving the old McAdoo crowd and the Know Nothings a reason to organize against you."

"I know perfectly well that you, as you read this letter, say to yourself quite honestly that you are not a candidate for 1928 and you can't be bothered with trying to control your fool friends," Roosevelt continued. "Nevertheless, you will be a candidate in 1928 whether you like it or not and I want to see you as strong a candidate as it is honestly possible to make you when the convention meets."[49]

He was right. Smith was a strong candidate in 1928, so strong, in fact, that would-be opponents like McAdoo ceded the field to him. He captured the party's nomination on the first ballot on the night of June 28, 1928, becoming the first Roman Catholic to win a major party's presidential nomination. As he did in 1924, Franklin Roosevelt placed Smith's name in nomination, even reprising his description of Smith as the Happy Warrior. Smith, his family, and close advisors were in Albany for the historic occasion, listening to Roosevelt and the roll call thanks to the magical new medium of radio. When the roll call ended and victory was secure, there were tears in the eyes of Alfred E. Smith, who learned about life and politics on the sidewalks of New York.

At long last, Charlie Murphy's most famous protégé, the best-loved son of Tammany Hall, was a candidate for president of the United States. A headline in the *New York Times* summed up this remarkable moment: "Alfred E. Smith's Rise from the City Streets Unparalleled in American History." So it was. Other presidential candidates had been born in humble circumstances. None had been born in a New York City tenement. Other presidents had come of age in cities. None had grown up in any place remotely like the Lower East Side. Other candidates started careers at a young age. None wrapped fish as a teenager to help pay the family bills.[50]

In his seconding speech for Smith, former Boston mayor Andrew J. Peters described himself as "a direct descendant of those who were among the earliest settlers of this country." He knew of no better way of celebrating his Pilgrim ancestors, he said, than to recognize Al Smith as the "best proof of democracy and its promise for the future."[51]

But large segments of American society profoundly disagreed, even ostensibly progressive journals such as *The Nation*, which withheld its endorsement from Smith in 1928 despite the editors' acknowledgment that he was "a symbol of tolerance in American life." For them, but not for Roosevelt, what mattered more than tolerance was Smith's unforgivable association with Tammany. "He is still the Tammany sachem who glories in that office and believes in that accursed institution against which stand charged a century of corruption, misgovernment, and uncalled-for human misery in the city of New York," the editors wrote. *The Nation*, like so many elite critics of Tammany, was incapable of perceiving Tammany's transformation during the first quarter of the twentieth century. Rather than cite the progressive achievements of Smith's years as governor, *The Nation* chose to summon through implication the ghost of Boss Tweed and other Tammany sinners to assail Smith's integrity.[52]

Reviled by the Right and abandoned by the Left—ironically, for some of the same reasons (temperance, Tammany, and the pope)—Al Smith never had a chance in the 1928 presidential election. Republican-led prosperity, which soon proved to be an illusion, certainly contributed to Herbert Hoover's resounding victory, but for many of Al Smith's supporters, the Happy Warrior was the victim of nativist bigotry from East to West, North to South. Smith even lost New York, his home state, by more than a hundred thousand votes—upstate nativists and antisaloon advocates came out in droves to keep the wet Catholic out of the White House.

The anti-Smith voters in New York nearly succeeded in keeping Franklin Roosevelt out of Albany as well. FDR was a reluctant warrior in 1928. Howe didn't think the time was right to run for governor, and neither did Eleanor Roosevelt, but Smith and his allies persuaded him on the eve of the state nominating convention. Tammany's Jimmy Walker, now the mayor of New York, placed his friend Frank's name in nomination. FDR won the race by about twenty-five thousand votes out of a total of more than four million cast. He risked much by coming to Smith's defense in the campaign's closing stages, lashing out at virulent anti-Catholic pamphlets circulating around the nation, particularly in the South. "I have seen circulars that were so unfit for publication that the people who wrote them and printed them and paid for them ought not to be put in jail, but ought to be put on the first ship and sent away from the United States," he told his audience. Roosevelt's anger was genuine, and it might well have cost him votes upstate.[53]

The wounds inflicted on Smith and his supporters took years to heal, if they ever did. Two days after the election, Woodrow Wilson's former aide, Joseph Tumulty, who had become friendly with many Tammany figures and had spoken at Tammany rallies, crossed paths with a friend's son on a street in Washington. The son was holding two pictures of Al Smith, saying that he "was going to place them in his room for memory's sake. The boy did not know it," Tumulty wrote, "but his remark left me with a gulp in my throat."

More than a decade later, Tumulty revisited the insults, slanders, and lies that were heaped upon Smith because he dared believe that a Catholic from an urban slum was qualified to be president of the United States. In a letter to Maryland Senator Millard Tydings, Tumulty summoned the memories of Smith's defeat as he sought to ensure than anybody who had had a hand in the campaign of hate was frozen out of the federal government. "The memories of the campaign of 1928 with its ugliness, its meanness, and its intolerance will live with me until the day I die," Tumulty wrote. "From every nook and cranny of the lower political world every contemptible means were resorted to . . . to destroy the man you and I supported, Governor Smith. No man who played a part in that campaign or subscribed to its maintenance is entitled to the smallest consideration at the hands of this administration."[54]

Even Smith's beloved wife, Katie, was the subject of scorn. The Republican Party circulated a pamphlet entitled *Mrs. Herbert Hoover: American Through and Through*, which implied that the daughter of Irish immigrants was something other than American, while a prominent Republican National committeewoman asked, with undisguised contempt, "Could you imagine Mrs. Smith in the White House?"[55]

From Smith's defeat and humiliation, however, came signs of the changes sweeping the nation and the Democratic Party. The new Democratic Party of urban residents and immigrant-stock constituents was created not in 1932, when FDR won the presidency, but in Smith's failed campaign of 1928. Smith captured a majority of votes in the nation's twelve largest cities; Republicans had won those cities four years earlier by 1.6 million votes. White ethnic neighborhoods in Boston, Chicago, and other major industrial cities saw large increases in the Democratic column as Jews, Italians, and Poles joined with the Irish in supporting a candidate who was, in spirit and in fact, one of them. The political realignment associated with the election of Franklin Roosevelt and the creation of the New Deal owed much to the personal narrative of Alfred E. Smith, a sachem of Tammany Hall. "Before the Roosevelt Revolution," wrote political scientist Samuel Lubell, "there was an Al Smith Revolution."[56]

It was Irish America's revolution, too, a revolution rooted in a transatlantic Irish narrative of hunger, powerlessness, and grievance; a revolution that created a more pluralistic, activist political culture in New York; a revolution achieved under the auspices of the nation's most famous political machine, Tammany Hall, and guided by a silent saloon-keeper whose father had escaped death and starvation in nineteenth-century Ireland.

TWELVE

‹·›⟹ ⟸‹·›

THE BATTLE OF TWO GOVERNORS

On a late November evening in 1930 not long after Franklin Delano Roosevelt was reelected governor of New York in a historic landslide, one of Charlie Murphy's protégés was summoned to dinner at the Executive Mansion on Eagle Street in Albany. Edward J. Flynn, the thirty-eight-year-old son of Irish immigrants, was the powerful Democratic Party boss of the Bronx—he took over the party there in 1922, at Murphy's behest, and restored order to an organization that was threatening to break apart because of feuds, rivalries, and uncertain leadership. He and Roosevelt got to know each other during the long Democratic National Convention in 1924, and they struck up a friendship that was not nearly as unlikely as the relationships Roosevelt had forged with some of Tammany's less-polished characters. Flynn, a graduate of Fordham Law School who may well have been born wearing a suit and tie, was not among the rowdy New Yorkers who hooted and hollered while William Jennings Bryan tried to explain away the Ku Klux Klan. He was cultivated, reserved, and studious, uncomfortable in the company of backslappers. "I was not an 'easy mixer,' indeed,

[I] found it quite difficult to move about with facility among strange people," Flynn wrote.[1]

Roosevelt called him "Eddie." There is no indication that Flynn called his new friend "Frank."

Flynn followed FDR to Albany in 1929, serving as the new governor's secretary of state. The title sounded impressive, but the duties were fairly prosaic. Flynn functioned as a political hunter and gatherer, stalking the state for information and gossip under the guise of overseeing fishing licenses and racehorses. At least, that's how Flynn interpreted his job. His predecessor as secretary of state had had a more grandiose vision of his duties, but Robert Moses was a more grandiose character. Al Smith had pleaded with FDR to retain Moses as secretary of state, but, after weeks of nonanswers, the new governor delivered his verdict: Moses would be fired—sort of. He continued to serve as the czar of the state park system, but not as an all-purpose adviser. "He rubs me the wrong way," FDR said of Moses. And so Franklin Roosevelt dismissed a man with impeccable reformer credentials and Ivy League degrees, replacing him with one of Charlie Murphy's men.[2]

In 1930, Republicans sought to capitalize on Flynn's presence in FDR's inner circle, circulating a campaign leaflet charging that "Governor Franklin D. Roosevelt, once the avowed enemy of Tammany . . . is now the champion of the organization of the infamous Tweed."[3]

The world of politics surely was turned upside down.

. . .

Ed Flynn's dinner in the Executive Mansion on that November evening in 1930 was an intimate affair—the party was limited to Flynn, Governor Roosevelt, and the governor's chain-smoking, gnomish personal assistant, Louis Howe, a onetime journalist who had devoted his life to furthering FDR's ambitions. The three men made polite conversation while dinner was served on a small table in front of one of the mansion's several fine fireplaces. After the meal was finished and the plates taken away, the three men retired to the library, where the governor got down to business.

"Eddie," Roosevelt said, turning his attention to his secretary of state, "my reason for asking you to stay overnight is that I believe I can be nominated for the Presidency in 1932 on the Democratic ticket."[*]

Flynn could not have been shocked, for the newspapers had been filled with speculation that another Roosevelt might be on his way to the White House, especially after FDR won reelection by three-quarters of a million votes in 1930. But there was much more to the FDR presidential boom than his landslide victory. The nation's economy was slumping and on its way to a catastrophic depression following the stock market crash of 1929. Times were bad enough in 1930—the national jobless rate was just under 9 percent—but they were about to get much worse, as unemployment reached 16 percent in 1931 and 24 percent in 1932. Banks failed, businesses closed, and hope disappeared from city streets and rural villages. Herbert Hoover, elected to the White House in a landslide over Al Smith in 1928, looked absolutely beatable as Roosevelt confided his ambitions to Flynn and Howe.

Roosevelt's announcement complicated Flynn's life, because FDR was not the only friend of his who was considered presidential material. Al Smith, whom Flynn had known longer than he'd known Roosevelt, was not finished with politics—or at least few Democrats believed that he was. The press referred to him as a potential candidate in 1932 despite the former governor's insistence that he was content to remain out of public life. Like so many New Yorkers, Flynn had a special place in his heart for Smith, the kid from the Fulton Fish Market who had risen to become a national figure.

In a larger sense, though, the prospect of a presidential campaign between two New York governors, Al Smith and Franklin Roosevelt, represented an absolute triumph for Tammany Hall, however uncomfortable it was bound to make Flynn and many others. Such a contest would showcase a new kind of politics in the Democratic Party—a politics that embraced cities, immigrants, ethnicity, pluralism, and the lunch-bucket liberalism that Charlie Murphy and his protégés had implemented in Albany during the first quarter of the twentieth century.

Few issues of ideology separated Smith and Roosevelt. The loom-ing contest between the two would inevitably focus on personality and electability, not the sort of fundamental differences that had separated Smith and McAdoo in 1924. Whatever else Flynn might have feared as he contemplated a presidential campaign between two of his friends, he might have taken comfort in knowing that the prospective candidates were fellow New Yorkers who had come of age during the height of Charles Murphy's influence over Albany and who had helped to trans-form the Democrats from the party of William Jennings Bryan and the Ku Klux Klan to a party that included urban Catholics and Jews (as well as Southern racists, to be sure). The Democratic Party was begin-ning to resemble Tammany Hall—urban bosses in Jersey City, Chicago, Boston, San Francisco, and Kansas City were important national play-ers who represented the children and grandchildren of immigrants, and many of these bosses shared the urban liberal agenda of greater regu-lation and stronger social-welfare measures that Al Smith had helped implement in New York.

Smith and Roosevelt were hardly the only New Yorkers who were key parts of the new Democratic Party. Robert Wagner, Smith's old friend from their days together in Albany, was elected to the U.S. Sen-ate in 1926 and was about to make his mark as one of the nation's most important lawmakers. Herbert Lehman, vice chairman of Tammany Hall's finance committee, was elected as FDR's lieutenant governor in 1928, becoming the first Jew elected to statewide office in New York. He, too, would go on to become a politician of national renown.

All four helped to implement the urban liberal agenda that trans-formed New York politics in the twentieth century. So, in that sense, Ed Flynn might have felt some satisfaction as he contemplated the prospect of his two friends running against each other for president in 1932, for they represented the new, pluralistic Democratic Party created, in part, by Tammany Hall. Although Flynn was not a member of Tammany—

as a Bronx resident, he was ineligible for membership in a group that ostensibly controlled only the Democratic Party of Manhattan—he served as an adjunct of the organization through his friendships and his enduring affection for Charles Murphy.

None of this, however, made his life easier as he considered what might happen in 1932.

. . .

Ed Flynn had been a frequent visitor to the Executive Mansion during the Smith years, and on one occasion he was dispatched to the mansion's reception area to stall the very powerful and very dry Josephus Daniels of North Carolina, onetime secretary of the navy, who apparently had shown up early for an appointment with Smith while the governor and his aides were fortifying themselves for another long day of work in Albany. Daniels's devotion to temperance was so passionate that he purged naval bases, officers' quarters, and all the ships at sea of anything stronger than cough medicine even before passage of Prohibition in 1920.

Smith told Flynn to keep Daniels at bay while he and his aides frantically removed highball glasses, beer mugs, and other signs of Tammany-style deliberations from the governor's office. (Smith no doubt was less concerned about evidence of copious tobacco consumption—after all, there was no law against smoke-filled rooms, and besides, Daniels was from North Carolina.) After a decent interval, Flynn led Daniels up the main stairway to Smith's second-floor office, where Prohibition had been restored.

Smith's humiliating defeat in 1928 made him something of a secular martyr among many Irish-Catholic New Yorkers, and Smith himself was not averse to viewing his defeat as a rejection of his religion, not his politics or his gravel-voiced, unapologetically urban persona. Many others agreed, although it seemed fair to note that Hoover's victory was as much a referendum on the Republican-led prosperity of the Roaring Twenties as it was on Smith's faith. Still, for Smith's many admirers, he was a victim of mindless bigotry, no longer a happy warrior but a wounded warrior whose scars required careful attention, respect, and that all-important virtue, loyalty.

As Franklin Roosevelt began to sketch out his plans for 1932, it fell to Flynn to deal with the delicate issue of Alfred E. Smith. The former governor had said he would not return to public life, and he seemed to be thriving as president of the Empire State Building Corporation, which was putting up the world's tallest building in a city of breadlines and shantytowns. Nevertheless, FDR felt obliged to let Smith know of his plans, and, just as important, he wanted to find out once and for all whether Smith had ambitions of his own. Roosevelt sent Flynn to see Smith before the 1932 campaign began in earnest, but the secretary of state was none too happy about it. "I hated to find myself in the position of a mediator in what had become a serious personal issue," Flynn wrote. But he was the obvious choice to have a candid talk with the former governor.[5]

When they met, Smith insisted again that he was through with politics. Family members had lost money in the stock-market crash. He had debts of his own. The Depression had taken its toll on him just as it had on so many other Americans. According to Flynn's account, Smith ruled out another presidential bid, freeing Flynn of any lingering obligations or guilt. Flynn committed himself—and his Bronx County organization—to Roosevelt's fledgling campaign.

And then everything changed. As the Depression grew worse in 1931, it became clear that Hoover and his fellow Republicans were on the verge of a historic defeat in 1932. Smith, by no means over his loss in 1928, saw a chance at redemption. As Smith's biographer, Robert Slayton, noted, the former governor still regarded Roosevelt as a pleasant but overmatched dilettante. Smith's most trusted aide, Belle Moskowitz, put it more bluntly. She told Roosevelt supporter Felix Frankfurter, "Many of us feel that the party needs a well-equipped candidate, able to lead." Refusing to even mention Roosevelt's name, she said that the "candidate . . . leading the field" did not offer "that kind of promise."[6]

Al Smith announced in February 1932 that he would accept the party's nomination for president if it were offered, but he would not campaign for it. Tammany quickly lined up behind him, even though Smith and the organization's new leader, Irish immigrant John Curry, were not particularly close. Flynn kept the Bronx in Roosevelt's column, a critical victory for the governor's campaign. New York City's Democrats were forced to choose sides between two New York Democrats: Smith and Roosevelt. The old Smith coalition of reformers and regulars broke apart, with hard feelings on both sides.

Sam Rosenman, a lawyer and assemblyman who had been close to Smith in the 1920s, and Smith's old friend Frances Perkins, who served as FDR's labor commissioner, sided with Roosevelt. Belle Moskowitz and master planner Robert Moses stayed at Smith's side. (This lineup was not particularly surprising, given that Rosenman and Perkins worked for FDR, while Moskowitz and Moses were pointedly dismissed from their posts after Roosevelt's election.) Meanwhile, Flynn and the Bronx were with FDR; Tammany and the city's three other Democratic organizations (Brooklyn, Queens, and Staten Island) sided with Smith.

The split between friends and allies caused no small amount of anguish in New York. James J. Hoey, a onetime Democratic state chairman and state legislator, and a longtime friend of Smith's, poured out his heart when Louis Howe asked him to endorse FDR. "You can understand my situation," he told Howe. "I have been so closely associated for more than a quarter of a century with Governor Smith that I do not feel as though I could take a stand in opposition to him publicly."

The key word, as Howe surely knew, was *publicly*. Hoey continued: "You know my sentiments, and I am doing everything I can in my own way to help the cause in which you are interested." Hoey, a middle-aged bachelor with thinning hair and a fleshy double chin, apparently helped the Roosevelt cause by serving as an informant for FDR in Smith's camp. In a "personal and confidential" letter to FDR's campaign manager, James Farley, Hoey reported on developments inside the six-member delegation from the Panama Canal Zone—information he received from the Smith camp. While one letter does not make a conspiracy, it does suggest that there may have been others, and it certainly demonstrates that Hoey was in touch with FDR's campaign even though he remained publicly loyal to Smith. Hoey's covert work on FDR's behalf would not go unrewarded.[7]

Hoey may have felt obliged to stand by Smith in public, but he was among a number of New York politicians growing alienated from Tammany's leadership. Ever since that glorious July 4 ceremony in 1929 when Governor Roosevelt himself had presided over the opening of the new Tammany Hall, the news had been all bad for the organization. A Tammany judge, Joseph F. Crater, disappeared in the midst of an investigation of malfeasance on the bench. (He was never found.) There was talk of renewed ties between Tammany figures and the city's underworld. Mayor Walker's love of the city's nightlife grew stale after the stock market crashed and the press reported fresh allegations of corruption in City Hall and in the city's judiciary. Roosevelt had little choice but to respond to a growing public outcry against Walker, leading to his appointment of an anti-Tammany judge, Samuel Seabury—the man who couldn't bring himself to vote for Al Smith's nomination as governor in 1918—to investigate city government. Seabury was a Tammany foe from central casting: He had the austere bearing of a cleric—perhaps not surprising, given that he was the descendant of an Anglican bishop—and he was utterly convinced of his own moral purity. And he was not wrong about Tammany's failings in the post-Murphy era.

The Tammany that had nurtured Al Smith and Robert Wagner, the Tammany that had won over Frances Perkins and Herbert Lehman, the Tammany that had led New York into a golden age of practical reform—that Tammany was slipping into the pages of history. In its place was an organization returning to stereotype, adrift ideologically and ethically with no new Al Smiths, no new Robert Wagners, to provide energy and ideas. Ironically, it was Jimmy Walker, soon to become a symbol of new Tammany excesses, who had seen trouble on the horizon years earlier, when Charlie Murphy was laid to rest. "The brains of Tammany Hall," Walker said, "lie in Calvary Cemetery."[8]

. . .

As the presidential campaign unfolded in the early months of 1932, it became clear that there would be no sentimental ending to the relationship between the two leading candidates, one the son of the Lower East Side and the other a scion of one of New York's great families. Al Smith and Franklin Roosevelt were determined to fight to the end for the party's nomination, to the distress of colleagues who believed the two New York governors ought to stand aside for the good of the party. William Gibbs McAdoo, at peace with the realization that he would never follow in the steps of his father-in-law, Woodrow Wilson, was among those who saw House Speaker John Nance Garner of Texas as an alternative to the battling New Yorkers.

"Unless the Democratic Party is willing to keep out of the Tammany mess in New York . . . by uniting on a man like Garner . . . I see nothing but another defeat ahead of us," McAdoo told Joseph Tumulty, the Jersey City politician who was Wilson's personal secretary. "The Smith and Roosevelt contest is bound to have the most-hurtful reactions."[9]

The 1932 Democratic National Convention in Chicago Stadium was not as contentious as the brutal affair in Madison Square Garden had been in 1924, but it had all the elements of a political civil war within the New York delegation and among urban Irish Catholics who were among the party's most reliable voters. Some believed passionately that Smith should have another chance, others believed just as firmly that Smith, through no fault of his own, would only lead the party to another disaster in November. The two New York governors, both of whom had won their offices with the help and support of Tammany Hall, took their fight to the convention floor in Chicago, where Roosevelt held a large but not insurmountable lead in the delegate count.

Leading the Roosevelt effort, along with the inevitable Louis Howe, were two New York Irish-Catholic politicians—Ed Flynn and a promising operative from rural Rockland County, James Farley—both of whom represented the Tammany tradition, even though they were not and never had been Tammany members. (Farley shared with his urban compatriots a common narrative. His grandparents were Famine immigrants and his father died in 1898 when Jim was nine years old, leaving behind a wife and five sons.) Farley had Smith's ebullience, Flynn had Charlie Murphy's quiet shrewdness. Farley was the glad-hander, ward heeler of the nation. Flynn was the strategist, the back-room deal-cutter.

While Farley managed Roosevelt's floor effort at the convention, Flynn worked behind the scenes with the likes of Senator Huey Long of Louisiana and Senator Cordell Hull of Tennessee to counter Al Smith's stop-Roosevelt strategy. As the maneuvering and jockeying were underway in Chicago's hotel rooms, Flynn received a message from Smith's manager, Joseph Proskauer. The former governor wanted to have a word with him.

It promised to be an awkward conversation. As Flynn entered Smith's room, conversation ceased and Smith's aides abruptly left. Just the two of them remained, two onetime allies, two men set on course for this day, for this time, by Silent Charlie Murphy.

"Ed," Smith said, "you are not representing the people of Bronx County in your support of Roosevelt. You know the people of Bronx County want you to support me."

Flynn conceded that Smith probably was right. But he had committed himself and his fellow delegates to Roosevelt months earlier, when Smith was not a candidate. It would be wrong, Flynn said, for his delegates to ditch FDR now simply because Smith was in the race. The two former allies continued to talk, and sometimes emotion got the better of them. Nearly twenty years later, Flynn recalled the conversation as "painful," because his friendship with Smith "had been much longer and more intimate than my friendship with Roosevelt."

But neither man gave ground. They shook hands, and Flynn left the room. Smith's closing handshake, he noticed, was not as firm, not as friendly, as it once had been.[10]

Franklin Roosevelt was nominated for president on the convention's fourth ballot, after John Garner, the prospective compromise candidate, agreed to serve as FDR's vice president in a back-room maneuver engineered just as Roosevelt seemed to be losing momentum. Garner brought with him the Texas and California delegations, which had been pledged to him. It was left to McAdoo, chairman of the Golden State delegation, to deliver the dramatic news of his state's switch from Garner to Roosevelt. As the man who fought Al Smith for 103 ballots back in 1924 rose to announce California's vote, Tammany delegates let him have it. Fairly or not, they remembered McAdoo as the Klan's man in 1924, as the self-styled progressive who could not summon the moral outrage to condemn the Ku Klux Klan but who saw no reason to disguise his contempt for Tammany. Boos cascaded from the rafters and from the floor itself as McAdoo tried to make himself heard. Finally, he said, "I don't care what the galleries think. California casts her forty-four votes for Governor Franklin D. Roosevelt!" Vengeance was never served so coldly, and with such effect. It was all over for Tammany Hall's Al Smith. Texas followed, and the rout for Roosevelt was on.[11]

As Roosevelt clinched the nomination, there was no motion from the vanquished candidate's forces to make the nomination unanimous, as tradition dictated. Al Smith simply couldn't allow it. He left Chicago that night, even as Roosevelt made his way from New York to Chicago to accept the nomination in person—something no candidate had ever done before.

For Al Smith, Chicago closed the curtain on his ambitions and on his leading role in American politics. The man he had regarded as an understudy was now a star.

· · ·

As a band struck up Franklin Roosevelt's boisterous campaign song, "Happy Days Are Here Again," and the nominee promised to deliver a new deal to the American people, another New Yorker left Chicago with dashed hopes, as just as Al Smith did. Samuel Seabury, the man Roosevelt had put in charge of investigating the Tammany administration of Mayor Jimmy Walker, had made the journey to Chicago for purposes

THE BATTLE OF TWO GOVERNORS ~ 279

that remained murky, even for veteran political observers. Although a practitioner of the "disinterested" school of politics and government, Seabury had always worn his ambitions on his well-tailored sleeve. He won several judicial races earlier in his career with Tammany's backing, and in 1916 he earned Tammany's nominal support to be a sacrificial-lamb candidate against incumbent Governor Charles Whitman, whom Charlie Murphy deemed to be unbeatable. And so he was.

In the weeks leading to the Chicago convention, Democratic delegates around the country opened their mailboxes to find complimentary copies of a new Seabury biography portraying him as the avenging angel of clean, disinterested, politics-free government. This publicity stunt, carried out in the middle of an election year, did not go unnoticed, and when Seabury showed up in Chicago with no apparent purpose, reporters speculated that he was there as a shadow candidate, just waiting to be asked in case divided Democrats needed an alternative to Roosevelt and Smith. Reporters were not alone in their suspicions. Years later, Ed Flynn charged that Seabury had hoped to thwart Roosevelt's presidential ambitions with his investigation of Tammany (and of Flynn—Seabury conducted a thorough review of Flynn's personal finances) and grab the nomination for himself.[19]

Whatever Seabury's motives, Tammany certainly had provided him with plenty of material as he looked into allegations of graft and judicial misconduct in Jimmy Walker's New York. The sheriff of New York County—a job once held by Honest John Kelly and the more honest Al Smith—was found to have accumulated nearly $400,000 in savings over seven years in a job that paid about $12,000 a year. Asked to explain himself, the sheriff referred to a tin box in his house that seemed to magically multiply currency. Seabury also revealed that the city had awarded a bus contract to a company that owned no buses but that had provided Mayor Walker with a personal line of credit. And a judge who had more than half a million dollars in savings told Seabury that he had taken out a large loan to help feed, clothe, and house no fewer than thirty-four relatives who were in his care.

As the Seabury investigation produced headline after headline detailing the Walker administration's lax ethics, attention turned to Franklin Roosevelt and the political dilemma he faced in his home state. He had the power to remove Walker as mayor, but if he did so, he was bound to further alienate Tammany supporters who had opposed his nomination. On the other hand, if he didn't act swiftly and decisively, Republicans surely would play the Tammany card in the general election, as they had done, unsuccessfully, during his gubernatorial reelection in 1930.

The Walker question—and the larger issue of FDR's relationship with Tammany Hall—had hung over Roosevelt's campaign in the buildup to the 1932 convention. Seabury's much-anticipated report arrived in the governor's mansion on a spring night in 1932, when Roosevelt was huddled with journalist and historian Claude Bowers. Bowers later wrote that Roosevelt was not nearly as outraged with Walker as Seabury was. The governor glanced through the findings and, according to Bowers, "expressed his opinion of the judge in language not printable." Although Walker admitted to accepting nearly $250,000 from a friend who invested his own money on the mayor's behalf, FDR did not seem convinced that he deserved removal, as Seabury recommended. "Never has a governor been asked to remove an elective officer on such evidence," Roosevelt said, according to Bowers.[13]

FDR stalled for time as he prepared for the Chicago convention, forwarding the report to Walker and asking him to respond to the charges. Walker responded, in a fashion, by delivering a defiant speech at the convention in favor of Smith's nomination. Weeks later, as pressure on candidate Roosevelt increased, Walker was summoned to Albany to undergo questioning by the governor himself. An explosive encounter seemed just days away as Roosevelt wrestled with an extraordinary dilemma. His election as president was nearly certain, but a misstep in his handling of Walker—and, by extension, Tammany Hall—could prove damaging. While the governor deliberated, Al Smith stepped in, taking aside his onetime colleague in Albany, Walker. With the national press watching Roosevelt's every move, Smith told Walker, "Jim, you're through." Walker announced his resignation on September 1, 1932. He soon set sail for Europe, telling reporters that he wanted to "get away from desks and telephones."[14]

. . .

As Jimmy Walker watched the skyline of the city he loved disappear into the horizon from the good ship *Conte Grande*, the question for the Tammany he left behind was this: How would it respond not only to the Seabury investigation but to all of the challenges it faced—from the financial emergency of the Depression to Franklin Roosevelt's imminent election as president?

The burden of setting Tammany Hall on a new course, or not, fell to a mild-mannered native of County Fermanagh, John Curry, who took over the organization in 1929 after Murphy's successor, George Olvany, resigned. A neatly dressed fifty-nine-year-old with thinning hair and a steel-gray mustache who was raised, improbably enough, on a farm on Manhattan's West Side, Curry served as a Tammany district leader during Murphy's glory years. After the organization's Executive Committee named him as the new boss in 1929, Curry promised that he would "carry out the politics in which I grew up." The man clearly was not paying attention, for he grew up at a time when Tammany scrupulously avoided the gross mistakes of its past, a time when it could attract men like Franklin Roosevelt's impeccable lieutenant governor, Herbert Lehman, son of a German-Jewish immigrant who founded the banking giant Lehman Brothers. Lehman entered civic life in part because he saw Al Smith as the model of a new kind of politics—tolerant, progressive, and urban. He saw the Ku Klux Klan's attacks on Smith in 1924 and 1928 as an assault not simply on Catholics but also on Jews like himself and all those who were deemed something less than authentically American. Lehman not only supported Smith, he also supported Tammany, joining the organization in the 1920s and serving as vice chairman of its finance committee.[15]

John Curry took over Tammany Hall as the organization's core constituents, his fellow Irish-Americans, continued their dispersal from the tenements of the Lower East Side to the more bucolic neighborhoods of the upper Bronx and western Queens. The number of immigrants, Irish and non-Irish, was in decline citywide, thanks to the lingering effects of the immigration restrictions of 1924. Curry would be called upon to make critical decisions about the organization's future, including its relationships with Roosevelt, Lehman, and Walker's successor in City Hall. Each of his decisions turned out to be disastrous, an almost willful rejection of the wisdom of his predecessors. Those decisions contributed as much to the organization's downfall as the more familiar narrative of New York's changing demographics and the advent of New Deal social programs. Some of the city's most prominent Irish politicians soon concluded that Tammany had outlived its usefulness—because, in the end, it had accomplished its mission.

· · ·

By law, the president of the Board of Aldermen became acting mayor when an incumbent left office early. So after Jimmy Walker resigned in 1932, the mantle of leadership fell to Joseph McKee, a former Latin and Greek teacher from the Bronx who was close to Ed Flynn, a fellow Fordham Law graduate. McKee had abandoned teaching for politics about a dozen years earlier, when he turned to a local Democratic district leader to help the destitute family of a dying friend. Help arrived, and a grateful McKee soon gave up education to become a neighborhood politician, the kind of person who came to the aid of families in need. In appearance, he was not unlike Walker—he was a good-looking man with well-groomed brown hair and a boyish face that made him seem younger than his forty-four years. But the resemblance ended there, as he made clear in his first act as mayor: He cut his own annual pay from $40,000 to $25,000.

McKee spent the next few months attempting to adjust the city's treasury to the Depression's grim realities. He demanded millions of dollars in budget savings, and for his effort Tammany's men on the city's

Board of Estimate—a quasi-legislative body consisting of the mayor, city comptroller, president of the Board of Aldermen, and the five borough presidents—diluted his budget-making powers. He complained about personnel costs but could not persuade Tammany to cut the city's payroll, which had doubled since 1918.

Unhappy with the new austerity in City Hall and still fuming over Walker's resignation, Tammany and its allies in the boroughs called for a special election to replace Walker on a more permanent basis. The Tammany candidate, John O'Brien, an undistinguished but likable jurist, won easily with John Curry's support.

Curry looked to extend his influence by blocking the nomination of Lieutenant Governor Lehman to succeed FDR as governor, even though Lehman had been a Tammany member. Curry apparently saw Lehman as a threat, a Tammany man who might be inclined to show off his independence once in power. Curry even concocted a scheme of political musical chairs, proposing to nominate Senator Robert Wagner for governor and to ship Lehman to Washington to take Wagner's place in the Senate. (Had Curry's plan worked, Wagner would not have been in the Senate to champion New Deal legislation, a chilling thought.) Al Smith intervened on Lehman's behalf, in essence telling Curry to fall in line or else. He did, sullenly.

The election of 1932 could have been a milestone in the rehabilitation and revitalization of Tammany Hall. Its embrace of pluralistic politics, its rejection of moralistic crusades like Prohibition, and its support for social welfare and government regulation were on the verge of transforming national politics. But its new leaders were petty and small, and its best people kept their distance.

All of that was put aside, however, on November 8, 1932, when the United States chose Franklin D. Roosevelt as its new president, a man who had been something of an auxiliary Tammany member during the Smith years. State voters elected Herbert Lehman, a card-carrying member of the organization, as governor. Another Tammany member, Robert Wagner, was reelected to a second term in the U.S.

Senate. In the city, the newly elected mayor, O'Brien, owed his career to Tammany.

The scene inside Tammany's ballroom was one of quiet jubilation. The new governor was gracious enough to stop by and mingle with Curry in a private room before heading uptown to congratulate the new president at his headquarters in the Biltmore Hotel. Senator Wagner stopped by as well, posing for a picture with Lehman and Curry before heading to his own headquarters. Mayor-elect O'Brien arrived and was ushered to the stage along with his wife and their five children, perhaps reminding the city that it was no longer in the hands of the philandering Walker. Tammany had seen few nights like this one. All of the pieces necessary for power and influence were in place—all the way to the White House. The lights outside the organization's new building brightened a city that otherwise had little to celebrate on that fall night. For when Tammany loyalists awoke the following morning, they returned to everyday life in a city where unemployment was nearly 25 percent; where fathers, mothers, and children lined up at dawn for bread; where the grandchildren of the Irish Famine wondered if, or when, the landlord might come to put them out on the street. Yes, these were hard times. But for one night anyway, Tammany could cheer.

It was, to be sure, a last hurrah.

A few weeks after the election, Al Smith appeared in front of Samuel Seabury as the long investigation of city government and Tammany drew to a close. Smith delivered a breathtaking lecture on the need to reform municipal government, leaving Seabury uncharacteristically speechless. The simultaneous existence of the city's five boroughs as five individual counties was inefficient and led to bloated payrolls, Smith said. Judges ought to be appointed by the mayor rather than nominated by political bosses. The City Council should be expanded to a two-house legislature to better serve as a check on mayoral power.

The city's press corps quickly hailed Al Smith as the city's savior. "The excited citizenry," wrote Arthur Krock in the *New York Times*, "hoped that this means the former Governor will lead a reform movement against Tammany at the Mayoralty election next year." A nonpartisan committee of civic elites, including the head of the city's Young Republican clubs, announced its intention to draft Smith as a mayoral candidate in 1933.[16]

Tammany and its boss, Curry, took Smith's suggestions in the spirit in which they were offered—as a stinging criticism of the organization's ethical and political drift back in time to the bad old days. A year later, Al Smith, the Happy Warrior himself, was booed at a Tammany Hall dinner.

THIRTEEN

LEGACIES

It was another Independence Day at Tammany Hall in the Great Depression year of 1937.

As usual, the sachems spared nothing to celebrate the occasion, although the ceremonies and speeches took place on Monday, July 5, to avoid conflict with more sacred observances on Sunday. The streets near Union Square were awash in red, white, and blue as Tammany's stalwarts by the hundreds strode past subway entrances along Fourteenth Street that could get them to the far reaches of Canarsie in Brooklyn and Parkchester in the Bronx. Many Tammany voters already had made that journey and not returned, and now they were beyond the reach of the precinct captain, the district leader, and the Hall itself.

But even as Tammany's influence began to wane, on this festive morning it could take credit for producing the greatest federal legislator of the Depression era, U.S. Senator Robert Wagner. Franklin Roosevelt's New Deal owed much to the vision and hard work of the German immigrant who had caught Charles Murphy's eye a generation earlier. As he took his place of honor on the banner-bedecked speakers' platform, Robert Wagner had to his credit two of the New Deal's signature reforms, the National Labor Relations Act (more commonly known as the Wagner Act), which gave unions greater collective bargaining powers, and the Social Security Act, for which he was a leading sponsor and advocate. There was more to come. In just a few months, Congress would pass the Wagner-Steagall Act, which created a federal housing agency and authorized the payment of housing subsidies to the poor. Never before had the federal government intervened so aggressively in the nation's housing market on behalf of the poor.

Al Smith might have been Tammany's favorite son, its martyr for the cause of political pluralism, but it was Robert Wagner who created the organization's greatest legislative legacy on a national level. Drawing on his experience in a Tammany-controlled state legislature, he wrote or sponsored milestone social-welfare laws that, for the first time, provided a national safety net for struggling families like his own. As an adult, Wagner looked back with little sentimentality at a childhood spent in a basement apartment in the heavily German neighborhood of Yorkville on the Upper East Side. "My boyhood was a pretty rough passage," he once recalled. All six Wagner children were sent to work at a young age to supplement their father's $5-a-week job as a janitor. Many Americans, he once told economist Leon Keyserling, his friend and aide, believed that anyone with character and determination could overcome difficult circumstances with hard work. "Leon," he said, "that's bunk. For every one who rises to the top, a thousand are destroyed."[1]

Wagner's role as one of the New Deal's leading liberals was defined on a single day, June 19, 1935, when the Senate passed the Social Security Act and the House passed the Wagner Act. The latter legislation rightly bore his name, because Wagner tirelessly championed the bill despite Franklin Roosevelt's initial opposition and then his studied neutrality. Labor Secretary Frances Perkins, who would have been familiar with Roosevelt's opaque political style, asserted that FDR "never lifted a finger" to win support for the pro-union bill. It was Wagner himself, calling on every trick he had learned as a young Tammany legislator, who singlehandedly won the bill's passage. "There would never have been a Wagner Act or anything like it at any time if the Senator had not spent himself in this cause to a degree which almost defies description," recalled Keyserling.[2]

Wagner's success in the Senate surely was a high point of Tammany's history, the natural conclusion of a process that began with a fire in a factory building in Greenwich Village in 1911, the capstone of narratives shared by men and women born in tenements during the Gilded Age who challenged the political, economic, and cultural assumptions of the nation's elites. Robert Wagner's contributions to the nation's new political order perhaps were not as dramatic as Al Smith's triumph at the 1928 Democratic National Convention or Tammany's fight against the Ku Klux Klan in 1924. But the laws he wrote and sponsored in the 1930s were milestones in American history, an overturning of the myth that a nation of rugged individuals needed nothing except a free market to ensure material success. The Wagner Act, Social Security, and the housing act were triumphs of a less-individualistic nation, a reflection of the values Wagner found in the political clubhouses and union halls of New York.

As the 1930s progressed, Wagner continued to advocate for new measures to broaden the era's commitment to social justice. He sponsored a strong antilynching bill (which FDR opposed, leading to its failure) and a special visa program designed to help twenty thousand Jewish children flee the Hitler regime in his native Germany (despite Wagner's efforts, the latter measure never made it to the Senate floor). His record of achievement was extraordinary, but even his failures were important—he could not singlehandedly stop the lynching of African-Americans or allow young Jews to escape Hitler, but by raising his voice on behalf of the oppressed, Robert Wagner earned a reputation as one of the twentieth century's greatest senators.

And he never saw a reason to deny his Tammany roots.

·   ·   ·

Dressed in a dark double-breasted suit on a humid summer morning, Robert Wagner was seated with his fellow U.S. senator and Tammany colleague Royal Copeland, who looked far more comfortable in a light suit, his jacket unbuttoned. Wagner slouched in his seat, while Copeland, an older man with round glasses and just the right amount of gray to suggest wisdom but not incapacity, sat erect, a picture of dignity. Wagner and Copeland may have been colleagues and longtime acquaintances, but they had very different views about their fellow New Yorker in the White House. Copeland had spoken out bitterly against FDR at Tammany's July 4 ceremony a year earlier, suggesting that the president—who was on his way to a smashing reelection victory in 1936—was becoming too powerful. This year, Copeland returned to that theme when he was called on to speak. Without mentioning the president by name, Copeland warned his audience of the power of unaccountable leaders. "We want no dictator in government, in industry, in social or community life," he said.

Wagner had no such foreboding thoughts to share. Instead, he focused his attention on the institution that had welcomed a hardworking immigrant into its innermost councils, an institution that still promoted and supported him, even amid the organization's divisions, feuds, and desperation.

Wagner's subject was Tammany Hall. Tellingly, his verbs were in the past tense, making his speech sound more like a eulogy than a call to arms. But it was noteworthy all the same, for it came from a senator who was well on his way to becoming a Capitol Hill legend.

Thirty years earlier, Wagner said, New York was a "backward and benighted state in social and welfare legislation. It forgot the lost souls tied day and night to the factory bench. But about that time, a small group from Tammany Hall were elected to serve in Albany. We remembered these lost souls and guided them to an earthly salvation. We passed law after law and made New York the shining mark for the world to emulate.

"Tammany Hall," Wagner continued, "may justly claim the title of the cradle of modern liberalism in America."

Wagner did not elaborate on his own role in passing law after law.

When he returned to his seat as fifteen hundred Tammany supporters cheered, State Supreme Court Justice Salvatore Cotillo, a fellow Tammany member who had served in Albany with Wagner, reminded the audience that Tammany's legislative legacy was the work of three men: Wagner, Al Smith, and James Foley, Charlie Murphy's son-in-law.[3]

Wagner's uplifting account of Tammany's history no doubt straightened the shoulders of stalwarts who remembered the glory days and who believed, despite an accumulation of evidence, that Tammany still had much to offer New York and the nation—much more than the dirge of a bagpipe, the sentimental lament of a fiddle, and the quiet murmuring of a wake. But their numbers were few, and getting fewer.

. . .

In the eight years that passed between the opening of the new Tammany Hall in 1929 and Robert Wagner's elegiacal tribute to the Tammany of yesteryear in 1937, the catastrophic Depression, changing demographics, population shifts, frayed alliances, and a disastrous split in the Democratic Party had combined to sap Tammany of its power, vitality, and ingenuity. Measured in raw politics, Tammany's influence clearly was in decline in 1937—its power base was shrinking, its leaders were divided, and its old allies were alienated or actively working against it. There was a new power in town, and his name was Fiorello La Guardia, a Yiddish-speaking Italian-Jewish Episcopalian son of immigrants with a rumpled everyman's demeanor and a sharp political intelligence that Tammany could only admire. He captured City Hall in 1933 with just 40 percent of the vote, but during the course of a memorable first term, he created an energetic new coalition of Italians, Jews, mainstream reformers, African-Americans, Puerto Ricans, and others who decided that Tammany did not have the answers to the questions the Great Depression posed. The chubby little man had a ferocious way of speaking and acting—he physically confronted a group of Tammany supporters on Election Day in 1933, calling them "thugs"—which made him unlike any reformer who had ever challenged Tammany. One of his biographers, Thomas Kessner, noted that the multilingual La Guardia "could campaign in five languages and on a hundred ancestral hatreds." Robert Moses, the master planner who owed his career to Tammany's Al Smith, sided with La Guardia and noted that the new mayor was capable of "exploiting racial and religious prejudices" in a way that surpassed the skills of "the bosses he despised and derided."[4]

Tammany had no response to the riddle of Fiorello La Guardia, for he was not in the starchy tradition of the blue-blooded reformers upon whom the organization had feasted in the past. He was, in a sense, a mirror image of Al Smith. He commanded the respect of professionals and experts, and he was a first-rate political showman who understood that urban politics was more than an exercise in bloodless, disinterested, decisionmaking. He read the comics over the radio during a newspaper strike; he showed up at fires and helped with rescues; he refused to move into the mayor's official residence, Gracie Mansion, preferring the comforts of his family's small East Harlem apartment; and he happily posed for pictures in an array of costumes—from his bathrobe (showing his down-home nature) to a grocer's white overalls (to promote a federal food stamp program). Such theatrics would have struck Seth Low, John Purroy Mitchel, and other one-term reform mayors as well beneath their precious dignity.[5]

In 1937, La Guardia was poised to do something no reformer had ever done in New York: win reelection to a second term as mayor. Some Tammany members, desperate to retake control of City Hall and its patronage, held out hope that Robert Wagner would put aside his Senate career and challenge the organization's most effective antagonist in the coming election. Just days after his Independence Day speech, however, Wagner announced that he would remain in the Senate. He and La Guardia had worked together on the federal housing bill. The Tammany senator and the reformist mayor shared a deep-seated belief in the new politics of the New Deal, and neither had an interest in unseating the other.

The prospect of another four years of passionate hostility from City

Hall was almost too much for Tammany to bear. But, even worse, La Guardia was only one of many ailments threatening the organization's very existence.

Tammany's power base, Manhattan, was declining when compared with the outer boroughs. Brooklyn was home to 2.6 million people, some eight hundred thousand more than Manhattan. Politicians respected numbers, so Brooklyn rightly became the center of political calculus in New York. But even smaller sections of the city could lay claim to a piece of Tammany's former power. The Bronx, so recently a bucolic afterthought in municipal affairs, had passed the million mark, thanks to the addition of 125,000 people since 1930. And now, with President Roosevelt's friend Ed Flynn considered the city's most influential Democrat, the Bronx had a firm grip on the ladle of New Deal patronage. Tammany Hall waited in quiet desperation at the far end of the table, hoping for a drop that never seemed to fall.

The Great Depression left Tammany bereft of ideas, although it was hardly alone in that regard, as the Hoover White House demonstrated. But as the city's private sector collapsed, tax revenue dried up, and banks demanded severe cuts in public spending, Tammany's leaders assured each other that this, too, would pass. But it only became worse after Jimmy Walker quit and a new Tammany administration took its place under Mayor O'Brien's equally feckless leadership. City Comptroller Charles Berry, a Tammany man, resisted calls to reduce the city's workforce in the face of burgeoning budget deficits, arguing that "any program which eliminates some city employees from the payroll . . . will of course increase the number of unemployed." Finally, though, as creditors hounded City Hall, Tammany let loose the dogs of austerity, but only after they were trained to follow the scent of teachers, hospital workers, clerks, and other city employees who had few ties to the organization. Reliably green-hued agencies, such as the Fire Department, faced the tamer beast of unpaid furloughs. The firefighters fought back in court and won.[6]

It is a rare political organization that can impose cutbacks in public spending and yet maintain popular support. Tammany was not one of them. Immigrant-stock voters had backed Tammany for many reasons other than a share of the spoils of office, but patronage certainly was critical in the care and feeding of its constituents. When spending cuts were ordered, Tammany made enemies of those who believed that a city job served as a buffer between their families and a breadline.

La Guardia took advantage of the anger, building his own personal political machine by appealing to the new New Yorkers, primarily Jews and Italians who may have voted for Tammany in the past but who embraced an alternative to the status quo at a time when breadlines snaked around city blocks and jobless men were living in shanties on the Great Lawn in Central Park. In New York in 1937, the number of Italian-born residents stood at about 440,000—double the number of Irish-born residents. Even more numerous were the Central and Eastern Europeans who had poured into the city before the immigration restrictions of 1924 effectively cut off the flood tide. Some 442,000 city residents were born in Russia, 237,000 were from Germany, and 238,000 were from Poland. Many of these Central and Eastern Europeans were Jews, and, when combined with native-born coreligionists, New York's Jewish population was nearly two million in the late 1930s.[7]

Jews and Italians had helped to swell the number of registered voters in New York by more than 40 percent in the 1920s, a quiet political revolution that demanded Tammany's attention. The organization's leaders were quick to recognize the growing power of Jewish voters, but they remained slow in reaching out to their fellow Catholics from Italy. When drawing up political boundaries, Tammany strategists often dispersed Italian neighborhoods, diluting their voting strength. It wasn't until 1931 that Tammany had its first Italian-American district leader, Albert Marinelli, and he won election to the post only after two of his allies suggested that the Irish incumbent's health would fare poorly if he remained in office.

Despite Tammany's neglect, Italians eagerly joined the Jews in supporting Tammany candidates such as Al Smith in the late 1920s. But as the Depression took its toll on the city's treasury and morale, the new immigrants and their children looked elsewhere for answers. Their search did not require a trip to the local political clubhouse or a ticket for the district leader's picnic. Families in the 1930s huddled around their radio consoles and heard for themselves the confident tones of their president and the energetic civic sermons of their mayor. These politicians and others spoke directly to the people, without the filter of a party organization. Mass culture erased old boundaries; radio, film, and other forms of entertainment made Tammany's spectacles less spectacular. "New Yorkers today do not sit on the front stoop . . . They do not think of themselves as residents of a particular group of blocks," lamented former congressman Herbert Claiborne Pell in a 1938 letter to Tammany's Jeremiah Mahoney. "This leaves the district captain working on a practically non-existent group."[8]

Events, personalities, demographics, and even some Tammany politicians like Mahoney were draining the organization of its vaunted power. In the years to come, journalists and historians would credit Tammany's decline in the 1930s to the New Deal, which replaced the smoke-filled clubhouse with professional bureaucrats, and to La Guardia, who sprayed Tammany with multilingual invective in the organization's old neighborhoods. What's more, Roosevelt put Flynn and La Guardia—not Tammany's bosses—in charge of federal funds for the massive public-works projects of the Depression era: the ambitious Triborough Bridge, one of the biggest projects of the 1930s; a new central post office in Flynn's Bronx; a new courthouse in Jamaica, Queens; a new ferry terminal on Ellis Island. Federal money built a new highway on Manhattan's East Side and expanded an airport in Queens. Tammany didn't get a piece of that action, either. The highway would be named in honor of Roosevelt; the airport bore La Guardia's name.

Roosevelt and La Guardia certainly were important factors in Tammany's fall from power in the 1930s. But they were not the only reasons for the organization's decline—after all, Tammany had managed to survive the hostility of presidents and mayors in the past. It faltered this time because of larger changes in the city's population and culture, because of a succession of weak leaders, and because Ed Flynn and Jeremiah Mahoney—both of them protégés of Charlie Murphy—decided that Tammany's mission was finished.

. . .

It began with Franklin Roosevelt's decision to run a third-party Democrat in the 1933 New York City mayoral campaign rather than support the incompetent leadership of Tammany Mayor John O'Brien, who was so slavish to the organization that when he was asked about the identity of his new police commissioner, he replied, "I don't know. They haven't told me yet." O'Brien was a decent man but an embarrassment, not the man to lead the city during the hardest of hard times. Roosevelt decided he had to go.[9]

The White House dispatched the trusty Flynn and the chairman of the Democratic National Committee, James Farley, to New York to challenge Tammany with an entity called the Recovery Party, whose candidate was Flynn's friend and the former acting mayor, Joseph McKee. The resulting split between Tammany's O'Brien and the Recovery Party's McKee led to La Guardia's election as a Republican. For Tammany, La Guardia's triumph was not just a loss but a humiliation: O'Brien mustered just 27 percent of the vote (compared with the 63 percent he had won in the special election of 1932) and finished dead last. Many embittered Tammany members blamed Roosevelt and Flynn for the electoral catastrophe, accusing both of betraying their party and turning over the city to the enemy.

Many, but not all. More realistic Tammany members recognized the odor of rot in their new building. They argued that Tammany had lost its way since the glory days of the 1920s, that it had failed to adapt to the unprecedented circumstances of the Depression and the city's new demographics. A longtime Tammany member, James Hoey—the Al Smith supporter who had forwarded information to the Roosevelt campaign in 1932—shocked the city's political order when he announced in late 1933 that the time had come for a "complete reorganization" of Tammany "under new leadership." Otherwise, he warned, "a new Democratic organization . . . will have to be set up in this city"—no idle threat after the Recovery Party campaign split the party. Hoey spoke with no small authority, for not only were his Tammany credentials impeccable but the Roosevelt administration had just appointed him to the key patronage post of collector of internal revenue for Lower Manhattan—a reward for his work on FDR's behalf during the 1932 campaign. Tammany's Executive Committee took the hint, firing its bungling leader, John Curry, and replacing him with James J. Dooling, a dapper forty-one-year-old described by Jeremiah Mahoney as "a nice boy with practically no ability."[10]

Dooling took over the organization at a time when its power was diminished and its influence profound. There was no contradiction between these two developments—indeed, the organization's loss of power was partly the result of its broad influence. Tammany no longer had a monopoly on stagecraft, organization, ethnic appeals, and populist rhetoric, for those trusty tools had been adapted for use by the most skillful reformer Tammany had ever faced, La Guardia. Under the mayor's leadership, the city's reformers finally realized how wrong they were to take their cues from the vaunted British writer James Bryce, who regarded American urban politics as the last refuge of the unschooled and unworthy. Tammany had long argued that voters—even those who spoke little or no English, even those unfamiliar with the political traditions of the Pilgrim fathers—were capable of determining and acting in their own best interests. In La Guardia, reformers finally had a candidate who could match Tammany's belief that voters need not take dictation from those who thought they knew best. The mayor, unlike so many of those who challenged Tammany in the past, reveled in his image as a political street-fighter: "I can out-demagogue any candidate I have met yet," he said. He was right. The reform movement finally had found a demagogue of their own.[11]

Tammany's influence was more than a matter of style and speech, more than gestures and symbols. Its leaders during the first quarter of the twentieth century had stripped the Progressive movement of its obsession with virtue and character, creating a model for New Deal reforms that fed the hungry because they were hungry, not because they were deemed worthy of assistance. No wonder, then, that Franklin Roosevelt insisted that the New Deal was a national version of the social-welfare measures signed into law in New York by Tammany's Al Smith in the 1920s.[12]

And that made the behavior of Smith, Senator Royal Copeland, and new Tammany boss James Dooling all the more puzzling in the critical year of 1937. Not long after Roosevelt's inauguration in 1933, when he condemned the "incompetence" of the nation's "money-changers"—rhetoric few would have expected to hear from State Senator Franklin Roosevelt in 1911—Smith turned against him with a bitterness that suggested more than mere politics was involved. Robert Wagner, watching from afar as his onetime "Tammany Twin" aligned with the right-wing Liberty League, privately complained that Smith had fallen under the influence of rich business leaders now that he was living among them on Fifth Avenue, across from Central Park. After publicly supporting Republican Alf Landon's doomed campaign against FDR in 1936, Smith was determined to embarrass the president in his own state in the 1937 mayoral race. He persuaded Tammany boss Dooling to back Copeland, whose loathing of Roosevelt matched Smith's, as the Democratic mayoral candidate against La Guardia. Dooling was among those who blamed Roosevelt for splitting the party and allowing La Guardia to win in 1933. He eagerly followed Smith's advice and announced his support for Copeland.

Tammany, however, no longer had the power to dictate the Democratic Party's choice for citywide office. Democrats who supported Roosevelt turned, tellingly, to another Tammany man, Jeremiah Mahoney, to rally behind President Roosevelt and the New Deal. Mahoney, widely admired in the city's Jewish community for attempting to organize a boycott of the 1936 Olympics in Nazi Germany, entered the mayoral race with relish. Tammany had fallen on hard times, he believed, and needed new leadership. "I would like to see a return to the days when Mr. Murphy was alive," Mahoney later told Claiborne Pell. "Then we did things more intelligently." Days after Mahoney entered the race, James Dooling died of apoplexy at the age of forty-four, and Tammany was leaderless again.[13]

The mayoral primary election of 1937 was a pivotal moment in Tammany's history, for it became a referendum not only on the New Deal but also on the new Democratic Party that Tammany itself had done so much to bring about. Royal Copeland campaigned as the voice of reaction, articulating the personal bitterness of his most prominent supporter, Al Smith. Mahoney campaigned as an avid New Dealer and an unabashed supporter of Franklin Roosevelt. "I will work in harmony with this administration because I am in sympathy with its objectives," he declared. During a rally at a Jewish senior citizens' home in Brooklyn, a supporter introduced Mahoney as "a friend of the greatest president of the United States." Mahoney linked arms with his running mates and danced while a cantor performed a song written in the candidate's honor. That was Tammany politics. Royal Copeland, the endorsed candidate of Tammany Hall, also entered the Republican primary to challenge La Guardia. He promised to lower taxes.[14]

Of the many humiliations heaped upon Tammany in Depression-era New York, none was as embarrassing as the mayoral primary of 1937, although its significance has been lost to history. Tammany's Jeremiah Mahoney, running explicitly against the "inept, selfish, and false" leaders of his own organization and as a proud New Dealer, defeated Tammany's Copeland in a landslide. Years later, Mahoney still relished the beating he delivered to the organization that had, in another era, under other leadership, provided him with his start in politics. "I had every reactionary in the Democratic Party in New York against me, and I beat Tammany Hall and the whole gang by one hundred and eighty-five thousand," he recalled with obvious pleasure.[15]

Mahoney went on to lose the general election to Fiorello La Guardia in a battle of two candidates who saw themselves as New Dealers. Ideologically, there was not a great deal of difference between Mahoney, product of Tammany Hall, and the organization's most effective foe, a man Mahoney later considered a friend. La Guardia's reelection was a political milestone for two reasons—first, he became the first anti-Tammany reform mayor to win a second term, and, second, the Tammany member who opposed him had no substantive argument to make against him. Mahoney tried, halfheartedly, to make hay of La Guardia's endorsement by the Communist Party. It went nowhere. La Guardia won, garnering 1.3 million votes to Mahoney's 889,000.

The Mahoney candidacy of 1937, a widely forgotten episode in the narrative of La Guardia's triumph of reform, showed that the mayor was hardly Tammany's only powerful antagonist. Tammany members themselves rebelled against Al Smith's bitterness and Copeland's turn to the right. District leaders, block captains, and rank-and-file members abandoned Copeland for Mahoney, whose campaign manager was another one of Charles Murphy's confidants, James Gerard, a distinguished former diplomat and failed U.S. Senate candidate in 1914. Like Mahoney, they saw the New Deal as the culmination of values and policies they had supported in New York for decades. They showed that Tammany still stood for progressive politics, even if its leaders no longer did.

The mayor himself must have noticed. Two years after winning reelection, the La Guardia administration became engulfed in a police corruption scandal, leading to the indictment of a sergeant and ten lieutenants for their involvement with a crooked bail-bond operation. It was just the sort of scandal that so many had associated with the worst elements of Tammany, and not without reason.

The mayor, whose zest for shooting Tammany's wounded was limitless, sought the services of a respected independent prosecutor to handle the officers' case. With the press watching closely, La Guardia won great praise when he chose a Tammany district leader to head the investigation—Jeremiah Mahoney.

And so a celebrated reformer picked a Tammany ward-heeler to investigate police corruption. New York politics was a complicated business, indeed.

. . .

Barely more than a decade had passed since Governor Franklin Roosevelt opened the new headquarters of the Tammany Society in the presence of the Empire State's most-powerful and best-known political leaders. By the early 1940s, as ward politics gave way to the urgent task of liberating the conquered nations of Europe and Asia, the Tammany building took on the musty aura of a neglected shrine. Where so recently men and women of divergent backgrounds had streamed into Tammany's ballroom for Election Night, now there was no great rush, no great excitement, as each election cycle brought dismal returns. La Guardia would never be dislodged, and as long as he was mayor, there would be no patronage from the city. More and more jobs required civil-service tests. Another avowed enemy, Robert Moses, was in charge of parks and public works, and he was no more likely than the mayor to consider Tammany's needs. The total of foreign-born New Yorkers plummeted to 28 percent in 1940—its lowest level, in terms of percentage, since the early nineteenth century, and far lower than when foreign-born residents made up more than half the city's population after the great surge following the Irish Famine. Neighborhood politics that had been Tammany's specialty seemed petty and small as Americans followed news of great battles in faraway places, with so many households wondering whether a loved one had made it through the day alive.

The iconoclastic Jeremiah Mahoney, his reputation only enhanced after his failed mayoral campaign, decided that only drastic action could save the remnants of what once was the preeminent Democratic organization in the nation. Mahoney proposed that Tammany Hall assume a new identity shorn of its colorful, controversial, and historic past. The organization, he said, should move out of Tammany Hall, the physical building owned by the technically separate Tammany Society, and reconstitute itself simply as the New York County Democratic Committee, purging all references to Tammany Hall. Members resisted, but soon the decision was made for them. The Tammany Society, the Hall's landlords, sold the building in 1943 to the International Ladies' Garment Workers' Union—an implacable Tammany foe and ally of the new American Labor Party, created to attract a new breed of independent-minded leftist voters.

Tammany Hall, the political organization, cleared out of Tammany Hall, the building, and moved uptown to the fifth floor of a building on Madison Avenue. The days of ballrooms filled with cheering men and women, of Election Night visits from mayors and governors and senators, of closed-door meetings attended by loyal and discreet block captains—those days were gone. The regalia, the banners, and the flags were put away. Those who had business with the top Democratic leaders of Manhattan found few reminders of the past amid the workaday desks and file cabinets and typewriters in the party's new headquarters. Indeed, the word *Tammany* was nowhere to be found. The door leading to the office was labeled *Democratic County Committee of New York County.*

Inside, there was just one glimpse of glory decorating the walls: a fine oil painting of Charles Francis Murphy.

. . .

So the Hall was gone. There would be a revival, even the restoration of the Tammany name, after La Guardia and Roosevelt were dead and the torch of leadership was passed to Carmine De Sapio, who in 1949 was named the organization's first non-Irish boss since Tweed. De Sapio's rise was yet another sign of the times, for the glory days of Gaelic Gotham were coming to an end, even as Irish immigrant William O'Dwyer captured City Hall in 1945 after La Guardia's three memorable terms. Fewer than one in ten New Yorkers was Irish in the 1940s. The descendants of the Emerald Isle's lost generations no longer lived on Oliver Street, where Al Smith came of age, or in the Bowery of Big Tim Sullivan, or in Hell's Kitchen, where the McManus Club still opened its doors to those with a favor to ask or a problem to solve. Sprawling new highways were about to lead to a new promised land of picket fences and backyards, far from the reach of a block captain or a district leader. Prosperity, the dearth of new immigrants to assimilate, and the continued growth of government programs left Tammany without a mission. Indeed, its mission had been accomplished: There were fewer people in the gutter and fewer people who saw themselves as part of an urban "rabble," as Al Smith described himself before he resettled uptown, far away from the Fulton Fish Market, the pushcarts, and the crowded tenements of his youth.

But even as its power waned in the 1940s, Tammany's influence was so ingrained that few noticed just how much it remained a vital part of American politics. Men and women who came of age at the height of Tammany's golden age, who saw its rough-hewn leaders not as proof of the public's ignorance but as legitimate voices of the city's streets, occupied places of local and national influence. Some were Tammany members, others worked cooperatively with Tammany figures, putting aside their own doubts and the contempt of their purer contemporaries. Frances Perkins, who wished she had been able to drink a beer with Big Tim Sullivan, presided over the Labor Department as the nation's first woman cabinet member. Samuel Rosenman, lent to Franklin Roosevelt's gubernatorial campaign in 1928 as a favor from Al Smith, continued to write the president's speeches and serve as one of his chief advisers. Tammany member Herbert Lehman served as governor of New York until 1942 and later served as a U.S. senator. Robert Wagner remained a lion of the Senate until he retired in 1948, and his law partner, Jeremiah Mahoney, continued to remain active in New York politics, happy to tell all who would listen that Charlie Murphy's Tammany had been at the forefront of American liberalism.

And then there was Ed Flynn, boss of the Bronx—unapologetic machine politician, patronage dispenser, favor-granter, and all-round political fixer. True, he was not a Tammany member, and indeed had contributed mightily to its decline in the 1930s, but even casual observers saw in Ed Flynn the spirit of Tammany's Charlie Murphy. "Nowadays, people who have known both men see a reflection of Murphy in almost everything Flynn does, even in the way he shakes hands," wrote Richard H. Rovere in *The New Yorker* in 1945.[16]

Flynn ran the Democratic National Committee for three years, resigning in 1943 in preparation for his appointment as Roosevelt's personal representative to Australia. But he withdrew his name amid a torrent of criticism for his connections to Tammany Hall and for a minor controversy over the installation of paving blocks at his vacation home in upstate Putnam County. (The blocks, which cost less than $50, were installed by city workers, which Flynn said he knew nothing about. He reimbursed the city for the expense.) "Mr. Flynn is a Tammany man," asserted the *Chicago Daily News* as it campaigned to block Flynn's posting to Australia. The White House was inundated with letters of protest, typical of which was one from Illinois that referred to "political scum like this fellow Flynn." Another writer saw Flynn's nomination as part of the Roosevelt administration's "appeasement of the Catholic Church."[17]

FDR never came to his friend's defense, but Flynn remained an important informal adviser to the Roosevelt White House, maintaining extensive correspondence about patronage and political intelligence with the president, his wife, and other officials. When he and his wife, Helen, visited the White House in the spring of 1944, he was shocked to find the president tired, disengaged, and irritable. After that visit, Flynn concluded that Roosevelt ought to forgo a fourth term. "I felt that he would never survive," Flynn later wrote. He asked Eleanor Roosevelt to do her best to persuade her husband to stand down. Not long afterward, Flynn was summoned to the White House again—not to plan a retirement party but to advise Roosevelt on the suddenly urgent question of the vice presidency.[18]

Throughout the summer of 1944, leading to the Democratic National Convention in Chicago, Flynn was absorbed in the question of Roosevelt's running mate—and, in his view, his inevitable successor. He decided, based on conversations with his fellow political professionals (a category that did not include most New Dealers), that Henry Wallace's continued presence on the ticket would cost Roosevelt votes and possibly the election. Flynn concluded that the increasingly leftist Wallace had become "the candidate of the radicals of the country."[19]

For Irish political professionals like Flynn, radicals of any stripe invariably were the sort of dreamers whose battles never ended well. Radicals, in Flynn's view, were worse than dangerous. They were amateurs. Flynn knew no more damning epithet.

Ed Flynn joined with Democratic National Committee chair Robert Hannegan, a Jesuit-trained lawyer from Missouri, Mayor Ed Kelly of Chicago, and several other professional politicians to stage an internal coup that overthrew Wallace as Roosevelt's running mate, replacing him with the more dependable, more professional Harry Truman, a poker-playing, straight-talking, bourbon-drinking two-term senator from Missouri. Truman rose from obscurity under the patronage of the Irish machine of Kansas City, led by Thomas Pendergast, convicted in 1939 of income-tax evasion. Truman was neither Irish nor Catholic, but, like Franklin Roosevelt, he came of age in a political culture that was both. He was not high on the list of potential nominees as Wallace's star faded in the run-up to the convention, but as Roosevelt delivered mixed signals about Wallace, the bosses took charge. For Flynn and his allies, the choice was clear. "If you went down the list as we did, you'd have seen that it had to be Truman," he said.[20]

So one of the twentieth century's most momentous political maneuvers, the selection of Franklin Roosevelt's successor, took place under the watchful eye of Charlie Murphy's man in the Bronx, Ed Flynn. Tammany's influence remained extraordinary, even in these, its dying days.

. . .

Al Smith spent his final years amid the polished splendor of Fifth Avenue, lonely and still picking at the wounds of 1928 and 1932. His friend Robert Moses made him a night watchman for the fine zoo he had built in Central Park, just across from Smith's apartment. The old warrior had his own key to the zoo, and his neighbors would tell stories of seeing Smith pass by at night on his way to see his friends behind bars. They never let him down, they never questioned his Americanism, they never asked about the pope. They tolerated his cigar smoke, his accent, the gold in his teeth. One of his favorite animals was a tiger—and, yes, he was called "Tammany." How could it have been otherwise? When Smith ambled across the street during regular hours and watched the children of New York gaze at the exotic beasts, he encouraged them to yell "La Guardia" at Tammany. The children were puzzled; the tiger was not. On cue, he bared his teeth. They were the only teeth Tammany had left.[21]

Nostalgia gave way to melancholy when Smith's wife, Katie, died in May 1944, a couple of days short of their forty-fourth wedding anniversary. A telegram from the White House arrived within hours. "I want you to know that I am thinking of you in your great loss and wish it were in my power to do something to lighten a grief so overwhelming," President Roosevelt wrote. The years, the rivalries, and the bitterness receded with a single gesture of kindness. Smith replied weeks later with a "Dear Frank" letter, assuring him that he was in "good shape." But he was not. He was taken to St. Vincent's Hospital in early August, suffering from heart and lung ailments. His condition became critical in early October. A dozen red roses arrived at his bedside, with notes from both Franklin and Eleanor Roosevelt. He died hours later, on October 4, 1944, at the age of seventy. The president of the United States released a statement calling Alfred Emanuel Smith a "hero."[22]

The organization that nurtured Smith outlived him, but not for long. In one of Ed Flynn's last triumphs before his own death in 1953, he helped arrange Tammany support for the mayoral candidacy of Robert F. Wagner Jr., who became mayor just a few years after the death of his father, the senator. The younger Wagner was the last mayor to win office with Tammany's approval, although that historic milestone came with an asterisk. With impeccable political instincts, Wagner ran for his third and final term as mayor in 1961 as the antimachine, antiboss, anti-Tammany candidate, a breathtaking piece of political chutzpah—and it worked. His patron, Carmine De Sapio, was defeated in a race for party district leader in Greenwich Village, meaning that he no longer had a seat in the party's Executive Committee. No boss had ever suffered such an ignominious defeat. He tried again, and again, and both times he lost to a young, lanky, reform-minded lawyer named Edward I. Koch. A new leader, Edward Costikyan, became head of the Democratic Party in Manhattan. He was not a member of Tammany.

The Hall was well and truly gone.

And so it died. With it, for better or for worse, perished a culture of extreme local politics, of a block-by-block, building-by-building organization, of methods that were irregular—as Frances Perkins so delicately put it—but responsive all the same. The Irish came to New York believing that the rules of politics were written to keep them powerless, as they had been in Ireland. When they saw the same class in New York observing the same rules, speaking the words of reform that sounded more like demands to conform, they saw no reason to turn their backs on politicians who recognized their opportunities and seized them, no reason to stand in judgment of rogues like Jimmy Walker and George Washington Plunkitt.

Once installed in power, the Irish in New York looked to government as a friend in need, a provider of last (or perhaps first) resort, as an advocate in a system constructed by others but now in their hands. They saw how power worked in Ireland. They knew that without power they might be left to starve in the name of abstract ideology. When they attained power in New York, they knew what to do with it—they made certain that they would not starve again, and that those who might allow it would be denied the power to do so.

It was an imperfect institution, Tammany, often egregiously so. Its alliances with gangsters and other crooked operators deserves history's rebuke. But after it was done and the Irish scattered to the suburbs, corruption and crooked deals did not disappear from municipal government. Mayors and lesser officials still paid attention to the needs of banking, real estate, and other interests, just as surely as Charles Murphy took care to look after the fortunes of the businessmen who befriended him over dinner at Delmonico's or who bought a fistful of tickets to John Ahearn's clambakes.

But the machine's absence left a void in New York, still a city of immigrants, and now, in the twenty-first century, many of these new-comers live in shadows that Tammany would have found unacceptable. Tens of thousands of immigrants without proper papers, without citizenship, unable to vote? Tammany's ward heelers would have seen them not as outcasts but as potential allies—and voters—and would have acted accordingly.

Gone, too, is the sense of participation, the connection among a block, an apartment house, a district, and those who represent them. Tammany provided spectacle, and while some of it may have been a screen for unsavory dealmaking, the chowders and the cruises and the festivals made Tammany's immigrant-stock constituents feel like New Yorkers—and Americans.

·   ·   ·

On a midwinter evening in early 1973, twenty members of the Anawanda Club trudged up two flights of well-worn stairs to spend one last night in Charlie Murphy's old political clubhouse. Some came with extra cash, because the club was auctioning off its last few possessions, with proceeds to be split among the club's sixty-three remaining members.[23]

The old men in the crowd spoke of other days, when the club sponsored an annual beefsteak dinner and the local politicians stopped by to shake hands and chew the political fat. It was a different neighborhood now, better in many ways. The old Gas House District had given way to dozens of low-rise brick apartment buildings put up in the 1940s to house World War II veterans and their families. They were decent people, hardworking and ambitious. But they didn't have the same connection to the neighborhood, the old men complained. The schoolteacher with a two-bedroom apartment in Stuyvesant Town, or the cop with the nice three-bedroom deal in Peter Cooper Village—as the apartment complexes were called—knew nothing about the old days, about the silent figure who took care of his voters under a gas lamp on Second Avenue. They saw no reason to come out on cold nights to talk politics in a second-floor clubhouse above a gin mill.

One of the few younger people in the crowd walked away with the club's poker chips for a bid of $2. An old-timer won a small bidding war for the club's grandfather clock. A minor city official paid $200, the highest amount bid on any object, for the rights to a six-foot portrait of Charles Francis Murphy.

What's the use? one of the old-timers said. He was answering a visitor's question—Why not keep the club going? Nobody cared anymore. Who, besides the holdouts in the room, knew that grand old Tammany Hall was just a few blocks to the south, unnoticed and forgotten? It was a new era. Time to move on.

As the auction ran out of steam, the oldtimers cast sideways glances when an eager young man plunked down ten bucks and said he wanted one of the club's pool tables. Then he put down a fiver and claimed the club's heavy old safe.

He then realized his problem: There was no way he was getting the table and the safe down those stairs. Not by himself.

The old ones knew what would happen next: He'd ask for help. And he'd get it.

No questions asked.

ACKNOWLEDGMENTS

This book is the outgrowth of my doctoral research at Rutgers University. It was my pleasure and honor to work with four distinguished scholars and writers, John Whiteclay Chambers II, my dissertation director, Warren Kimball, David Greenberg, and Mark Edward Lender. My colleagues at Kean University were tremendously supportive. Thanks to Dr. Dawood Farahi, Kean's president, Audrey Kelly, Matt Caruso, Erin Alghandoor, Joey Moran, Karen Harris, and the entire History Department, especially Christopher Bellitto.

There surely is a special place in the afterlife reserved for those who staff archives and special collections. My thanks to all who assisted me, especially Brendan Dolan at the Archives of Irish America at New York University's Glucksman Ireland House, Alan Delozier at Seton Hall University's Monsignor Field Archives and Special Collections Center, Scott Taylor at Georgetown University Library, and the staffs of the New York Public Library, the New York Historical Society, the Columbia University Rare Book and Manuscript Library, the Franklin D. Roosevelt Library, the New York State Library and Archives, the Archives of the Archdiocese of New York, the American Irish Historical Society, the Library of Congress, and the National Library of Ireland.

I am indebted to historians and writers who have tried to complicate and broaden our understanding of Tammany Hall and of Irish-American politics, including J. Joseph Huthmacher, John Buenker, Nancy Joan Weiss, Kenneth Ackerman, Leo Hershkowitz, Edward Levine, Kerby Miller, Francis Barry, Richard Welch, Mary C. Kelly, Thomas Fleming, and Jay Dolan. A word of gratitude, too, for the late Daniel Patrick Moynihan, with whom I had several memorable conversations about Tammany history during the 1990s.

My debt to Peter Quinn is beyond words. Thanks, too, to Arthur Carter and Peter Kaplan for their friendship.

My editor, Katie Adams, has an extraordinary eye and remarkable patience. My thanks to Bob Weil, publishing director of Liveright, for his confidence and support. I'm grateful to copyeditor Kathleen Brandes, and to the publicity and marketing staff at W. W. Norton.

My agent, John Wright, could not be a better friend.

My wife, Eileen Duggan, and our children, Kate and Conor, now know more about Tammany Hall than they ever thought possible. Talk about patience!

NOTES

INTRODUCTION

1. *New York Times,* July 5, 1929.
2. Nathan Glazer and Daniel Patrick Moynihan, *Beyond the Melting Pot: The Negroes, Puerto Ricans, Jews, Italians, and Irish of New York City* (Cambridge, MA: MIT Press, 1970), p. 224.
3. William L. Riordon, *Plunkitt of Tammany Hall: A Series of Very Plain Talks on Very Practical Politics* (New York: Signet, 1995), pp. 25–26.
4. Lincoln Steffens, *The Shame of the Cities* (New York: Hill & Wang, 1957), p. 201.
5. *The Outlook,* February 21, 1903.
6. See, among others, Noel Ignatiev, *How the Irish Became White* (New York: Routledge, 1995); *Freeman's Journal and Catholic Register,* July 8, 1854.
7. *New York Times,* October 24, 1906.
8. Undated broadside, New-York Historical Society Broadside Collection.
9. Cecil Woodham-Smith, *The Great Hunger* (London: H. Hamilton, 1962), p. 156; *Littell's Living Age,* vol. 171, No. 2211 (November 6, 1886).
10. The figure comes from Robert James Scally, *The End of Hidden Ireland: Rebellion, Famine, and Emigration* (New York: Oxford University Press, 1995), p. 13.
11. See Sterling Stuckey, *Slave Culture: Nationalist Theory and the Foundations of Black America* (Oxford: Oxford University Press, 1987); Deborah Gray White, *Ar'n't I a Woman? Female Slaves in the Plantation South* (New York: W. W. Norton, 1999); John Thornton, *Africa and Africans in the Making of the Atlantic World, 1400–1800* (Cambridge: Cambridge University Press, 1998).
12. John Byrne to William Bourke Cockran, October 20, 1898, William Bourke Cockran Papers, Box 1, New York Public Library. (Cockran's name appears in some sources as Cochran, perhaps because the latter is a more familiar spelling.) Ironically, it was Richard Croker, the Irish immigrant head of Tammany,

who blocked the appointment of Byrne's friend, a judge named Daly. See un-dated memo in Edwin Kilroe Papers, Box 20, Columbia University Special Col-lections. Cockran broke with Croker over the Daly nonappointment.

13. Allen Nevins and Milton Halsey Thomas, eds., *The Diaries of George Templeton Strong*, vol. 1 (New York: Macmillan, 1952), p. 348.

14. Scally, *The End of Hidden Ireland*, p. 14.

One: "TAMMANY HALL BELONGS TO US"

1. Descriptions of the events in Tammany Hall on April 24, 1817, can be found in the *New York Evening Post*, April 25 and 26, 1817.

2. Fergus O'Ferrall, *Catholic Emancipation: Daniel O'Connell and the Birth of Irish Democracy, 1820–30* (Dublin: Gill and Macmillan, 1985), p. 190.

3. Drawn from a firsthand account published anonymously in the *New York Eve-ning Post*, April 26, 1817.

4. Lyman H. Butterfield, ed., *Adams Family Correspondence*, vol. II (Cambridge: Harvard University Press, 1963), pp. 229–30.

5. Tammany Hall's early years are covered in Oliver E. Allen, *The Tiger: The Rise and Fall of Tammany Hall* (Reading, MA: Addison-Wesley, 1993); Jerome Mushkat, *Tammany: The Evolution of a Political Machine, 1789–1865* (Syracuse, NY: Syracuse University Press, 1971); Gustavus Myers, *The History of Tam-many Hall* (Ithaca, NY: Cornell University Press, 1991; reprint of 1901 edition); and M. A. Werner, *Tammany Hall* (New York: Greenwood Press, 1968).

6. Werner, *Tammany Hall*, p. 10.

7. Gustavus Myers, *The History of Tammany Hall*, p. 23. (Myers, a noted journalist and socialist activist, published the book himself because he could not find a publisher. A revised edition was published by Boni and Liveright in 1917.)

8. *Examiner*, April 23, 1814; Myers, *The History of Tammany Hall*, p. 69.

9. *New York Evening Post*, November 21, 1827; Thomas Addis Emmet, *A Memoir of Thomas Addis and Robert Emmet* (New York: Emmet Press, 1905), p. 490.

10. Werner, *Tammany Hall*, p. 46.

11. A receipt for the contribution from New York is contained in a letter from O'Connell's Catholic Association to James McNevin, January 30, 1829, Daniel O'Connell Papers, MS 5242, National Library of Ireland. The recipient most likely was William James MacNeven.

12. *United States Catholic Miscellany*, April 11, 1829.

Two: MASS POLITICS

1. Robert Kee, *Ireland: A History* (London: Fakenham Press, 1980), p. 75.

2. Joseph P. Tumulty, *Woodrow Wilson as I Know Him* (New York: Doubleday, 1921), p. 2.

3. Michael MacDonagh, *The Life of Daniel O'Connell* (London: Cassell and Com-pany, 1903), p. 16.

4. O'Ferrall, *Catholic Emancipation*, p. 37.

5. Angus Macintyre, *The Liberator: Daniel O'Connell and the Irish Party 1830–1847* (London: Hamish Hamilton, 1965), p. 7.

6. Catholics in mainland Britain did not have the vote at this time. The number

of freeholders is from R. F. Foster, *Modern Ireland, 1600–1972* (New York: Penguin, 1989), p. 302.

7. Denis Gwynn, *Daniel O'Connell* (Cork, Ireland: Cork University Press, 1947), p. 170.

8. *Blackwood's Magazine*, May 1827, p. 575.

9. Richard Warner, *Catholic Emancipation, Incompatible With The Safety Of the Established Religion, Liberty, Laws and Protestant Succession of the British Empire* (London: C. J. G. & F. Rivington, 1829).

10. Irene Whelan, *The Bible War in Ireland: The 'Second Reformation' and the Polarization of Protestant-Catholic Relations, 1800–1840* (Madison, WI: University of Wisconsin Press, 2005), p. 85.

11. Thomas Wyse, *Historical Sketch of the Late Catholic Association of Ireland*, vol. 1 (London: A. J. Valpy, 1829), p. 234.

12. Wyse, *Historical Sketch*, vol. 1, pp. 235, 267.

13. Petition found in Thomas Wyse Papers, MS 15,024, National Library of Ireland, Dublin.

14. R. Ott to Winston Barron, undated; Pat Powers to Wyse, May 17, 1826; John Power to Wyse, April 18, 1826, Thomas Wyse Papers, MS 15,023, National Library of Ireland.

15. See John Magin's schedule in Thomas Wyse Papers, MS 15,028, National Library of Ireland.

16. See O'Ferrall, *Catholic Emancipation*, pp. 130–33.

17. *Dublin Evening Post*, July 1, 1826; Thomas Bartlett, *The Fall and Rise of the Irish Nation* (Dublin: Rowman and Littlefield, 1992), p. 343.

18. See O'Connell Papers, Records of the Catholic Association, National Library of Ireland: Minutes of the Relief Committee, January 31, 1827, MS 5242; C. M. Murphy to O'Connell, December 20, 1828, MS 5242; Richard Walsh to Edward Dwyer, January 29, 1828, MS 5243; Minutes of the Relief Committee, November 8, 1828, MS 5243; Hayden to Thomas Wyse, August 4, 1826, Thomas Wyse Papers, MS 15,023, National Library of Ireland.

19. *Dublin Evening Post*, July 1, 1828.

20. *Irish Shield*, May 5, 1829.

21. Figures from Foster, *Modern Ireland*, p. 302. The number of freeholders was increased to just over sixty thousand after the franchise was expanded in 1832; *Dublin Evening Post*, July 6, 1826.

22. *Dublin Evening Post*, September 6, 1830; O'Ferrall, *Catholic Emancipation*, p. 215.

23. John Hughes to James Harper, May 17, 1844, reprinted in Lawrence Kehoe, ed., *Complete Works of the Most Rev. John Hughes, DD* (New York: Lawrence Kehoe, 1866), vol. 1, p. 451.

24. The Whitman reference can be found in Tyler Anbinder, *Five Points: The Nineteenth Century New York Neighborhood That Invented Tap Dance, Stole Elections, and Became the World's Most Notorious Slum* (New York: Free Press, 2001), p. 185. For the Hone reference, see Philip Hone, *The Diary of Philip Hone* (New York: Dodd, Mead, 1889), vol. 1, p. 659. For the Brownson quote, see Vincent Peter Lannie, "Profile of an Immigrant Bishop: The Early Career of John Hughes," *Pennsylvania History*, vol. 32, no. 4 (October 1965), p. 378.

25. Hughes speech at Carroll Hall, March 30, 1841, published in Kehoe, *Complete Works*, p. 256.
26. Richard Shaw, *Dagger John: The Unquiet Life and Times of Archbishop John Hughes of New York* (New York: Paulist Press, 1977), pp. 141–42.
27. Shaw, *Dagger John*, p. 139.
28. Hughes to Seward, August 29, 1840, Hughes Papers, Box 4 (Reel 2), Archives of the Archdiocese of New York, Yonkers, NY.
29. Hughes address at Carroll Hall, October 29, 1841, in Kehoe, *Complete Works*, vol. 1, p. 272.
30. Glazer and Moynihan, *Beyond the Melting Pot*, p. 227; Hughes to Harper, May 17, 1844, published in Kehoe, *Complete Works*, vol. 1, p. 462.
31. Hughes to Patrick Collins of the Public School Society, September 15, 1840, Minutes of the Board of Trustees of the Public School Society, New-York Historical Society.
32. Hughes to unknown recipient (addressed as "Right Rev. and Dear Brother in Christ"), August 27, 1840, Hughes Papers, Box 4, Archives of the Archdiocese of New York.
33. Kehoe, *Complete Works*, vol. 1, pp. 100, 54, and 73. For the number of financiers on the PSS board, see Martin L. Meenagh, "Archbishop John Hughes and the New York Schools Controversy of 1840–43," *American Nineteenth Century History*, vol. 5, no. 1 (Spring 2004), p. 49.
34. Seward to Hughes, September 11, 1840, Hughes papers, Box 4 (Reel 2), Archives of the Archdiocese of New York.
35. John Hassard, *The Life of John Hughes: First Archbishop of New York* (New York: Arno Press, 1969), p. 234.
36. Kehoe, *Complete Works*, vol. 1, pp. 136, 134.
37. Shaw, *Dagger John*, pp. 163, 151–52.
38. Kehoe, *Complete Works*, vol. 1, pp. 143–83.
39. *U.S. Catholic Miscellany*, November 14, 1840; *New York Observer*, November 7, 1840.
40. Shaw, *Dagger John*, p. 159; Lee Benson, *The Concept of Jacksonian Democracy: New York as a Test Case* (Princeton, NJ: Princeton University Press, 1961), p. 188.
41. *Freeman's Journal*, April 17, 1841.
42. Kehoe, *Complete Works*, vol. 1, pp. 280–81.
43. Sean Wilentz, *Chants Democratic: New York City and the Rise of the American Working Class, 1788–1850* (New York: Oxford University Press, 2004), p. 330.
44. Hughes to Seward, March 22, 1842, Box 4 (Reel 3), Archives of the Archdiocese of New York.
45. Diane Ravitch, *The Great School Wars: A History of the New York City Public Schools* (Baltimore: Johns Hopkins University Press, 2000).
46. See *Freeman's Journal*, April 9 and May 7, 1842.
47. Anbinder, *Five Points*, p. 155.
48. John Hughes, *The Catholic Chapter in the History of the United States: A Lecture*, quoted in Walter G. Sharrow, "John Hughes and a Catholic Response to Slavery in Antebellum America," *The Journal of Negro History*, vol. 57, no. 3 (July 1972), p. 261.
49. *Freeman's Journal*, August 7, 1841.

50. Kehoe, *Complete Works*, vol. 1, pp. 269, 276.
51. Figures from Robert Ernst, *Immigrant Life in New York City, 1825-1863* (Syracuse, NY: Syracuse University Press, 1994), p. 135; Shaw, *Dagger John*, p. 185.
52. Constitution and Bylaws of the American Republican Party, James Harper Papers, Box 1, New York Public Library; *The Crisis: An Appeal to our Countrymen on the subject of Foreign Influence in the United States* (New York: n.p., 1844), p. 5.
53. John Hughes to James Harper, May 17, 1844, reprinted in Kehoe, ed., *Complete Works*, vol. 1, p. 452.
54. Hassard, *The Life of John Hughes*, pp. 277–78.
55. Shaw, *Dagger John*, p. 197.
56. Hughes to Harper, May 17, 1844, printed in Kehoe, ed., *Complete Works*, vol. 1, p. 344.

Three: THE GREAT HUNGER

1. *New York Tribune*, October 4, 1845.
2. Cormac O Grada, *The Great Irish Famine* (London: Macmillan, 1989), p. 25. For a study of how the potato became a staple for the European poor, see Redcliffe N. Salaman, *The History and Social Influence of the Potato* (Cambridge: Cambridge University Press, 1985). Salaman also investigates the causes of the potato failure in Ireland and its devastating consequences.
3. These figures are quoted in nearly all works about the Famine, including Christine Kinealy, *This Great Calamity: The Irish Famine 1845–52* (Dublin: Gill and Macmillan, 2006), pp. 295–96.
4. See Maurice Halbwachs, *On Collective Memory* (Chicago: University of Chicago Press, 1992). For a critique of Halbwachs, see Jeffrey K. Olick, *The Politics of Regret: On Collective Memory and Historical Responsibility* (New York: Routledge, 2007).
5. *Hansard*, vol. 89 (February 1847), pp. 994–95; Shelley Barber, ed., *The Prendergast Letters: Correspondence from Famine-Era Ireland, 1840–1850* (Amherst: University of Massachusetts Press, 2006), pp. 98, 140, 119.
6. *The Times* (London), October 10, 1847.
7. Glazer and Moynihan, *Beyond the Melting Pot*, p. 224.
8. *Census for the State of New York for 1855* (Albany: 1857) showed that the city's total population was 622,924, the number of Irish-born, 175,735, and the total number of foreign-born, 325,646.
9. Christine Kinealy, *A Death-Dealing Famine: The Great Hunger in Ireland* (London: Pluto Press, 1997), pp. 141–42.
10. Kinealy, *A Death-Dealing Famine*, p. 4. Historian Peter Gray has described Trevelyan and other British policymakers as "moralists" who saw the famine as a providential judgment on the character of the Irish-Catholic poor. See Gray, *Famine, Land and Politics: British Government and Irish Society, 1843–50* (Dublin: Irish Academic Press, 2001).
11. Charles Edward Trevelyan, *The Irish Crisis* (London: Longman, Brown, Green & Longmans, 1848), p. 184.
12. G. P. Gooch, ed., *The Later Correspondence of Lord John Russell, 1840–1878*, vol. 1 (London: Longmans, Green, 1925), pp. 161–62; *The Economist*, January 30, 1847.

13. Trevelyan, *The Irish Crisis*, p. 187.

14. Kinealy, *This Great Calamity*, p. 196; Trevelyan, *The Irish Crisis*, p. 90.

15. "A Lecture on the Antecedent Causes of the Irish Famine in 1847," in Kehoe, *Complete Works*, vol. 1, pp. 544–58.

16. James Donnelly, *The Great Irish Potato Famine* (Phoenix Mill, UK: Sutton Publishing Ltd., 2001), pp. 181–82; Kerby Miller, *Emigrants and Exiles: Ireland and the Irish Exodus to North America* (New York: Oxford University Press, 1985), pp. 195–96, 297.

17. Joseph J. Rubin and Charles H. Brown, eds., *Walt Whitman of the New York Aurora* (State College: Pennsylvania State University Press, 1950), pp. 58–59.

18. See Hasia Diner's essay, "The Era of the Great Migration," in Ronald H. Bayor and Timothy J. Meagher, eds., *The New York Irish* (Baltimore: Johns Hopkins University Press, 1996), p. 91.

19. Joseph Huthmacher, in "Urban Liberalism and the Age of Reform," *Mississippi Valley Historical Review* 49 (1962), and John Buenker, in *Urban Liberalism and Progressive Reform* (New York: W. W. Norton, 1973), date the beginnings of urban liberalism to the early twentieth century.

20. Lee Benson identified New York politics in 1844 as a clash between two groups of elite officeholders who used the rhetoric of ethnicity and religious difference to mobilize voters. See Benson, *The Concept of Jacksonian Democracy*.

21. *New York Times*, June 22, 1887.

22. See Mick Mulcrone's essay, "The Famine and Collective Memory," in Arthur Gribben, ed., *The Great Famine and the Irish Diaspora in America* (Amherst: University of Massachusetts Press, 1999), p. 225.

23. *New York Times*, March 27, 1920.

24. See *The Reminiscences of Jeremiah T. Mahoney*, Columbia Center for Oral History, p. 195. Although Mahoney referred to his personal support for specific social reforms, his comments came during a general discussion of the working-class background of Robert Wagner and other Tammany figures.

25. *New York Times*, April 2, 1852.

26. *Irish-American*, June 4, 1868; see *Irish World*'s coverage of food shortages in Ireland, August 30, 1870, and in India, August 25, 1877.

27. *New York American*, January 5, 1910.

28. Undated speech, William Bourke Cockran Papers, New York Public Library, Box 30.

29. See Thomas Flanagan's essay, "The Irish in John Ford's Films," in Michael Coffey, ed., *The Irish in America* (New York: Hyperion, 1997), pp. 190–95. Ford, according to Flanagan, said that the film's narrative was "similar to the famine in Ireland, when they threw the people off the land and left them wandering on the roads to starve—part of the Irish tradition." See also William Kennedy, *Riding the Yellow Trolley Car: Selected Nonfiction* (New York: Viking, 1993), pp. 51–52.

30. Dennis Smith, "A Soul for the Civil Service," in Coffey, ed., *The Irish in America*, p. 165; Fire Department of New York roster, January 1, 1888, found in the New York City Fire Museum; author's tally.

31. Adrian Cook, *The Armies of the Street: The New York City Draft Riots of 1863* (Lexington: University Press of Kentucky, 1982), p. 43; Bayor and Meagher, *The New York Irish*, p. 95; *New York Times*, September 17, 1869.

NOTES 317

32. *New York Tribune*, March 2, 1850.

33. *New York Herald*, October 18, 1854; *New York Times*, February 18, 1855.

34. *New York Evening Post*, November 10, 1857.

35. Ibid., October 23, 1857; *New York Times*, October 10, 1857.

36. Wood was elected mayor in 1854, reelected in 1856, defeated in a special election in 1857, and elected again in 1859. He lost reelection in 1861 but was elected to Congress in 1862. For Wood's estimate of his fortune, see Wood to James Buchanan, September 8, 1858, Buchanan Papers, Historical Society of Pennsylvania.

37. *New York Times*, July 17, 1857.

38. Wood's biographer, Jerome Mushkat, noted that Wood voted with pro-slavery forces on fifty-six roll-call votes in the House of Representatives in 1841, by far the most of any Northern member of Congress. See Mushkat, *Fernando Wood: A Political Biography* (Kent, OH: Kent State University Press, 1990), p. 15.

39. *New York Evening Post*, October 23, 1857; *Documents of the Board of Aldermen of the City of New York*, vol. 23, Mayor's Message, July 7, 1856 (New York: Chas. W. Baker, 1856).

40. *Irish News*, November 14, 1857.

41. *New York Evening Post*, *New York Times*, *New York Sun*, October 23, 1857.

42. *New York Evening Post*, October 23, 1857; Amy Bridges, *A City in the Republic: Antebellum New York and the Origins of Machine Politics* (Cambridge: Cambridge University Press, 1984), p. 118; Anbinder, *Five Points*, p. 244.

43. Mushkat, *Fernando Wood*, pp. 78–79.

Four: CIVIL WAR

1. Chief Engineer's Annual Report, 1850, published in the *New York Herald*, September 6, 1850. The annual report did not cover a calendar year, but rather late 1849 through late 1850.

2. Kenneth Ackerman, *Boss Tweed: The Rise and Fall of the Corrupt Pol Who Conceived the Soul of Modern New York* (New York: Carroll & Graf, 2005), p. 83.

3. Tyler Anbinder, *Nativism and Slavery: The Northern Know Nothings and the Politics of the 1850s* (New York: Oxford University Press, 1992), p. 13.

4. *New York Times*, October 11, 1852.

5. *New York Tribune*, November 10, 1853.

6. *New York Times*, October 30, 1854. The *Times* reprinted Seymour's letter, originally published in the Albany *Atlas*, noting that the letter was not dated but seemed to be written during the 1852 gubernatorial campaign.

7. For more on the role of saloons in nineteenth-century urban areas, see Jon M. Kingsdale, "The 'Poor Man's Club': Social Functions of the Urban Working-Class Saloon," *American Quarterly*, vol. 25, no. 4 (October 1973). See also Mark Edward Lender and James Kirby Martin, *Drinking in America: A History* (New York: The Free Press, 1982).

8. David G. Croly, *Seymour and Blair: Their Lives and Services* (New York: Richardson and Company, 1868), pp. 34–35.

9. *New York Times*, April 22, 1854.

10. *Freeman's Journal*, July 1, 1854.

11. The figure is from Anbinder, *Nativism and Slavery*, p. 43.

12. Ibid., p. 107.

13. *Freeman's Journal*, July 8, 1854; *Irish World*, August 12, 1871; June 6, 1874.

14. William M. Tweed to James J. Murphy, February 5, 1855, Tweed Papers, New-York Historical Society.

15. Tweed to Murphy, January 20 and February 5, 1855, Tweed Papers, New-York Historical Society.

16. *Congressional Globe*, 34th Congress, 1st Session, pp. 967–69.

17. *Speech by John Kelly in Reply to the Charges of Hon. Thomas R. Whitney against Catholicism*, delivered in the House, August 9,1855 (Washington: Union Office, 1856).

18. David Potter, *The Impending Crisis* (New York: Harper & Row, 1976), p. 252.

19. *Speech by John Kelly in Reply to the Charges of Hon. Thomas R. Whitney.*

20. *New York Tribune*, May 17, 1858.

21. Some scholars—including Ignatiev (cited above); David Roediger, *Working Toward Whiteness: How America's Immigrants Became White* (New York: Basic Books, 2006); and Theodore W. Allen, *The Invention of the White Race: Racial Oppression and Society Control* (New York: Verso, 1994)—have theorized that the Irish sought to prove their whiteness in order to gain acceptance from the Anglo-Protestant mainstream. This is a curious divergence from modern scholarship, which tends to emphasize the ways in which oppressed groups retain their identity while resisting or negotiating with their would-be oppressors. The leading journalists, Protestant preachers, and elite reformers of the Gilded Age no doubt would have been amused to learn that the Irish desperately wished to cast aside their "otherness"—which included their Catholicism—in order to fit into mainstream New York society.

22. References to the Irish as slaves abound in O'Connell's speeches. Just one example: In the introduction to a collection of his letters, O'Connell referred to Ireland as the "bond slave of Britain." See O'Connell, *Letters to the Reformers of England on the Reform Bill for Ireland* (London: J. Ridgway, 1832), p. 8.

23. "Erin, Oh Erin," and "The Minstrel Boy" by Thomas Moore, in Seamus Deane, ed., *The Field Day Anthology of Irish Writing* (Derry: Field Day Publications, 1991), pp. 1061, 1064.

24. Patricia Ferreira, "All But 'A Black Skin and Wooly Hair': Frederick Douglass' Witness of the Irish Famine," *American Studies International*, vol. 37, no. 2 (June 1999), pp. 78–80.

25. O'Ferrall, *Catholic Emancipation*, p. 50.

26. *Irish-American*, November 14, 1863; October 29, 1853.

27. *Irish World*, August 12, 1871.

28. Richard Shaw, *Dagger John*, p. 137; *Irish-American*, October 28, 1849.

29. Most Protestants, of course, were of English or Scottish background, while the Catholics were, by and large, the island's native Gaelic population.

30. *Freeman's Journal*, October 6, 1860.

31. Mushkat, *Tammany*, p. 334.

32. Mushkat, *Fernando Wood*, p. 136.

33. *New York Herald*, July 14, 1863.

34. This summary of the violence is based on reports in the *New York Times* on July 14, 15, and 16, 1863.

35. Iver Bernstein, *The New York City Draft Riots: Their Significance for American*

Society and Politics in the Age of Civil War (New York: Oxford University Press, 1990), p. 69.

36. Hughes to Seward, July 19, 1863, Hughes Papers, Roll 2, Archives of the Archdiocese of New York.

37. *Irish World*, May 5, 1871.

38. Ackerman, *Boss Tweed*, p. 63.

39. See Tweed to Tilden, December 30 and October 8, 1868, Samuel Tilden Papers, Box 25, New York Public Library.

40. Myers, *The History of Tammany Hall*, p. 279.

Five: A TAMMANY RIOT

1. For details of the exiles' journey and entrance into New York Harbor, see John Devoy, *Recollections of an Irish Rebel* (New York: Charles Young, 1929), pp. 329–31, and Jeremiah O'Donovan Rossa, *Rossa's Recollections* (New York: Mariners Harbor, 1894), as well as accounts in the *Irish World*, January 22, 1871, and the *New York Herald*, January 21, 1871. See also Devoy's journal in John Devoy Papers, MS 18,004, National Library of Ireland, Dublin

2. *Gaelic American*, March 7, 1925.

3. *New York Times*, February 9, 1871.

4. Ibid., November 6, 1856.

5. *Irish World*, October 3, 1874.

6. Figures from Ackerman, *Boss Tweed*, p. 87.

7. *New York Times*, April 14, 1871.

8. Ibid., June 20, 1871.

9. Ibid., July 8, 1871.

10. Celebrations of July 12 continue in Northern Ireland today, although tensions have been reduced since the beginning of the Irish peace process in the 1990s.

11. *New York Tribune*, July 14, 1870; see also the *Tribune* and *Times* coverages of the riot, July 14, 15; *Irish-American*, July 23, 1870.

12. See the letters pages in the *New York Herald*, the *New York Times*, and the *New York Sun*, July 12 and 13, 1871. See also Michael A. Gordon, *The Orange Riots: Irish Political Violence in New York City, 1870 and 1871* (Ithaca, NY: Cornell University Press, 2009), pp. 79–82.

13. *New York Herald*, July 11, 1871.

14. *New York Tribune*, July 12, 1871.

15. *New York Times*, July 11, 1871; *New York Tribune*, July 11, 1871.

16. *New York Tribune*, July 12, 1871.

17. Ibid.

18. *New York Sun*, July 13, 1871.

19. Gordon, *The Orange Riots*, p. 113.

20. *Irish World*, July 22, 1871.

21. Gordon, *The Orange Riots*, p. 164; *New York Sun*, July 14, 1871; *Harper's Weekly*, July 29, 1871.

22. *New York Tribune*, July 16, 1871; *New York Herald*, July 16, 1871; Gordon, *The Orange Riots*, p. 159.

23. See a postmortem tribute to Plunkitt in the *New York Times*, November 20, 1924. The *Times* was skeptical of Plunkitt's account, for he also claimed that

Mayor Hall ordered him to take charge of the volatile situation before it exploded into violence. Plunkitt was a twenty-nine-year-old alderman at the time. For "The Church of Aggression," see *New York Times*, March 10, 1871.

24. Ibid., July 22–29, 1871. See also Ackerman, *Boss Tweed*, p. 170. Ironically, the so-called Tweed Courthouse remains in use in the twenty-first century, serving as headquarters of the city Department of Education as of 2011.

25. *The Nation*, August 24, 1871; September 7, 1871.

26. *New York Times*, September 25, 1871.

27. *Harper's Weekly*, September 30, 1871.

28. *New York Times*, September 26, 1871.

29. Ibid., November 9, 1871.

Six: TAMMANY'S IRISH RECONSTRUCTION

1. *New York Tribune*, November 4, 1877.

2. Andrew D. White, "The Government of American Cities," *Forum* (December 1890), p. 214. The article was later retitled "City Affairs Are Not Political."

3. Francis S. Barry, *The Scandal of Reform: The Grand Failures of New York's Political Crusaders and the Death of Nonpartisanship* (New Brunswick, NJ: Rutgers University Press, 2009), p. 34; White, "The Government of American Cities," p. 215.

4. *New York Times*, December 26, 1874.

5. See, for example, a cartoon entitled "The Catholics Are Coming" in *Puck*, October 27, 1880. For a full treatment of *Puck*'s importance in Gilded Age New York, see Samuel J. Thomas, "Mugwump Cartoonists, the Papacy, and Tammany Hall in America's Gilded Age," in *Religion and American Culture: A Journal of Interpretation*, vol. 14, no. 2 (Summer 2004).

6. Daniel Cassidy, *How the Irish Invented Slang: The Secret Language of the Crossroads* (Petrolia, CA: CounterPunch Books, 2007), p. 174.

7. For a breakdown of Manhattan's Assembly districts in 1880, see Enumeration Districts of the 1st Supervisors District of New York, accessible at www.bklyn-genealogy-info.com/Ward/1880NYC.1.html.

8. Riordon, *Plunkitt of Tammany Hall*, pp. 92–93.

9. *New York Times*, November 2, 1872.

10. *Irish World*, November 16, 1872; *New York Times*, November 7, 1872.

11. John Kelly to unnamed recipient, November 20, 1875; Samuel Tilden to John Kelly, August 1873 (undated), Samuel Tilden Papers, Box 15, New York Public Library.

12. *New York Times*, October 7, 1874.

13. Edwin G. Burrows and Mike Wallace, *Gotham: A History of New York City to 1898* (New York: Oxford University Press, 1999), p. 1025.

14. *New York Times*, September 23, 1874.

15. Ibid., November 7, 1874.

16. Telegram from Kelly to Tilden, May 24, 1875, Samuel Tilden Papers, Box 15, New York Public Library; undated telegram, Kelly to James Fox, Samuel Tilden Papers, Box 15, New York Public Library. Kelly also opposed construction of the Brooklyn Bridge (after first supporting the plan), beginning in 1878. He believed it was too costly and would help Brooklyn more than New York.

17. Alexander C. Flick, *Samuel Jones Tilden: A Study in Political Sagacity* (New York: Dodd, Mead, 1939), p. 262.
18. *New York Times*, February 23, 1875.
19. Michael McGerr, *The Decline of Popular Politics: The American North, 1865–1928* (New York: Oxford University Press, 1986), p. 46.
20. Ibid., p. 46; Barry, *The Scandal of Reform*, p. 34.
21. Sven Beckert, "Democracy and its Discontents: Contesting Suffrage Rights in Gilded Age New York," *Past and Present*, vol. 174, no. 1 (2002), p. 137.
22. Ibid., p. 140.
23. The proposed amendment covered all cities in New York state. Those with twenty-five thousand residents or fewer were subjected to no new restrictions. Qualifications were lower in cities with populations of twenty-five thousand to a hundred thousand.
24. David Quigley, *Second Founding: New York City, Reconstruction, and the Making of American Democracy* (New York: Hill and Wang, 2004), p. 158; Barry, *The Scandal of Reform*, p. 35.
25. *Irish World*, April 21, 1877.
26. *Commercial and Financial Chronicle*, April 28, 1877.
27. *New York Post*, October 30, 1877.
28. *New York Tribune*, October 24, 1877. For more on Swallowtail disaffection with Kelly, see Seymour J. Mandelbaum, *Boss Tweed's New York* (Chicago: Ivan R. Dee, 1990), pp. 172–74.
29. *New York Times*, July 15, 1877.
30. *New York Post*, November 5, 1877; *New York Times*, November 2, 1877.
31. *Irish-American*, November 3, 1877.
32. *New York Times*, October 30, 1877.
33. *Irish-American*, November 17, 1877.
34. *New York Times*, September 11, 1880.
35. Rev. Joseph Hartwell, *Romanism in Politics: What it Costs—Tammany Hall the Stronghold of Rome* (New York: Phillips & Hunt, 1887), pp. 1, 14.
36. Marquis James, *Merchant Adventurer: The Story of W. R. Grace* (Wilmington, DE: Scholarly Resources, 1993), p. 12.
37. *New York Tribune*, October 26, 1880.
38. *New York Herald*, October 24, 1880; *New York Tribune*, October 27, 1880.
39. *New York Sun*, November 1, 1880.
40. *New York Sun*, November 1, 1880.
41. Louis Eisenstein and Elliot Rosenberg, *A Stripe of Tammany's Tiger* (New York: Robert Speller & Sons, 1966), p. 15.
42. *New York Times*, November 3, 1880.

Seven: CHALLENGING THE GILDED AGE

1. The Mick Moloney Collection of Irish-American Music and Popular Culture, Box 48, Archives of Irish America, Bobst Library, New York University. The song is undated, but a reference to General Grant (not quoted) would indicate that the song was written before Grant's death in 1885.
2. John G. Sproat, *The Best Men: Liberal Reformers in the Gilded Age* (New York: Oxford University Press, 1968), p. 62.

3. George Henry Shibley, *Majority Rule in Combination with Representative Government in City, State and Nation* (Washington, DC: American Federation of Labor, 1902), p. 75.
4. *New York Times*, October 4, 1881.
5. Ibid.
6. James, *Merchant Adventurer*, p. 173.
7. *New York Times*, July 14, 1877.
8. *New York World*, April 15, 1883.
9. Arthur Mann, *Yankee Reformers in the Urban Age: Social Reform in Boston, 1880–1900* (New York: Harper Torchbooks, 1954), p. 105.
10. Quote from *Facts for the People: A Report of the Anti-Monopoly League of the State of New York* (New York, 1883), pp. 9, 38; Chauncey Mitchell Depew, *My Memories of Eighty Years* (New York: Charles Scribner's Sons, 1921), p. 124.
11. *Official Proceedings of the Democratic National Convention 1884* (New York: Douglas Taylor's Democratic Printing House, 1884), pp. 126–28.
12. Ibid., pp. 134, 139.
13. Ibid., p. 176.
14. See the *Irish World and American Industrial Liberator*, February 5, 1881, for a description of its campaign in Ireland.
15. Eric Foner, "Class, Ethnicity and Radicalism in the Gilded Age: The Land League and Irish America," *Marxist Perspectives*, vol. 2 (1978), p. 156; *New York Times*, January 27, 1886.
16. Foner, "Class, Ethnicity and Radicalism in the Gilded Age," p. 156.
17. For more on the importance of the Central Labor Union and its connection to land reform in Ireland, see David Scobey, "Boycotting the Politics Factory: Labor Radicalism and the New York City Mayoral Election of 1884," *Radical History Review*, 28–30, 1984. (The title incorrectly described the article's focus, the mayoral race of 1886.)
18. Kenneth C. Wenzer, ed., *Henry George, The Transatlantic Irish, and Their Times* (Bingley, UK: JAI Press, 2009), p. 523; Robert D. Cross, *The Emergence of Liberal Catholicism in America* (Cambridge: Harvard University Press, 1958), p. 118.
19. *New York Times*, June 6, 1886.

Eight: TO HELL WITH REFORM

1. *New York Tribune*, July 24, 1903.
2. Figures from Burrows and Wallace, *Gotham*, pp. 1110–12, and *Federation*, a quarterly publication of the Federation of Churches and Christian Organizations in New York City, June 1920.
3. *New York Times*, April 24, 1886.
4. Edward T. O'Donnell, "Though Not an Irishman: Henry George and the American Irish," *American Journal of Economics and Sociology*, vol. 56, no. 4 (October 1997), p. 414.
5. *New York Times*, October 12, 1886.
6. Archbishop Corrigan to Rev. Edward McGlynn, October 26, 1886, Archbishop Michael Corrigan Papers, Box 10, Seton Hall University Special Collections.
7. Burrows and Wallace, *Gotham*, p. 1108.
8. Ibid., p. 1106.

9. Thomas Wyse Papers, MS 15,036, National Library of Ireland; also published as an appendix to Wyse's previously cited *Historical Sketch of the Late Catholic Association of New York*, vol. 2, pp. 114–56.

10. Eisenstein and Rosenberg, *A Stripe of Tammany's Tiger*, p. 15.

11. *New York Times*, August 1, 1893.

12. See John Ahearn's obituary: *New York Times*, December 20, 1920.

13. *New York Times*, December 23, 1902.

14. Grady quote: *New York Times*, November 4, 1901. Schurz: ibid., May 7, 1897.

15. *Harper's Weekly*, April 16, 1870.

16. Maureen Fitzgerald, *Habits of Compassion: Irish Catholic Nuns and the Origins of New York's Welfare System, 1830–1920* (Chicago: University of Illinois Press, 2006), p. 135.

17. Ibid., p. 121.

18. *New York Times*, July 12, 1894.

19. Membership rolls from the Kilroe Tammany Collection, New-York Historical Society; *Tammany Times*, July 4, 1903.

20. *Federation*, a quarterly publication of the Federation of Churches and Christian Organizations in New York City, June 1920.

21. *New York Times*, September 4, 1894.

22. Ibid., August 28, 1893.

23. Ibid., August 14, 1878.

24. See *New York Times*, September 24, 1900, for an account of a meeting of the CLU during which Tammany-affiliated union leaders addressed several topics.

25. Richard Croker to Hugh Grant, January 31, 1889, Hugh Grant Papers, New-York Historical Society; *New York Times*, February 7, 1889.

26. Biographical details of all Assembly members in 1893 can be found in *The Red Book: An Illustrated Legislative Manual of the State of New York* (Albany: James B. Lyon, 1892), New York State Library, Albany.

27. *New York Times*, August 7, 1893.

28. Ibid., August 15, 1893.

29. Ibid., August 7, 1893.

30. *Evening World*, February 15, 1892.

31. Goldwin Smith, "Why Send More Irish to America?" *The Nineteenth Century*, vol. 13, no. 76 (June 1883).

32. T. W. Russell, "American Sidelights on Home Rule," *Fortnightly* (March 1893), p. 351; Sydney Brooke, "Tammany Hall," *The Monthly Review* (November 1901), p. 102.

33. *New York Times*, March 29, 1875.

34. Ibid., February 19, 1886.

35. James Bryce, *The American Commonwealth*, abridged (Philadelphia: John D. Morris, 1906), p. 241.

36. *New York Times*, November 10, 1904.

37. Hartwell, *Romanism in Politics*, pp. 8, 22, 23.

38. *New York Times*, June 9, 1886.

39. Ibid., May 21, 1914; *The Academy*, December 18, 1909, p. 845.

40. *New York Times*, June 27, 1900.

41. William Bourke Cockran Papers, Box 7, New York Public Library.

42. *New York Times*, March 14, 1892; November 2 and 3, 1894.

43. Warren Sloat, *A Battle for the Soul of New York: Tammany Hall, Police Corruption, Vice, and the Reverend Charles Parkhurst's Crusade Against Them* (New York: Cooper Square Press, 2002), pp. 360, 368.

44. *New York Times*, November 30, 1894; December 1, 1893.

45. Richard Zacks, *Island of Vice: Theodore Roosevelt's Doomed Quest to Clean Up Sin-Loving New York* (New York: Doubleday, 2012), p. 71; *New York Times*, May 7, 1895.

46. Barry, *The Scandal of Reform*, p. 61.

47. Zacks, *Island of Vice*, p. 137.

48. *Report of the Special Commission of the Assembly Appointed to Investigate the Public Offices and Appointments of the City of New York* (Albany, NY: J. B. Lyon, 1900), vol. II, pp. 353–54. See also *New York Sun*, April 15, 1899.

49. *New York Times*, April 24, 1896.

50. Barry, *The Scandal of Reform*, p. 60.

51. Gerald Kurland, *Seth Low: The Reformer in an Urban and Industrial Age* (New York: Twayne Publishers, 1971), p. 106.

52. *New York Times*, October 14, 1897.

Nine: AN ADMIRABLE ORGANIZATION?

1. Details on the life of young Charles Francis Murphy come from coverage of his death and funeral in late April 1924 in the *New York Times*, the *New York American*, the *New York Sun*, and the *New York Evening World*. See also Nancy Joan Weiss, *Charles Francis Murphy, 1858–1924: Respectability and Responsibility in Tammany Politics* (Northampton, MA: Smith College Press, 1968). Weiss's short study of Murphy is a masterful attempt to go beyond stereotypes of Tammany bosses in general and of Murphy in particular. See also Harold Zink, *City Bosses in the United States* (Durham, NC: Duke University Press, 1930). Murphy's district was the 12th Assembly district in the early 1890s. It was later reconfigured into the 18th Assembly district.

2. Riordon, *Plunkitt of Tammany Hall*, p. 78.

3. *New York Times*, February 22, 1914.

4. *New York Evening World*, April 25, 1924.

5. Lothrop Stoddard, *Master of Manhattan: The Life of Richard Croker* (New York: Longmans, Green, 1931), p. 203; Theodore Roosevelt, *An Autobiography* (New York: Charles Scribner's Sons, 1920), p. 272.

6. Coverage of Hall's death was extensive. See *New York Tribune*, January 18 and 19, 1901; *New York World*, January 18, 1901; and *New York Times*, January 19 and 20, 1901.

7. *New York Times*, November 1, 1901; *The Outlook*, November 16, 1901.

8. *New York Times*, December 24, 1901.

9. Ibid., November 7, 1901.

10. Weiss, *Charles Francis Murphy*, pp. 28–29.

11. *New York Times*, October 4, 1902.

12. Edward J. Flynn, *You're the Boss: The Practice of American Politics* (New York: Collier Books, 1962), p. 46.

13. *The Reminiscences of Arthur Krock*, Columbia Center for Oral History, p. 3.

14. Gene Fowler, *Beau James: The Life and Times of Jimmy Walker* (New York: The Viking Press, 1949), p. 85.

15. Steffens, *The Shame of the Cities*, p. 205.
16. *New York World*, February 14 and 15, 1914.
17. Jean Edward Smith, *FDR* (New York: Random House, 2007), p. 78.
18. Riordon, *Plunkitt of Tammany Hall*, p. 17.
19. The New York Reform Club papers, Annual Report of the Treasurer, 1912, New York Public Library.
20. Richard Welling Papers, Box 13, New York Public Library.
21. *New York Tribune*, May 26, 1918; *New York Evening Telegram*, August 2, 1918.
22. Steffens, *The Shame of the Cities*, p. 205.
23. John M. Allswang makes this point in his book *Bosses, Machines, and Urban Voters* (Baltimore: Johns Hopkins University Press, 1986), p. 75.
24. For more on Folks, see Dorothy M. Brown and Elizabeth McKeown, *The Poor Belong to Us: Catholic Charities and American Welfare* (Cambridge: Harvard University Press, 1997).
25. *New York Times*, October 1, 1903.
26. Ibid., November 3, 1903.
27. Buenker, *Urban Liberalism and Progressive Reform*, p. 122.
28. Richard A. Greenwald, *The Triangle Fire, the Protocols of Peace, and Industrial Democracy in Progressive Era New York* (Philadelphia: Temple University Press, 2005), p. 417.
29. Werner, *Tammany Hall*, pp. 506–7.
30. *The Reminiscences of Frances Perkins*, p. 240.
31. Frances Perkins, *The Roosevelt I Knew* (New York: Viking Press, 1946), p. 23; *The Reminiscences of Jeremiah T. Mahoney*, p. 63.
32. *The Reminiscences of Frances Perkins*, p. 110.
33. Weiss, *Charles Francis Murphy*, p. 75; Alfred E. Smith, *Up to Now: An Autobiography* (New York: Viking Press, 1929), p. 121.
34. An English-language transcript of *Rerum Novarum* is available on the Vatican website: www.vatican.va/holy_father/leo_xiii/encyclicals; *The Reminiscences of Jeremiah T. Mahoney*, p. 195; Margaret O'Brien Steinfels, ed., *American Catholics, American Culture: Tradition and Resistance* (Lanham, MD: Sheed and Ward, 2004), p. 15.
35. *The Reminiscences of Jeremiah T. Mahoney*, pp. 13, 63.
36. Labor historian Richard A. Greenwald argued that the FIC's power came from one source: Tammany Hall. See his book *The Triangle Fire*, p. 157.
37. Blaine A. Brownell and Warren E. Stickle, eds., *Bosses and Reformers* (Boston: Houghton Mifflin, 1973), p. 27.
38. Riordon, *Plunkitt of Tammany Hall*, p. 28.
39. This account is taken from *The Reminiscences of Frances Perkins*, p. 213.

Ten: MURPHY'S LAW

1. *New York Telegram*, June 23, 1912.
2. *Official Report of the Proceedings of the Democratic National Convention, 1912* (Chicago: Peterson Linotyping Co., 1912), pp. 2, 6.
3. *New York Times*, June 25, 1912.
4. Ibid., June 28, 1912.
5. Mary B. Bryan, ed., *The Memoirs of William Jennings Bryan* (Philadelphia: John C. Winston, 1925), p. 178.

6. *New York Times*, July 3, 1912.

7. Weiss, *Charles Francis Murphy*, p. 71.

8. *New York Times*, July 30, 1912.

9. Greenwald, *The Triangle Fire*, p. 164.

10. *The Outlook*, May 17, 1913, p. 84.

11. Mahoney mentioned this in several passages of his oral history. See *The Reminiscences of Jeremiah T. Mahoney*, Columbia Center for Oral History, pp. 3, 106, 107, 194.

12. Civic League material from the Kilroe Collection of Tammany Material, Box 26, Columbia University Special Collections.

13. The Sunday baseball controversy was reported in the *New York Times*, March 20, 1918.

14. *New York Times*, June 24, 1913.

15. Ibid., May 3, 1913; April 19, 1913.

16. Robert F. Wesser, *A Response to Progressivism: The Democratic Party and New York Politics: 1902–1918* (New York: New York University Press, 1986), p. 125.

17. Wesser, *A Response to Progressivism*, p. 125.

18. *New York Times*, May 9, 1913.

19. Ibid., October 30, 1913.

20. *New York Tribune*, November 5, 6, 1913.

21. *New York Sun*, November 6, 1913.

22. *The Reminiscences of Frances Perkins*, Columbia Center for Oral History, p. 287.

23. *New York Times*, November 5, 1915.

24. *Debate on the Treaty between Great Britain and Ireland, signed in London on the 6th December, 1921: Sessions 14 December 1921 to 10 January 1922*. Accessed through CELT: Corpus of Electronic Texts Edition, January 15, 2013, http://www.ucc .ie/celt/published/E900003-001/index.html.

25. David Fitzpatrick, *Harry Boland's Irish Revolution* (Cork, Ireland: Cork University Press, 2003), p. 266.

26. For more on McKeown, see *New York World*, June 14, 1921. See also Thomas Smith (on Murphy's behalf) to Bourke Cockran, June 21, 1921, and Bourke Cockran to Murphy, June 28, 1921, Cockran Papers, Box 10, New York Public Library.

27. *Westminster Review*, November 1910, p. 497.

28. *New York Times*, December 9 and 7, 1913.

29. Thomas D. McCarthy to Colonel House, November 16, 1914, Joseph Tumulty Papers, Box 44, Library of Congress.

30. *New York Tribune*, November 5, 1913; Smith, *Up to Now*, p. 139.

31. Slayton, *Empire Statesman*, p. 109.

32. *New York Times*, October 2, 1917.

33. *New York Tribune*, November 7, 1917.

34. Slayton, *Empire Statesman*, p. 111.

35. Alfred Connable and Edward Silverfarb, *Tigers of Tammany Hall: Nine Men Who Ran New York* (New York: Holt, Rinehart and Winston, 1967), p. 262.

36. *New York Times*, October 4, 1944.

37. Weiss, *Charles Francis Murphy*, p. 77.

38. For correspondence between Cockran and Murphy on disarmament, see Cockran Papers, Box 5, New York Public Library. For Murphy's quote and the *Times*'s comment, see *New York Times*, December 27, 1920.

39. *The Reminiscences of Jeremiah T. Mahoney*, p. 46.

40. Murphy's funeral and Roosevelt's comment were covered in the *New York Times*, April 26, 1924.

Eleven: FRANK AND AL

1. Smith to Roosevelt, November 8, 1920; Roosevelt to Smith, November 9, 1920, FDR Family, Business and Personal Papers, Box 5, FDR Library, Hyde Park, NY.

2. Robert K. Murray, *The 103rd Ballot: Democrats and the Disaster in Madison Square Garden* (New York: Harper & Row, 1976), p. 287.

3. *New York Globe*, June 2, 1911.

4. *The Reminiscences of Jeremiah T. Mahoney*, Columbia Center for Oral History, p. 181.

5. For more on the bishops' proposals, see Joseph M. McShane, *"Sufficiently Radical": Catholicism, Progressivism, and the Bishops' Program of 1919* (Washington, DC: Catholic University Press, 1986).

6. See Speaker Thaddeus Sweet's speech in the *Journal of the Assembly of the State of New York, 142nd Session* (Albany: J. B. Lyon Co., 1919), pp. 9–11.

7. See the introduction to *Report of the Reconstruction Commission to Governor Alfred E. Smith on Retrenchment and Reorganization in the State Government* (Albany: J. B. Lyon Co., 1919). For Smith's remarks, see Henry Moskowitz, ed., *Progressive Democracy: Addresses and State Papers of Alfred E. Smith* (New York: Harcourt, Brace, 1928), p. 92.

8. *The Reminiscences of Joseph Proskauer*, Columbia Center for Oral History, p. 5.

9. FDR to Smith, February 4, 1930, FDR Gubernatorial Papers, FDR Library, Hyde Park.

10. Ibid.

11. Smith, *FDR*, p. 78.

12. Ibid., p. 77; Christopher M. Finan, *Alfred E. Smith: The Happy Warrior* (New York: Hill & Wang, 2002), pp. 237–38.

13. Smith, *FDR*, p. 81.

14. This common argument can be seen in Kenneth S. Davis, *FDR: The Beckoning of Destiny, 1882–1928* (New York: G. P. Putnam's Sons, 1972), p. 257.

15. *New York Times*, January 23 and April 1, 1911.

16. For his correspondence on such issues as temperance, Sunday baseball, and Sunday business closings, see FDR's Senate Papers, Boxes 8 and 9, FDR Library, Hyde Park. Jean Edward Smith noted that several newspapers reported Sullivan's vote, but none referred to any role that Roosevelt played in summoning Sullivan to the floor. The *Senate Journal*, as Smith notes, recorded only votes, not the debate. Smith concluded that Howe's version was false. See Smith, *FDR*, p. 82.

17. FDR to Smith, September 15, 1922, FDR Family, Business and Personal Papers, Box 5, FDR Library, Hyde Park.

18. Perkins, *The Roosevelt I Knew*, p. 13.

19. Ibid.; Memo, July 7, 1938, President's Personal File 290, FDR Papers; Frank Freidel, *Franklin D. Roosevelt: A Rendezvous with Destiny* (New York: Little, Brown, 1990), p. 533.

20. Quoted in J. Joseph Huthmacher, *Senator Robert F. Wagner and the Rise of Urban Liberalism* (New York: Atheneum, 1971), p. 137. Huthmacher, who coined the term *urban liberalism* to describe the ideology of machine politicians during the Progressive Era, makes it clear that Murphy exerted tremendous influence over Wagner during the latter's formative years. (Huthmacher did not identify the political figure he quoted.)

21. See, for example, Freidel, *Franklin D. Roosevelt: A Rendezvous with Destiny*, p. 537.

22. *New York Times*, December 3, 1898.

23. *New York Sun, New York Times*, July 5, 1917.

24. For comments by The McManus and Walker, see Frank Freidel, *Franklin D. Roosevelt: The Apprenticeship* (Boston: Little, Brown, 1952), p. 373.

25. See FDR to Smith, October 14, 1918, and Smith to FDR, October 19, 1918, Family, Business and Personal Papers, Box 5, FDR Library, Hyde Park. Frank Freidel argued that FDR's enthusiasm for Smith was lukewarm at best, but he did not mention FDR's offer to speak on Smith's behalf, a generous gesture in a tight election. See Freidel, *Franklin D. Roosevelt: The Apprenticeship*, p. 370, fn.

26. James Canneron Jr., "Al Smith—Catholic, Tammany, Wet," *The Nation*, July 4, 1928.

27. Franklin D. Roosevelt, *The Happy Warrior: Alfred E. Smith* (Boston: Houghton Mifflin, 1928), pp. 7–8.

28. Davis, *FDR: The Beckoning of Destiny, 1882–1928*, p. 610.

29. *New York Tribune*, September 14, 1913. Historians Richard Hofstadter and Otis L. Graham Jr. noted that some progressives who were active during the Wilson years came to regard Roosevelt's New Deal as an "outrageous departure from everything they had known and valued," in Hofstader's words, leading them to conclude that "overpowering alien influences" were to blame for the "subversion" of the progressive agenda. See Hofstadter, *The Age of Reform* (New York: Vintage Books, 1955), pp. 303–4. See also Graham Jr., *The Old Progressives and the New Deal* (New York: Oxford University Press, 1967).

30. Madison Grant, *The Passing of the Great Race* (New York: Scribner's, 1922), p. 5.

31. For more on Cotillo, see Thomas M. Henderson, "Immigrant Politician: Salvatore Cotillo, Progressive Ethnic," *International Migration Review*, vol. 13, no. 1 (Spring 1979).

32. John Devoy, leader of New York's Irish nationalist community from 1871 until his death in 1928, challenged Senator John Sharp Williams of Mississippi when Williams complained about the political agendas of hyphenated Americans in 1911. "Aren't the Anglo-Saxons hyphenated?" Devoy asked. See Devoy's account of the meeting in the *Gaelic American* newspaper, March 1, 1924.

33. William Bourke Cockran to Hebrew Immigrant Aid Society of America, April 27, 1921, Cockran Papers, Box 10; see also undated speech, Cockran Papers, Box 30, New York Public Library.

34. *New York Times*, March 9, 1924.

35. Ibid., April 19, 1924; Edward Flynn to Eleanor Roosevelt, March 23, 1943, President's Official File, 1892, Box 2, FDR Library, Hyde Park.

36. Clip from the *Fellowship Forum*, n.d. [1928], Private Papers of Alfred E. Smith, Box 1, New York State Library. *Time* magazine noted that in 1928, when Smith was a presidential candidate, the *Fellowship Forum* "showed a greater increase in gross revenue than any other U.S. publication." See *Time*, November 12, 1928.

37. Tumulty to Smith, April 24, 1924, Joseph Tumulty Papers, Box 74, Library of Congress.
38. *New York Times*, April 26, 1924.
39. Ibid., April 27, 1924.
40. See Babe Ruth to FDR, May 9, 1924, Papers Pertaining to the Campaign of 1924, FDR Library, Hyde Park.
41. *New York Tribune*, June 27, 1924.
42. Murray, *The 103rd Ballot*, p. 145; *New York Times*, October 23 and November 4, 1923; June 24, 1924.
43. Murray, *The 103rd Ballot*, p. 159.
44. *New York Times* on July 3, 1924, presented a transcript of Bryan's speech. It does not include the phrase "you do not represent the future of this country." The phrase has been attributed to Bryan in several books, including Slayton, *Empire Statesman*, p. 214, and Oscar Handlin, *Al Smith and His America* (Boston: Little, Brown, 1958), p. 123.
45. Smith, *Up to Now*, p. 338.
46. See pamphlet by Evans in the Official Papers of Alfred E. Smith, Folder 200–341, New York State Archives, Albany, NY. Smith kept a large file of material relating to the Klan.
47. Undated clip from the *New York World*, Official Papers of Alfred E. Smith, Folder 200-4-2, New York State Archives, Albany, NY.
48. FDR to Smith, December 29, 1925, FDR Family, Business and Personal Papers, Box 5, FDR Library, Hyde Park.
49. FDR to Smith, September 17, 1926, FDR Family, Business and Personal Papers, Box 5, FDR Library, Hyde Park.
50. Slayton, *Empire Statesman*, p. 257; *New York Times*, June 29, 1928.
51. *New York Times*, June 29, 1928.
52. "Should Liberals Vote for Smith?" *The Nation*, vol. 127, no. 3299 (September 26, 1928). The editors did not answer their own question, advising readers to decide for themselves whether to vote for Smith or the Socialist Party candidate, Norman Thomas, who was a contributor to the magazine.
53. *New York Times*, October 18, 1928.
54. Joseph Tumulty to Thomas McCarthy, November 8, 1928; Joseph Tumulty to Millard Tydings, March 28, 1939, Joseph Tumulty Papers, Boxes 69, 60, Library of Congress. In his letter to Tydings, Tumulty sought to block the appointment of a contributor to Hoover's campaign for a minor office.
55. Slayton, *Empire Statesman*, p. 315.
56. Ibid., p. 325.

Twelve: THE BATTLE OF TWO GOVERNORS

1. Flynn, *You're the Boss*, p. 98.
2. Robert A. Caro, *The Power Broker: Robert Moses and the Fall of New York* (New York: Vintage, 1975), p. 296.
3. "Roosevelt and Tammany Hall: Heretofore and Up to Now," found in Vertical File, Box O, FDR Papers, FDR Library, Hyde Park.
4. Flynn, *You're the Boss*, p. 96.
5. Ibid., pp. 99–100.

6.   Slayton, *Empire Statesman*, p. 366.
7.   James J. Hoey to Louis Howe, April 7, 1932; Hoey to James Farley, May 4, 1932, James A. Farley Papers, Box 1, Library of Congress.
8.   Weiss, *Charles Francis Murphy*, p. 92.
9.   William Gibbs McAdoo to Joseph Tumulty, February 24, 1932, Joseph Tumulty Papers, Box 69, Library of Congress.
10. Flynn, *You're the Boss*, p. 108.
11. *New York Times*, July 2, 1932.
12. *The Reminiscences of Edward J. Flynn*, Columbia Center for Oral History, p. 13, *New York Times*, June 19, 1932.
13. Claude Bowers to Edward J. Flynn, October 16, 1947, Edward J. Flynn Papers, Box 1, FDR Library, Hyde Park.
14. Allen, *The Tiger*, p. 253; *New York Times*, September 11, 1932.
15. Curry quote: Allen, *The Tiger*, p. 239. The Tammany letterhead lists Lehman as vice chair of the committee. See, for example, George Olvany to James A. Farley, November 9, 1927, James Farley Papers, Box 1, Library of Congress.
16. *New York Times*, December 4, 5, 1932.

Thirteen: LEGACIES

1.   Huthmacher, *Senator Robert F. Wagner and the Rise of Urban Liberalism*, p. 13; Oral History of Leon Keyserling, Harry S. Truman Presidential Library, pp. 24–25. Available at http://www.trumanlibrary.org/oralhist/keyserl.htm.
2.   Huthmacher, *Senator Robert F. Wagner*, pp. 190, 197.
3.   *New York Times*, July 6, 1937.
4.   Thomas Kessner, *Fiorello H. La Guardia and the Making of Modern New York* (New York: McGraw-Hill, 1989), p. 249.
5.   La Guardia, his wife, and their two children eventually did move to Gracie Mansion during La Guardia's third term.
6.   For more on public-payroll cuts, see Steven P. Erie, *Rainbow's End: Irish-Americans and the Dilemmas of Urban Machine Politics, 1840–1985* (Berkeley: University of California Press, 1988), pp. 107–39, and Terry Golway, *So Others Might Live: The FDNY since 1700* (New York: Basic Books, 2002), p. 191. For Berry's quote, see *New York Times*, September 25, 1932.
7.   Ira Rosenwaite, *Population History of New York City* (Syracuse, NY: Syracuse University Press, 1972), p. 98.
8.   Jeremiah Mahoney to Herbert Claiborne Pell, October 14, 1938, Papers of Herbert Claiborne Pell, Box 13, FDR Library, Hyde Park.
9.   Allen, *The Tiger*, p. 255.
10. *New York Times*, November 16, 1933; *The Reminiscences of Jeremiah T. Mahoney*, p. 144, Columbia Center for Oral History.
11. Thomas Kessner, *Fiorello H. La Guardia*, p. 415.
12. According to Frances Perkins, FDR said that nearly everything he did at the federal level was "like things Al Smith did as Governor of New York." See Perkins, *The Roosevelt I Knew*, p. 150.
13. Herbert Claiborne Pell to Jeremiah T. Mahoney, May 9, 1938, Box 13, FDR Library, Hyde Park.1
14. *New York Times*, September 12, August 23, 1937.

15. *The Reminiscences of Jeremiah T. Mahoney,* Columbia Center for Oral History, p. 77.

16. Richard H. Rovere, "Nothing Much to It," *New Yorker,* September 8, 1945.

17. The letters of protest and news clips can be found in the President's Official File, 5224, Box 1, FDR Library, Hyde Park.

18. Flynn, *You're the Boss,* p. 194.

19. Ibid., p. 195.

20. Richard H. Rovere, "A Man for This Age, Too," *New York Times Magazine,* April 11, 1965.

21. This account is based on Robert Caro's poignant description of Al Smith's final years in *The Power Broker,* pp. 381–83, and the documentary "The Irish in America: Long Journey Home," directed by Thomas Lennon and shown on PBS in 1997.

22. Telegram from Roosevelt to Smith, May 4, 1944; Smith to Roosevelt, June 29, 1944, President's Personal File, PPF 676, FDR Library, Hyde Park; *New York Times,* October 5, 1944.

23. This account is based on a *New York Times* article, January 21, 1973.

BIBLIOGRAPHY

LETTERS AND MANUSCRIPT COLLECTIONS

Republic of Ireland

NATIONAL LIBRARY OF IRELAND, DUBLIN

Papers of Daniel O'Connell (Records of the Catholic Association)
Papers of John Devoy
Papers of Farnham Family
Papers of Alice Stopford Greene
Papers of Thomas Wyse

United States

AMERICAN CATHOLIC HISTORY RESEARCH CENTER, CATHOLIC UNIVER-
SITY OF AMERICA, WASHINGTON DC

Fenian Brotherhood Papers

AMERICAN IRISH HISTORICAL SOCIETY, NEW YORK

Papers of Daniel Cohalan
Friends of Irish Freedom Papers

ARCHIVES OF THE ARCHDIOCESE OF NEW YORK, YONKERS, NY

Papers of John Hughes

ARCHIVES OF THE UNIVERSITY OF NOTRE DAME, NOTRE DAME, INDIANA

Records of the Society for the Propagation of the Faith

COLUMBIA UNIVERSITY RARE BOOK AND MANUSCRIPT LIBRARY, NEW YORK

Edwin Patrick Kilroe Papers and Collection of Tammaniana

FRANKLIN D. ROOSEVELT LIBRARY, HYDE PARK, NY

Papers of Edward J. Flynn
Papers of Harry Hopkins
Official Papers of Louis Howe
Papers of Herbert Claiborne Pell
Papers of Eleanor Roosevelt
Papers of Franklin D. Roosevelt, including:
    Family, Business and Personal Papers
    Papers Pertaining to the Campaign of 1924
    Papers as Governor of New York
    Papers as State Senator from New York
    President's Personal File
    President's Official File
    President's Secretary's File
    Vertical File

GEORGETOWN UNIVERSITY LIBRARY, SPECIAL COLLECTIONS, WASHINGTON, DC

Papers of Robert F. Wagner

HISTORICAL SOCIETY OF PENNSYLVANIA, PHILADELPHIA

Papers of James Buchanan

LIBRARY OF CONGRESS, WASHINGTON, DC

Papers of Joseph Tumulty
Papers of James A. Farley

MONSIGNOR FIELD ARCHIVES AND SPECIAL COLLECTIONS, SETON HALL UNIVERSITY, SOUTH ORANGE, NJ

Papers of Michael A. Corrigan

MUNICIPAL REFERENCE LIBRARY, NEW YORK CITY

Annual Report of the Fire Department of the City of New York, 1912
Papers of John Purroy Mitchel and James J. Walker

NEW YORK FIRE MUSEUM

Roster of the Fire Department of New York, 1888

NEW-YORK HISTORICAL SOCIETY

Collection of material relating to Tammany Hall, the Tammany Society, and New York politics
Minutes of the Trustees of the Public School Society
Papers of Hugh Grant
Papers of William Tweed

NEW YORK PUBLIC LIBRARY, NEW YORK CITY

Papers of William Bourke Cockran

Papers of James Harper
Papers of the New York Reform Club
Papers of Samuel Tilden
Papers of Frank Walsh
Papers of Richard Welling (Citizens Union correspondence)

NEW YORK STATE ARCHIVES, ALBANY

Public Papers of Alfred E. Smith

NEW YORK STATE LIBRARY, MANUSCRIPTS AND SPECIAL COLLECTIONS, ALBANY

Papers of Martin Glynn
Private Papers of Alfred E. Smith

NEW YORK UNIVERSITY ARCHIVES OF IRISH AMERICA

The Mick Moloney Collection of Irish-American Music and Popular Culture

ORAL HISTORY INTERVIEWS

COLUMBIA CENTER FOR ORAL HISTORY, COLUMBIA UNIVERSITY, NEW YORK

Reminiscences of Edward J. Flynn, Arthur Krock, Jeremiah T. Mahoney, Frances Perkins, and Joseph Proskauer

GOVERNMENT PUBLICATIONS

Documents of the Board of Aldermen of the City of New York, vol. 23 (New York: Chas. W. Baker, 1856).
Journal of the Assembly of the State of New York, 142nd Session (Albany: J. B. Lyon Co., 1919).
Official Proceedings of the Democratic National Convention 1884 (New York: Douglas Taylor's Democratic Printing House, 1884).
Official Report of the Proceedings of the Democratic National Convention, 1912 (Chicago: Peterson Linotyping Co., 1912).
Preliminary Report of the Factory Investigating Commission, vol. 2 (Albany: J. B. Lyon Co., 1912).
Report of the Reconstruction Commission to Governor Alfred E. Smith on Retrenchment and Reorganization in the State Government (Albany: J. B. Lyon Co., 1919).
Report to the Select Committee on Alleged New York Election Frauds, Made to the House of Representatives, Fortieth Congress, Third Session (Washington, DC, 1869).
Report of the Special Committee of the Assembly Appointed to Investigate the Public Offices and Appointments of the City of New York, vol. 2 (Albany: J. B. Lyon Co., 1900).
Special Report on the New York and Brooklyn Surface Railroad Strikes by the Board of Mediation and Arbitration (Albany: Troy Press, 1889).
Speech by John Kelly in Reply to the Charges of Hon. Thomas R. Whitney against Catholicism, delivered in the House, August 9, 1855 (Washington: Union Office, 1856).
The Red Book: An Illustrated Legislative Manual of the State of New York (Albany: James B. Lyon, 1892).

PUBLISHED COLLECTIONS OF CORRESPONDENCE AND DOCUMENTS

Gooch, G. P. ed. *The Later Correspondence of Lord John Russell, 1840–1878*. Vol. I. London: Longmans, Green, 1925.

Kehoe, Lawrence, ed. *Complete Works of the Most Rev. John Hughes, DD*. Vols. I and II. New York: Lawrence Kehoe, 1866.

Moskowitz, Henry, ed. *Progressive Democracy: Addresses and State Papers of Alfred E. Smith*. New York: Harcourt, Brace, 1928.

O'Connell, Maurice. *The Correspondence of Daniel O'Connell*. Vols. I and II. Shannon, Ireland: Irish University Press, 1973.

Rosenman, Samuel, ed. *The Public Papers and Addresses of Franklin D. Roosevelt*. New York: Macmillan, 1939.

BOOKS: MEMOIRS, BIOGRAPHIES, GENERAL HISTORIES

Ackerman, Kenneth. *Boss Tweed: The Rise and Fall of the Corrupt Pol Who Conceived the Soul of Modern New York*. New York: Carroll & Graf, 2005.

Adams, Peter. *The Bowery Boys: Street Corner Radicals and the Politics of Rebellion*. Westport, CT: Praeger, 2005.

Allen, Oliver E. *The Tiger: The Rise and Fall of Tammany Hall*. Reading, MA: Addison-Wesley, 1993.

Allen, Theodore W. *The Invention of the White Race: Racial Oppression and Society Control*. New York: Verso, 1994.

Allswang, John M. *Bosses, Machines, and Urban Voters*. Baltimore: Johns Hopkins University Press, 1986.

Anbinder, Tyler. *Five Points: The Nineteenth Century New York Neighborhood That Invented Tap Dance, Stole Elections, and Became the World's Most Notorious Slum*. New York: Free Press, 2001.

————. *Nativism and Slavery: The Northern Know Nothings and The Politics of the 1850s*. New York: Oxford University Press, 1992.

Barber, Shelley, ed. *The Prendergast Letters: Correspondence from Famine-Era Ireland, 1840–1850*. Amherst: University of Massachusetts Press, 2006.

Bardon, Jonathan. *A History of Ulster*. Belfast: Blackstaff Press, 1992.

Barry, Francis S. *The Scandal of Reform: The Grand Failures of New York's Political Crusaders and the Death of Nonpartisanship*. New Brunswick, NJ: Rutgers University Press, 2009.

Bartlett, Thomas. *The Fall and Rise of the Irish Nation*. Dublin: Rowman and Littlefield, 1992.

Bayor, Ronald H., and Timothy J. Meagher, eds. *The New York Irish*. Baltimore: Johns Hopkins University Press, 1996.

Benson, Lee. *The Concept of Jacksonian Democracy: New York as a Test Case*. Princeton, NJ: Princeton University Press, 1961.

Bernstein, Iver. *The New York City Draft Riots: Their Significance for American Society and Politics in the Age of Civil War*. New York: Oxford University Press, 1990.

Bodnar, John. *The Transplanted*. Bloomington: Indiana University Press, 1987.

Bowers, Claude Gernade. *The Irish Orators: A History of Ireland's Fight for Freedom*. Indianapolis: Bobbs-Merrill, 1916.

Brace, Charles Loring. *The Dangerous Classes of New York and Twenty Years' Work Among Them*. New York: Wynkoop & Hallenbeck, 1872.

Bridges, Amy. *A City in the Republic*. Cambridge: Cambridge University Press, 1984.

Brown, Dorothy M., and Elizabeth McKeown. *The Poor Belong to Us: Catholic Charities and American Welfare*. Cambridge: Harvard University Press, 1997.

Brownell, Blaine A., and Warren E. Stickle, eds. *Bosses and Reformers*. Boston: Houghton Mifflin, 1973.

Bryan, Mary B., ed. *The Memoirs of William Jennings Bryan*. Philadelphia: John C. Winston, 1925.

Bryce, James. *The American Commonwealth* (abridged). Philadelphia: John D. Morris, 1906.

Buenker, John. *Urban Liberalism and Progressive Reform*. New York: W. W. Norton, 1973.

Butterfield, Lyman H., ed. *Adams Family Correspondence*. Vol. 2. Cambridge: Harvard University Press, 1963.

Cannato, Vincent J. *American Passage: The History of Ellis Island*. New York: Harper, 2009.

Caro, Robert. *The Power Broker: Robert Moses and the Fall of New York*. New York: Vintage, 1975.

Chambers, John Whiteclay, II. *The Tyranny of Change: America in the Progressive Era, 1980–1920*. New Brunswick, NJ: Rutgers University Press, 2000.

Clark, Samuel, and James S. Donnelly Jr., eds. *Irish Peasants: Violence and Political Unrest, 1780–1914*. Madison: University of Wisconsin Press, 1983.

Coffey, Michael, ed. *The Irish in America*. New York: Hyperion, 1997.

Connable, Alfred, and Edward Silverfarb. *Tigers of Tammany Hall*. New York: Holt, Rinehart and Winston, 1967.

Connolly, James J. *The Triumph of Ethnic Progressivism: Urban Political Culture in Boston, 1900–1925*. Cambridge: Harvard University Press, 1998.

Cook, Adrian, *The Armies of the Street: The New York City Draft Riots of 1863*. Lexington: University Press of Kentucky, 1989.

Cook, Fred J. *American Political Bosses and Machines*. New York: Franklin Watts, 1973.

Croly, David G. *Seymour and Blair: Their Lives and Services*. New York: Richardson and Company, 1868.

Cross, Robert D. *The Emergence of Liberal Catholicism in America*. Cambridge: Harvard University Press, 1958.

Davis, Kenneth S. *FDR: The Beckoning of Destiny, 1882–1928*. New York: G. P. Putnam's Sons, 1972.

Deane, Seamus, ed. *The Field Day Anthology of Irish Writing*, Vol. 2. Derry, Northern Ireland: Field Day Publications, 1991.

Depew, Chauncey Mitchell. *My Memories of Eighty Years*. New York: Charles Scribner's Sons, 1921.

Devoy, John, *Recollections of an Irish Rebel*. New York: Charles Young, 1929.

Diner, Hasia R. *We Remember With Reverence and Love: American Jews and the Myth of Silence After the Holocaust, 1945–1962*. New York: New York University Press, 2009.

Diner, Steven J. *A Very Different Age: Americans of the Progressive Era*. New York: Hill and Wang, 1998.

Dolan, Jay P. *The Immigrant Church*. Notre Dame, IN: University of Notre Dame Press, 1992.

Dorsett, Lyle W. *Franklin D. Roosevelt and the City Bosses.* Port Washington, NY: Kennikat Press, 1977.

Dyer, Thomas G. *Theodore Roosevelt and the Idea of Race.* Baton Rouge: Louisiana State University Press, 1992.

Eisenstein, Louis, and Elliot Rosenberg. *A Stripe of Tammany's Tiger.* New York: Robert Speller & Sons, 1966.

Emmet, Thomas Addis. *A Memoir of Thomas Addis and Robert Emmet.* New York: Emmet Press, 1905.

Erie, Steven P. *Rainbow's End: Irish-Americans and the Dilemmas of Urban Machine Politics, 1840–1985.* Berkeley: University of California Press, 1988.

Ernst, Robert. *Immigrant Life in New York City, 1825–1863.* Syracuse, NY: Syracuse University Press, 1994.

Fanning, Charles, ed. *Mr. Dooley and the Chicago Irish: The Autobiography of a Nineteenth-Century Ethnic Group.* Washington, DC: Catholic University Press of America, 1976.

Fenster, Julie M. *FDR's Shadow: Louis Howe, The Force That Shaped Franklin and Eleanor Roosevelt.* New York: Palgrave Macmillan, 2009.

Finan, Christopher M. *Alfred E. Smith: The Happy Warrior.* New York: Hill & Wang, 2002.

Fisher, James T. *On the Irish Waterfront: The Crusader, the Movie, and the Soul of the Port of New York.* Ithaca, NY: Cornell University Press, 2009.

Fitzgerald, Maureen. *Habits of Compassion: Irish Catholic Nuns and the Origins of New York's Welfare System, 1830–1920.* Chicago: University of Illinois Press, 2006.

Fleming, Thomas. *Mysteries of My Father.* Hoboken, NJ: Wiley, 2005.

Flynn, Edward J. *You're the Boss: The Practice of American Politics.* New York: Collier Books, 1962.

Foster, R. F. *Modern Ireland, 1600–1972.* New York: Penguin, 1989.

Fowler, Gene. *Beau James: The Life and Times of Jimmy Walker.* New York: Viking Press, 1949.

Freidel, Frank. *Franklin D. Roosevelt: The Apprenticeship.* Boston: Little, Brown, 1952.

———. *Franklin D. Roosevelt: A Rendezvous with Destiny.* New York: Little, Brown, 1990.

Gibson, Florence. *Attitudes of the New York Irish.* New York: Columbia University Press, 1951.

Glazer, Nathan, and Daniel Patrick Moynihan. *Beyond the Melting Pot: The Negroes, Puerto Ricans, Jews, Italians, and Irish of New York City.* Cambridge, MA: MIT Press, 1963.

Gordon, Michael A. *The Orange Riots: Irish Political Violence in New York City, 1870 and 1871.* Ithaca, NY: Cornell University Press, 2009.

Graham, Otis L., Jr. *The Old Progressives and the New Deal.* New York: Oxford University Press, 1967.

Grant, Madison. *The Passing of the Great Race.* New York: Scribner's, 1922.

Gray, Peter. *Famine, Land and Politics: British Government and Irish Society, 1843–1850.* Dublin: Irish Academic Press, 2001.

Greenwald, Richard A. *The Triangle Fire, the Protocols of Peace, and Industrial Democracy in Progressive Era New York.* Philadelphia: Temple University Press, 2005.

Gribben, Arthur, ed. *The Great Famine and the Irish Diaspora in America.* Amherst: University of Massachusetts Press, 1999.

Gwynn, Denis. *Daniel O'Connell*. Cork, Ireland: Cork University Press, 1947.

Hahn, Steven. *A Nation Under Our Feet: Black Political Struggles in the Rural South from Slavery to the Great Migration*. Cambridge, MA: Belknap Press, 2003.

Halbwachs, Maurice. *On Collective Memory*. Chicago: University of Chicago Press, 1992.

Hamby, Alonzo L. *Man of the People: A Life of Harry S. Truman*. New York: Oxford University Press, 1995.

Hammack, David C. *Power and Society: Greater New York at the Turn of the Century*. New York: Columbia University Press, 1982.

Handlin, Oscar. *The Uprooted: The Epic Story of the Great Migration that Made the American People*. Boston: Little, Brown, 1951.

————. *Al Smith and His America*. Boston: Little, Brown, 1958.

Hartwell, Joseph. *Romanism in Politics: What it Costs—Tammany Hall the Stronghold of Rome*. New York: Phillips & Hunt, 1887.

Hawley, Willis D., and Michael Lipsky, eds. *Theoretical Perspectives on Urban Politics*. Englewood Cliffs, NJ: Prentice-Hall, 1976.

Hayden, Tom, ed. *Irish Hunger: Personal Reflections on the Legacy of the Famine*. Boulder, CO: Roberts Rinehart, 1997.

Henderson, Thomas M. *Tammany Hall and the New Immigrants: The Progressive Years*. New York: Arno Press, 1976.

Hershkowitz, Leo. *Tweed's New York: Another Look*. New York: Anchor Press, 1977.

Higham, John. *Strangers in the Land: Patterns of American Nativism, 1860–1925*. New Brunswick, NJ: Rutgers University Press, 2004.

Hofstadter, Richard. *The Age of Reform*. New York: Vintage Books, 1955.

Hone, Philip. *The Diary of Philip Hone*. Vol. 1. New York: Dodd, Mead, 1889.

Huthmacher, J. Joseph. *Senator Robert F. Wagner and the Rise of Urban Liberalism*. New York: Atheneum, 1971.

Ignatiev, Noel. *How the Irish Became White*. New York: Routledge, 1995.

James, Marquis. *Merchant Adventurer: The Story of W. R. Grace*. Wilmington, DE: Scholarly Resources, 1993.

Jonnes, Jill. *Conquering Gotham: Building Penn Station and Its Tunnels*. New York: Penguin, 2008.

Kee, Robert. *The Most Distressful Country*. London: Penguin, 1972.

————. *Ireland: A History*. London: Fakenham Press, 1980.

Kelly, Mary C. *The Shamrock and the Lily: The New York Irish and the Creation of a Transatlantic Identity, 1845–1921*. New York: Peter Lang, 2007.

Kennedy, William. *Riding the Yellow Trolley Car: Selected Nonfiction*. New York: Viking, 1993.

Kessner, Thomas. *Fiorello H. LaGuardia and the Making of Modern New York*. New York: McGraw-Hill, 1989.

Kimball, Warren. *The Juggler*. Princeton, NJ: Princeton University Press, 1991.

Kinealy, Christine. *This Great Calamity: The Irish Famine 1845–52*. Dublin: Gill and Macmillan, 2006.

————. *Daniel O'Connell and the Anti-Slavery Movement*. London: Pickering & Chatto, 2010.

————. *A Death-Dealing Famine: The Great Hunger in Ireland*. London: Pluto Press, 1997.

Kurland, Gerald. *Seth Low: The Reformer in an Urban and Industrial Age*. New York: Twayne Publishers, 1971.

LaCerra, Charles. *Franklin Delano Roosevelt and Tammany Hall of New York.* New York: University Press of America, 1997.

Larkin, Emmet, ed. *Alexis de Tocqueville's Journey in Ireland.* Washington, DC: Catholic University of America Press, 1990.

Laxton, Edward. *The Famine Ships.* New York: Henry Holt, 1998.

Lee, J. J., and Marion Casey, eds. *Making the Irish American: History and Heritage of the Irish in the United States.* New York: New York University Press, 2006.

Lender, Mark Edward, and James Martin Kirby. *Drinking in America: A History.* New York: Free Press, 1987.

Levine, Edward M. *The Irish and Irish Politicians: A Study of Cultural and Social Alienation.* Notre Dame, IN: University of Notre Dame Press, 1966.

Lubell, Samuel. *The Future of American Politics.* Garden City, NY: Doubleday, 1951.

MacDonagh, Michael. *The Life of Daniel O'Connell.* London: Cassell and Company, 1903.

Macintyre, Angus. *The Liberator: Daniel O'Connell and the Irish Party 1830–1847.* London: Hamish Hamilton, 1965.

Mandelbaum, Seymour J. *Boss Tweed's New York.* Chicago: Ivan R. Dee, 1990.

Mann, Arthur. *Yankee Reformers in the Urban Age: Social Reform in Boston, 1880–1900.* New York: Harper Torchbooks, 1954.

McCaffrey, Lawrence J. *The Irish Catholic Diaspora in America.* Washington, DC: Catholic University of America Press, 1997.

McClellan, George B. *The Gentleman and the Tiger.* Philadelphia: J. B. Lippincott, 1956.

McCormick, Richard L. *The Party Period and Public Policy: American Politics from the Age of Jackson to the Progressive Era.* New York: Oxford University Press, 1986.

McCullough, David. *Truman.* New York: Simon & Schuster, 1992.

McGerr, Michael. *The Decline of Popular Politics: The American North, 1865–1928.* New York: Oxford University Press, 1986.

McGreevy, John T. *Catholicism and American Freedom: A History.* New York: W. W. Norton, 2003.

McMahon, Sean. *A Short History of Ireland.* Cork, Ireland: Mercier Press, 1996.

McShane, Joseph M. *"Sufficiently Radical": Catholicism, Progressivism, and the Bishops' Program of 1919.* Washington, DC: Catholic University of America Press, 1986.

Merton, Robert K. *Social Theory and Social Structure.* New York: Free Press, 1968.

Miller, Kerby. *Emigrants and Exiles: Ireland and the Irish Exodus to North America.* New York: Oxford University Press, 1985.

Mitchell, Margaret, *Gone With the Wind.* New York: Macmillan, 1936.

Mitgang, Herbert. *The Man Who Rode the Tiger: The Life and Times of Judge Samuel Seabury.* New York: J. B. Lippincott, 1963.

Moley, Raymond J. *The First New Deal.* New York: Harcourt, Brace and World, 1966.

Morris, Charles. *American Catholic.* New York: Times Books, 1997.

Morse, Samuel F. B. *Foreign Conspiracy Against the Liberties of the United States.* New York: American and Foreign Christian Union, 1855.

Murray, Robert K. *The 103rd Ballot: Democrats and the Disaster in Madison Square Garden.* New York: Harper & Row, 1976.

Mushkat, Jerome. *Fernando Wood: A Political Biography.* Kent, OH: Kent State University Press, 1990.

Myers, Gustavus. *A History of Tammany Hall.* New York: Boni & Liveright, 1917.

Nevins, Allen. *Herbert Lehman and His Era.* New York: Scribner, 1963.

————— and Milton Halsey Thomas, eds. *The Diaries of George Templeton Strong*. New York: Macmillan, 1952.

O'Brien, Conor Cruise. *Parnell and His Party*. London: Oxford University Press, 1957.

O'Brien, William, and Desmond Ryan, eds. *Devoy's Post Bag*, Vol. 1. Dublin: Fallon, 1948.

O'Connell, Daniel. *Letters to the Reformers of England on the Reform Bill for Ireland*. London: J. Ridgway, 1832.

O'Ferrall, Fergus. *Catholic Emancipation: Daniel O'Connell and the Birth of Irish Democracy, 1820–30*. Dublin: Gill and Macmillan, 1985.

O Grada, Cormac. *The Great Irish Famine*. London: Macmillan, 1989.

—————. *Black '47 and Beyond: The Great Irish Famine in History, Economy, and Memory*. Princeton, NJ: Princeton University Press, 1996.

Olick, Jeffrey K. *The Politics of Regret: On Collective Memory and Historical Responsibility*. New York: Routledge, 2007.

O Tuathaigh, Gearoid. *Ireland before the Famine 1798–1848*. Dublin: Gill and Macmillan, 1972.

Perkins, Frances. *The Roosevelt I Knew*. New York: Viking Press, 1946.

Perry, Elisabeth Israels. *Belle Moskowitz*. New York: Oxford University Press, 1987.

Poirteir, Cathal. *Famine Echoes*. Dublin: Gill and Macmillan, 1995.

—————, ed. *The Great Irish Famine*. Cork, Ireland: Mercier Press, 1995.

Potter, David. *The Impending Crisis*. New York: Harper & Row, 1976.

Potter, George W. *To the Golden Door: The Story of the Irish in Ireland and America*. Boston: Little, Brown, 1960.

Quigley, David. *Second Founding: New York City, Reconstruction, and the Making of American Democracy*. New York: Hill and Wang, 2004.

Quinn, Peter. *Looking for Jimmy: Journeys in Search of Irish America*. New York: Overlook, 2006.

Ravitch, Diane. *The Great School Wars: A History of the New York City Public Schools*. Baltimore: Johns Hopkins University Press, 2000.

Riordon, William L., ed. *Plunkitt of Tammany Hall: A Series of Very Plain Talks on Very Practical Politics*. New York: Signet Classics, 1995.

Rodgers, Daniel. *Atlantic Crossings*. Cambridge, MA: Belknap Press, 2000.

Roediger, David. *Working Toward Whiteness: How America's Immigrants Became White*. New York: Basic Books, 2006.

Roosevelt, Franklin D. *The Happy Warrior: Alfred E. Smith*. Boston: Houghton Mifflin, 1928.

Roosevelt, Theodore. *An Autobiography*. New York: Charles Scribner's Sons, 1920.

Rosenwaite, Ira. *Population History of New York City*. Syracuse, NY: Syracuse University Press, 1972.

Rossa, Jeremiah O'Donovan. *Rossa's Recollections*. New York: Mariners Harbor, 1894.

Rubin, Joseph J., and Charles H. Brown, eds. *Walt Whitman of the New York Aurora*. State College: Pennsylvania State University Press, 1950.

Ryan, Desmond. *The Fenian Chief*. Coral Gables: University of Miami Press, 1967.

Ryan, Mary P. *Civic Wars: Democracy and Public Life in the American City During the Nineteenth Century*. Berkeley: University of California Press, 1998.

Salaman, Redcliffe N. *The History and Social Influence of the Potato*. Cambridge: Cambridge University Press, 1985.

Savage, Sean J. *Roosevelt the Party Leader: 1932–1945*. Lexington: University of Kentucky Press, 1991.

Scally, Robert James. *The End of Hidden Ireland: Rebellion, Famine, and Emigration.* New York: Oxford University Press, 1994.

Schlesinger, Arthur M., Jr. *The Age of Roosevelt, Volume I: The Crisis of the Old Order.* Boston: Houghton Mifflin, 1957.

Scroop. Daniel. *Mr. Democrat: Jim Farley, the New Deal, and the Making of Modern American Politics.* Ann Arbor: University of Michigan Press, 2006.

Shannon, William V. *The American Irish: A Political and Social Portrait.* New York: Macmillan, 1963.

Shaw, Richard. *Dagger John: The Unquiet Life and Times of Archbishop John Hughes of New York.* New York: Paulist Press, 1977.

Shibley, George Henry. *Majority Rule in Combination with Representative Government in City, State, and Nation.* Washington, DC: American Federation of Labor, 1902.

Short, K. R. M. *The Dynamite War.* Atlantic Highlands, NJ: Humanities Press, 1979.

Silbey, Joel H., Allan G. Bogue, William H. Flanigan, eds. *The History of American Electoral Behavior.* Princeton, NJ: Princeton University Press, 1978.

Slayton, Robert. *Empire Statesman: The Rise and Redemption of Al Smith.* New York: Free Press, 2001.

Sloat, Warren. *A Battle for the Soul of New York: Tammany Hall, Police Corruption, Vice, and Reverend Charles Parkhurst's Crusade Against Them.* New York: Cooper Square Press, 2002.

Smith, Alfred E. *Up to Now: An Autobiography.* New York: Viking Press, 1929.

Smith, Jean Edward. *FDR.* New York: Random House, 2007.

Stave, Bruce M., and Sondra Astor Stave. *Urban Bosses, Machines, and Progressive Reformers.* Malabar, FL: Robert E. Krieger Publishing, 1984.

Steffens, Lincoln. *Autobiography.* New York: Harcourt, Brace, 1930.

———. *The Shame of the Cities.* New York: Hill and Wang, 1957.

Steinfels, Margaret O'Brien, ed. *American Catholics, American Culture: Tradition and Resistance.* Lanham, MD: Sheed and Ward, 2004.

Stoddard, Lothrop. *Master of Manhattan: The Life of Richard Croker.* New York: Longmans, Green, 1931.

Stoughton, John. *William Wilberforce.* New York: A. C. Armstrong & Son, 1880.

Stuckey, Sterling. *Slave Culture: Nationalist Theory and the Foundations of Black America.* Oxford: Oxford University Press, 1987.

Taylor, Nick. *American-Made: The Enduring Legacy of the WPA, When FDR Put the Nation to Work.* New York: Bantam Books, 2008.

Thornton, John. *Africa and Africans in the Making of the Atlantic World, 1400–1800.* Cambridge: Cambridge University Press, 1998.

Toibin, Colm, and Diarmaid Ferriter. *The Irish Famine: A Documentary.* London: Profile Books, 2004.

Trevelyan, Charles Edward. *The Irish Crisis.* London: Longman, Brown, Green & Longmans, 1848.

Tumulty, Joseph P. *Woodrow Wilson As I Know Him.* New York: Doubleday, 1921.

Valone, David A. *Ireland's Great Hunger: Relief, Representation, and Remembrance*, Vol. 2. Lanham, MD: University Press of America, 2010.

Vaughn, W. E., ed. *New History of Ireland.* Vol. 5. Oxford: Clarendon Press, 1989.

Von Drehle, David. *Triangle: The Fire That Changed America.* New York: Grove Press, 2003.

Walters, Ronald G. *American Reformers, 1815–1860.* New York: Hill and Wang, 1997.

Ward, Geoffrey C. *A First-Class Temperament: The Emergence of Franklin Roosevelt*. New York: Harper & Row, 1989.

Warner, Richard. *Catholic Emancipation, Incompatible with the Safety of the Established Religion, Liberty, Laws and Protestant Succession of the British Empire*. London: C. J. G. & F. Rivington, 1829.

Weiss, Nancy Joan. *Charles Francis Murphy, 1858–1924: Respectability and Responsibility in Tammany Politics*. Northampton, MA: Smith College Press, 1968.

Welch, Richard F. *King of the Bowery: Big Tim Sullivan, Tammany Hall, and New York City from the Gilded Age to the Progressive Era*. Madison, NJ: Fairleigh Dickinson University Press, 2008.

Wenzer, Kenneth C., ed. *Henry George, the Transatlantic Irish, and Their Times*. Bingley, UK: JAI Press, 2009.

Werner, M. A. *Tammany Hall*. New York: Greenwood Press, 1968.

Wesser, Robert F. *A Response to Progressivism: The Democratic Party and New York Politics: 1902–1918*. New York: New York University Press, 1986.

Whelan, Irene. *The Bible War in Ireland: The 'Second Reformation' and the Polarization of Protestant-Catholic Relations, 1800–1840*. Madison: University of Wisconsin Press, 2005.

White, Deborah Gray. *Ar'n't I a Woman? Female Slaves in the Plantation South*. New York: W. W. Norton, 1999.

Wilentz, Sean. *Chants Democratic: New York City and the Rise of the American Working Class, 1788-1850*. New York: Oxford University Press, 2004.

Woodham-Smith, Cecil. *The Great Hunger*. London: H. Hamilton, 1962.

Wyse, Thomas. *Historical Sketch of the Late Catholic Association of Ireland*. Vols. 1 and 2. London, A. J. Valpy, 1829.

Zacks, Richard. *Island of Vice: Theodore Roosevelt's Doomed Quest to Clean Up Sin-Loving New York*. New York: Doubleday, 2002.

Zink, Harold. *City Bosses in the United States*. Durham, NC: Duke University Press, 1930.

ARTICLES

Beckert, Sven. "Democracy and its Discontents: Contesting Suffrage Rights in Gilded Age New York." *Past and Present*, no. 174 (February 2002).

Cannon, James Jr. "Al Smith—Catholic, Tammany, Wet." *The Nation*, July 4, 1928.

Chalmers, Leonard. "Fernando Wood and Tammany Hall: The First Phase." *New-York Historical Society Quarterly* 52 (October 1968).

Cornwell, Elmer, Jr. "Bosses, Machines, and Ethnic Groups." *Annals of the American Academy of Political and Social Science* 353 (May 1964).

Croker, Richard. "Tammany Hall and the Democracy." *North American Review* 154, no. 423 (February 1892).

Ferreira, Patricia. "All But 'A Black Skin and Wooly Hair': Frederick Douglass' Witness of the Irish Famine." *American Studies International* 37, no. 2 (June 1999).

Foner, Eric. "Class, Ethnicity and Radicalism in the Gilded Age: The Land League and Irish-America." *Marxist Perspectives* 2 (1978).

Godkin, E. L. "A Key to Municipal Reform." *North American Review* 151, no. 407 (October 1890).

Henderson, Thomas. "Immigrant Politician: Salvatore Cotillo, Progressive Ethnic." *International Migration Review* 13, no. 1 (Spring 1979).

Huthmacher, J. Joseph. "Urban Liberalism and the Age of Reform." *Mississippi Valley Historical Review* 49 (1962).

———. "Charles Evans Hughes and Charles Francis Murphy: The Metamorphosis of Progressivism." *New York History* (January 1965).

Kingsdale, Jon M. "The 'Poor Man's Club': Social Functions of the Urban Working-Class Saloon." *American Quarterly* 25, no. 4 (October 1973).

Lannie, Vincent Peter. "Profile of an Immigrant Bishop: The Early Career of John Hughes." *Pennsylvania History* 32, no. 4 (October 1965).

Lui, Adonica Y. "The Machine and Social Policies: Tammany Hall and the Politics of Public Outdoor Relief, New York City, 1874–1898." *Studies in American Political Development* 9, no. 2 (September 1995).

Meenagh, Martin L. "Archbishop John Hughes and the New York Schools Controversy of 1840–43," *American Nineteenth Century History* 5, no. 1 (Spring 2004).

O Grada, Cormac. "Famine, Trauma, and Memory." *Bealoideas: The Journal of the Folklore Society of Ireland*, no. 69 (2001).

O'Toole, Fintan. "What Haunted Eugene O'Neill." *New York Review of Books*, November 8, 2007.

Scobey, David. "Boycotting the Politics Factory: Labor Radicalism and the New York City Mayoral Election of 1884." *Radical History Review*, 28–30 (1984).

Sharrow, Walter G. "John Hughes and a Catholic Response to Slavery in Anetbellum America." *Journal of Negro History* 57, no. 3 (July 1972).

Stead, William T. "Mr. Richard Croker and Greater New York." *Review of Reviews* 16 (October 1897).

Thomas, Samuel J. "Mugwump Cartoonists, the Papacy, and Tammany Hall in America's Gilded Age." *Religion and American Culture: A Journal of Interpretation* 14, no. 2 (Summer 2004).

Wesser, Robert F. "Charles Evans Hughes and the Urban Sources of Political Progressivism." *New-York Historical Society Quarterly* 40 (October 1966).

Whelan, Kevin. "The Memories of 'The Dead.' " *Yale Journal of Criticism* 15, no. 1 (Spring 2002).

White, Andrew D. "The Government of American Cities." *Forum* (December 1890).

SOURCES ACCESSED ONLINE

Debate on the Treaty between Great Britain and Ireland, signed in London on the 6th December, 1921. Accessed through CELT, www.ucc.ie/celt/published/E900003-001/index/html.

Herbert H. Lehman Collections, Columbia University, http://lehman.cul.columbia.edu/

Oral History of Leon Keyserling, Harry S. Truman Library, http://www.trumanlibrary.org/oralhist/keyserl.html.

NEWSPAPERS AND PERIODICALS

United Kingdom

Blackwood's Magazine
Fortnightly

Hansard
The Economist
The Guardian
The Monthly Review
The Nineteenth Century
The Times (London)
Westminster Review

Republic of Ireland

Dublin Evening Mail
Dublin Evening Post
The Nation

United States

ALBANY, NEW YORK

Knickerbocker News

CHARLESTON, SOUTH CAROLINA

U.S. Catholic Miscellany

NEW YORK CITY

Commercial and Financial Chronicle
Federation
Freeman's Journal and Catholic Register
Gaelic American
Harper's Weekly
Irish-American
Irish Citizen
Irish News
Irish Shield
Irish World
Journal of Commerce
New York American
New York Evening Post
New York Herald
New York Observer
New York Sun
New York Times
New York Tribune
New York World
Puck
The Independent
The Nation
The New Yorker
Truth Teller
United Irishmen

WASHINGTON, DC
Congressional Globe

UNPUBLISHED PAPER

"Us Against Them," delivered by Thomas Fleming at "Understanding the Irish in
New Jersey: A Symposium on Irish and Irish-American Research Perspectives,"
Drew University, Madison, New Jersey, November 6, 2009.

INDEX

ABOUT THE AUTHOR

TERRY GOLWAY was a journalist for thirty years, writing for the *New York Observer,* the *New York Times,* and other venues. He holds a PhD in American history from Rutgers University and is currently the director of the Kean University Center for History, Politics, and Policy in New Jersey.